CW01670070

The Gothic Reader

The Gothic Reader

A Critical Anthology

Edited by Martin Myrone

Tate Publishing

First published 2006 by order
of the Tate Trustees by
Tate Publishing, a division
of Tate Enterprises Ltd,
Millbank, London SW1P 4RG
www.tate.org.uk/publishing

© Tate 2006

Sigmund Freud (pp.167–70):
© Sigmund Freud Copyrights,
by arrangement with Paterson
Marsh Ltd.

M.R. James (pp.175–7, p.310): with
thanks to the estate of M.R. James

Ernest Jones (p.170–3)
© The Estate of Ernest Jones

H.P. Lovecraft (pp.179–80)
reproduced by permission of Arkham
House Publishers, Inc., and Arkham's
agents, JABberwocky Literary Agency,
PO Box 4558, NY 11104-0558

All rights reserved. No part of
this book may be reprinted or
reproduced or utilised in any form
or by any electronic, mechanical
or other means, now known or
hereafter invented, including
photocopying and recording,
or in any information storage or
retrieval system, without permission
in writing from the publishers

The moral rights of the authors
have been asserted

British Library Cataloguing
in Publication Data
A catalogue record for this book
is available from the British Library

ISBN-10: 1-85437-599-7
ISBN-13: 978-184537-599-5

Distributed in the United States
and Canada by Harry N. Abrams,
Inc., New York

Designed by
Matt Brown, DesignBranch
Printed by
T J International Ltd, Padstow

Contents

Christopher Frayling
We live in Gothic times…

The City of Bath is full of monuments to the 'great British tradition' of literature in the eighteenth and nineteenth centuries: little metal plaques attached to the sides of Georgian Crescent buildings, like theatre programmes adorning neo-classical stage-sets. Jane Austen at number 4, Sydney Place; Edmund Burke at 11, North Parade; Henry Fielding at Widcombe Lodge; Walter Scott at 6, South Parade. These weathered metal plaques are woven through the beige stone walls of the city. In the mid-1970s, I wrote to Bath City Council in an attempt to introduce a new name to the pantheon. If Jane Austen and Walter Scott were up there with the greats, what about Mary Shelley, the author of *Frankenstein*, who actually wrote much of her celebrated novel in the centre of the city? I wrote to the Council suggesting that they place a metal plaque '*Frankenstein* was created here by Mary Shelley, autumn 1816–spring 1817' on the site of what used to be 5, Abbey Churchyard, just above the Roman Baths. For although the creation scene of *Frankenstein* had first been told by Mary Godwin (as she then was) on the night of 17 or 18 June 1816 in a holiday villa overlooking Lake Geneva — beginning like a folktale with the words 'it was on a dreary night of November' — she turned the story into a full-length novel between October 1816 and February 1817 in Bath. While Mary Godwin elaborated on her fireside idea of a young scientist who engages in spare-parts surgery — by adding Victor Frankenstein's education at Ingolstadt, explorer Robert Walton's letters on his expedition to the North Pole and the creature's autobiography — she was simultaneously being given tuition in drawing and painting (by a 'Mr West'), developing her interest in popular science by attending talks by Dr Wilkinson in the Lecture Rooms on Kingston Parade, and experiencing intense pressure from William Godwin to get married to Percy Shelley. It seemed to me, therefore, that the Bath environment might well have had an influence on the final shape of *Frankenstein*. But Bath City Council remained unconvinced. They wrote back saying that Jane Austen and Henry Fielding seemed more in keeping with their image of the Georgian City. In any case, they added, wasn't *Frankenstein* really more to do with Hollywood than England? The plaque would surely lower the tone: Boris Karloff and Beau Nash did not belong in the same universe.

Jane Austen had, famously, satirised the craze for Gothic fiction — which had peaked in England during the 1790s — in *Northanger Abbey*, published posthumously a few months before *Frankenstein* at Christmas 1817 (though mainly written in the late 1790s, a time when twenty-five Gothics were being published every year — an average of over 35 per cent of *all* the novels being issued). In the genteel surroundings of Bath's recently rebuilt Pump Room round the corner from 5, Abbey Churchyard, her two heroines had discussed the latest bloodcurdling romances with all the breathless excitement of today's seventeen-year-olds texting each other about the latest schlock-horror movies:

'I will read you their names directly; here they are in my pocket book. *Castle of Wolfenbach, Clermont, Mysterious Warnings, Necromancer of the Black Forest, Midnight Bell, Orphan of the Rhine* and *Horrid Mysteries*...'

'But are they all *horrid*? Are you sure they are all horrid?'

These titles were not made up: they had all recently been published in the wake of Ann Radcliffe's huge success with the reading public from *A Sicilian Romance* (1790) onwards. Six of them had German connections, and German tales of terror, often with plots hinging on secret societies or conspiracies, were indeed popular during the later stages of the French Revolution; one of them — Regina Roche's *Clermont* (1798) — had been panned as a tired remix of Mrs Radcliffe's early work. *Northanger Abbey* remains a witty and clever commentary on what young female readers saw in Gothic novels, at a time when real terrors were happening just across the Channel. But, in the end, Jane Austen was singing from the same hymn-sheet as Bath City Council. As was Henry Fielding, who introduced book eight of *Tom Jones* (1749) with some jokes about the sorts of authors who resorted to horrors and wonders to make their fictions interesting. Let's hear it for the middling people.

I thought of writing back; and pointing out how Bath has traditionally celebrated William Beckford — author of the 'oriental-Gothic' *Vathek* (1786), and designer of the most sexually suggestive building in the City. Had the Councillors ever *read Vathek*? At one notably over-the-top moment in the story, Beckford has the caliph's scantily clad mother admit 'my taste for dead bodies and everything like mummy, is decided'. Or perhaps I could write to the Councillors and point out how the sainted Edmund Burke had, in his *A Philosophical Enquiry into... the Sublime and Beautiful* (1757), provided the — admittedly often spurious — aesthetic credo for the many Gothic novelists who wanted to appear respectable as well as earn unrespectable amounts of money both at the same time. But it would probably have been a waste of paper.

Because looking back, my exchange of letters was about much more than just a metal plaque: it was about the critical respectability of Jane Austen and Henry Fielding and Walter Scott and — in the mid-1970s — the continuing unrespectability of Gothic novels and the many guilty pleasures to be had from them. Gothic novels were not quite pukka. They held up a curious, haunted mirror to the true-to-life mainstream of English literature — Leavis's great tradition — and as for their authors, they certainly did not qualify for entry into English Literature's all-male county cricket eleven. File under 'the popular novel' instead, the sort of material Queenie Leavis — rather than F.R. — wrote about.

With a few honourable exceptions, the commentators who had written in any depth about Gothic novels at that time tended to be eccentric bibliophiles and collectors (Montague Summers' *Gothic Bibliography* (1940), running to 621 pages, was often displayed in upmarket antiquarian bookshops although a number of entries did not in fact exist), or veteran art critics with long memories who still reckoned that the Gothics had in some sense been precursors of the dream-language of Surrealism, and who spoke darkly of 'the castle question'. I can remember talking with a fellow research student (who was preparing a doctorate on medieval architecture, as it happens), who seemed a little queasy about the titles of the books I was ordering in the old round Reading Room of the British Museum. The titles resembled Jane Austen's must-read list, only they were all vampire stories. 'Admit it', said the research student, 'you're writing about horror literature for the money, aren't you?' There couldn't possibly be any other reason.

The honourable exceptions, written by literary historians in those days rather than literary critics, were still Edith Birkhead's *The Tale of Terror*, which had first been published in 1921, Devendra P. Varma's *The Gothic Flame* (1957) — which found in the novels 'the same sinister overtones and the same solemn grandeur' as in twelfth-century Gothic cathedrals — and Mario Praz's *The Romantic Agony*, which had first been issued in 1933 but which had recently become widely available in paperback. Praz adopted a boisterously thematic approach — The Persecuted Woman/The Fatal Woman; Milton's Satan/The Byronic Vampire; and so on — which was taken up at this time by aficionados of Hammer Films and British Gothic cinema. Praz also edited the standard anthology *Three Gothic Novels* (1968), which unproblematically included *Frankenstein* under that heading when it isn't really a Gothic novel at all — though Mary Shelley, from 1831 onwards, did market it as such with her celebrated retrospective *Introduction*, full of thunderstorms and creaking doors and bad vibrations. *Three Gothic Novels* had the Frankfurt version of Fuseli's painting *The Nightmare* on its cover.

Apart from these, the prejudice against horror fiction was firmly entrenched — as a conditioned reflex, almost. It was a form of fiction that was deliberately sensationalist; with heroes, heroines and villains who were merely puppets — acting out dramas which had no serious connection with the facts or morals of everyday life — in narratives which were disjoined and irrational; an ephemeral fad with formulaic conventions (antiquated castles, hidden secrets, hauntings, aristocratic villains, put-upon maidens, eighteenth-century heroes and heroines projected back into historical environments) which only deserved to survive as a cult, at best a symptom of nasty consumerism at the end of the eighteenth century and since. Edmund Burke wrote approvingly of 'the terrible sublime' as an antidote to mental lethargy and boredom. Horace Walpole, seven years later, agreed that 'Terror, the author's principal engine, prevents the story from ever languishing'. So this was sensationalism for sensationalism's sake, best read or viewed late at night when the critical faculties are half asleep. Jane Austen's novels, by contrast, could be read in daylight.

Writers in the genre evidently thought otherwise during the mid-1970s. Stephen King's *'Salem's Lot* (1975) and Anne Rice's *Interview with the Vampire* (1976) successfully resurrected the undead from their Victorian coffins, the one by transplanting the creatures to contemporary small-town America, the other by giving the vampire a psychology for the first time. These books were eventually to achieve semi-legitimate status. But a new collection of Gothic stories was about to enter the literary canon, and through the front door. The idea of writing to Bath City Council was concocted with the novelist Angela Carter, who also lived in the city. And at precisely that time, she was beginning to write about how this long-marginalised form of literature from the past was becoming central to what we would now call the postmodernist era — challenging clichés by exaggerating them, reworking the old stories in a culture of quotations and questioning some of the value systems of the accepted apostolic succession in the arts. In Gothic fiction, Angela Carter wrote in 1974, 'characters and events are exaggerated beyond reality, to become symbols, ideas, passions... style will tend to become ornate and unnatural — and thus operate against the perennial human desire [especially in Britain] to believe the word as fact... (the Gothic) retains a singular moral function — that of provoking unease'. So some art made you feel good; some transgressive art made you feel uneasy. The Gothic should be placed and was beginning to be placed, she concluded, in relation to realism in literature and the visual arts and at the same time associated with fantasy and the fantastic, with the realms of imagination and desire: novels needn't deal with domestic life and everyday experience after all; their truth could lie elsewhere. The genre may have started life with Horace Walpole and neo-medievalism — a haunted castle, giant pieces of armour, an avenging ghost, a disputed inheritance — but the Gothic had since turned into something more pervasive: an aesthetic. This aesthetic had strong links with the realist-sentimental novels of the Abbé Prévost, Samuel Richardson and Jean-Jacques Rousseau which preceded it — I originally experienced Gothic novels though my doctorate on Rousseau's *Julie ou La Nouvelle Héloïse* — but it was beginning to be seen as standing in stark opposition to 'safe' literary realism. Angela Carter was delighted to see, as she put it, that 'the *fin* in this particular *siècle* was beginning rather earlier than usual'. For, as she added, "we live in Gothic times..."

A couple of years later, in 1976 — to exemplify these ideas — Angela Carter wrote a radio play called *Vampirella*, which was subsequently turned into a magical short story in her collection *The Bloody Chamber* — the collection which also included *The Company of Wolves*, a transcription of Little Red Riding Hood as seen from the point of view of a resourceful pubescent girl. The story was called *The Lady of the House of Love*, and both play and story were written when I was starting to research in earnest Gothic fiction in general and the literature of vampires in particular. In fact, in the early summer of 1976 — which happened to be the five-hundredth anniversary of the death of Vlad the Impaler, Vlad Dracula the prince of Wallachia who unwittingly bequeathed his name to the infamous vampire Count, when Bram Stoker discovered it in a footnote to a book he was reading on holiday in Whitby — I visited the Carpathian Mountains in Central Romania to unearth some visual and historical material for a proposed book on the vampire in literature.

The book was to be one of a new series of 'Gollancz Fantasy and Macabre' — in a distinctive black and red jacket — and Angela Carter was contributing to the series as well, with *The Passion of New Eve*. The distinctive 'look' of the series was abruptly abandoned shortly after our two books were issued: public libraries, symbolically enough, preferred the traditional and instantly recognisable yellow Gollancz jacket. Black and red — allied to the words 'Fantasy and Macabre' — did not inspire the same trust. But in 1976, I had the strange experience of having my research trip Gothicised before my very eyes. The central character in the play *Vampirella* and *The Lady of the House of Love* is a dashing young public-school chap called Hero who rashly decides to go on a tour of the land beyond the forest, Transylvania, on his bicycle. Angela's story was very loosely based on my escapade — and it grew out of the many midnight conversations we had at that time about the attraction of Gothic metaphors for female writers and readers, the Gothic aesthetic, and the Marquis de Sade's contention that the craze was a by-product of the French Revolution — 'it was necessary to call upon hell to arouse interest' (Angela was beginning her work on *The Sadean Woman: An Exercise in Cultural History*). Also about the bloodline of the literary Count Dracula, and about Sawney Beane the Midlothian cannibal and amateur anarchist, a particularly choice specimen whose favourite meal was roast leg of Justice of the Peace. Hero in both play and story is rather naïve and over-enthusiastic, has studied the good old English tradition of literature at university, and above all believes that words are facts. Indeed, when confronted with the delectable vampire countess, Dracula's daughter, who turns out to be more cat-like than bat-like, he reassures himself by clinging hard to the world of empirical reality:

> Soon it will be morning; the crowing of the mundane cock and the first light will dissolve this gothic dream with the solvent of the natural. Yes, perhaps I shall take her to Vienna; and we shall clip off her finger nails and take her to a good dentist, to deal with her fangs. Perhaps, perhaps... one day, when she is cured... mother, I want you to meet... There are some things that, even if they are true, we must not believe them.

In the end, what protects Hero from a fate worse than death is not the traditional weapons of religion (holy water and the crucifix) or even of folklore and the old religion (garlic and a wooden stake) but the fact that he has been brought up to repress his imagination, and he simply doesn't recognise a real bloodsucker when he sees one. Desire is best coped with by having a cold shower. This lack of a Gothic imagination gives his heroism to the hero. Clearly, Angela thought I had been overdosing on Richardson and Rousseau and that I was not yet fully attuned, personally or professionally, to the *transgressive* aspects of the Gothic. When I finally read *The Lady of the House of Love*, in manuscript, I could experience my real-life researches in Transylvania being transformed into the magic language of the Gothic: the exaggeration and melodrama, the ornate style, the revisiting and reordering of well-worn generic conventions, the sense of a story which has often been told before, the sensational subject-matter, the conscious anachronisms, the projection of Hero into alien territory, the castle and its surrounding thicket, the villainess as taboo-breaker, the deliberate contrast between everyday material reality and a richly symbolic universe, the playfulness, the Gothic novel as being — in part — about itself, highly aware of its own fictionality. While she was writing the story, I recall Angela asking me about what happened to the borders of Transylvania round the time of the First World War, only realising later that she was thinking about the terse last line of her story: 'Next day, his regiment embarked for France'. Which signalled the end of feudalism, countesses and princes and inhabited castles and the rise of twentieth-century demons. Throughout the story the 'gothic dream' is contrasted with 'the solvent of the natural' and the technological inventions of the Enlightenment.

Thirty years after *The Lady of the House of Love* and my preparations for *The Vampyre*, literary-critical attitudes towards Gothic novels have changed utterly, as have their cultural contexts. The International Gothic Association website now lists some fifty-three courses on the subject at undergraduate and postgraduate levels, at forty-four universities around the globe — mainly in Britain and especially the USA, but also in Australia, Bulgaria, China, France, Germany and Taiwan. At the same time, as themes within the wider culture, the Gothic, horror and fantasy have never been so widespread and deep-rooted — at least not since England in the 1790s. "We are indeed", as Angela Carter put it, now living "in Gothic times". The sublime — in Burke's sense — has become one of the dominant aesthetics of the age. Burke defined the sublime, for him the most satisfying aesthetic experience of all — and an essential antidote to the predictable and the mundane — as a confrontation between the viewer or reader and extreme phenomena which triggers the emotion of terror; a strange and all-embracing mix of desire and loathing, pain and pleasure. In his list of reliable stimuli he included ruined temples, dark landscapes, howling wildernesses, gloomy forests, vicious animals, raging storms, gaping chasms and rough seas — a list that could almost be a menu for the horror novels and paintings that were shortly to come, a Burke's peerage of terror. Were he writing today, his list might still include some awe-inspiring natural phenomena — travel to dangerous places, extreme sports in remote settings, the pleasure of ruins, encountering a big animal in the wild — but even these have become in some ways predictable and mundane through endless mechanical and electronic reproduction. We experience these things, mediated through the photographs we have seen of them. So Burke's list would perhaps be just as likely to include phenomena from within the culture as well as from within 'nature': in no particular order, celluloid slashers, gross special effects, roller-coaster movies, the shift from late-night B movies to mainstream spectaculars, violent rap lyrics, bestselling doorstep horror novels where the devil inhabits the central-heating unit, further up the scale writings by Angela Carter, Toni Morrison, Margaret Atwood and Joyce Carol Oates, Damien Hirst's dead cows in formaldehyde which left the artist 'feeling like Dr Frankenstein', the Chapman brothers reworking Goya's *Disasters of War*, the neo-conceptual *Sensation!* generation for whom a well-stocked mind seems to consist of a large collection of horror videos and some xeroxed extracts from Jean Baudrillard, multimedia retreads of nineteenth-century Gothics, computer games, themed restaurants and clubs, the Goth subculture, plus of course that dizzying expansion of academic interest. The Gothic has shuffled back to centre stage, this time round revelling in its own clichés — which maybe would disqualify the contemporary genre from Burke's list of sublime stimuli after all, except for that very first confrontation when — as Burke put it — 'the mind is so utterly filled with its object, that it cannot entertain any other'. When the mind is literally blown.

It is astonishing how resilient the old stories have proved to be. Even in Alfred Hitchcock's film *Psycho* (1960), the prototype for all subsequent slasher movies, there is still the castle on the hill in the form of a clapboard gingerbread-Gothic Californian mansion. So 'the castle question' continues to intrigue us, even when there is a motel down the path and showers in every suite. The associated Dracula myth has proved so flexible that in Francis Ford Coppola's lush, big-budget remake (1992), Van Helsing becomes the fundamentalist bad guy and the Count becomes the last romantic. Charles Dickens wisely wrote of ghosts in *A Christmas Tree* (1850) that 'it is worthy of remark [that they are] reducible to a very few general types and classes; for, ghosts walk in a beaten track'. The same could certainly be said of contemporary popular horror novels and films. Which incidentally shows that the foundations of the genre — in literary and visual form — are of much more than antiquarian interest. Some people reckon, as writer Geoffrey O'Brien has observed, that these foundations are:

> ... crucial to a genre that seems to define itself by constantly recapitulating everything it has been ... To watch many horror movies is in some sense to watch the same movie over and over: they are drawn to their past in the same way that their characters are compelled to go back to the ancestral crypt... The rest is ornament and variations on a theme, a matter of more masks or bigger masks or more convincingly detailed masks.

This super-movie (and super-novel) has survived many variations in the twentieth century, since the Surrealists first saw the Gothic as 'fathoming the secret depths of history': the expressionism of the 1920s and the camp expressionism of the 1930s; the drive-in triple features of the 1950s; the rise of Hammer Films, where British cinema discovered sex and the gore was presented for the first time in chocolate box colours; the Italian pop surrealism of the 1960s; the psycho killers and seriously dysfunctional families of the 1970s and 1980s; the shift from margin to mainstream in the 1990s; above all, the change from pre-Second World War horror (where normal society was where the heroes and heroines lived) to post-Seventies horror (where the horror has become a form of liberation, and normality has itself become strange).

Throughout all this history within popular culture, the more masks and bigger masks and more detailed masks have taken on a life of their own. And as a result the atmosphere surrounding horror films (and those doorstep horror novels) from the beginning has been that of a carnival sideshow — not quite respectable, a glimpse of another world where transgressive things happen, often a bit tacky (let's face it) and above all an experience which does not quite live up to the poster, the promotional gimmicks and the slightly strange showman standing outside the tent. As cultural historian David J. Skal has pointed out, the culture of horror has always had as much to do with carnival-style promotional gimmicks as with the films themselves — just like Dr Caligari standing outside his sideshow at Holstenwall Fair, and inviting the hapless students in to see the somnambulist Cesare with a lot of hype and a life-sized poster which looks as though it was painted by Edvard Munch. Even in the eighteenth century, Gothic novels challenged — sometimes deliberately — the high ground of culture, and were later to problematise high/low distinctions. The carnival gimmicks used by horror movies seldom use the same campaign tactics as what used to be called mainstream Hollywood films: the names of the stars, the quality of the production, the timeliness of the story. Instead they blare out a warning or a challenge usually in the colour yellow: 'Warning! The Monster demands a mate!'; 'When the Screen Screams You'll Scream Too...'; 'You'll wish it were only a nightmare' and my personal favourite (from Robert Aldrich's *Whatever Happened to Baby Jane?*) 'Sister, sister/oh so fair/why is there blood/all over your hair?' These are tales of terror, and unashamed of it. The promotional gimmicks are the modern-day equivalent of all those playful prefaces — starting with Horace Walpole's for *Otranto* — with their counterfeit origins, lost manuscripts, false archaisms and bogus translations. Realist novels did not require these playful gimmicks: their high moral purpose could surely speak for itself.

Stephen King tells the story of film producers Samuel Z. Arkoff and James H. Nicholson, who were the kings of AIP drive-in movies between 1954 and 1968. Their pre-production style was simple and effective. They would think up a catchy title, trawl interest in it, then produce an even more catchy poster, trawl interest in that, and only then — if there was enough take-up — would they begin to think about actually making a film. Title first, poster second, film third. Producer William Castle, in the late 1950s, added a few carnival refinements of his own: the offer of medical treatment, for those who found the horror too much; insuring audiences with Lloyds of London if any of them should die during *Macabre*; some cinema seats wired to produce mild electric shocks for *The Tingler*. His autobiography was called *Step Right Up! I'm Gonna Scare the Pants Off America*.

Astonishingly, some of the visuals used in these campaigns and movies came indirectly — often very indirectly — from the world of visual art. The monster played by Karloff in James Whale's *Frankenstein* (1931) became not a new Adam, but a thing of scars and stitches and skewers — probably based by makeup designer Jack Pierce on a memorable image of mad aristocrats entitled *The Chinchillas* from Goya's series of prints *Caprichos/Caprices* (1799). The monster's female victim — being carried or lying in terror on a bed — in *Frankenstein* and progeny as often as not derived from Fuseli's painting *The Nightmare*. Skull Island in *King Kong* is from Böcklin's *Isle of the Dead*. Norman Bates' Gothic mansion deliberately echoes Edward Hopper's *House by the Railroad*. The *Alien* design is blood kin to Francis Bacon's *Figures at the base of a Crucifixion*. Edvard Munch's *Scream* is everywhere, as is the gnarled dying oak tree and waxing moon from Caspar David Friedrich's *Two Men Contemplating the Moon*. The shadow of Friedrich lies over most of *Nosferatu*, And so on. Much of the art has come from Northern Europe in the late eighteenth and nineteenth centuries, carried by émigré production designers and art directors.

In the end, the patter of the carnival barker seems to boil down to this: he assumes we want to be terrified; he assumes we want to see, from the relative safety of our cinema seat, the horror that normally would not dare to speak its name; he assumes — like Edmund Burke — that we enjoy 'desire with loathing strangely mixed' or 'the tempestuous loveliness of terror', as Coleridge and Shelley put it. Charles Dickens' fat boy in *The Pickwick Papers* expressed the thing more bluntly: 'I wants to make your flesh creep'. We believe these old, old stories and we don't believe them, both at the same time. We approach them as we do the carnival magician in *The Wizard of Oz*, even when we have realised he is the charlatan behind the curtain.

Much of the recent critical debate about Gothic novels — and horror cinema — has tended to mask or perhaps exorcise this basic function of the genre, which is to scare its readers and viewers in enjoyable ways, by solemnly deconstructing the words on the page or the images on the screen into the psychological or socio-political elements which may lie beneath them: in other words, by reading what is between the lines rather than what is on them. As Jerrold E. Hogle has recently written, in his *Introduction* to the *Cambridge Companion to Gothic Fiction* (2002):

> No other form of writing or theatre is as insistent as Gothic on juxtaposing potential revolution and possible reaction — about gender, sexuality, race, class, the colonizers versus the colonized, the physical versus the metaphysical, and abnormal versus normal psychology — and leaving both extremes sharply before us and far less resolved than the conventional endings in most of these works claim them to be.

The eccentric bibliomania of the 1930s and 1940s, and the old-style literary history which paralleled it, even the careful speculations by Angela Carter on the 'singular moral function' of the Gothic and her own practice as a novelist, have made way for an embattled kind of defiance of the literary establishment (whatever that may now be) with its great tradition and Enlightenment ideas and preference for the realist tradition. The specific enemy is Augustan/neo-classical writers and critics; the more general enemy is most literary critics pre-1985. This defiance chimes with the diffuse 'postmodernism' which has been in the ether at the same time — postmodernism with its hall of mirrors, its fascination with simulacra, forgeries and the artificial, its suspicion of 'natural' appearances and its emphasis on intertextuality rather than authorial intention; the twilight of the real has proved spookily appropriate to the Gothic. It all seemed so promosing, when Angela wrote about it. Maybe today's defiance is also, in part, a defensiveness — like aspects of Film Studies in the same years, which began by explaining visual images but soon preferred to explain them away, as if the commentators were scared of enjoying themselves. Where the Gothic novel is concerned, the key intellectual context is identity politics in the late twentieth century — gender, race, post-colonialism — and the key entry points have been Freud's essay on *The Uncanny* (1919), about how familiar desires and fears particularly scare us when they reappear in unfamiliar guises, and Julia Kristeva's *Powers of Horror* (1980), about how the repressed is 'abjected' or discarded onto the Other and how 'the abject' can challenge the deepest roots of our identity. Also influential have been essays by Roland Barthes and Umberto Eco, on 'open texts' which break the flow and emphasise the arbitrariness of the sign and 'closed texts' which simply contribute to the flow and present the word as fact: many Gothic novels may *seem* closed but are *really* open.

So Gothic novels have become texts, above all other forms of fiction, where 'the repressed' can return, where 'the abject' can be disguised, and where social and political anxieties can be displaced — waiting for critics from today's more liberated perspectives to disinter them. There have been debates about definitions of 'the Gothic' — should the term apply, strictly speaking, only to the period between 1764 (*The Castle of Otranto*) and 1816 (*Frankenstein*) or maybe 1820 (Maturin's *Melmoth the Wanderer*), or should it have much broader application to the heirs of the Gothic in twentieth- and twenty-first-century popular culture? John Ruskin famously wrote, in his *Seven Lamps of Architecture*, 'I use the word Gothic in the most extended sense as broadly opposed to classical — that it admits a richness of record altogether unlimited'. Many today would agree. Also there have been debates between those who prefer to emphasise psychoanalytical approaches (as applied to authors *and* readers) and those who are more interested in the redescription of immediate historical contexts — such as the rise of consumerism with its ephemeral choices and shifting fashions, the expansion of the reading public, the commercialisation of publishing, the complex impact of the French Revolution, the politics of gender in the late eighteenth century, all of them presenting a new challenge to fixed social hierarchies. The context of gender has led — at its best — to a welcome reappraisal of the work of Ann Radcliffe from the points of view of women's property rights and family structures in a patriarchal age. It has also led to the less welcome concept of something called 'female Gothic', which apparently empowered its authors through more subtle and sublimated forms of horror than the grosser male version; and to the absorption of *Frankenstein* into the Gothic web. Psychoanalytical approaches have found Bram Stoker's *Dracula* (1897) to be particularly fertile territory, the site of every imaginable middle class anxiety about politics, race, gender and especially sexuality with the Count turning into an all-purpose Other. In the 1950s, the Freudian critic Maurice Richardson referred to *Dracula* as '. . . a kind of incestuous, necrophilious, oral-anal-sadistic all-in wrestling match', a parable of Oedipal conflict (the Count as big daddy), repressed sexual desires, and the dilution of sexual drive. But he was not being entirely serious. Today, no-one seems to be certain whether *Dracula* is in the end about repression or empowerment: it all depends on whether you are on the side of 'the crew of light' or the vampires. As Chris Baldick and Robert Mighall have wisely written, about such approaches to literary deconstruction:

> From psychoanalysis, such Gothic Criticism has taken the model of middle-class respectability divided against itself, deeply driven by and in conflict with uncontrollable forces; from post-structuralism it has taken the model of 'violent hierarchies', in which the dominant constructs its identity by the constant suppression of the subordinate; and from neo-Marxist theory it has taken a model of the 'political unconscious', the unsaid of a given historical period, which modern criticism is called upon to articulate, finding in the past 'subversive' validations of the desires and agendas of the present...

This judgement is harsh, but it certainly fits some of the more extreme contributions to the burgeoning sub-discipline of Gothic Studies. Baldick and Mighall conclude that it is as if literary criticism itself has become a Gothic project creating its own melodramas through which to confront villains within the crumbling hierarchies of the academy. One welcome side effect of this general reappraisal of the Gothic has been in publishing: reissues of important or obscure texts and documents in useful critical editions; critical debates in the form of substantial anthologies of articles by leading scholars in the field, such as the Oxford and Cambridge *Companions*. But these have been confined to the discipline of literary studies. What has been lacking up to now has been a collection of texts with a much broader historical scope — ranging from canonical Gothic right through to twentieth-century ideas and contemporary culture, challenging fundamentalist conceptions of 'the Gothic' on the way — which aims to reincorporate the visual arts into the subject-area, through texts and illustrations. What happened to the Gothic between publication of *The Castle of Otranto* on Christmas Day 1764 and the irresistible rise of Ann Radcliffe in the 1790s? Scholars have rightly emphasised the importance of isolated 'moments' such as the debates among critics about the history and significance of 'romance' in the 1780s, but the slow take-up of the lessons of *Otranto* still requires explanation. And where exactly did Ann Radcliffe get her landscapes from?

One answer to both is that from the mid-1770s onwards several of the younger generation of visual artists in Britain began exploring Gothic themes — deliberate exaggerations of neo-classicism and of gendered bodily types, tableaux of the supernatural taken from the tragedies of Shakespeare (notably the witches and the dagger from *Macbeth*; the King's nightmare from the tent scene of *Richard III*; the ghost on the battlements from *Hamlet*), rediscoveries — and sometimes inventions — of national traditions of fantasy from the worlds of folklore and fairytale, horrific incidents, wild landscapes, castles and dungeons all justified with reference to 'the sublime' and canonical literature. This led to a critical debate — parallel to equivalent questions of 'romance' — about the moral and aesthetic legitimacy of such themes and imagery. Up to now, literary scholars have tended on the whole to confine their interest in visual art to the cover illustrations of their books (an obligatory Fuseli or sometimes a Friedrich). By the same token, art historians working on closely related fields (the paintings of among others James Barry, Maria and Richard Cosway, George Romney, Benjamin West and above all Henry Fuseli and William Blake; the politics of the Royal Academy; the meanings and value of 'culture'; the Gothic Revival) have generally overlooked the ever-swelling body of new cultural and literary studies of the Gothic. This collection of texts and images aims to start redressing the balance, using 'Gothic' as an art-historical term. It also aims to bring together practitioner-texts by canonical writers and critics, with theoretical material from commentators and journalists of the period — and since. Some of the late eighteenth-century debates, for example about 'terror Gothic' and 'horror Gothic', the atmospheric and the explicit, are still very much around, albeit using very different vocabularies. Others, on the aesthetic functions of horror and fantasy, have changed beyond all recognition, especially since the publication of Freud's *The Uncanny* and Ernest Jones' more detailed *On the Nightmare*: we can now have thoughts about terror and horror which were literally unthinkable in the late eighteenth century. By collating some of the earliest accounts of the Gothic with more recent ones, hidden continuities and discontinuities can be opened up for debate. Some critics have stressed the 'medieval' aspects of the Gothic novel post-*Otranto*, and related these in a direct way to the Gothic Revival in architecture and design: others have noted that very few Gothic novels in fact had a 'medieval' setting and that connections with the Gothic Revival are tenuous at best. Discuss. Finally, *The Gothic Reader* examines through texts and illustrations, the invention of a new figure on the cultural landscape, the wild, inspired artist: from the late eighteenth-century craze for artists' biographies to confessional autobiographies to the sickly dreams of Edgar Allan Poe and H.P. Lovecraft, the artist himself or herself has become the subject of fantasy. Haunted paintings and artefacts became a staple of Gothic fiction from the mid- nineteenth century onwards, long before Oscar Wilde and *Dorian Gray*.

Horace Walpole, in April 1765, wrote of the 'liberty to expatiate through the boundless realms of invention' which his 'Gothic Story' had made possible. The Gothic — as a critical, historical, literary and visual subject — has certainly contained legions, and we hope this *Reader* will help to extend the field even further. For much of the nineteenth century and some of the twentieth, the Gothic was waiting in the wings. Now it is centre stage. The last time I visited William Beckford's Tower, up Lansdown Hill in Bath, I was greeted by the sight of an Italian film-crew shooting a soft-porn Satanist sequence for a horror movie in the graveyard where the author of *Vathek* is buried. At least, I *think* that is what they were doing. It really is time for Bath City Council to reconsider. Apart from anything else, postmodernism is beginning to get tired.

A Companion to the Gothic, ed. David Punter (Oxford, 2001) and *The Cambridge Companion to Gothic Fiction*, ed. Jerrold E. Hogle (Cambridge, 2002) proved very useful in preparing this *Introduction*. An earlier version of part of it appeared in *Topic Magazine* (issue 2, Cambridge, Fall 2002, pp. 76–83).

The Gothic: A Sampling of Some Key Texts and Images

As a modern critical term, 'Gothic' has meant the literature of horror and fantasy that developed in the late eighteenth century, specifically with the publication of Horace Walpole's *The Castle of Otranto* (1764), and which remained a vastly popular and energetic literary form until the eve of the Victorian era. Later efforts in this field have more contentiously been called 'Gothic', though there may be little argument that Edgar Allan Poe and Bram Stoker represent, if not a direct continuation of the 'classic' Gothic literature of the end of the eighteenth century, a significant reinvigoration of this literary form. Yet the term is also widely employed in relation to modern and contemporary literature in the English language and otherwise, cinema, art, and cultural criticism. It may be taken to refer to certain, structural, tendencies to distortion, the grotesque, and uncanny, rather than a definable, limited genre. As the scholarly industry around the Gothic has proliferated, so Gothicisms have multiplied, so that we might now consider a vast array of historical, generic and geographical versions of the Gothic.

In the relatively small compass of this present volume, it would be impossible to make a representative selection of passages and short tales that might satisfy any definition of the Gothic, even the most restrictive. What we present here is the opportunity to taste some of the more shocking, intriguing and telling moments of horror, fantasy and the weird to be found within what we will temporarily allow ourselves to believe can be defined as 'the Gothic tradition', and to introduce some defining visual images which draw on, echo or anticipate this literary phenomenon. Naturally, we have sought to introduce excerpts from what are most widely considered to be the canonical works — trusting that there is no one who would dispute that Walpole, Radcliffe, Lewis and Mary Shelley might be productively considered as 'Gothic' authors of one kind or another. But with the texts by Burke and Blake, Smollett and Steele, and with the presence of these usually overlooked images, we hope to offer a sense of possibility for a more wide-ranging exploration of the horrific, bizarre and uncanny in art.

1.1

A Horrifying Oriental Tale

The Guardian (1713) was among the early essay-periodicals that helped define a modern, bourgeois literary culture in the eighteenth century. Such succinct, witty writing helped to articulate a new cultural self-awareness among a largely urban class, who drew their status and material comfort from professional activities and business rather than aristocratic land-ownership. Somewhat detached from the traditions of high culture, the writers of these journals were at liberty to revise and refresh the principles of good taste and the compass of good manners.

Like *The Tatler* (1709–11) and *Spectator* (1711–12), the periodical featured short stories, both original and based on traditional sources, as well as cultural criticism, philosophy and discussions of manners, morals and mores. 'The History of Santon Barsisa' is a story found in Turkish, Arabic and Persian tradition; it had most recently appeared in Jacob Tonson's *Turkish Tales* (1708). Although the author of this version — presumed to be Richard Steele — is careful to assure the reader that it fits with the Christian morality of the essay journal as a whole, the tale's bleakness and the rather startling physicality of the conclusion introduce a note of amorality more usually associated with later Gothic narratives.

Significantly, this story was cited by Matthew Lewis as among the prime points of inspiration for his defining Gothic novel *The Monk* (1796).

31 August 1713

Richard Steele 1672–1729
The Guardian, no.148

There is a kind of Apothegm, which I have frequently met with in my Reading, to this purpose; *That there are few, if any Books, out of which a Man of Learning may not extract something for his use*. I have often experienced the Truth of this Maxim, when, calling in at my Bookseller's, I have taken the Book next to my Hand off the Counter, to employ the Minutes I have been obliged to linger away there, in waiting for one Friend or other. Yesterday, when I came there, the *Turkish Tales* happened to lie in my way; upon opening of that amusing Author, I happened to dip upon a short Tale, which gave me a great many serious Reflections. The very same Fable may fall into the Hands of great many Men of Wit and Pleasure, who, 'tis probable, will read it with a sneer; but since it may as probably Divert and Instruct a great many Persons of plain and virtuous Minds, I shall make no scruple of making it the Entertainment of this Day's Paper. The Moral to be drawn from it is intirely Christian, and is so very obvious, that I shall leave to every Reader the Pleasure of picking it out for himself. I shall only premise, to obviate any Offence that may be taken, that a great many Notions in the *Mahometan* Religion are borrowed from the *Holy Scripture*.

The History of Santon Barsisa

There was formerly a *Santon* whose Name was *Barsisa*, which for the Space of an hundred Years very fervently apply'd himself to Prayer; and scarce ever went out of the Grotto in which he made his Residence, for fear of exposing himself to the Danger of offending God. He fasted in the Day-time, and watch'd in the Night; all the Inhabitants of the Country had such a great Veneration for him, and so highly valu'd his Prayers, that they commonly apply'd to him when they had any Favour to beg of Heaven. When he made Vows for the Health of a sick Person, the Patient was immediately cur'd.

It happen'd that the Daughter of the King of that Country fell into a dangerous Distemper, the Cause of which the Physicians could not discover, yet they continu'd prescribing Remedies by guess; but instead of helping the Princess, they only augmented her Disease. In the mean time the King was inconsolable, for he passionately lov'd his Daughter; wherefore one Day, finding all Human Assistance vain, he declar'd it as his Opinion, that the Princess ought to be sent to the *Santon Barsisa*.

All the *Beys* applauded his Sentiment, and the King's Officers conducted her to the *Santon*; who, notwithstanding his frozen Age, could not see such a Beauty without being sensibly mov'd. He gaz'd on her with Pleasure, and the Devil, taking this Opportunity, whisper'd in his Ear thus; *O* Santon! *don't let slip such a fortunate Minute: Tell the king's Servants that it is requisite for the Princess to pass this Night in the Grotto, to see whether it will please God to cure her; that you will put up a Prayer for her, and that they need only come to fetch her to Morrow.*

How weak is Man! The *Santon* follow'd the Devil's Advice, and did what he suggested to him. But the Officers, before they would yield to leave the Princess, sent one of their Number to know the King's Pleasure. That Monarch, who had an entire Confidence in *Barsisa*, never in the least scrupled the trusting of his Daughter with him. *I consent*, said he, *that she stay with that Holy Man, and that he keep her as long as he pleases: I am wholly satisfy'd on that Head.*

When the Officers had receiv'd the King's Answer they all retired, and the Princess remain'd alone with the Hermit. Night being come, the Devil presented himself to the *Santon*, saying, *Canst thou let slip so favourable an Opportunity with so charming a Creature? Fear not her telling of the Violence you offer her; if she were even so indiscreet as to reveal it, who will believe her? The Court, the City, and all the World are too much prepossessed in your Favour, to give any Credit to such a Report. You may do any thing unpunish'd, when arm'd by the great Reputation for Wisdom which you have acquir'd.* The unfortunate *Barsisa* was so weak as to hearken to the Enemy of Mankind. He approach'd the Princess, took her into his Arms, and in a Moment cancell'd a Virtue of an hundred Years Duration.

He had no sooner perpetrated his Crime, than a thousand avenging Horrors haunted him Night and Day. He thus accosts the Devil: *O Wretch!* says he, *'tis thou which hast destroy'd me! Thou hast encompass'd me for a whole Age, and endeavoured to seduce me; and now at last thou hast gain'd thy End. O* Santon! answer'd the Devil, *don't reproach me with the Pleasure thou hast enjoy'd. Thou mayest repent: But what is unhappy for you is that the Princess is impregnated, and thy Sin will become publick: thou wilt become the Laughing stock of those who admire and reverence thee at present, and the King will put thee to an ignominious Death.*

Barsisa, terrify'd by this Discourse, says to the Devil, *What shall I do to prevent the Publication of my Shame? To hinder the Knowledge of your Crime you ought to commit a fresh one,* answer'd the Devil: *Kill the Princess, bury her at the Corner of the Grotto, and when the King's Messengers come to Morrow, tell them you have cur'd her, and that she went from the Grotto very early in the Morning: They will believe you, and search for her all over the City and Country; the King her Father will be in great Pain for her, but after several vain Searches, it will wear off.*

The Hermit, abandon'd by God, pursuant to this advice kill'd the Princess, bury'd her in a Corner of the Grotto, and the next Day told the Officers what the Devil bid him to say. They made diligent Enquiry for the King's Daughter, but not being able to hear of her, they despair'd of finding her, when the Devil told them all their Search for the Princess was vain; and relating what had pass'd betwixt her and the *Santon*, he told them the place where she was interred. The Officers immediately went to the

Grotto, seiz'd *Barsisa*, and found the Princess's Body in the Place to which the Devil had directed them; whereupon they took up the Corps, and carry'd that and the *Santon* to the Palace.

When the King saw his Daughter dead, and was inform'd of the whole Event, he broke out into Tears and bitter Lamentations; and assembling the Doctors, he laid out the *Santon's* Crime before them, and ask'd their Advice how he should be punish'd. All the Doctors condemn'd him to Death, upon which the King order'd him to be hang'd: Accordingly a Gibbet was erected: the Hermit went up the Ladder, and when he was going to be turn'd off, the Devil whisper'd in his Ear these Words: *O* Santon! *if you will worship me I will extricate you out of this Difficulty, and transport you two thousand Leagues from hence, into a Country where you shall be reverenc'd by Men, as much as you were before this Adventure. I am content,* says *Barsisa; deliver me, and I will worship thee. Give me first a Sign of Adoration,* replies the Devil; whereupon the *Santon* bow'd his Head, and said, *I give myself to you*. The Devil then raising his Voice, said, *O* Barsisa*,, I am satisfy'd; I have obtain'd what I desir'd:* And with these Words spitting in his Face, he disappear'd; and the deluded *Santon* was hang'd.

1.2

Horrid Imprisonments

The following two selections present episodes of profound Gothic horror, although extracted from novels of a quite different character. Tobias Smollett's *The Adventures of Ferdinand Count Fathom* (1753) represents the robustly entertaining, picareque novel of adventure which won wide favour in the mid-eighteenth century. This scene, in which the hero is trapped in a locked room with a dead body, was understood at a very early date to anticipate the horribly morbid encounters characteristic of the full-blooded Gothic novel (see below, p.130). Sterne's *A Sentimental Journey* (1768) is a complexly ironic and knowing fiction, that was part of, and commented on, the cult of 'sensibility' -the affectation of deep feeling and profound sensitivity to nature that formed the tireless subject of essays, novels, poems and, in due course, ridicule, from the 1750s. The text follows the travels of an Anglican parson, Yorick, around France, as he encounters various moving scenes and affecting personal stories. Here, threatened with imprisonment in Paris because he lacked the proper passport, Yorick meditates upon the fate of a prisoner in the infamous Bastille, in order to conjure up a suitable sense of dread and fear.

1753

Tobias Smollett 1721–71
The Adventures of Ferdinand Count Fathom

Fathom, whose own principles taught him to be suspicious, and ever upon his guard against the treachery of his fellow-creatures, could have dispensed with this instance of her care in confining her guest to her chamber, and began to be seized with strange fancies, when he observed that there was no bolt on the inside of the door, by which he might secure himself from intrusion. In consequence of these suggestions, he proposed to take an accurate survey of every object in the apartment, and in the course of his inquiry, had the mortification to find the dead body of a man, still warm, who had been lately stabbed, and concealed beneath several bundles of straw.

Such a discovery could not fail to fill the breast of our hero, with unspeakable horror; for he concluded that he himself would undergo the same fate before morning, without the interposition of a miracle in his favour. In the first transports of his dread, he ran to the window with a view to escape by that outlet, and found his flight effectually obstructed by divers strong bars of iron. Then his heart began to palpitate, his hair to bristle up, and his knees to totter; his thoughts teemed with presages of death and destruction; his conscience rose up in judgment against him, and he underwent a severe paroxysm of dismay and distraction. His spirits were agitated into a state of fermentation that produced a species of resolution a-kin to that which is inspired by brandy or other strong liquors, and by an impulse that seemed supernatural, he was immediately hurried into measures for his own preservation.

What upon a less interesting occasion his imagination durst not propose, he now executed without scruple or remorse: he undressed the corpse that lay bleeding among the straw, and, conveying it to the bed in his arms, deposited it in the attitude of a person who sleeps at his ease; then he extinguished the light, took possession of the place from whence the body had been removed, and holding a pistol ready cocked in each hand, waited for the sequel with that determined purpose, which is often the immediate production of despair. About midnight he heard the sound of feet ascending the ladder, the door was softly opened, he saw the shadow of two men stalking towards the bed, a dark lanthorn being unshrouded, directed their aim to the supposed sleeper, and he that held it, thrust a poniard to his heart; the force of the blow made a compression on the chest, and a sort of groan issued from the windpipe of the defunct; the stroke was repeated, without producing a repetition of the note, so that the assassins concluded the work was effectually done, and retired for the present, with a design to return and rifle the deceased at their leisure.

Never had our hero spent a moment in such agony, as he felt during this operation; the whole surface of his body was covered with a cold sweat, and his nerves were relaxed with an universal palsy: in short, he remained in a trance that, in all probability, contributed to his safety; for, had he retained the use of his senses, he might have been discovered by the transports of his fear. The first use he made of his retrieved recollection was to perceive that the assassins had left the door open in their retreat; and he would have instantly availed himself of this their neglect, by sallying out upon them, at the hazard of his life, had not he been restrained by a conversation he overheard in the room below, importing that the ruffians were going to set out upon another expedition, in hopes of finding more prey: they accordingly departed, after having laid strong injunctions upon the old woman, to keep the door fast locked during their absence; and Ferdinand took his resolution without farther delay. So soon as by his conjecture, the robbers were at a sufficient distance from the house, he rose from his lurking-place, moved softly towards the bed, and rummaging the pockets of the deceased, found a purse well stored with ducats, of which, together with a silver watch and a diamond ring, he immediately possessed himself without scruple; then descending with great care and circumspection, into the lower apartment, stood before the old beldam, before she had the least intimation of his approach.

Accustomed as she was to the trade of blood, the hoary hag did not behold this apparition without giving signs of infinite terror and astonishment, believing it was no other than the spirit of her second guest who had been murdered; she fell upon her knees, and began to recommend herself to the protection of the saints, crossing herself with as much devotion, as if she had been entitled to the particular care and attention of Heaven. Nor did her anxiety abate, when she was undeceived in this her supposition, and understood it was no phantom, but the real substance of the stranger, who without staying to upbraid her with the enormity of her crimes, commanded her on pain of immediate death to produce his horse, to which being conducted, he set her upon the saddle without delay, and mounting behind, invested her with the management of the reins, swearing in a most peremptory tone, that the only chance she had for her life, was in directing him safely to the next town; and that so soon as she should give him the least cause to doubt her fidelity in the performance of that task, he would, on the instant, act the part of her executioner.

This declaration had its effect upon the withered Hecate, who, with many supplications for mercy and forgiveness, promised to guide him in safety to a certain village at the distance of two leagues, where he might lodge in security, and be provided with a fresh horse, or other convenience, for pursuing his intended route. On these conditions, he told her, she might deserve his clemency, and they accordingly took their departure together, she being placed astride upon the saddle, holding the bridle in one hand, and a switch in the other; and our adventurer sitting on the crupper, superintending her conduct, and keeping the muzzle of a pistol close at her ear. In this equipage, they travelled across part of the same wood, in which his guide had forsaken him; and it is not to be supposed, that he passed his time in the most agreeable reverie, while he found himself involved in the labyrinth of those shades, which he considered as the haunts of robbery and assassination.

Common fear was a comfortable sensation to what he felt in this excursion. The first steps he had taken for his preservation, were the effects of neer instinct, while his faculties were extinguished or suppressed by despair; but, now as his reflection began to recur, he was haunted by the most intolerable apprehensions. Every whisper of the wind through the thickets, was swelled into the hoarse menaces of murder, the shaking of the boughs was construed into the brandishing of poignards, and every shadow of a tree, became the apparition of a ruffian eager for blood. In short, at each of these occurrences, he felt what was infinitely more tormenting than the stab of a real dagger; and at every fresh filip of his fear, he acted as remembrancer to his conductress, in a new volley of imprecations, importing that her life was absolutely connected with his opinion of his own safety.

Human nature could not longer subsist under such complicated terror: at last he found himself clear of the forest, and was blessed with the distant view of an inhabited place: he then began to exercise his thoughts upon a new subject. He debated with himself, whether he should make a parade of his intrepidity and public spirit, by disclosing his atchievement, and surrendering his guide to the penalty of the law; or leave the old hag and her accomplices to the remorse of their own consciences, and proceed quietly on his journey to Paris, in undisturbed possession of the prize he had already obtained. This last step he determined to take, upon recollecting that in the course of his information, the story of the murdered stranger would infallibly attract the attention of justice, and in that case, the effects he had borrowed from the defunct, must be refunded for the benefit of those who had a right to the succession. This was an argument which our adventurer could not resist; he foresaw that he should be stript of his acquisition, which he looked upon as the fair fruits of his valour and sagacity; and moreover, be detained as an evidence against the robbers, to the manifest detriment of his affairs: perhaps too, he had motives of conscience that dissuaded him from bearing witness against a set of people, whose principles did not much differ from his own.

Influenced by such considerations, he yielded to the first importunity of the beldam, whom he dismissed at a very small distance from the village, after he had earnestly exhorted her to quit such an atrocious course of life, and attone for her past crimes, by sacrificing her associates to the demands of justice. She did not fail to vow a perfect reformation, and to prostrate herself before him, for the favour she had found; then she betook

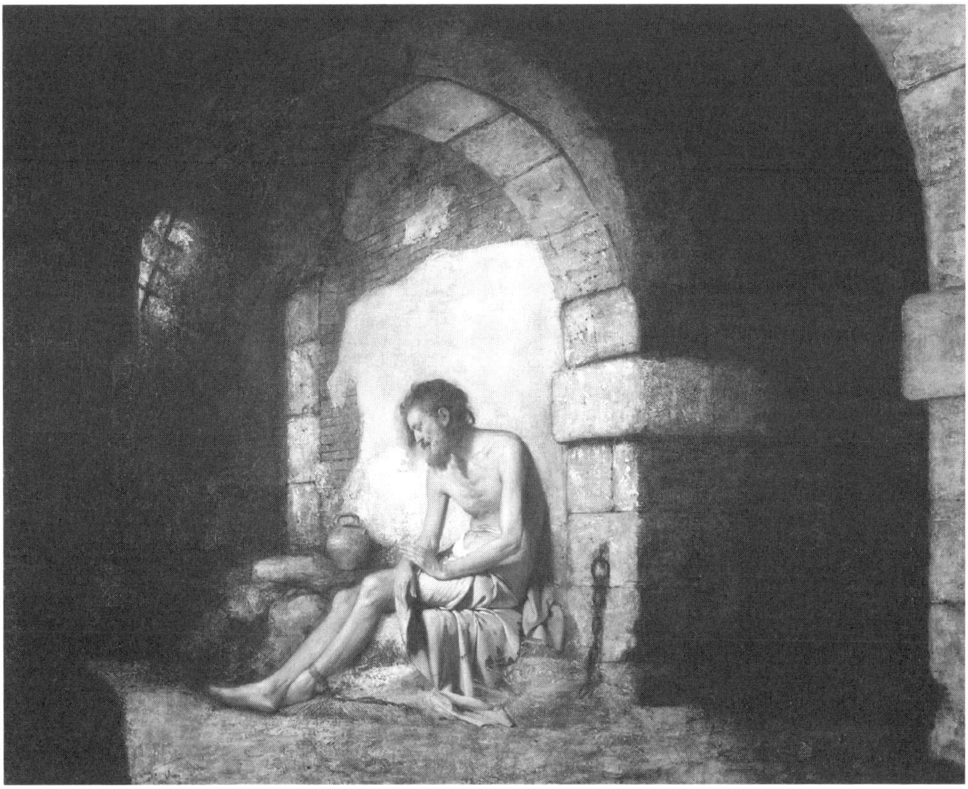

1
Joseph Wright of Derby
The Captive, after Sterne, c.1774
Oil on canvas 102 × 127.5 cm
Vancouver Art Gallery

herself to her habitation, with full purpose of advising her fellow-murderers to repair with all dispatch to the village, and impeach our hero, who wisely distrusting her professions, stayed no longer in the place, than to hire a guide for the next stage, which brought him to the city of Chalons sur Marne.

1768

Laurence Sterne 1713–68
A Sentimental Journey through France and Italy by Mr Yorick

The Captive. Paris

The bird in his cage pursued me into my room; I sat down close to my table, and leaning my head upon my hand, I began to figure to myself the miseries of confinement. I was in a right frame for it, and so I gave full scope to my imagination.

I was going to begin with the millions of my fellow creatures born to no inheritance but slavery; but finding, however affecting the picture was, that I could not bring it near me, and that the multitude of sad groups in it did but distract me.—

— I took a single captive, and having first shut him up in his dungeon, I then look'd through the twilight of his grated door to take his picture.

I beheld his body half wasted away with long expectation and confinement, and felt what kind of sickness of the heart it was which arises from hope deferr'd. Upon looking nearer I saw him pale and feverish: in thirty years the western breeze had not once fann'd his blood — he had seen no sun, no moon in all that time — nor had the voice of friend or kinsman breathed through his lattice — his children —

—But here my heart began to bleed — and I was forced to go on with another part of the portrait.

He was sitting upon the ground upon a little straw, in the furthest corner of the dungeon, which was alternately his chair and bed: a little calender of small sticks were laid at the head notch'd all over with the dismal days and nights he had pass'd there — he had one of these little sticks in his hand, and with a rusty nail he was etching another day of misery to add to the heap. As I darkened the little light he had, he lifted up a hopeless eye towards the door, then cast it down — shook his head, and went on with the work of affliction. I heard his chains upon his legs, as he turn'd his body to lay his little stick upon the bundle — He gave a deep sigh — I saw the iron enter into his soul — I burst into tears — I could not sustain the picture of confinement which my fancy had drawn — I startled up from my chair...

The Castle of Otranto

Horace Walpole's novel *The Castle of Otranto* (1764) has always been considered the first proper Gothic tale, and a singularly important point of reference for the fictions which followed in this vein. Walpole (1717–97) was a connoisseur, collector and antiquarian, who had made some forays into public life but was more largely occupied with his private concerns. Greatest among these was developing the fantastically ornate Gothic fantasia of Strawberry Hill, perhaps the most important building of the mid-eighteenth century Gothic revival, inspired, by Walpole's own account, by a dream fuelled by his medieval preoccupations (see p.220). Walpole's fiction was first published as a translation of an old manuscript, as described in the Preface, thus enacting a curiously, characteristically Gothic deception. The author's identity was, though, well-known by the time of the second edition of 1765. The new Preface to that second edition appears here on p.136.

Walpole's text conjugates most of the important preoccupations of the Gothic literature of the next decades: a sickly but profound fascination with the Catholic past, bizarre architectural spaces, ghosts and hauntings, sexual perversion and violent revenge, dressed in an overheated, often mock-Shakespearean language. All these elements are apparent in the section excerpted here. The plot, implausible in the extreme, concerns the bizarre death of the son of Manfred, the lord of Otranto, Conrad, crushed by a gigantic helmet which appears from nowhere, and his near-incestuous pursuit of Conrad's bride-to-be, Isabella.

1764

Horace Walpole 1717–97
The Castle of Otranto

Preface to the first edition

The following work was found in the library of an ancient Catholic family in the north of *England*. It was printed at *Naples*, in the black letter, in the year 1529. How much sooner it was written does not appear. The principal incidents are such as were believed in the darkest ages of Christianity; but the language and conduct have nothing that savours of barbarism. The style is of the purest *Italian*. If the story was written near the time when it is supposed to have happened, it must have been between 1095, the era of the first crusade, and 1243, the date of the last, or not long afterwards. There is no other circumstance in the work that can lead us to guess at the period in which the scene is laid: The names of the actors are evidently fictitious, and probably disguised on purpose: Yet the *Spanish* names of the domestics seem to indicate, that this work was not composed, until the establishment of the *Arragonian* Kings in *Naples* had made *Spanish* appellations familiar in that country. The beauty of the diction, and the zeal of the author [moderated, however, by singular judgment] concur to make me think that the date of the composition was little antecedent to that of the impression. Letters were then in the most flourishing state in *Italy*, and contributed to dispel the empire of superstition, at that time so forcibly attacked by the reformers. It is not unlikely that an artful priest might endeavour to turn their own arms on the innovators; and might avail himself of his abilities as an author to confirm the populace in their ancient errors and superstitions. If this was his view, he has certainly acted with signal address. Such a work as the following would enslave a hundred vulgar minds beyond half the books of controversy that have been written from the days of *Luther* to the present hour.

This solution of the author's motives is, however, offered as a mere conjecture. Whatever his views were, or whatever effects the execution of them might have, his work can only be laid before the public at present as a matter of entertainment. Even as such, some apology for it is necessary. Miracles, visions, necromancies, dreams, and other preternatural events, are exploded now even from romances. That was not the case when our author wrote; much less when the story itself is supposed to have happened. Belief in every kind of prodigy was so established in those dark ages, that an author would not be faithful to the *manners* of the times who should omit all mention of them. He is not bound to believe them himself, but he must represent his actors as believing them.

If this *air* of the *miraculous* is excused, the reader will find nothing else unworthy of his perusal. Allow the possibility of the facts, and all the actors comport themselves as persons would do in their situation. There is no bombast, no similes, flowers, digressions, or unnecessary descriptions. Everything tends directly to the catastrophe. Never is the reader's attention relaxed. The rules of the drama are almost observed throughout the conduct of the piece. The characters are well drawn and still better maintained. Terror, the author's principal engine, prevents the story from ever languishing; and it is so often contrasted by pity, that the mind is kept up in a constant vicissitude of interesting passions.

Some persons may perhaps think the characters of the domestics too little serious for the general cast of the story; but besides their opposition to the principal personages, the art of the author is very observable in his conduct of the subalterns. They discover many passages essential to the story, which could not be well brought to light but by their naïveté and simplicity: In particular, the womanish terror and foibles of *Bianca*, in the last chapter, conduce essentially towards advancing the catastrophe.

It is natural for a translator to be prejudiced in favour of his adopted work. More impartial readers may not be so much struck with the beauties of this piece as I was. Yet I am not blind to my author's defects. I could wish he had grounded his plan on a more useful moral than this; that *the sins of fathers are visited on their children to the third and fourth generation*. I doubt whether, in his time, any more than at present, ambition curbed its appetite of dominion from the dread of so remote a punishment. And yet this moral is weakened by that less direct insinuation, that even such anathema may be diverted by devotion to St. *Nicholas*. Here the interest of the Monk plainly gets the better of the judgment of the author. However, with all its faults, I have no doubt but the *English* reader will be pleased with a sight of this performance. The piety that reigns throughout, the lessons of virtue that are inculcated, and the rigid purity of the sentiments, exempt this work from the censure to which romances are but too liable. Should it meet with the success I hope for, I may be encouraged to reprint the original *Italian*, though it will tend to depreciate my own labour. Our language falls far short of the charms of the *Italian*, both for variety and harmony. The latter is peculiarly excellent for simple narrative. It is difficult in *English to relate* without falling too low or rising too high; a fault obviously occasioned by the little care taken to speak pure language in common conversation. Every *Italian* or *Frenchman* of any rank piques himself on speaking his own tongue correctly and with choice. I cannot flatter myself with having done justice to my author in this respect: His style is as elegant, as his conduct of the passions is masterly. It is pity that he did not apply his talents to what they were evidently proper for, the theatre.

I will detain the reader no longer, but to make one short remark. Though the machinery is invention, and the names of the actors imaginary, I cannot but believe, that the ground-work of the story is founded on truth. The scene is undoubtedly laid in some real castle. The author seems frequently, without design, to

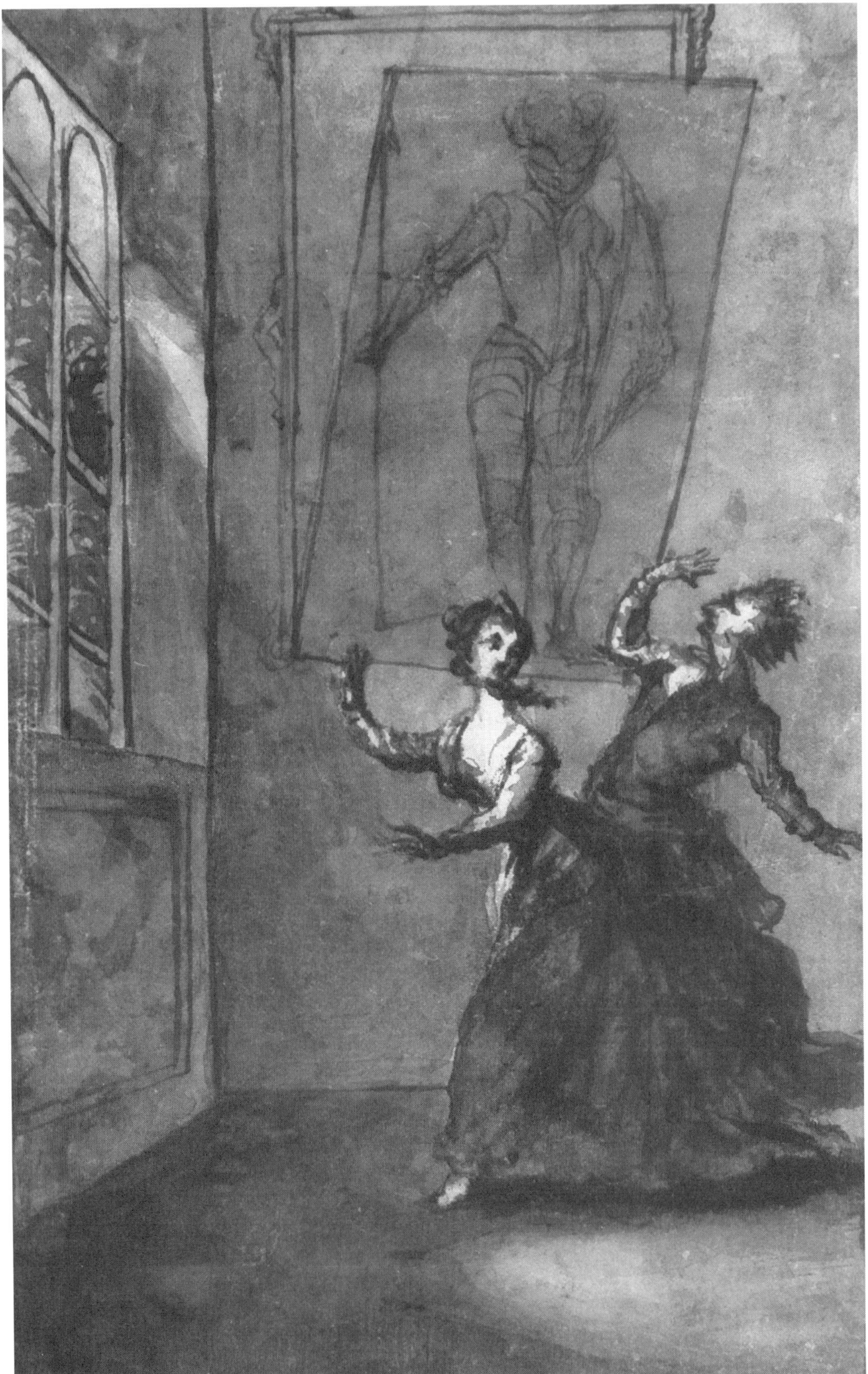

2
Susanna Duncombe
The Ghost Scene from 'The Castle of Otranto'
Pencil, pen and ink and wash on paper 18.7 × 11 cm
Tate. Presented by Mrs Joan Highmore Blackhall and Dr R.B. McConnell 1986

describe particular parts. *The chamber*, says he, *on the right-hand; the door on the left-hand; the distance from the chapel to* Conrad's *apartment:* These and other passages are strong presumptions that the author had some certain building in his eye. Curious persons, who have leisure to employ in such researches, may possibly discover in the *Italian* writers the foundation on which our author has built. If a catastrophe, at all resembling that which he describes, is believed to have given rise to this work, it will contribute to interest the reader, and will make the castle of *Otranto* a still more moving story.

Chapter 1

In the meantime, the care and zeal of the young Ladies had brought the Princess *Hippolita* to herself, who amidst the transports of her own sorrow frequently demanded news of her Lord, would have dismissed her attendants to watch over him, and at last enjoined *Matilda* to leave her, and visit and comfort her father. *Matilda*, who wanted no affectionate duty to *Manfred*, though she trembled at his austerity, obeyed the orders of *Hippolita*, whom she tenderly recommended to *Isabella*; and inquiring of the domestics for her father, was informed that he was retired to his chamber, and had commanded that nobody should have admittance to him. Concluding that he was immersed in sorrow for the death of her brother, and fearing to renew his tears by the sight of his sole remaining child, she hesitated whether she should break in upon his affliction; yet solicitude for him, backed by the commands of her mother, encouraged her to venture disobeying the orders he had given, a fault she had never been guilty of before. The gentle timidity of her nature made her pause for some minutes at his door. She heard him traverse his chamber backwards, and forwards with disordered steps; a mood which increased her apprehensions. She was, however, just going to beg admittance, when *Manfred* suddenly opened the door; and as it was now twilight, concurring with the disorder of his mind, he did not distinguish the person, but asked angrily, who it was? *Matilda* replied, trembling My dearest father, it is I, your daughter. *Manfred*, stepping back hastily, cried, Begone, I do not want a daughter; and flinging back abruptly, clapped the door against the terrified *Matilda*.

She was too well acquainted with her father's impetuosity to venture a second intrusion. When she had a little recovered the shock of so bitter a reception, she wiped away her tears to prevent the additional stab that the knowledge of it would give to *Hippolita*, who questioned her in the most anxious terms on the health of *Manfred*, and how he bore his loss. *Matilda* assured her he was well, and supported his misfortune with manly fortitude.

But will he not let me see him? said Hippolita mournfully; will he not permit me to blend my tears with his, and shed a mother's sorrows in the bosom of her Lord? Or do you deceive me, *Matilda*? I know how *Manfred* doted on his son: Is not the stroke too heavy for him? has he not sunk under it? You do not answer me — alas! I dread the worst! — Raise me, my maidens; I will, I will see my Lord. Bear me to him instantly: he is dearer to me even than my children.

Matilda made signs to Isabella to prevent *Hippolita's* rising; and both those lovely young women were using their gentle violence to stop and calm the Princess, when a servant, on the part of *Manfred*, arrived and told *Isabella* that his Lord demanded to speak with her.

With me! cried *Isabella*. Go,' said *Hippolita*, relieved by a message from her Lord: *Manfred* cannot support the sight of his own family. He thinks you less disordered than we are, and dreads the shock of my grief. Console him, dear *Isabella*, and tell him I will smother my own anguish rather than add to his.

As it was now evening, the servant who conducted *Isabella*, bore a torch before her. When they came to *Manfred*, who was walking impatiently about the gallery, he started, and said hastily, take away that light, and begone. Then shutting the door impetuously, he flung himself upon a bench against the wall, and bade *Isabella* sit by him. She obeyed trembling. I sent for you, Lady, said he,—and then stopped under great appearance of confusion. My Lord! — Yes, I sent for you on a matter of great moment, resumed he. Dry your tears, young Lady — you have lost your bridegroom. — Yes, cruel fate! and I have lost the hopes of my race! But *Conrad* was not worthy of your beauty. — How, my Lord!' said *Isabella*; sure you do not suspect me of not feeling the concern I ought: my duty and affection would have always — 'Think no more of him,' interrupted *Manfred*; he was a sickly, puny child, and *H*eaven has perhaps taken him away, that I might not trust the honours of my house on so frail a foundation. The line of *Manfred* calls for numerous supports. My foolish fondness for that boy blinded the eyes of my prudence — but it is better as it is. I hope, in a few years, to have reason to rejoice at the death of *Conrad*.

Words cannot paint the astonishment of *Isabella*. At first she apprehended that grief had disordered *Manfred*'s understanding. Her next thought suggested that this strange discourse was designed to ensnare her: She feared that *Manfred* had perceived her indifference for his son: and in consequence of that idea she replied Good my Lord, do not doubt my tenderness: my heart would have accompanied my hand. *Conrad* would have engrossed all my care; and wherever fate shall dispose of me, I shall always cherish his memory, and regard your Highness and the virtuous *Hippolita* as my parents. Curse on *Hippolita*! cried *Manfred*. 'Forget her from this moment, as I do. In short, Lady, you have missed a husband undeserving of your charms: They shall now be better disposed of. Instead of a sickly boy, you shall have a husband in the prime of his age, who will know how to value your beauties, and who may expect a numerous offspring. Alas, My Lord! said *Isabella*, my mind is too sadly engrossed by the recent catastrophe in your family to think of another marriage. If ever my father returns, and it shall be his pleasure, I shall obey, as I did when I consented to give my hand to your son: But until his return, permit me to remain under your hospitable roof, and employ the melancholy hours in assuaging yours, *Hippolita*'s, and the fair *Matilda*'s affliction.'

I desired you once before, said *Manfred* angrily, not to name that woman: from this hour she must be a stranger to you, as she must be to me. In short, Isabella, since I cannot give you my son, I offer you myself. — Heavens! cried Isabella, waking from her delusion, what do I hear? You! my Lord! You! My father-in-law! the father of *Conrad*! the husband of the virtuous and tender Hippolita! — I tell you, said *Manfred* imperiously, *Hippolita* is no longer my wife; I divorce her from this hour. Too long has she cursed me by her unfruitfulness: My fate depends on having sons, — and this night I trust will give a new date to my hopes. At those words he seized the cold hand of *Isabella*, who was half dead with fright and horror. She shrieked, and started from him. Manfred rose to pursue her, when the moon, which was now up, and gleamed in at the opposite casement, presented to his sight the plumes of the fatal helmet, which rose to the height of the windows, waving backwards and forwards in a tempestuous manner, and accompanied with a hollow and rustling sound. *Isabella*, who gathered courage from her situation, and who dreaded nothing so much as *Manfred*'s pursuit of his declaration, cried Look! My Lord; see, Heaven itself declares against your impious intentions! — Heaven nor Hell shall impede my designs, said *Manfred*, advancing again to seize the Princess. At that instant the portrait of his grandfather, which hung over the bench where they had been sitting, uttered a deep sigh, and heaved its breast. *Isabella*, whose back was turned to the picture, saw not the motion, nor knew whence the sound came, but started, and said Hark, my Lord! What sound was that? and at the same time made towards the door. *Manfred*, distracted between the flight of *Isabella*, who had now reached the stairs, and yet unable to keep his eyes from the picture, which began to move, had, however, advanced some steps after her, still looking backwards on the portrait, when he saw it quit its panel, and descend on the floor with a grave and melancholy air. Do I dream? cried *Manfred*, returning, or are the devils themselves in league against me? Speak, infernal spectre! Or, if thou art my grandsire, why dost thou too conspire against thy wretched descendant, who too dearly pays for — e'er he could finish the sentence, the vision sighed again, and made a sign to Manfred to follow him. Lead on! cried *Manfred*; I will follow thee to the gulf of perdition. The spectre marched sedately, but dejected, to the end of the gallery, and turned into a chamber on the right-hand. *Manfred* accompanied him at a little distance, full of anxiety and horror, but resolved. As he would have entered the chamber, the door was clapped to with violence by an invisible hand. The Prince, collecting courage from this delay, would have forcibly burst open the door with his foot, but found that it resisted his utmost efforts. Since Hell will not satisfy my curiosity, said *Manfred*, I will use the human means in my power for preserving my race; *Isabella* shall not escape me.

The Lady, whose resolution had given way to terror the moment she had quitted *Manfred*, continued her flight to the bottom of the principal staircase. There she stopped, not knowing whither to direct her steps, nor how to escape from the impetuosity of the Prince. The gates of the castle she knew were locked, and guards placed in the court. Should she, as her heart prompted her, go and prepare *Hippolita* for the cruel destiny that awaited her; she did not doubt but *Manfred* would seek her there, and that his violence would incite him to double the injury he meditated, without leaving room for them to avoid the impetuosity of his passions. Delay might give him time to reflect on the horrid measures he had conceived, or produce some circumstance in her favour, if she could for that night at least-avoid his odious purpose. — Yet where conceal herself! *H*ow avoid the pursuit he would infallibly make throughout the castle!

As these thoughts passed rapidly through her mind, she recollected a subterraneous passage which led from the vaults of the castle to the church of St *Nicholas*. Could she reach the altar before she was over-taken, she knew even *Manfred's* violence would not date profane the sacredness of the place; and she determined, if no other means of deliverance offered, to shut herself up for ever among the holy virgins, whose convent was contiguous to the cathedral. In this resolution, she seized a lamp that burned at the foot of the staircase, and hurried towards the secret passage.

The lower part of the castle was hollowed out into several intricate cloysters; and it was not easy for one under so much anxiety to find the door that opened into the cavern. An awful silence reigned throughout those subterraneous regions, except now and then some blasts of wind that shook the doors she had passed, and which, grating on the rusty hinges, were re-echoed through that long labyrinth of darkness. Every murmur struck her with new terror; — yet more she dreaded to hear the wrathful voice of *Manfred* urging his domestics to pursue her. She trod as softly as impatience would give her leave,— yet frequently stopped and listened to hear if she was followed. In one of those moments she thought she heard a sigh. She shuddered, and recoiled a few paces. In a moment she thought she heard the step of some person. Her blood curdled; she concluded it was *Manfred*. Every suggestion, that horror could inspire, rushed into her mind. She condemned her rash flight, which had thus exposed her to his rage in a place where her cries were not likely to draw anybody to her assistance.— Yet the sound seemed not to come from behind,— if *Manfred* knew where she was, he must have followed her: She was still in one of the cloyters, and the steps she had heard were too distinct to proceed from the way she had come. Cheared with this reflection, and hoping to find a friend in whoever was not the Prince; she was going to advance, when a door that stood ajar, at some distance to the left, was opened gently: But, e'er her lamp, which she held up, could discover who opened it, the person retreated precipitately on seeing the light.

Isabella, whom every incident was sufficient to dismay, hesitated whether she should proceed. Her dread of *Manfred* soon outweighed every other terror. The very circumstance of the person avoiding her, gave her a sort of courage. It could only be, she thought, some domestic belonging to the castle. Her gentleness had never raised her an enemy, and conscious innocence made her hope that, unless sent by thePrince's order to seek her, his servants would rather assist than prevent her flight. Fortifying herself with these reflections, and believing by what she could observe, that she was near the mouth of the subterraneous cavern, she approached the door that had been opened; but a sudden gust of wind, that met her at the door, extinguished her lamp, and left her in total darkness.

Words cannot paint the horror of the Princess's situation. Alone in so dismal a place, her mind impressed with all the terrible events of the day, hopeless of escaping, expecting every moment the arrival of *Manfred*, and far from tranquil on knowing she was within reach of somebody, she knew not whom, who for some cause seemed concealed thereabouts, all these thoughts crowded on her distracted mind, and she was ready to sink under her apprehensions. She addressed herself to every Saint in heaven, and inwardly implored their assistance. For a considerable time she remained in an agony of despair. At last, as softly as was possible, she felt for the door, and, having found it, entered trembling into the vault, from whence she had heard the sigh and steps. It gave her a kind of momentary joy to perceive an imperfect ray of clouded moonshine gleam from the roof of the vault, which seemed to be fallen in, and from whence hung a fragment of earth or building, she could not distinguish which, they appeared to have been crushed inwards. She advanced eagerly towards this chasm, when she discerned a human form, standing close against the wall.

She shrieked ...

1.4

Vathek

The son of a vastly wealthy plantation-owner and politician, William Beckford (1759–1844) enjoyed a life of enormous material privilege, marred by painful social isolation. Driven out of British society after the disclosure of a homosexual romance in 1784, Beckford took refuge on the Continent where he remained for many years.

Beckford made several enormously important contributions to the 'Gothic' as a cultural phenomenon in the widest sense. His compilation of fantasy biographies of artists, printed in 1780 while he was still a teenager, makes forays into the grotesque and outlandish (see text 4.2). His Oriental tale, *Vathek*, excerpted here, is considered as among the very greatest examples of Gothic literature. An extended exercise in sensual indulgence of the most bizarre, perverse and excessive kind, the novel presents the reader with a barrage of images and sensations. Beckford's greatest Gothic creation was, though, the house of Fonthill, designed after his return from the Continent in 1796 as a medieval abbey on an overwhelming scale and filled with fantastical art and fittings (see pp.221–6).

1786

William Beckford 1759–1844
The History of the Caliph Vathek

At the name of Carathis, Vathek recollected the tablets he had received from his mother; who assured him they were fraught with preternatural qualities; and advised him to consult them as emergencies might require. Whilst he was engaged in turning them over; he heard a shout of joy, and a loud clapping of hands. The curtains of his pavilion were soon drawn back; and he beheld Bababalouk, followed by a troop of his favourites; conducting two dwarfs; each a cubit high; who had brought between them a large basket of melons, oranges, and pomegranates. They were singing in the sweetest tones the words that follow: 'We dwell on the top of these rocks, in a cabin of rushes and canes; the eagles envy us our nest: a small spring supplies us with water for the Abdest, and we daily repeat prayers, which the Prophet approves. We l ove you, O commander of the faithful! our master, the good Emir Fakreddin, loves you also: he reveres, in your person, the vicegerent of Mahomet. Little as we are, in us he confides: he knows our hearts to be as good as our bodies are contemptible; and hath placed us here to aid those who are bewildered on these dreary mountains. Last night, whilst we were occupied within our cell, in reading the holy Koran, a sudden hurricane blew out our lights, and rocked our habitation. For two whole hours, a palpable darkness prevailed; but we heard sounds at a distance, which we conjectured to proceed from the bells of a Cafila, passing over the rocks. Our ears were soon filled with deplorable shrieks, frightful roarings, and the sound of tymbals. Chilled with terror, we concluded that the Deggial, with his exterminating angels, had sent forth his plagues on the earth. In the midst of these melancholy reflections, we perceived flames of the deepest red glow in the horizon; and found ourselves, in a few moments, covered with flakes of fire. Amazed at so strange an appearance, we took up the volume dictated by the blessed Intelligence, and, kneeling, by the light of the fire that surrounded us, we recited the verse which says, "Put no trust in any thing but the mercy of Heaven: there is no help, save in the holy Prophet: the mountain of Kaf itself may tremble; it is the power of Allah only that cannot be moved." After having pronounced these words, we felt consolation; and our minds were hushed into a sacred repose. Silence ensued, and our ears clearly distinguished a voice in the air; saying: "Servants of my faithful servant! go down to the happy valley of Fakreddin: tell him that an illustrious opportunity now offers to satiate the thirst of his hospitable heart. The commander of true believers is, this day, bewildered amongst these mountains, and stands in need of thy aid." — We obeyed, with joy, the angelic mission; and our master, filled with pious zeal, hath culled with his own hands these melons, oranges, and pomegranates. He is following us, with a hundred dromedaries, laden with the purest waters of his fountains; and is coming to kiss the fringe of your consecrated robe, and implore you to enter his humble habitation, which, placed amidst these barren wilds, resembles an emerald set in lead.' The dwarfs, having ended their address, remained still standing, and, with hands crossed upon their bosoms, preserved a respectful silence.

Vathek, in the midst of this curious harangue, seized the basket; and, long before it was finished, the fruits had dissolved in his mouth. As he continued to eat, his piety increased; and, in the same breath, he recited his prayers and called for the Koran, and sugar.

Such was the state of his mind, when the tablets, which were thrown by, at the approach of the dwarfs, again attracted his eye. He took them up; but, was ready to drop on the ground when he beheld, in large red characters, these words inscribed by Carathis, which were, indeed, enough to make him tremble: 'Beware of old Doctors and their puny messengers of but one cubit high: distrust their pious frauds; and, instead of eating their melons, impale on a spit, the bearers of them. Shouldest thou be such a fool as to visit them, the portal of the subterranean palace will shut in thy face; and with such force as shall shake thee asunder: thy body shall be spit upon, and bats will engender in thy belly.'

'To what tends this ominous rhapsody?' cries the Caliph; 'and must I, then, perish in these deserts, with thirst, whilst I may refresh myself in the delicious valley of melons and cucumbers? — Accursed be the Giaour, with his portal of ebony! he hath made me dance attendance, too long, already. Besides; who shall prescribe laws to me? — I, forsooth, must not enter any one's habitation! Be it so: but what one can I enter that is not my own!' Bababalouk, who lost not a syllable of this soliloquy, applauded it with all his heart; and the Ladies, for the first time, agreed with him in opinion.

The dwarfs were entertained; caressed; and seated, with great ceremony, on little cushions of satin. The symmetry of their persons, was a subject of admiration; not an inch of them was suffered to pass unexamined. Knick-knacks and dainties were offered in profusion; but all were declined, with respectful gravity. They climbed up the sides of the Caliph's seat, and, placing themselves each on one of his shoulders, began to whisper prayers in his ears. Their tongues quivered like the leaves of a poplar; and the patience of Vathek was almost exhausted; when the acclamations of the troops announced the approach of Fakreddin; who was come with a hundred old grey beards, and as many Korans and dromedaries. They instantly set about their ablutions, and began to repeat the Bismillah. Vathek, to get rid of these officious monitors, followed their example; for, his hands were burning.

The good Emir, who was punctiliously religious, and likewise a great dealer in compliments; made an harangue, five times more prolix and insipid, than his little harbingers had already delivered. The Caliph, unable any longer to refrain, exclaimed, 'For the love of Mahomet, my dear Fakreddin, have done! let us proceed to your valley, and enjoy the fruits that *H*eaven hath vouchsafed you.' The hint of proceeding put all into motion. The venerable attendants of the Emir set forward, somewhat slowly, but Vathek, having ordered his little pages, in private, to goad on the dromedaries; loud fits of laughter broke forth from the cages; for the unwieldy curvetting of these poor beasts, and the ridiculous distress of their superannuated riders, afforded the ladies no small entertainment.

They descended, however, unhurt into the valley; by the easy slopes, which the emir had ordered to be cut in the rock; and, already, the murmuring of streams and the rustling of leaves began to catch their attention. The cavalcade soon entered a path, which was skirted by flowering shrubs, and extended to a vast wood of palm-trees, whose branches overspread a building of hewn stone. This edifice was crowned with nine domes, and adorned with as many portals of bronze, on which was engraven the following inscription: 'This is the asylum of pilgrims; the refuge of travellers; and the depository of secrets from all parts of the world.'

Nine pages, beautiful as the day, and decently clothed in robes of Egyptian linen very long and very modest; were standing at each door. They received the whole retinue with an easy and inviting air. Four of the most amiable, placed the Caliph, on a magnificent taktrevan; four others, somewhat less graceful, took charge of Bababalouk, who capered for joy, at the snug little cabin that fell to his share; the pages that remained, waited on the rest of the train.

When everything masculine was gone out of sight, the gate of a large inclosure, on the right, turned on its harmonious hinges; and a young female, of a slender form, came forth. Her light brown hair floated, in the hazy breeze of the twilight. A troop of young maidens, like the Pleiades, attended her on tip-toe. They hastened to the pavilions that contained the Sultanas; and the young lady, gracefully bending, said to them: 'Charming Princesses, everything is ready: we have prepared beds for your repose, and strewed your apartments with jasmine: *N*o insects will keep off slumber from visiting your eye-lids; we will dispel them with a thousand plumes. Come, then, amiable Ladies! refresh your delicate feet and your ivory limbs, in baths of rosewater; and, by the light of perfumed lamps, your servants will amuse you with tales.'

The Sultanas accepted with pleasure, these obliging offers; and followed the young lady to the Emir's Harem; where we must, for a moment, leave them...

1.5

The Nightmare

In 1782 the Anglo-Swiss painter Henry Fuseli (1741–1825) exhibited his first version of *The Nightmare* (Detroit Institute of Arts) at the annual exhibition of contemporary art held by the Royal Academy in London. As the press reviews excerpted below testify, contemporaries were mystified, fascinated and a little shocked at this image.

Showing a young woman laying back on a sofa, with a monstrous imp sitting on her chest, the painting has elicited a vast array of interpretations — relating this image to scientific ideas about bad dreams, literary and folk tradition, classical art, or to Fuseli's personal sexual anxieties.

The painting is unlikely to ever be simply explained away; instead, Fuseli seems to have calculated an image that would endure precisely because it evades simple explication. He painted variations of this composition throughout his career; a version was on his easel at the time of his death. The version illustrated here was painted around 1789, and was reproduced as an illustration to Erasmus Darwin's poem 'The Botanic Garden,' a protracted rhyming rumination on the vegetable world and the processes of botanical reproduction. This version has become perhaps the best known, being famously used as the cover of Penguin Books' *Three Gothic Novels* (1964), and cropping up on album covers, caricatures, and as the frontispiece to Ernest Jones' *On the Nightmare* (1931) (excerpted below, Part Two, p.170).

3
Henry Fuseli
The Nightmare, c.1790–1
Oil on canvas 75.5 × 64 cm
Freies Deutches Hochstift/
Frankfurter Goethes-Museum

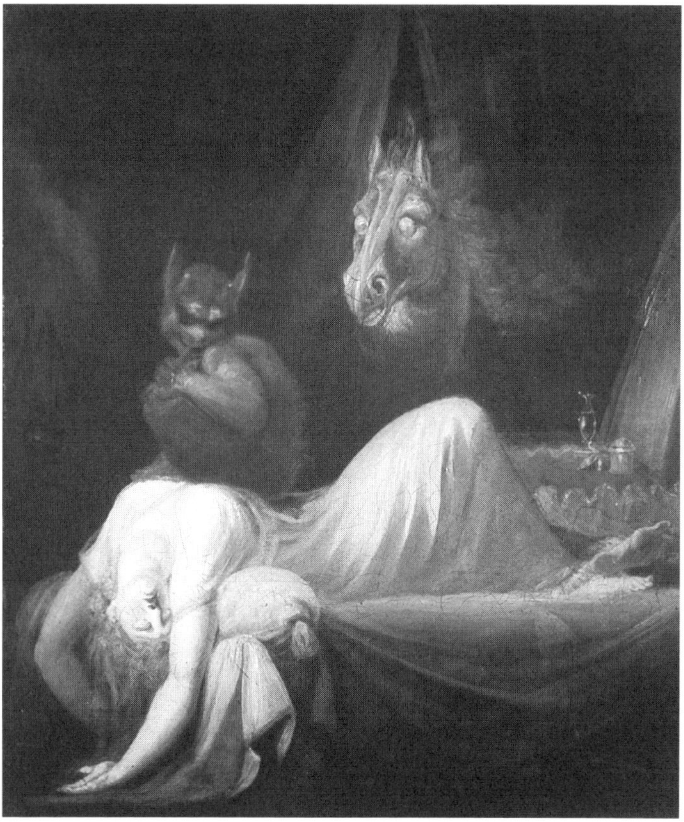

1 May 1782

The Gazetteer

Night Mare

Any artist who *personifies an idea upon canvas*, has at least the merit of imagination. The present picture seems to be not only well conceived, but well executed — it describes a beautiful young woman asleep upon her back, with her head and arms hanging over the couch she lies upon; and in this situation the Night Mare, in the form of an imp, is pressing her stomach. The whole produces the effect very powerfully, and the foreshortening of the head, neck, and arms, seem to be given in the true style of drawing.

9 May 1782

The Morning Chronicle

No.64. The Night Mare, by Mr Fuiseli like all his productions, has strong marks of genius about it; but hag-riding is too unpleasant a thought to be agreeable to any one, and is unfit for furniture or reflection. — Qui bono?

8 May 1782

The Morning Herald

There is a wildness of conception in Mr Fuseli's picture of the Night Shade at the Royal Academy, which teems with that usual concomitant of genius, inaccuracy.

He has introduced a mare's head into the piece, to

characterize his subject. Now the personification of that disorder, which attacks the human frame in sleep, is borrowed from a word of northern origin; *Mair* or Mêre, a witch or sorceress.

Shakespeare's Mad Tom mentions her in that character from some legendary ballad, not unknown, perhaps, to the ingenious compiler of the reliques of our ancient English poetry.

> "St Withold footed thrice the wold,
> He met the Night Mare and her nine-fold;
> Rid her alight and her troth plight,
> And aroynt thee, witch, aroynt thee!"
> *Lear, Act III. Scene IV*

1789

From Erasmus Darwin *The Loves of the Plants*

...on his Night-Mare, through the evening fog,
Flits the squab fiend o'er fen, and lake, and bog,
Seeks some love-wilder'd Maid with sleep oppress'd,
Alights, and grinning sits upon her breast.
—Such as of late amid the murky sky
Was mark'd by *Fuseli's* poetic eye;
Whose daring tints, with *Shakespear's* happiest grace,
Gave to the airy phantom form and place —
Back o'er her pillow sinks her blushing head,
Her snow-white limbs hang helpless from the bed;
While with quick sighs, and suffocative breath,
Her interrupted heart-pulse swims in death.
—Then shrieks of captured towns, and widows' tears,
Pale lovers stretch'd upon their blood-stain'd biers,
The Headlong precipice that thwarts her flight,
The trackless desert, the cold starless night,
And stern-ey'd Murderer with his knife behind,
In dread succession agonize her mind.
O'er her fair limbs convulsive tremors fleet,
Start in her hands, and struggle in her feet;
In vain to scream with quivering lips she tries,
And strains in palsy'd lids her tremulous eyes;
In vain she *wills* to run, fly, swim, walk, creep;
The *Will* presides not in the bower of *Sleep*.
-On her fair bosom sits the Demon-Ape
Erect, and balances his bloated shape;
Rolls in their marble orbs his Gorgon-eyes,
And drinks with leathern ears her tender cries.

1.6

The French Revolution

The earliest Gothic fictions and poetry were created during a period of increasing optimism and material wealth in Britain. The period from the 1740s to the 1760s saw a succession of British military victories, ensuring the nation's imperial expansion. Yet during this period there was also a sense of unease about the fate of the nation, the fear that the luxuriance and sickly decay which had affected the ancient empires would be repeated in the modern age. The war with Revolutionary America (1775–83) seemed to confirm as much. It is from this date that the appeal of Gothic romance became all the more charged. Yet traumatic as the events of that war were, the period of the French Revolution (1789–99) seemed to mark a total transformation of the world. Although initially greeted with enthusiasm in Britain, as it appeared to make available to the long-oppressed people of absolutist France the political liberties secured to Britons by their revolutions of the seventeenth century, the mood turned during 1791 and especially with the execution of Louis XVI in 1792. Burke's *Reflections on the Revolution in France* (1790) was singularly important in ensuring fear about the course of events. Revolution seemed to many to be running out of hand, turning into mob-rule, chaos and monstrous violence. The Gothic emerged as an important means of understanding and representing the unprecedented events of the Revolution; only Gothic motifs of horror, peril and imprisonment seemed equal to the chaotic events of the day.

Excerpted here are Burke's sensationalist account of the arrest of Louis XVI and his family, and two poetic responses to the breaking open of the Bastille — the infamous Paris prison which had long been seen as the emblem of French absolutist oppression; one from the visionary poet William Blake (1757–1827), the other from the more conventional, although politically committed, sentimental novelist Helen Maria Williams (1761–1827).

1790

Edmund Burke 1729–97
Reflections on the Revolution in France

This address was made with much good-nature and affection, to be sure. But among the revolutions in France, must be reckoned a considerable revolution in their ideas of politeness. In England we are said to learn manners at second-hand from your side of the water, and that we dress our behaviour in the frippery of France. If so, we are still in the old cut; and have not so far conformed to the new Parisian mode of good breeding, as to think it quite in the most refined strain of delicate compliment (whether in condolence or congratulation) to say, to the most humiliated creature that crawls upon the earth, that great public benefits are derived from the murder of his servants, the attempted assassination of himself and of his wife, and the mortification, disgrace, and degradation, that he has personally suffered. It is a topic of consolation which our ordinary of Newgate would be too humane to use to a criminal at the foot of the gallows. I should have thought that the hangman of Paris, now that he is liberalized by the vote of the National Assembly, and is allowed his rank and arms in the Herald's College of the rights of men, would be too generous, too gallant a man, too full of the sense of his new dignity, to employ that cutting consolation to any of the persons whom the leze nation might bring under the administration of his *executive powers*.

A man is fallen indeed, when he is thus flattered. The anodyne draught of oblivion, thus drugged, is well calculated to preserve a galling wakefulness, and to feed the living ulcer of a corroding memory. Thus to administer the opiate potion of amnesty, powdered with all the ingredients of scorn and contempt, is to hold to his lips, instead of 'the balm of hurt minds', the cup of human misery full to the brim, and to force him to drink it to the dregs.

Yielding to reasons, at least as forcible as those which were so delicately urged in the compliment on the new year, the king of France will probably endeavor to forget these events, and that compliment. But history, who keeps a durable record of all our acts, and exercises her awful censure over the proceedings of all sorts of sovereigns, will not forget either those events, or the aera of this liberal refinement in the intercourse of mankind. History will record, that on the morning of the 6th of October 1789, the king and queen of France, after a day of confusion, alarm, dismay, and slaughter, lay down, under the pledged security of public faith, to indulge nature in a few hours of respite, and troubled melancholy repose. From this sleep the queen was first startled by the sentinel at her door, who cried out to her, to save herself by flight — that this was the last proof of fidelity he could give — that they were upon him, and he was dead. Instantly he was cut down.

A band of cruel ruffians and assassins, reeking with his blood, rushed into the chamber of the queen, and pierced with a hundred strokes of bayonets and poniards the bed, from whence this persecuted woman had but just time to fly almost naked, and through ways unknown to the murderers had escaped to seek refuge at the feet of a king and husband, not secure of his own life for a moment.

This king, to say no more of him, and this queen, and their infant children (who once would have been the pride and hope of a great and generous people) were then forced to abandon the sanctuary of the most splendid palace in the world, which they left swimming in blood, polluted by massacre, and strewed with scattered limbs and mutilated carcasses. Thence they were conducted into the capital of their kingdom. Two had been selected from the unprovoked, unresisted, promiscuous slaughter, which was made of the gentlemen of birth and family who composed the king's body guard. These two gentlemen, with all the parade of an execution of justice, were cruelly and publicly dragged to the block, and beheaded in the great court of the palace. Their heads were stuck upon spears, and led the procession; whilst the royal captives who followed in the train were slowly moved along, amidst the horrid yells, and shrilling screams, and frantic dances, and infamous contumelies, and all the unutterable abominations of the furies of hell, in the abused shape of the vilest of women. After they had been made to taste, drop by drop, more than the bitterness of death, in the slow torture of a journey of twelve miles, protracted to six hours, they were, under a guard, composed of those very soldiers who had thus conducted them through this famous triumph, lodged in one of the old palaces of Paris, now converted into a Bastile for kings.

Is this a triumph to be consecrated at altars? to be commemorated with grateful thanksgiving? to be offered to the divine humanity with fervent prayer and enthusiastick ejaculation? — These Theban and Thracian orgies, acted in France and applauded only in the Old Jewry, I assure you, kindle prophetic enthusiasm in the minds but of very few people in this kingdom; although a saint and apostle, who may have revelations of his own and who has so completely vanquished all the mean superstitions of the heart, may incline to think it pious and decorous to compare it with the entrance into the world of the Prince of Peace, proclaimed in an holy temple by a venerable sage, and not long before not worse announced by the voice of angels to the quiet innocence of shepherds.

1791

William Blake 1757–1827
The French Revolution

The dead brood over Europe, the cloud and vision descends over chearful France;
O cloud well appointed! Sick, sick: the Prince on his couch, wreath'd in dim
And appalling mist; his strong hand outstretch'd, from his shoulder down the bone
Runs aching cold into the scepter too heavy for mortal grasp. No more
To be swayed by visible hand, nor in cruelty bruise the mild flourishing mountains.
Sick the mountains, and all their vineyards weep, in the eyes of the kingly mourner;
Pale is the morning cloud in his visage. Rise, Necker: the ancient dawn calls us
To awake from slumbers of five thousands years. I awake, but my soul is in dreams;
From my window I see the old mountains of France, like aged men, fading away.
Troubled, leaning on Necker, descends the King, to his chamber of council; shady mountains
In fear utter voices of thunder; the woods of France embosom the sound;
Clouds of wisdom prophetic reply, and roll over the palace roof heavy,
Forty men: each conversing with woes in the infinite shadows of his soul,
Like our ancient fathers in regions of twilight, walk, gathering round the King;
Again the loud voice of France cries to the morning, the morning prophecies to its clouds.
For the Commons convene in the Hall of the Nation. France shakes! And the heavens of France
Perplex'd vibrate round each careful countenance! Darkness of old times around them
Utters loud despair, shadowing Paris; her grey towers groan, and the Bastile trembles.
In its terrible towers the Governor stood, in dark fogs list'ning the horror;
A thousand his soldiers, old veterans of France, breathing red clouds of power and dominion,
Sudden seiz'd with bowlings, despair, and black night, he stalk'd like a lion from tower
To tower, his howlings were heard in the Louvre; from court to court restless he dragg'd
His strong limbs; from court to court curs'd the fierce torment unquell'd,
Howling and giving the dark command; in his soul stood the purple plague,
Tugging his iron manacles, and piercing through the seven towers dark and sickly,
Panting over the prisoners like a wolf gorg'd; and the den nam'd Horror held a man
Chain'd hand and foot, round his neck an iron band, bound to the impregnable wall.
In his soul was the serpent coil'd round in his heart, hid from the light, as in a cleft rock;
And the man was confin'd for a writing prophetic: in the tower nam'd Darkness, was a man
Pinion'd down to the stone floor, his strong bones scarce cover'd with sinews; the iron rings
Were forg'd smaller as the flesh decay'd, a mask of iron on his face hid the lineaments
Of ancient Kings, and the frown of the eternal lion was hid from the oppressed earth.
In the tower named Bloody, a skeleton yellow remained in its chains on its couch
Of stone, once a man who refus'd to sign papers of abhorrence; the eternal worm
Crept in the skeleton. In the den nam'd Religion, a loathsome sick woman, bound down
To a bed of straw; the seven diseases of earth, like birds of prey, stood on the couch,
And fed on the body. She refus'd to be whore to the Minister, and with a knife smote him.
In the tower nam'd Order, an old man, whose white beard cover'd the stone floor like weeds
On margin of the sea, shrivel'd up by heat of day and cold of night; his den was short
And narrow as a grave dug for a child, with spiders webs wove, and with slime
Of ancient horrors cover'd, for snakes and scorpions are his companions; harmless they breathe
His sorrowful breath: he, by conscience urg'd, in the city of Paris rais'd a pulpit,
And taught wonders to darken'd souls. In the den nam'd Destiny a strong man sat,
His feet and hands cut off, and his eyes blinded; round his middle a chain and a band
Fasten'd into the wall; fancy gave him to see an image of despair in his den,
Eternally rushing round, like a man on his hands and knees, day and night without rest.
He was friend to the favourite. In the seventh tower, nam'd the tower of God, was a man
Mad, with chains loose, which he dragg'd up and down; fed with hopes year by year, he pined
For liberty; vain hopes: his reason decay'd, and the world of attraction in his bosom
Center'd, and the rushing of chaos overwhelm'd his dark soul. He was confin'd
For a letter of advice to a King, and his ravings in winds are heard over Versailles.
But the dens shook and trembled, the prisoners look up and assay to shout; they listen,
Then laugh in the dismal den, then are silent, and a light walks round the dark towers.
For the Commons convene in the Hall of the Nation; like spirits of fire in the beautiful
Porches of the Sun, to plant beauty in the desart craving abyss, they gleam
On the anxious city; all children new-born first behold them; tears are fled,
And they nestle in earth-breathing bosoms. So the city of Paris, their wives and children,

Look up to the morning Senate, and visions of sorrow leave pensive streets.
But heavy brow'd jealousies lower o'er the Louvre, and terrors of ancient Kings
Descend from the gloom and wander thro' the palace, and weep round the King and his Nobles.
While loud thunders roll, troubling the dead, Kings are sick throughout all the earth,
The voice ceas'd: the Nation sat: And the triple forg'd fetters of times were unloos'd.
The voice ceas'd: the Nation sat: but ancient darkness and trembling wander thro' the palace...

1790

Helen Maria Williams 1761–1827
from *Julia, A Novel*

The Bastille, a Vision

I.1 'Drear cell! along whose lonely bounds,
Unvisited by light,
Chill silence dwells with night,
Save where the clanging fetter sounds!
Abyss, where mercy never came,
Nor hope, the wretch can find;
Where long inaction wastes the frame,
And half annihilates the mind!

I.2 'Stretch'd helpless in this living tomb,
O haste, congenial death!
Seize, seize this ling'ring breath,
And shroud me in unconscious gloom —
Britain! thy exil'd son no more
Thy blissful vales shall see;
Why did I leave thy hallow'd shore,
Distinguish'd land, where all are free?'

I.3 Bastille! within thy hideous pile,
Which stains of blood defile.—
Thus rose the captive's sighs,
Till slumber seal'd his weeping eyes —
Terrific visions hover near!
He sees an awful form appear!
Who drags his step to deeper cells,
Where stranger wilder horror dwells.

II.1 'Oh, tear me from these haunted walls,
Or those fierce shapes controul!
Lest madness seize my soul —
That pond'rous mask of iron falls,
I see.' — 'Rash mortal, ha! beware,
Nor breathe that hidden name!
Should those dire accents wound the air,
Know death shall lock thy stiff'ning frame.

II.2 'Hark! that loud bell which sullen tolls!
It wakes a shriek of woe.
From yawning depths below;
Shrill through this hollow vault it rolls!
A deed was done in this black cell
Unfit for mortal ears!
A deed was done, when toll'd that knell,
No human heart could live and hear!

II.3 'Rouse thee from thy numbing trance,
Near yon thick gloom advance;
The solid cloud has shook;
Arm all thy soul with strength to look. —
Enough! thy starting locks have rose,
Thy limbs have fail'd, thy blood has froze;
On scenes so foul, with mad affright,
I fix no more thy fastened sight.'

III.1 'Those troubled phantoms melt away!
I lose the sense of care —
I feel the vital air —
I see, I *see* the light of day! —
Visions of bliss! eternal powers!
What force has shook those hated walls?
What arm has rent those threat'ning towers?
It falls- the guilty fabric falls!'

III.2 'Now, favoured mortal, now behold!
To soothe thy captive state,
I ope the book of fate,
Mark what its registers unfold!
Where this dark pile in chaos lies,
With nature's execrations hurl'd,
Shall Freedom's sacred temple rise,
And charm an emulating world!

III.3 'Tis her awak'ning voice commands
Those firm, those patriot bands,
Arm'd to avenge her cause,
And guard her violated laws! —
Did ever earth a scene display
More glorious to the eye of day,
Than millions with according mind,
Who claim the rights of human kind?

IV.1 'Does the fam'd Roman page sublime,
An hour more bright unroll,
To animate the soul,
Than this, lov'd theme of future time? —
Posterity, with rev'rence meet,
The consecrated act shall hear;
Age shall the glowing tale repeat,
And youth shall drop the burning tear!

IV.2 'The peasant, while he fondly sees
His infants round the hearth,
Pursue their simple mirth,
Or emulously climb his knees,
No more bewails their future lot,
By tyranny's stern rod oppress'd;
While Freedom guards his straw-roof'd cot,
And all his useful toils are blest.

IV.3 'Philosophy! oh share the meed
Of Freedom's noblest deed!
'Tis thine each truth to scan,
Guardian of bliss, and friend of man!
'Tis thine all human wrongs to heal,
'Tis thine to love all nature's weal;
To give each gen'rous purpose birth,
And renovate the gladden'd earth.'

1.7

Radcliffe's Romances

Ann Radcliffe (1764–1823) was probably the most materially successful and critically respected of the Gothic novelists. In a succession of lengthy fictions, beginning with *The Castles of Athlin and Dunbayne* (1789) and *The Romance of the Forest* (1791), Radcliffe detailed convoluted romances and ghostly narratives, returning to the romantic scenery of Italy and Southern Germany and the trappings of Catholicism, as subjects of fascination, admiration and horror. Much was made in these novels of the landscape and architectural settings, evoked in long — to some critics, overlong — descriptive passages. Equally important, and much-remarked upon by contemporaries and critics now, is Radcliffe's rejection of actual supernatural interventions. While there are ghostly voices, strange sounds, and seeming apparitions, these are all ultimately resolved to have material explanations. This combination of rationalism, Catholic superstition, irrationalism and romance proved irresistible to generations of readers, and still at the end of the nineteenth century we find that it is this author, almost uniquely from among the early Gothic novelists, who remained read and appreciated (see text 2.8).

Excerpted here are the two texts which critics consider to be Radcliffe's major achievements. The passage from *The Mysteries of Udolpho* (1794) reveals her combination of romantic adventure and the evocation of vast landscape settings; the section of *The Italian* (1797) reproduced here, her fascination with the rituals of the Catholic church and the supposedly horrid powers of its Inquisition.

1794

From Ann Radcliffe 1764–1823
The Mysteries of Udolpho

At a little distance, was discovered a rude and dangerous passage, formed by an enormous pine, which, thrown across the chasm, united the opposite precipices, and which had been felled probably by the hunter, to facilitate his chace of the izard, or the wolf. The whole party, the guides excepted, shuddered at the prospect of crossing this alpine bridge, whose sides afforded no kind of defence, and from which to fall was to die. The guides, however, prepared to lead over the mules, while Blanche stood trembling on the brink, and listening to the roar of the waters, which were seen descending from rocks above, overhung with lofty pines, and thence precipitating themselves into the deep abyss, where their white surges gleamed faintly in the moon-light. The poor animals proceeded over this perilous bridge with instinctive caution, neither frightened by the noise of the cataract, or deceived by the gloom, which the impending foliage threw athwart their way. It was now, that the solitary torch, which had been hitherto of little service, was found to be an inestimable treasure; and Blanche, terrified, shrinking, but endeavouring to re-collect all her firmness and presence of mind, preceded by her lover and supported by her father, followed the red gleam of the torch, in safety, to the opposite cliff.

As they went on, the heights contracted, and formed a narrow pass, at the bottom of which, the torrent they had just crossed, was heard to thunder. But they were again cheered by the bark of a dog, keeping watch, perhaps, over the flocks of the mountains, to protect them from the nightly descent of the wolves. The sound was much nearer than before, and, while they rejoiced in the hope of soon reaching a place of repose, a light was seen to glimmer at a distance. It appeared at a height considerably above the level of their path, and was lost and seen again, as if the waving branches of trees sometimes excluded and then admitted its rays. The guides hallooed with all their strength, but the sound of no human voice was heard in return, and, at length, as a more effectual means of making themselves known, they fired a pistol. But, while they listened in anxious expectation, the noise of the explosion was alone heard, echoing among the rocks, and it gradually sunk into silence, which no friendly hint of man disturbed. The light, however, that had been seen before, now became plainer, and, soon after, voices were heard indistinctly on the wind; but, upon the guides repeating the call, the voices suddenly ceased, and the light disappeared.

The Lady Blanche was now almost sinking beneath the pressure of anxiety, fatigue and apprehension, and the united efforts of the Count and St. Foix could scarcely support her spirits. As they continued to advance, an object was perceived on a point of rock above, which, the strong rays of the moon then falling on

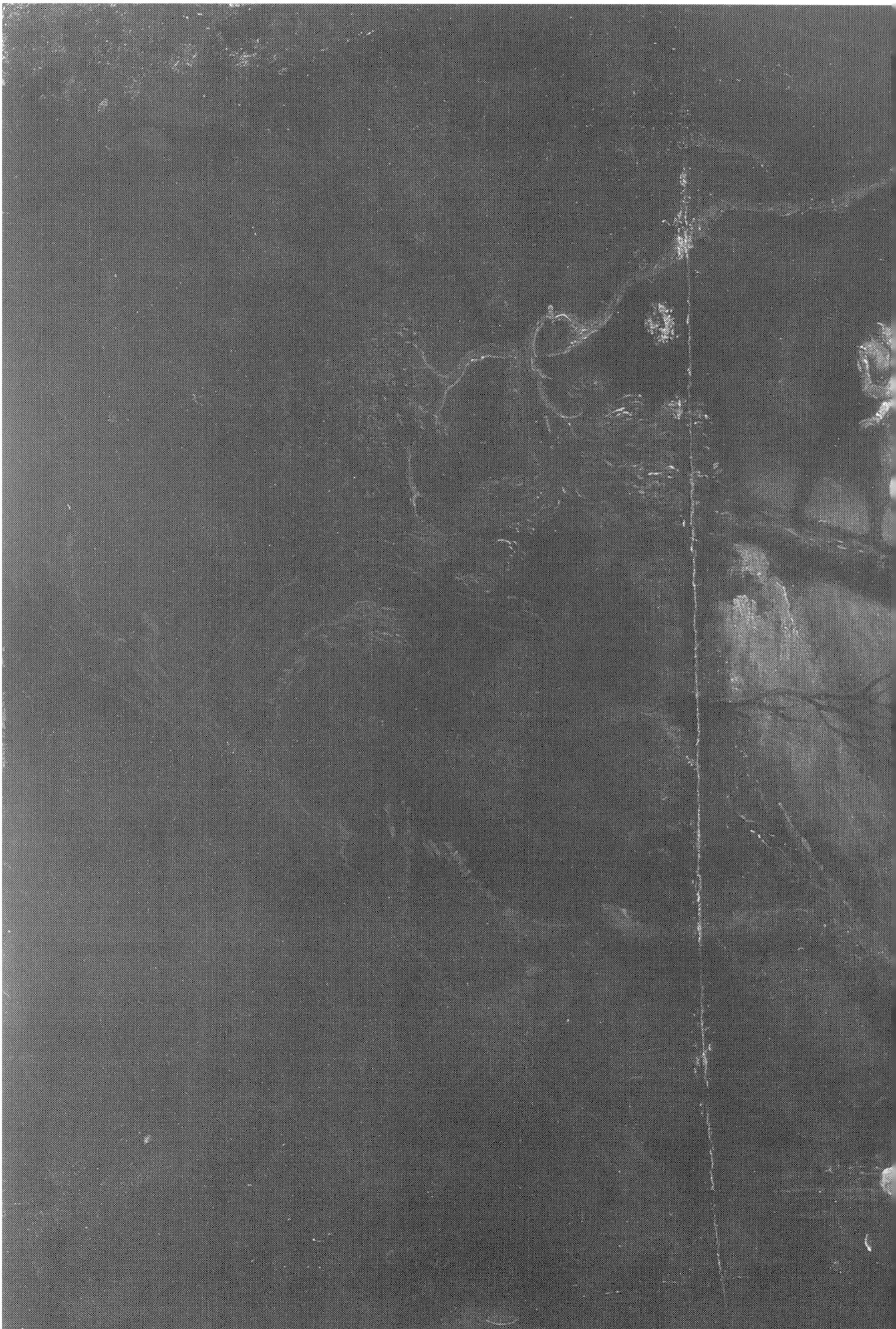

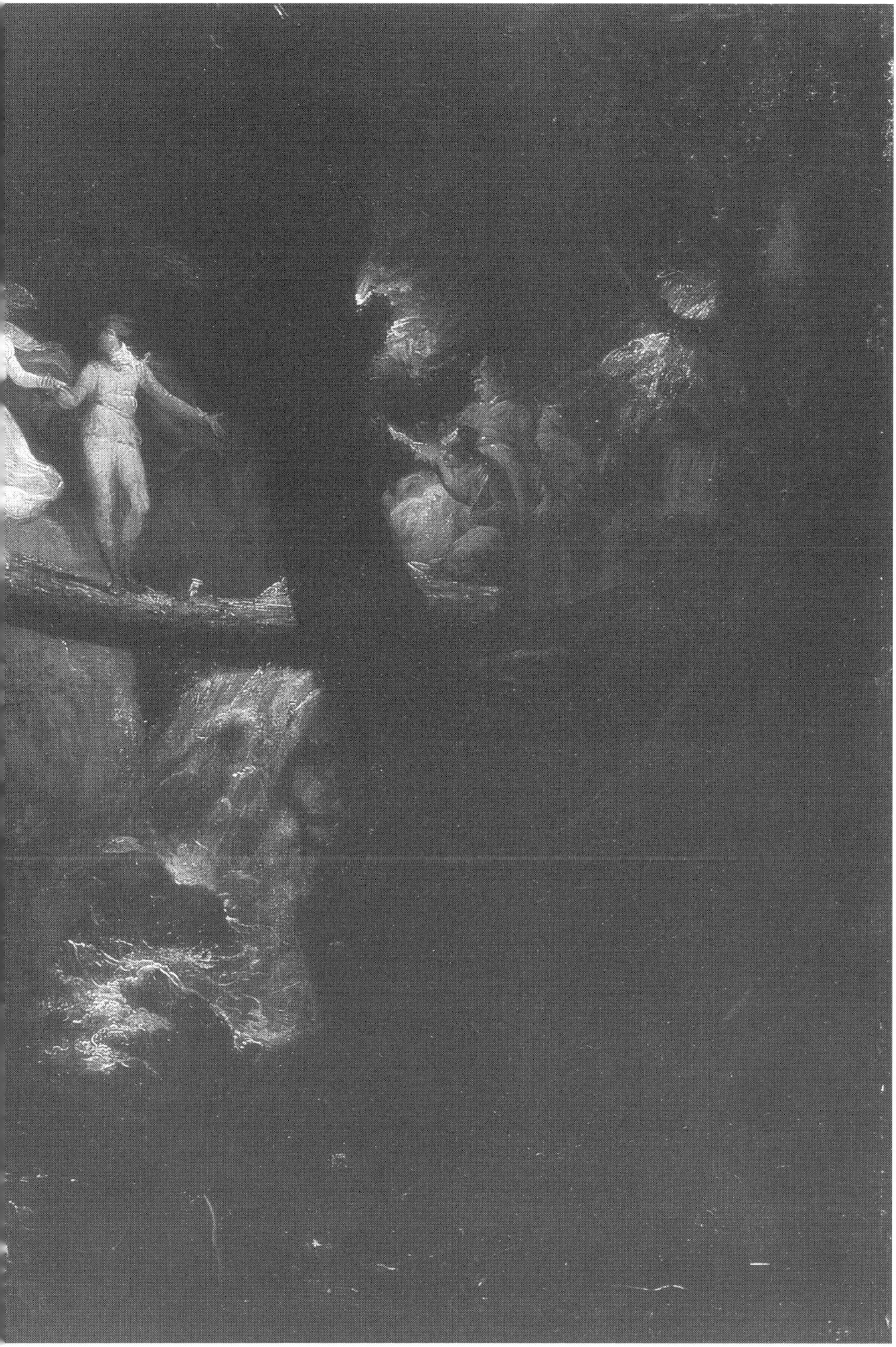

4 (pp. 56–7)
Nathaniel Grogan
Lady Blanche Crosses the Ravine Guided by the Count and St Foix: A Scene from 'The Mysteries of Udolpho', late 1790s
Oil on canvas 76.9 × 108 cm
National Gallery of Ireland, Dublin

it, appeared to be a watch-tower. The Count, from its situation and some other circumstances, had little doubt, that it was such, and believing, that the light had proceeded from thence, he endeavoured to re-animate his daughter's spirits by the near prospect of shelter and repose, which, however rude the accommodation, a ruined watch-tower might afford.

'Numerous watch-towers have been erected among the Pyrenees,' said the Count, anxious only to call Blanche's attention from the subject of her fears; 'and the method, by which they give intelligence of the approach of the enemy, is, you know, by fires, kindled on the summits of these edifices. Signals have thus, sometimes, been communicated from post to post, along a frontier line of several hundred miles in length. Then, as occasion may require, the lurking armies emerge from their fortresses and the forests, and march forth, to defend, perhaps, the entrance of some grand pass, where, planting themselves on the heights, they assail their astonished enemies, who wind along the glen below, with fragments of the shattered cliff, and pour death and defeat upon them. The ancient forts, and watch-towers, overlooking the grand passes of the Pyrenées, are carefully preserved; but some of those in inferior stations have been suffered to fall into decay, and are now frequently converted into the more peaceful habitation of the hunter, or the shepherd, who, after a day of toil, retires hither, and, with his faithful dogs, forgets, near a cheerful blaze, the labour of the chace, or the anxiety of collecting his wandering flocks, while he is sheltered from the nightly storm.'

'But are they always thus peacefully inhabited?' said the Lady Blanche.

'No,' replied the Count, 'they are sometimes the asylum of French and Spanish smugglers, who cross the mountains with contraband goods from their respective countries, and the latter are particularly numerous, against whom strong parties of the king's troops are sometimes sent. But the desperate resolution of these adventurers, who, knowing, that, if they are taken, they must expiate the breach of the law by the most cruel death, travel in large parties, well armed, often daunts the courage of the soldiers. The smugglers, who seek only safety, never engage, when they can possibly avoid it; the military, also, who know, that in these encounters, danger is certain, and glory almost unattainable, are equally reluctant to fight; an engagement, therefore, very seldom happens, but, when it does, it never concludes till after the most desperate and bloody conflict. You are inattentive, Blanche,' added the Count: 'I have wearied you with a dull subject; but see, yonder, in the moon-light, is the edifice we have been in search of, and we are fortunate to be so near it, before the storm bursts.

Blanche, looking up, perceived, that they were at the foot of the cliff, on whose summit the building stood, but no light now issued from it; the barking of the dog too had, for some time, ceased, and the guides began to doubt, whether this was really the object of their search. From the distance, at which they surveyed it, shewn imperfectly by a cloudy moon, it appeared to be of more extent than a single watch-tower; but the difficulty was how to ascend the height, whose abrupt declivities seemed to afford no kind of path-way.

While the guides carried forward the torch to examine the cliff, the Count, remaining with Blanche and St. Foix at its foot, under the shadow of the woods, endeavoured again to beguile the time by conversation, but again anxiety abstracted the mind of Blanche; and he then consulted, apart with St. Foix, whether it would be advisable, should a path be found, to venture to an edifice, which might possibly harbour banditti. They considered, that their own party was not small, and that several of them were well armed; and, after enumerating the dangers, to be incurred by passing the night in the open wild, exposed, perhaps, to the effects of a thunder-storm, there remained not a doubt, that they ought to endeavour to obtain admittance to the edifice above, at any hazard respecting the inhabitants it might harbour; but the darkness, and the dead silence, that surrounded it, appeared to contradict the probability of its being inhabited at all.

A shout from the guides aroused their attention, after which, in a few minutes, one of the Count's servants returned with intelligence, that a path was found, and they immediately hastened to join the guides, when they all ascended a little winding way cut in the rock among thickets of dwarf wood, and, after much toil and some danger, reached the summit, where several ruined towers, surrounded by a massy wall, rose to their view, partially illumined by the moon-light. The space around the building was silent, and apparently forsaken, but the Count was cautious; 'Step softly,' said he, in a low voice, 'while we reconnoitre the edifice.'

Having proceeded silently along for some paces, they stopped at a gate, whose portals were terrible even in ruins, and, after a moment's hesitation, passed on to the court of entrance, but paused again at the head of a terrace, which, branching from it, ran along the brow of a precipice. Over this, rose the main body of the edifice, which was now seen to be, not a watch-tower, but one of those ancient fortresses, that, from age and neglect, had fallen to decay. Many parts of it, however, appeared to be still entire; it was built of grey stone, in the heavy Saxon-gothic style, with enormous round towers, buttresses of proportionable strength, and the arch of the large gate, which seemed to open into the hall of the fabric, was round, as was that of a window above. The air of solemnity, which must so strongly have characterized the pile even in the days of its early strength, was now considerably heightened by its shattered battlements and half-demolished walls, and by the huge masses of ruin, scattered in its wide area, now silent and grass grown. In this court of entrance stood the gigantic remains of an oak, that seemed to have flourished and decayed with the building, which it still appeared frowningly to protect by the few remaining branches, leafless and moss-grown, that crowned its trunk, and whose wide extent told how enormous the tree had been in a former age. This fortress was evidently once of great strength, and, from its situation on a point of rock, impending over a deep glen, had been of great power to annoy, as well as to resist; the Count, therefore, as he stood surveying it, was somewhat surprised, that it had been suffered, ancient as it was, to sink into ruins, and its present lonely and deserted air excited in his breast emotions of melancholy awe. While he indulged, for a moment, these emotions, he thought he heard a sound of remote voices steal upon the stillness, from within the building, the front of which he again surveyed with scrutinizing eyes, but yet no light was visible. He now determined to walk round the fort, to that remote part of it, whence he thought the voices had arisen, that he might examine whether any light could be discerned there, before he ventured to knock at the gate; for this purpose, he entered upon the terrace, where the remains of cannon were yet apparent in the thick walls, but he had not proceeded many paces, when his steps were suddenly arrested by the loud barking of a dog within, and which he fancied to be the same, whose voice had been the means of bringing the travellers thither. It now appeared certain, that the place was inhabited, and the Count returned to consult again with St. Foix, whether he should try to obtain admittance, for its wild aspect had somewhat shaken his former resolution; but, after a second consultation, he submitted to the considerations, which before determined him, and which were strengthened by the discovery of the dog, that guarded the fort, as well as by the stillness that pervaded it. He, therefore, ordered one of his servants to knock at the gate, who was advancing to obey him, when a light appeared through the loop-hole of one of the towers, and the Count called loudly, but, receiving no answer, he went up to the gate himself, and struck upon it with an iron-pointed pole, which had assisted him to climb the steep. When the echoes had ceased, that this blow had awakened, the renewed barking, — and there were now more than one dog, — was the only sound, that was heard. The Count stepped back, a few paces, to observe whether the light was in the tower, and, perceiving, that it was gone, he returned to the portal, and had lifted the pole to strike again, when again he fancied he heard the murmur of voices within, and paused to listen. He was confirmed in the supposition, but they were too remote, to be heard otherwise than in a murmur, and the Count now let the pole fall heavily upon the gate; when almost immediately a profound silence followed. It was apparent, that the people within had heard the sound, and their caution in admitting strangers gave him a favourable opinion of them. 'They are either hunters or shepherds,' said he, 'who, like ourselves, have probably sought shelter from the night within these walls, and are fearful of admitting strangers, lest they should prove robbers. I will endeavour to remove their fears.' So saying, he called aloud, 'We are friends, who ask shelter from the night.' In a few moments, steps were heard within, which approached, and a voice then enquired — 'Who calls?'...

1797

Ann Radcliffe 1764–1823
The Italian

A long interval elapsed, during which the stillness of the place was sometimes interrupted by a closing door, and, at others, by indistinct sounds, which yet appeared to Vivaldi like lamentations and extorted groans. Inquisitors, in their long black robes, issued, from time, to time from the passages, and crossed the hall to other avenues. They eyed the prisoners with curiosity, but without pity. Their visages, with few exceptions, seemed stamped with the characters of demons. Vivaldi could not look upon the grave cruelty, or the serocious impatience, their countenances severally expressed, without reading in them the fate of some fellow creature, the fate, which these men seemed going, even at this moment, to confirm; and, as they passed with soundless steps, he shrunk from observation, as if their very looks possessed some supernatural power, and could have struck death. But he followed their fleeting figures, as they proceeded on their work of horror, to where the last glimmering ray faded into darkness, expecting to see other doors of other chambers open to receive them. While meditating upon these horrors, Vivaldi lost every selfish consideration in astonishment and indignation of the sufferings, which the frenzied wickedness of man prepares for man, who, even at the moment of infliction, insults his victim with assertions of the justice and necessity of such procedure. 'Is this possible!' said Vivaldi internally, 'Can this be in human nature! — Can such horrible perversion of right be permitted! Can man, who calls himself endowed with reason, and immeasurably superior to every other created being, argue himself into the commission of such horrible folly, such inveterate cruelty, as exceeds all the acts of the most irrational and ferocious brute. Brutes do not deliberately slaughter their species; it remains for man only, man, proud of his prerogative of reason, and boasting of his sense of justice, to unite the most terrible extremes of folly and wickedness!'

Vivaldi had been no stranger to the existence of this tribunal; he had long understood the nature of the establishment, and had often received particular accounts of its customs and laws; but, though he had believed before, it was now only that conviction appeared to impress his understanding. A new view of human nature seemed to burst, at once, upon his mind, and he could not have experienced greater astonishment, if this had been the first moment, in which he had heard of the institution. But, when he thought of Ellena, considered that she was in the power of this tribunal, and that it was probable she was at this moment within the same dreadful walls, grief, indignation, and despair

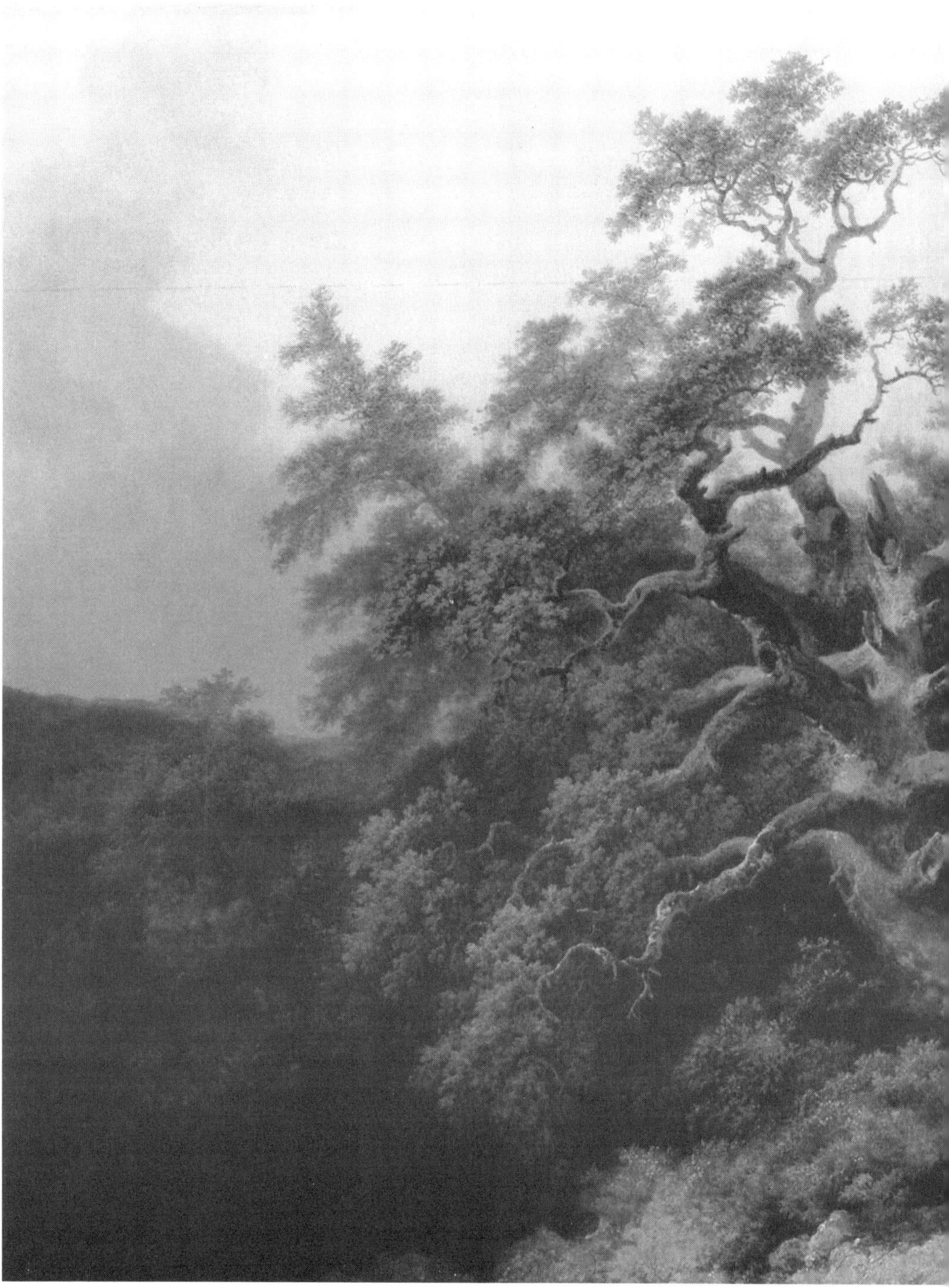

5
Philip James de Loutherbourg
Travellers Attacked by Banditti, 1781
Oil on canvas 67.3 × 105.1 cm
Tate. Purchased 1967

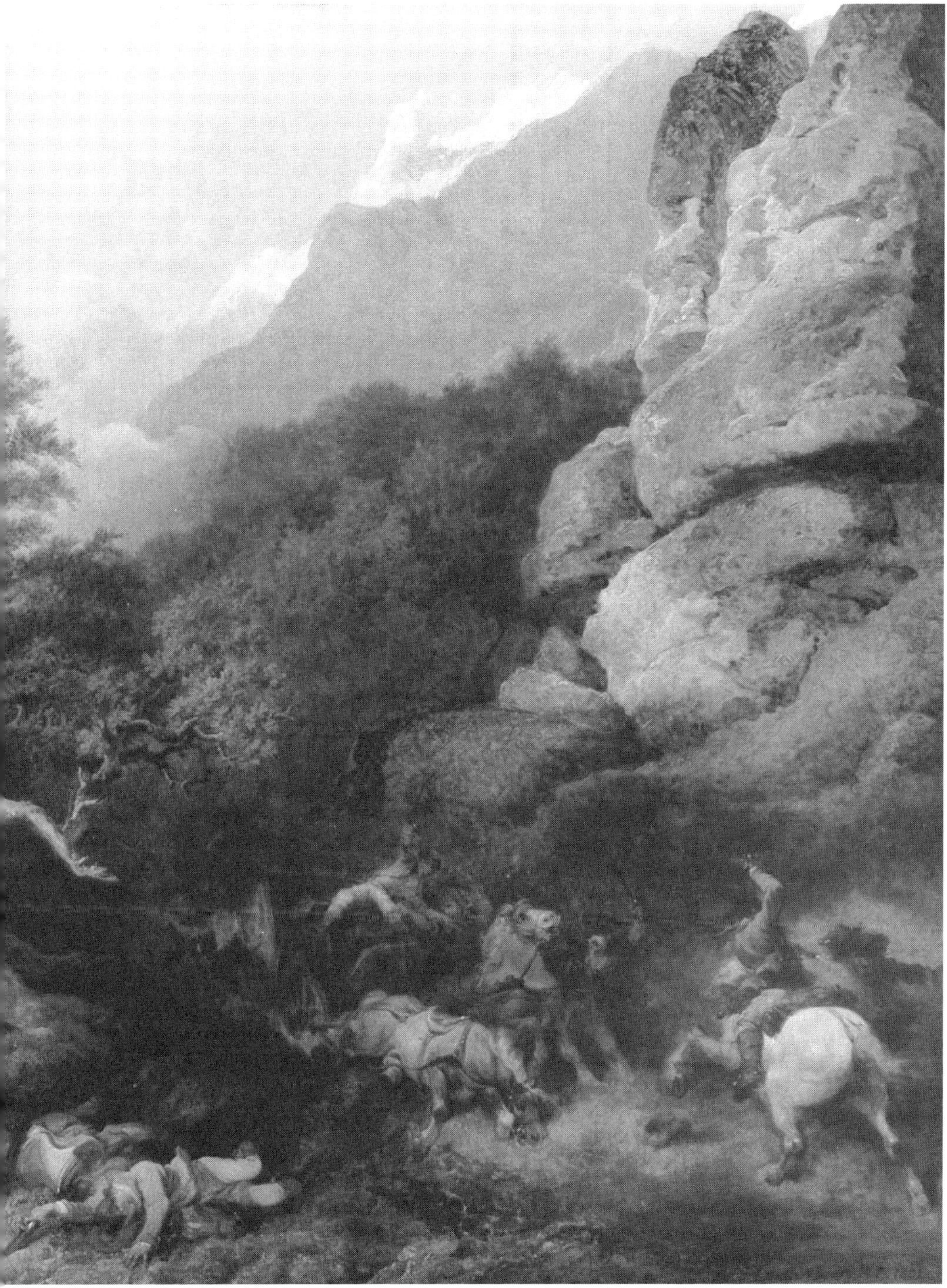

irritated him almost to frenzy. He seemed suddenly animated with supernatural strength, and ready to attempt impossibilities for her deliverance. It was by a strong effort for self command, that he forbore bursting the bonds, which held him, and making a desperate attempt to seek her through the vast extent of these prisons. Reflection, however, had not so entirely forsaken him, but that he saw the impossibility of succeeding in such an effort, the moment he had conceived it, and he forbore to rush upon the certain destruction, to which it must have led. His passions, thus restrained, seemed to become virtues, and to display themselves in the energy of his courage and his fortitude. His soul became stern and vigorous in despair, and his manner and countenance assumed a calm dignity, which seemed to awe, in some degree, even his guards. The pain of his wounds was no longer felt; it appeared as if the strength of his intellectual self had subdued the infirmities of the body, and, perhaps, in these moments of elevation, he could have endured the torture without shrinking.

Paulo, meanwhile, mute and grave, was watchful of all that passed; he observed the revolutions in his master's mind, with grief first, and then with surprize, but he could not imitate the noble fortitude, which now gave weight and steadiness to Vivaldi's thoughts. And when he looked on the power and gloom around him, and on the visages of the passing Inquisitors, he began to repent, that he had so freely delivered his opinion of this tribunal, in the presence of its agents, and to perceive, that if he played up the kind of tune he had threatened, it would probably be the last he should ever be permitted to perform in this world.

At length, the chief officer descended the stair-case, and immediately bade Vivaldi follow him. Paulo was accompanying his master, but was withheld by the guard, and told he was to be disposed of in a different way. This was the moment of his severest trial; he declared he would not be separated from his master.

'What did I demand to be brought here for,' he cried, 'if it was not that I might go shares with the Signor in all his troubles? This is not a place to come to for pleasure, I warrant; and I can promise ye, gentlemen, I would not have come within an hundred miles of you, if it had not been for my master's sake.'

The guards roughly interrupted him, and were carrying him away, when Vivaldi's commanding voice arrested them. He returned to speak a few words of consolation to his faithful servant, and, since they were to be separated, to take leave of him.

Paulo embraced his knees, and, while he wept, and his words were almost stifled by sobs, declared no force should drag him from his master, while he had life; and repeatedly appealed to the guards, with — 'What did I demand to be brought here for? Did ever any body come here to seek pleasure? What right have you to prevent my going shares with my master in his troubles?'

'We do not intend to deny you that pleasure, friend,' replied one of the guards!

'Don't you? Then heaven bless you!' cried Paulo, springing

from his knees, and shaking the man by the hand with a violence, that would nearly have dislocated the shoulder of a person less robust.

'So come with us,' added the guard, drawing him away from Vivaldi. Paulo now became outrageous, and, struggling with the guards, burst from them, and again fell at the feet of his master, who raised and embraced him, endeavouring to prevail with him to submit quietly to what was inevitable, and to encourage him with hope.

'I trust that our separation will be short,' said Vivaldi, 'and that we shall meet in happier circumstances. My innocence must soon appear.'

'We shall never, never meet again, Signormio, in this world,' said Paulo, sobbing violently, 'so don't make me hope so. That old Abbess knows what she is about too well to let us escape; or she would not have catched us up so cunningly as she did; so what signifies innocence! O! if my old lord, the Marchese, did but know where we are!'

Vivaldi interrupted him, and turning to the guards said, 'I recommend my faithful servant to your compassion; he is innocent. It will some time, perhaps, be in my power to recompence you for any indulgence you may allow him, and I shall value it a thousand times more highly, than any you could shew to myself! Farewell, Paulo, — farewell! Officer, I am ready.'

'O stay! Signor, for one moment — stay!' said Paulo.

'We can wait no longer,' said the guard, and again drew Paulo away, who looking piteously after Vivaldi, alternately repeated, Farewel, dear maestro! farewel dear, dear maestro!' and 'What did I demand to be brought here for? What did I demand to be brought here for? — what was it for, if not to go shares with my maestro?' till Vivaldi was beyond the reach of sight and of hearing.

Vivaldi, having followed the officer up the stair-case, passed through a gallery to an anti-chamber, where, being delivered into the custody of some persons in waiting, his conductor disappeared beyond a folding door, that led to an inner apartments. Over this door was an inscription in Hebrew characters, traced in blood-colour. Dante's inscription on the entrance of the infernal regions, would have been suitable to a place, where every circumstance and feature seemed to say, *'Hope, that comes to all, comes not here!'*

Vivaldi conjectured, that in this chamber they were preparing for him the instruments, which were to extort a confession; and though he knew little of the regular proceedings of this tribunal, he had always understood, that the torture was inflicted upon the accused person, till he made confession of the crime, of which he was suspected. By such a mode of proceeding, the innocent were certain of suffering longer than the guilty; for, as they had nothing to confess, the Inquisitor, mistaking innocence for obstinacy, persevered in his inflictions, and it frequently happened that he compelled the innocent to become criminal, and assert a falsehood, that they might be released from anguish, which they could no longer sustain. Vivaldi considered this circumstance undauntedly; every faculty of his soul was bent up to firmness and endurance. He believed that he understood the extent of the charge, which would be brought against him, a charge as false, as a specious confirmation of it, would be terrible in it's consequence both to Ellena and himself. Yet every art would be practised to bring him to an acknowledgment of having carried off a nun, and he knew also, that, since the prosecutor and the witnesses are never confronted with the prisoner in cases of severe accusation, and since their very names are concealed from him, it would be scarcely possible for him to prove his innocence. But he did not hesitate an instant whether to sacrifice himself for Ellena, determining rather to expire beneath the merciless inflictions of the Inquisitors, than to assert a falsehood, which must involve her in destruction.

The officer, at length, appeared, and, having beckoned Vivaldi to advance, uncovered his head, and bared his arms. He then led him forward through the folding door into the chamber; having done which, he immediately withdrew, and the door, which shut out Hope, closed after him...

1.8

The Monk

The Monk (1796) was the literary sensation of the age, and represents the high — and to some eyes low — point of the Gothic novel. Packed with gruesome and outrageous images, shocking themes of sexual violence and perversion, and narrative convolution, the tale was fabricated by Matthew Gregory Lewis (1775–1818) while he was still a teenager. Massively popular, once news of his authorship spread, the novel became the focus of a moral panic (see text 5.3). Lewis was wealthy — an heir to a fortune made on the sugar plantations in the West Indies — and he took a seat in Parliament in 1796. Better was expected of such a blessed youth from the more sternly moral kinds of critic. Accordingly, the fourth official edition of 1798 was expurgated, and retitled *Ambrosio, or The Monk*. However, it was said that uncut editions were available with the most offensive passages highlighted for ease of use! Admired by De Sade and latterly the Surrealists, Lewis's text was one of the relatively few occasions when the Gothic novel achieved the ability to genuinely shock sensibilities and transgress social norms; more rarely still, it retains something of that power.

Excerpted here are a notorious chapter from the second volume, which critics singled out as demonstrating the blasphemous content of this fiction (and which T.J. Mathias thought could be prosecuted as obscene; see p.291), and a particularly horrid section from the last part of the text, extracted from the first-person description of the terrible imprisonment of the heroine Agnes.

1796

Matthew Gregory Lewis 1775–1818
The Monk

From Vol.2, Chapter 7

One evening, when he had found Elvira almost perfectly restored to health, he quitted her earlier than was his usual custom. Not finding Antonia in the antichamber, he ventured to follow her to her own. It was only separated from her mother's by a closet, in which Flora, the waiting-woman, generally slept. Antonia sat upon a sopha with her back towards the door, and read attentively. She heard not his approach, till he had seated himself by her. She started, and welcomed him with a look of pleasure: then rising, she would have conducted him to the sitting-room; but Ambrosio, taking her hand, obliged her by gentle violence to resume her place. She complied without difficulty: she knew not that there was more impropriety in conversing with him in one room than another. She thought herself equally secure of his principles and her own; and having replaced herself upon the sopha, she began to prattle to him with her usual ease and vivacity.

He examined the Book which she had been reading, and had now placed upon the table. It was the Bible.

'How!' said the friar to himself, 'Antonia reads the Bible, and is still so ignorant?'

But, upon a further inspection, he found that Elvira had made exactly the same remark. That prudent mother, while she admired the beauties of the sacred writings, was convinced that, unrestricted, no reading more improper could be permitted a young woman. Many of the narratives can only tend to excite ideas the worst calculated for a female breast: every thing is called plainly and roundly by its name; and the annals of a brothel would scarcely furnish a greater choice of indecent expressions. Yet this is the book which young women are recommended to study, which is put into the hands of children, able to comprehend little more than those passages of which they had better remain ignorant, and which but too frequently inculcates the first rudiments of vice, and gives the first alarm to the still sleeping passions. Of this was Elvira so fully convinced, that she would have preferred putting into her Daughter's hands '*Amadis de Gaul*,' or '*The Valiant Champion, Tirante the White*;' and would sooner have authorised her studying the lewd exploits of *Don Galaor*, or the lascivious jokes of the *Damsel Plazer di mi vida*. She had in consequence made two resolutions respecting the Bible. The first was, that Antonia should not read it till she was of an age to feel its beauties, and profit by its morality. The second, that it should be copied out with her own hand, and all improper passages either altered or omitted. She had adhered to this determination, and such was the Bible which Antonia was reading: it had been lately delivered to her, and she perused it with an avidity, with a delight that was inexpressible. Ambrosio perceived his mistake, and replaced the book upon the table.

Antonia spoke of her mother's health with all the enthusiastic joy of a youthful heart.

'I admire your filial affection,' said the abbot; 'It proves the excellence and sensibility of your character; it promises a treasure to him whom Heaven has destined to possess your affections. The Breast, so capable of fondness for a parent, what will it feel for a lover? Nay, perhaps, what feels it for one even now? Tell me, my lovely daughter, have you known what it is to love? Answer me with sincerity: forget my habit, and consider me only as a friend.'

'What it is to love?' said she, repeating his question; 'Oh! yes, undoubtedly; I have loved many, many people.'

'That is not what I mean. The love of which I speak can be felt only for one. Have you never seen the man whom you wished to be your husband?'

'Oh! no, indeed!'

This was an untruth, but she was unconscious of its falsehood: she knew not the nature of her sentiments for Lorenzo; and never having seen him since his first visit to Elvira, with every day his image grew less feebly impressed upon her bosom: besides, She thought of an husband with all a virgin's terror, and negatived the friar's demand without a moment's hesitation.

'And do you not long to see that man, Antonia? Do you feel no void in your heart, which you fain would have filled up? Do you heave no sighs for the absence of some one dear to you, but who that some one is you know not? Perceive you not that what formerly could please, has charms for you no longer? that a thousand new wishes, new ideas, new sensations, have sprang in your bosom, only to be felt, never to be described? Or, while you fill every other heart with passion, is it possible that your own remains insensible and cold? It cannot be! That melting eye, that blushing cheek, that enchanting voluptuous melancholy which at times overspreads your features — all these marks belie your words: you love, Antonia, and in vain would hide it from me.'

'Father, you amaze me! What is this love of which you speak? I neither know its nature, nor, if I felt it, why I should conceal the sentiment.'

'Have you seen no man, Antonia, whom though never seen before, you seemed long to have sought? whose form, though a stranger's, was familiar to your eyes? the sound of whose voice soothed you, pleased you, penetrated to your very soul? in whose presence you rejoiced, for whose absence you lamented? With whom your heart seemed to expand, and in whose bosom, with confidence unbounded, you reposed the cares of your own? Have you not felt all this, Antonia?'

'Certainly I have: the first time that I saw you, I felt it.'

Ambrosio started. Scarcely dared he credit his hearing.

'Me, Antonia?' he cried, his eyes sparkling with delight and impatience, while he seized her hand, and pressed it rapturously to his lips. 'Me, Antonia? You felt these sentiments for me?'

'Even with more strength than you have described. The very moment that I beheld you, I felt so pleased, so interested! I waited so eagerly to catch the sound of your voice; and when I heard it, it seemed so sweet! it spoke to me a language till then so unknown! Methought, it told me a thousand things which I wished to hear! It seemed as if I had long known you; as if I had a right to your friendship, your advice, and your protection. I wept when you departed, and longed for the time which should restore you to my sight.'

'Antonia! my charming Antonia!' exclaimed the monk, and caught her to his bosom: 'Can I believe my senses? Repeat it to me, my sweet girl! Tell me again that you love me, that you love me truly and tenderly!'

'Indeed, I do: let my mother be excepted, and the world holds no one more dear to me!'

At this frank avowal Ambrosio no longer possessed himself; wild with desire, he clasped the blushing trembler in his arms. He fastened his lips greedily upon hers, sucked in her pure delicious breath, violated with his bold hand the treasures of her bosom, and wound around him her soft and yielding limbs. Startled, alarmed, and confused at his action, surprise at first deprived her of the power of resistance. At length recovering herself, she strove to escape from his embrace.

'Father! — Ambrosio!' she cried, 'release me, for God's sake!'

But the licentious monk heeded not her prayers: he persisted in his design, and proceeded to take still greater liberties. Antonia prayed, wept, and struggled: terrified to the extreme, though at what she knew not, she exerted all her strength to repulse the friar, and was on the point of shrieking for assistance, when the chamber door was suddenly thrown open. Ambrosio had just sufficient presence of mind to be sensible of his danger. Reluctantly he quitted his prey, and started hastily from the couch. Antonia uttered an exclamation of joy, flew towards the door, and found herself clasped in the arms of her mother.

From Vol.3, Chapter 4

'My supposed death was attended with the greatest agonies. Those moments which I believed my last were embittered by the domina's assurances that I could not escape perdition; and as my eyes closed, I heard her rage exhale itself in curses on my offence. The horror of this situation, of a death-bed from which hope was banished, of a sleep from which I was only to wake to find myself the prey of flames and furies, was more dreadful than I can describe. When animation revived in me, my soul was still impressed with these terrible ideas. I looked round with fear, expecting to behold the ministers of divine vengeance. For the first hour, my senses were so bewildered, and my brain so dizzy, that I strove in vain to arrange the strange images which floated in

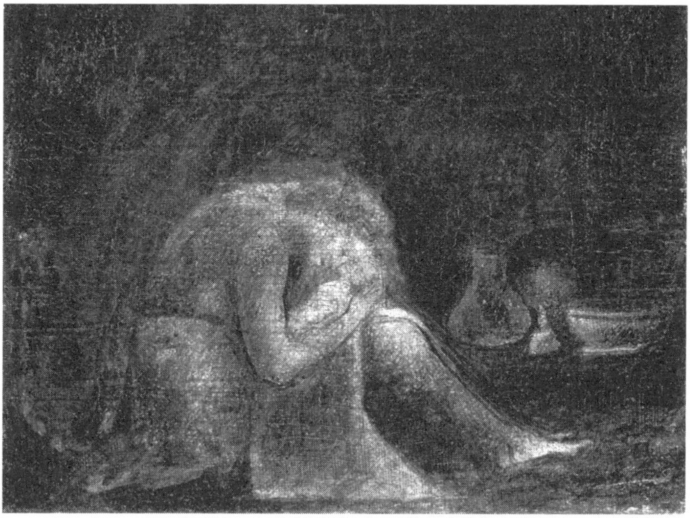

6
Catherine Blake
Agnes, *c.*1800
Tempera on canvas
13.7 × 18.1 cm
The Fitzwilliam Museum, Cambridge

wild confusion before me. If I endeavoured to raise myself from the ground, the wandering of my head deceived me. Every thing around me seemed to rock, and I sank once more upon the earth. My weak and dazzled eyes were unable to bear a nearer approach to a gleam of light, which I saw trembling above me. I was compelled to close them again, and remain motionless in the same posture.

A full hour elapsed, before I was sufficiently myself to examine the surrounding objects. When I did examine them, what terror filled my bosom! I found myself extended upon a sort of wicker couch. It had six handles to it, which doubtless had served the nuns to convey me to my grave. I was covered with a linen cloth: several faded flowers were strown over me: On one side lay a small wooden crucifix: on the other, a rosary of large beads. Four low narrow walls confined me. The top was also covered, and in it was fitted a small grated door, through which was admitted the little air which circulated in this miserable place. A faint glimmering of light, which streamed through the bars, permitted me to distinguish the surrounding horrors. I was oppressed by a noisome suffocating smell; and perceiving that the grated door was unfastened, I thought that I might possibly effect my escape. As I raised myself with this design, my hand rested upon something soft: I grasped it, and advanced it towards the light. Almighty God! what was my disgust! my consternation! In spite of its putridity, and the worms which preyed upon it, I perceived a corrupted human head, and recognised the features of a nun who had died some months before! I threw it from me, and sank almost lifeless upon my bier.

When my strength returned, this circumstance, and the consciousness of being surrounded by the loathsome and mouldering bodies of my companions, increased my desire to escape from my fearful prison. I again moved towards the light. The grated door was within my reach. I lifted it without difficulty:

probably it had been left unclosed to facilitate my quitting the dungeon. Aiding myself by the irregularity of the walls, some of whose stones projected beyond the rest, I contrived to ascend them, and drag myself out of my prison. I now found myself in a vault tolerably spacious. Several tombs, similar in appearance to that whence I had just escaped, were ranged along the sides in order, and seemed to be considerably sunk within the earth. A sepulchral lamp was suspended from the roof by an iron chain, and shed a gloomy light through the dungeon. Emblems of death were seen on every side: skulls, shoulder-blades, thigh-bones, and other reliques of mortality were scattered upon the dewy ground. Each tomb was ornamented with a large crucifix, and in one corner stood a wooden statue of St. Clare. To these objects I at first paid no attention: a door, the only outlet from the vault, had attracted my eyes. I hastened towards it, having wrapped my winding-sheet closely round me. I pushed against the door, and to my inexpressible terror found that it was fastened on the outside.

I guessed immediately, that the prioress, mistaking the nature of the liquor which she had compelled me to drink, instead of poison had administered a strong opiate. From this I concluded that, being to all appearance dead, I had received the rites of burial, and that deprived of the power of making my existence known, it would be my fate to expire of hunger. This idea penetrated me with horror, not merely for my own sake, but that of the innocent creature who still lived within my bosom. I again endeavoured to open the door, but it resisted all my efforts. I stretched my voice to the extent of its compass, and shrieked for aid. I was remote from the hearing of every one. No friendly voice replied to mine. A profound and melancholy silence prevailed through the vault, and I despaired of liberty. My long abstinence from food now began to torment me. The tortures which hunger inflicted on me, were the most painful and insupportable: yet they seemed to increase with every hour which past over my head. Sometimes I threw myself upon the ground, and rolled upon it wild and desperate: sometimes starting up, I returned to the door, again strove to force it open, and repeated my fruitless cries for succour. Often was I on the point of striking my temple against the sharp corner of some monument, dashing out my brains, and thus terminating my woes at once. But still the remembrance of my baby vanquished my resolution. I trembled at a deed, which equally endangered my child's existence and my own. Then would I vent my anguish in loud exclamations and passionate complaints; and then again my strength failing me, silent and hopeless I would sit me down upon the base of St. Clare's statue, fold my arms, and abandon myself to sullen despair. Thus passed several wretched hours. Death advanced towards me with rapid strides, and I expected that every succeeding moment would be that of my dissolution. Suddenly a neighbouring tomb caught my eye: a basket stood upon it, which till then I had not observed. I started from my seat: I made towards it as swiftly as my exhausted frame would permit. How eagerly did I seize the basket, on finding it to contain a loaf of coarse bread and a small bottle of water!

I threw myself with avidity upon these humble aliments. They had to all appearance been placed in the vault for several days. The bread was hard, and the water tainted; yet never did I taste food to me so delicious. When the cravings of appetite were satisfied, I busied myself with conjectures upon this new circumstance. I debated whether the basket had been placed there with a view to my necessity. Hope answered my doubts in the affirmative. Yet who could guess me to be in need of such assistance? If my existence was known, why was I detained in this gloomy vault? If I was kept a Prisoner, what meant the ceremony of committing me to the tomb? Or if I was doomed to perish with hunger, to whose pity was I indebted for provisions placed within my reach? A friend would not have kept my dreadful punishment a secret: neither did it seem probable that an enemy would have taken pains to supply me with the means of existence. Upon the whole I was inclined to think that the domina's designs upon my life had been discovered by some one of my partisans in the convent, who had found means to substitute an opiate for poison; that she had furnished me with food to support me, till She could effect my delivery; and that she was then employed in giving intelligence to my relations of my danger, and pointing out a way to release me from captivity. Yet why then was the quality of my provisions so coarse? How could my friend have entered the vault without the domina's knowledge? and if she had entered, why was the door fastened so carefully? These reflections staggered me: yet still this idea was the most favourable to my hopes, and I dwelt upon it in preference.

My meditations were interrupted by the sound of distant foot-steps. They approached, but slowly. Rays of light now darted through the crevices of the door. Uncertain whether the persons who advanced came to relieve me, or were conducted by some other motive to the vault, I failed not to attract their notice by loud cries for help. Still the sounds drew near. The light grew stronger. At length with inexpressible pleasure I heard the key turning in the lock. Persuaded that my deliverance was at hand, I flew towards the door with a shriek of joy. It opened: but all my hopes of escape died away, when the prioress appeared followed by the same four nuns who had been witnesses of my supposed death. They bore torches in their hands, and gazed upon me in fearful silence.

I started back in terror. The domina descended into the vault, as did also her companions. She bent upon me a stern resentful eye, but expressed no surprise at finding me still living. She took the seat which I had just quitted. The door was again closed, and the nuns ranged themselves behind their superior, while the glare of their torches, dimmed by the vapours and dampness of the vault, gilded with cold beams the surrounding monuments. For some moments all preserved a dead and solemn silence. I stood at some distance from the prioress. At length she beckoned me to advance. Trembling at the severity of her aspect, my strength scarce sufficed me to obey her. I drew near, but my limbs were unable to support their burthen. I sank upon my knees, I clasped my hands, and lifted them up to her for mercy, but had no power to articulate a syllable.

She gazed upon me with angry eyes.

'Do I see a penitent, or a criminal?' She said at length; 'Are those hands raised in contrition for your crimes, or in fear of meeting their punishment? Do those tears acknowledge the justice of your doom, or only solicit mitigation of your sufferings? I fear me, 'tis the latter!'

She paused, but kept her eye still fixed upon mine.

'Take courage,' she continued; 'I wish not for your death, but your repentance. The draught which I administered, was no poison, but an opiate. My intention in deceiving you, was to make you feel the agonies of a guilty conscience, had death overtaken you suddenly while your crimes were still unrepented. You have suffered those agonies; I have brought you to be familiar with the sharpness of death, and I trust that your momentary anguish will prove to you an eternal benefit. It is not my design to destroy your immortal soul, or bid you seek the grave, burthened with the weight of sins unexpiated. No, daughter, far from it; I will purify you with wholesome chastisement, and furnish you with full leisure for contrition and remorse. Hear then my sentence; The ill-judged zeal of your friends delayed its execution, but cannot now prevent it. All Madrid believes you to be no more; your relations are thoroughly persuaded of your death, and the nuns your partizans have assisted at your funeral. Your existence can never be suspected. I have taken such precautions as must render it an impenetrable mystery. Then abandon all thoughts of a world from which you are eternally separated, and employ the few hours which are allowed you in preparing for the next.'

This exordium led me to expect something terrible. I trembled, and would have spoken to deprecate her wrath; but a motion of the domina commanded me to be silent. She proceeded:

'Though of late years unjustly neglected, and now opposed by many of our misguided sisters (whom Heaven convert!) it is my intention to revive the laws of our order in their full force. That against incontinence is severe, but no more than so monstrous an offence demands. Submit to it, daughter, without resistance; you will find the benefit of patience and resignation in a better life than this. Listen then to the sentence of St.Clare. —Beneath these vaults there exist prisons, intended to receive such criminals as yourself: artfully is their entrance concealed, and she who enters them, must resign all hopes of liberty. Thither must you now be conveyed. Food shall be supplied you, but not sufficient for the indulgence of appetite: you shall have just enough to keep together body and soul, and its quality shall be the simplest and coarsest. Weep, daughter, weep, and moisten your bread with your tears: God knows that you have ample cause for sorrow! Chained down in one of these secret dungeons, shut out from the world and light for ever, with no comfort but religion, no society but repentance; thus must you groan away the remainder of your days. Such are St. Clare's orders; submit to them without repining. Follow me!'

Thunder-struck at this barbarous decree, my little remaining strength abandoned me. I answered only by falling at her feet, and bathing them with tears. The domina, unmoved by my affliction, rose from her seat with a stately air: she repeated her commands in an absolute tone; but my excessive faintness made me unable to obey her. Mariana and Alix raised me from the ground, and carried me forwards in their arms. The prioress moved on, leaning upon Violante, and Camilla preceded her with a torch. Thus passed our sad procession along the passages, in silence only broken by my sighs and groans. We stopped before the principal shrine of St. Clare. The statue was removed from its pedestal, though how I knew not. The nuns afterwards raised an iron grate till then concealed by the image, and let it fall on the other side with a loud crash. The awful sound, repeated by the vaults above and caverns below me, roused me from the despondent apathy in which I had been plunged. I looked before me; an abyss presented itself to my affrighted eyes, and a steep and narrow stair-case, whither my conductors were leading me. I shrieked, and started back. I implored compassion, rent the air with my cries, and summoned both heaven and earth to my assistance. In vain! I was hurried down the stair-case, and forced into one of the cells which lined the cavern's sides.

My blood ran cold, as I gazed upon this melancholy abode. The cold vapours hovering in the air, the walls green with damp, the bed of straw so forlorn and comfortless, the chain destined to bind me for ever to my prison, and the reptiles of every description which as the torches advanced towards them, I descried hurrying to their retreats, struck my heart with terrors almost too exquisite for nature to bear. Driven by despair to madness, I burst suddenly from the nuns who held me; I threw myself upon my knees before the prioress, and besought her mercy in the most passionate and frantic terms.

'If not on me,' said I, 'look at least with pity on that innocent being, whose life is attached to mine! Great is my crime, but let not my child suffer for it! My baby has committed no fault. Oh! spare me for the sake of my unborn offspring, whom ere it tastes life, your severity dooms to destruction!'

The prioress drew back hastily; she forced her habit from my grasp, as if my touch had been contagious.

'What!' she exclaimed with an exasperated air; 'What! Dare you plead for the produce of your shame? Shall a creature be permitted to live, conceived in guilt so monstrous? Abandoned woman, speak for him no more! Better that the wretch should perish than live: begotten in perjury, incontinence, and pollution, it cannot fail to prove a prodigy of vice. Hear me, thou guilty!

Expect no mercy from me, either for yourself or brat. Rather pray that Death may seize you before you produce it; or, if it must see the light, that its eyes may immediately be closed again for ever! No aid shall be given you in your labour; bring your offspring into the world yourself, feed it yourself, nurse it yourself, bury it yourself: God grant that the latter may happen soon, lest you receive comfort from the fruit of your iniquity!'

This inhuman speech, the threats which it contained, the dreadful sufferings foretold to me by the domina, and her prayers for my infant's death, on whom though unborn I already doted, were more than my exhausted frame could support. Uttering a deep groan, I fell senseless at the feet of my unrelenting enemy. I know not how long I remained in this situation; but I imagine that some time must have elapsed before my recovery, since it sufficed the prioress and her nuns to quit the cavern. When my senses returned, I found myself in silence and solitude. I heard not even the retiring foot-steps of my persecutors. All was hushed, and all was dreadful! I had been thrown upon the bed of straw: The heavy chain which I had already eyed with terror, was wound around my waist, and fastened me to the wall. A lamp glimmering with dull melancholy rays through my dungeon, permitted my distinguishing all its horrors. It was separated from the cavern by a low and irregular wall of stone. A large chasm was left open in it which formed the entrance, for door there was none. A leaden crucifix was in front of my straw couch. A tattered rug lay near me, as did also a chaplet of beads; and not far from me stood a pitcher of water, and a wicker-basket containing a small loaf, and a bottle of oil to supply my lamp.

With a despondent eye did I examine this scene of suffering: when I reflected that I was doomed to pass in it the remainder of my days, my heart was rent with bitter anguish. I had once been taught to look forward to a lot so different! At one time my prospects had appeared so bright, so flattering! Now all was lost to me. Friends, comfort, society, happiness, in one moment I was deprived of all! Dead to the world, dead to pleasure, I lived to nothing but the sense of misery. How fair did that world seem to me, from which I was for ever excluded! How many loved objects did it contain, whom I never should behold again! As I threw a look of terror round my prison, as I shrunk from the cutting wind which howled through my subterraneous dwelling, the change seemed so striking, so abrupt, that I doubted its reality. That the duke de Medina's niece, that the destined bride of the marquis de las Cisternas, one bred up in affluence, related to the noblest families in Spain, and rich in a multitude of affectionate friends — that she should in one moment become a captive, separated from the world for ever, weighed down with chains, and reduced to support life with the coarsest aliments — appeared a change so sudden and incredible, that I believed myself the sport of some frightful vision. Its continuance convinced me of my mistake with but too much certainty. Every morning I looked for some relief from my suffering: every morning my hopes were disappointed.

At length I abandoned all idea of escaping, I resigned myself to my fate, and only expected liberty when she came the companion of death.

My mental anguish, and the dreadful scenes in which I had been an actress, advanced the period of my labour. In solitude and misery, abandoned by all, unassisted by art, uncomforted by friendship, with pangs which if witnessed would have touched the hardest heart, was I delivered of my wretched burthen. It came alive into the world; but I knew not how to treat it, or by what means to preserve its existence. I could only bathe it with tears, warm it in my bosom, and offer up prayers for its safety. I was soon deprived of this mournful employment: the want of proper attendance, my ignorance how to nurse it, the bitter cold of the dungeon, and the unwholesome air which inflated its lungs, terminated my sweet babe's short and painful existence. It expired in a few hours after its birth, and I witnessed its death with agonies which beggar all description.

But my grief was unavailing. My infant was no more; nor could all my sighs impart to its little tender frame the breath of a moment. I rent my winding-sheet, and wrapped in it my lovely child. I placed it on my bosom, its soft arm folded round my neck, and its pale cold cheek resting upon mine. Thus did its lifeless limbs repose, while I covered it with kisses, talked to it, wept, and moaned over it without remission, day or night. Camilla entered my prison regularly once every twenty-four hours, to bring me food. In spite of her flinty nature, she could not behold this spectacle unmoved. She feared that grief so excessive would at length turn my brain; and in truth I was not always in my proper senses. From a principle of compassion she urged me to permit the corse to be buried: but to this I never would consent. I vowed not to part with it while I had life: its presence was my only comfort, and no persuasion could induce me to give it up. It soon became a mass of putridity, and to every eye was a loathsome and disgusting object, to every eye but a mother's. In vain did human feelings bid me recoil from this emblem of mortality with repugnance. I withstood, and vanquished that repugnance. I persisted in holding my infant to my bosom, in lamenting it, loving it, adoring it! Hour after hour have I passed upon my sorry couch, contemplating what had once been my child: I endeavoured to retrace its features through the livid corruption, with which they were overspread. During my confinement this sad occupation was my only delight; and at that time worlds should not have bribed me to give it up. Even when released from my prison, I brought away my child in my arms. The representations of my two kind friends,' — [Here she took the hands of the marchioness and Virginia, and pressed them alternately to her lips] — at length persuaded me to resign my unhappy infant to the grave. Yet I parted from it with reluctance. However, reason at length prevailed; I suffered it to be taken from me, and it now reposes in consecrated ground...

1.9

Gothic Poems

Poetry has an important place in the Gothic literature of the 1790s and 1800s. The poems that appeared through Lewis's *The Monk* were considered by many to be the finest elements of that book, and rather more acceptable than the horrific descriptions and ideas to be found in the main text. Lewis produced a compilation of poems, translations and mock-translations by himself and collaborators, notably Walter Scott (1771-1832), in 1801: *Tales of Wonder.* This combined Oriental fantasies, tales of Gothic Romance and horrible imagery in a manner that proved irresistible to contemporary readers, and was reprinted, emulated and ripped-off numerous times.

Scott's 'The Fire King' was published in *Tales of Wonder*. It was written to request, for Lewis wanted a group of poems dealing with elemental spirits for his compilation. By Scott's own account, his contribution to what he flippantly termed 'Lewis's stock of horribles' was casually knocked out one boozy evening after dinner. Nonetheless, the poem was a considerable success and the story was dramatized in 1801. 'Ghasta' is a youthful effort by Percy Bysshe Shelley (1792-1822), produced late in 1809 or 1810 when he was still a teenager. Gothic readings such as the *Tales of Wonder* exerted a significant influence on the poets and writers of the 'Romantic' era, and Shelley's 'Ghasta' is expressly an imitation of the kinds of poems to be found in Lewis's collection and its imitators.

1799

Walter Scott 1771–1832

The Fire King

BOLD knights and fair dames, to my harp give an ear,
Of love, and of war, and of wonder to hear;
And you haply may sigh, in the midst of your glee,
At the tale of Count Albert and fair Rosalie.

O see you that castle, so strong and so high?
And see you that lady, the tear in her eye?
And see you that palmer, from Palestine's land,
The shell on his hat, and the staff in his hand?

'Now palmer, gray palmer, O tell unto me,
What news bring you home from the Holy Countrie;
And how goes the warfare by Galilee's strand,
And how fare our nobles, the flower of the land?'—

'O well goes the warfare by Gallilee's wave,
For Gilead, and Nablous, and Ramah we have;
And well fare our nobles by Mount Libanon,
For the Heathen have lost, and the Christians have won.'

A fair chain of gold mid her ringlets there hung;
That chain O'er the palmer's gray locks has she flung
'Oh! palmer, gray palmer, this chain be thy fee,
For the news thou hast brought from the East Countrie.

'And palmer, good palmer, by Gallilee's wave,
O saw ye Count Albert, the gentle and brave?
When the Crescent went back, and the Red-cross rush'd on
O saw ye him foremost on Mount Libanon?'—

'O lady, fair lady, the tree green it grows;
O lady, fair lady, the stream pure it flows;
Your castle stands strong, and your hopes soar on high
But lady, fair lady, all blossoms to die.

'The green boughs they wither, the thunderbolt falls,
It leaves of your castle but levin-scorch'd walls;
The pure stream runs muddy; the gay hope is gone;
Count Albert is taken on Mount Libanon.

'O she's ta'en a horse, should be fleet at her speed;
And she's ta'en a sword, should be sharp at her need;
And she has ta'en shipping for Palestine's land,
To ransom Count Albert from Soldanrie's hand.

Small thought had Count Albert on fair Rosalie,
Small thought on his faith, on his knighthood, had he
A heathenish damsel his light heart had won,
The Soldan's fair daughter on Mount Lebanon.

'Oh! Christian, brave Christian, my love would'st thou be?
Three things must thou do ere I hearken to thee
Our laws and our worship on thee shalt thou take;
And this thou shalt first do for Zulema's sake.

'And, next, in the cavern, where burns evermore
The mystical flame which the Curdmans adore,
Alone, and in silence, three nights shalt thou wake;
And this thou shalt next do for Zulema's sake.

'And, last, thou shalt aid us with council and hand,
To drive the Frank robber from Palestine's land;
For my lord and my love then Count Albert I'll take,
When all this is accomplished for Zulema's sake.'—

He has thrown by his helmet and cross-handled sword,
Renouncing his knighthood, denying his Lord;
He has ta'en the green caftan, and turban put on,
For the love of the maiden of fair Libanon.

And in the dread cavern, deep deep under ground,
Which fifty steel gates and steel portals surround,
He has watched until day-break, but sight saw he none,
Save the flame burning bright on its altar of stone.

Amazed was the princess, the Soldan amazed,
Sore murmured the priests as on Albert they gazed;
They searched all his garments, and, under his weeds,
They found, and took from him, his rosary beads.

Again in the cavern, deep deep under ground,
He watched the lone night, while the winds whistled round;
Far off was their murmur, it came not more nigh,
The flame burn'd unmoved, and naught else did he spy.

Loud murmured the priests, and amazed was the king,
While many dark spells of their witchcraft they sing:
They search'd Albert's body, and, lo! on his breast
Was the sign of the Cross, by his father impressed.

The priests they eraze it with care and with pain,
And the recreant returned to the cavern again;
But, as he descended, a whisper there fell! -
It was his good angel, who bade him farewell! —

High bristled his hair, his heart flutter'd and beat,
And he turned him five steps, half resolved to retreat;
But his heart it was harden'd, his purpose was gone,
When he thought on the maiden of fair Libanon.

Scarce pass'd he the archway, the threshold scarce trod,
When the winds from the four points of heaven were abroad;
They made each steel portal to rattle and ring,
And, borne on the blast, came the dread Fire-King.

Full sore rock'd the cavern, whene'er he drew nigh,
The fire on the altar blazed bick'ring and high;
In volcanic explosions the mountains proclaim
The dreadful approach of the Monarch of Flame.

Unmeasured in height, and undistinguish'd in form,
His breath it was lightning, his voice it was storm;
I ween the stout heart of Count Albert was tame,
When he saw in his terrors the Monarch of Flame.

In his hand a broad faulchion blue-glimmer'd through smoke,
And Mount Lebanon shook, as the Monarch he spoke;—
'With this brand shalt thou conquer, thus long, and no more,
Till thou bend to the Cross, and the Virgin adore.'—

The cloud-shrouded arm gives the weapon — and see!
The recreant receives the charmed gift on his knee.
The thunders growl distant, and faint gleam the fires,
As, borne on his whirlwind, the phantom retires.

Count Albert has armed him the Paynim among,
Though his heart it was false, yet his arm it was strong;
And the Red-cross wax'd faint, and the Crescent came on,
From the day he commanded on Mount Libanon,

From Lebanon's forests to Gallilee's wave,
The sands of Samaar drank the blood of the brave;
Till the Knights of the Temple, and Knights of Saint John,
With Salem's King Baldwin, against him came on.

The war-cymbals clatter'd, the trumpets replied,
The lances were couch'd, and they closed on each side;
And horsemen and horses Count Albert o'erthrew,
Till he pierced the thick tumult King Baldwin unto.

Against the charmed blade which Count Albert did wield,
The fence had been vain of the King's Red-cross shield;
But a Page thrust him forward the monarch before,
And cleft the proud turban the renegade wore.

So fell was the dint, that Count Albert stoop'd low
Before the crossed shield, to his steel saddle-bow;
And scarce had he bent to the Red-Cross his head,
—*'Bonne grace, notre Dame,'*— he unwittingly said.

Sore sigh'd the charmed sword, for its virtue was o'er,
It sprung from his grasp, and was never seen more;
But true men have said, that the lightning's red wing
Did waft back the brand to the dread Fire-King.

He clenched his set teeth, and his gauntletted hand;
He stretch'd with one buffet that page on the strand
As back from the stripling the broken casque roll'd,
You might see the blue eyes, and the ringlets of gold!

Short time had Count Albert in horror to stare
On those death-swimming eye-balls and blood-clotted hair;
For down came the Templars, like Cedron in flood,
And dyed their long lances in Saracen blood.

The Saracens, Curdmans, and Ishmaelites yield
To the scallop, the saltier, and crossletted shield;
And the eagles were gorged with the infidel dead,
From Bethsaida's fountains to Naphthali's head.

The battle is over on Bethsaida's plain. —
Oh! who is yon Paynim lies stretched 'mid the slain?
And who is yon Page lying cold at his knee?
Oh! who but Count Albert and fair Rosalie.

The Lady was buried in Salem's bless'd bound,
The Count he was left to the vulture and hound:
Her soul to high mercy our Lady did bring;
His went on the blast to the dread Fire-King.

Yet many a minstrel in harping can tell,
How the Red Cross it conquer'd, the Crescent it fell;
And lords and gay ladies have sigh'd, mid their glee,
At the Tale of Count Albert and fair Rosalie.

7
Henry Fuseli
The Fire King appears to Count Albert, c.1801–10
Oil on canvas 99 × 124 cm
Victoria and Albert Museum, London

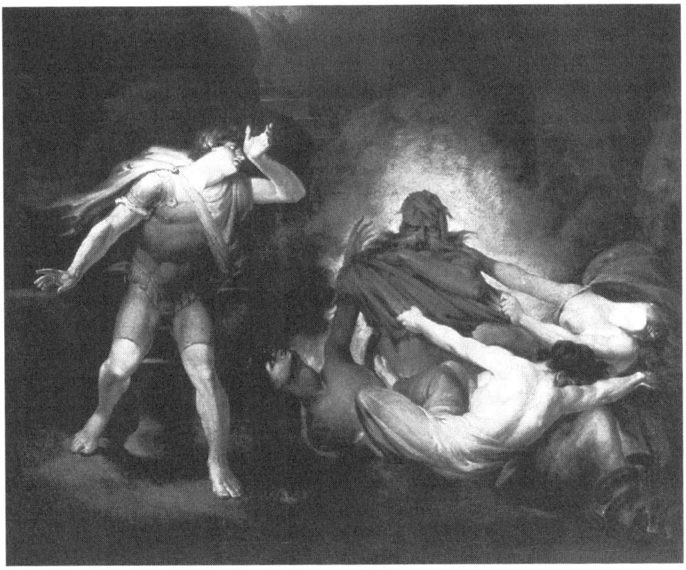

c. 1809–10

Percy Bysshe Shelley 1792–1822
Ghasta or, The Avenging Demon!!!

The idea of the following tale was taken from a few unconnected German Stanzas. The principal Character is evidently the Wandering Jew, and although not mentioned by name, the burning Cross on his forehead undoubtedly alludes to that superstition, so prevalent in the part of Germany called the Black Forest, where this scene is supposed to lie.

Hark! the owlet flaps her wing,
In the pathless dell beneath,
Hark! night ravens loudly sing,
Tidings of despair and death. —

Horror covers all the sky,
Clouds of darkness blot the moon,
Prepare! for mortal thou must die,
Prepare to yield thy soul up soon —

Fierce the tempest raves around,
Fierce the volleyed lightnings fly,
Crashing thunder shakes the ground,
Fire and tumult fill the sky. —

Hark! the tolling village bell,
Tells the hour of midnight come,
Now can blast the powers of Hell,
Fiend-like goblins now can roam —

See! his crest all stained with rain,
A warrior hastening speeds his way,
He starts, looks round him, starts again,
And sighs for the approach of day.

See! his frantic steed he reins,
See! he lifts his hands on high,
Implores a respite to his pains,
From the powers of the sky.

He seeks an Inn, for faint from toil,
Fatigue had bent his lofty form,
To rest his wearied limbs awhile,
Fatigued with wandering and the storm.

* * *

Slow the door is opened wide —
With trackless tread a stranger came,
His form Majestic, slow his stride,
He sate, nor spake, — nor told his name —

Terror blanched the warrior's cheek,
Cold sweat from his forehead ran,
In vain his tongue essayed to speak, —
At last the stranger thus began:

'Mortal! thou that saw'st the sprite,
Tell me what I wish to know,
Or come with me before 'tis light,
Where cypress trees and mandrakes grow.

'Fierce the avenging Demon's ire,
Fiercer than the wintry blast,
Fiercer than the lightning's fire,
When the hour of twilight's past' —

The warrior raised his sunken eye.
It met the stranger's sullen scowl,
'Mortal! Mortal! thou must die,'
In burning letters chilled his soul.

Warrior
Stranger! whoso'er you are,
I feel impelled my tale to tell —
Horrors stranger shalt thou hear,
Horrors drear as those of Hell.

O'er my Castle silence reigned,
Late the night and drear the hour,
When on the terrace I observed,
A fleeting shadowy mist to lower. —

Light the cloud as summer fog,
Which transient shuns the morning beam;
Fleeting as the cloud on bog,
That hangs or on the mountain stream. —

Horror seized my shuddering brain,
Horror dimmed my starting eye.
In vain I tried to speak, — In vain
My limbs essayed the spot to fly —

At last the thin and shadowy form,
With noiseless, trackless footsteps came, —
Its light robe floated on the storm,
Its head was bound with lambent flame.

In chilling voice drear as the breeze
Which sweeps along th' autumnal ground,
Which wanders through the leafless trees,
Or the mandrake's groan which floats around.

'Thou art mine and I am thine,
'Till the sinking of the world,
I am thine and thou art mine,
'Till in ruin death is hurled —

'Strong the power and dire the fate,
Which drags me from the depths of Hell,
Breaks the tomb's eternal gate,
Where fiendish shapes and dead men yell,

'Haply I might ne'er have shrank
From flames that rack the guilty dead,
Haply I might ne'er have sank
On pleasure's flowery, thorny bed —

— But stay! no more I dare disclose,
Of the tale I wish to tell,
On Earth relentless were my woes,
But fiercer are my pangs in Hell —

'Now I claim thee as my love,
Lay aside all chilling fear,
My affection will I prove,
Where sheeted ghosts and spectres are!

'For thou art mine, and I am thine,
'Till the dreaded judgement day,
I am thine, and thou art mine —
Night is past — I must away.'

Still I gazed, and still the form
Pressed upon my aching sight,
Still I braved the howling storm,
When the ghost dissolved in night. —

Restless, sleepless fled the night,
Sleepless as a sick man's bed,
When he sighs for morning light,
When he turns his aching head, —

Slow and painful passed the day.
Melancholy seized my brain,
Lingering fled the hours away,
Lingering to a wretch in pain. —

At last came night, ah! horrid hour,
Ah! chilling time that wakes the dead,
When demons ride the clouds that lower,
-The phantom sat upon my bed.

In hollow voice, low as the sound
Which in some charnel makes its moan,
What floats along the burying ground,
The phantom claimed me as her own.

Her chilling finger on my head,
With coldest touch congealed my soul —
Cold as the finger of the dead,
Or damps which round a tombstone roll —

Months are passed in lingering round,
Every night the spectre comes,
With thrilling step it shakes the ground,
With thrilling step it round me roams —

Stranger! I have told to thee,
All the tale I have to tell —
Stranger! canst thou tell to me,
How to 'scape the powers of Hell? —

Stranger
Warrior! I can ease thy woes,
Wilt thou, wilt thou, come with me —
Warrior! I can all disclose,
Follow, follow, follow me.

Yet the tempest's duskiest wing,
Its mantle stretches o'er the sky,
Yet the midnight ravens sing,
'Mortal! Mortal! thou must die.'

At last they saw a river clear,
That crossed the heathy path they trod,
The Stranger's look was wild and drear,
The firm Earth shook beneath his nod —

He raised a wand above his head,
He traced a circle on the plain,
In a wild verse he called the dead,
The dead with silent footsteps came.

A burning brilliance on his head,
Flaming filled the stormy air,
In a wild verse he called the dead,
The dead in motley crowd were there. —

'Ghasta! Ghasta! come along,
Bring thy fiendish crowd with thee,
Quickly raise th' avenging Song,
Ghasta! Ghasta! come to me.'

Horrid shapes in mantles gray,
Flit athwart the stormy night,
'Ghasta! Ghasta! come away,
Come away before 'tis light.'

See! the sheeted Ghost they bring,
Yelling dreadful o'er the heath,
Hark! the deadly verse they sing,
Tidings of despair and death!

The yelling Ghost before him stands,
See! she rolls her eyes around,
Now she lifts her bony hands,
Now her footsteps shake the ground.

Stranger
Phantom of Theresa say,
Why to earth again you came,
Quickly speak, I must away!
Or you must bleach for aye in flame, —

Phantom
Mighty one I know thee now,
Mightiest power of the sky,
Know thee by thy flaming brow,
Onow thee by thy sparkling eye.

That fire is scorching! Oh! I came,
From the caverned depth of Hell,
My fleeting false Rodolph to claim,
Mighty one! I know thee well. —

Stranger
Ghasta! seize yon wandering sprite,
Drag her to the depth beneath,
Take her swift, before 'tis light,
Take her to the cells of death!

Thou that heardst the trackless dead,
In the mouldering tomb must lie,
Mortal! look upon my head,
Mortal! Mortal! thou must die.

Of glowing flame a cross was there,
Which threw a light around his form,
Whilst his lank and raven hair,
Floated wild upon the storm.—

The warrior upwards turned his eyes,
Gazed upon the cross of fire,
There sat horror and surprise,
There sat God's eternal

A shivering through the Warrior flew,
Colder than the nightly blast,
Colder than the evening dew,
When the hour of twilight's past. —

Thunder shakes th' expansive sky,
Shakes the bosom of the heath,
'Mortal! Mortal! thou must die' —
The warrior sank convulsed in death.

JANUARY 1810

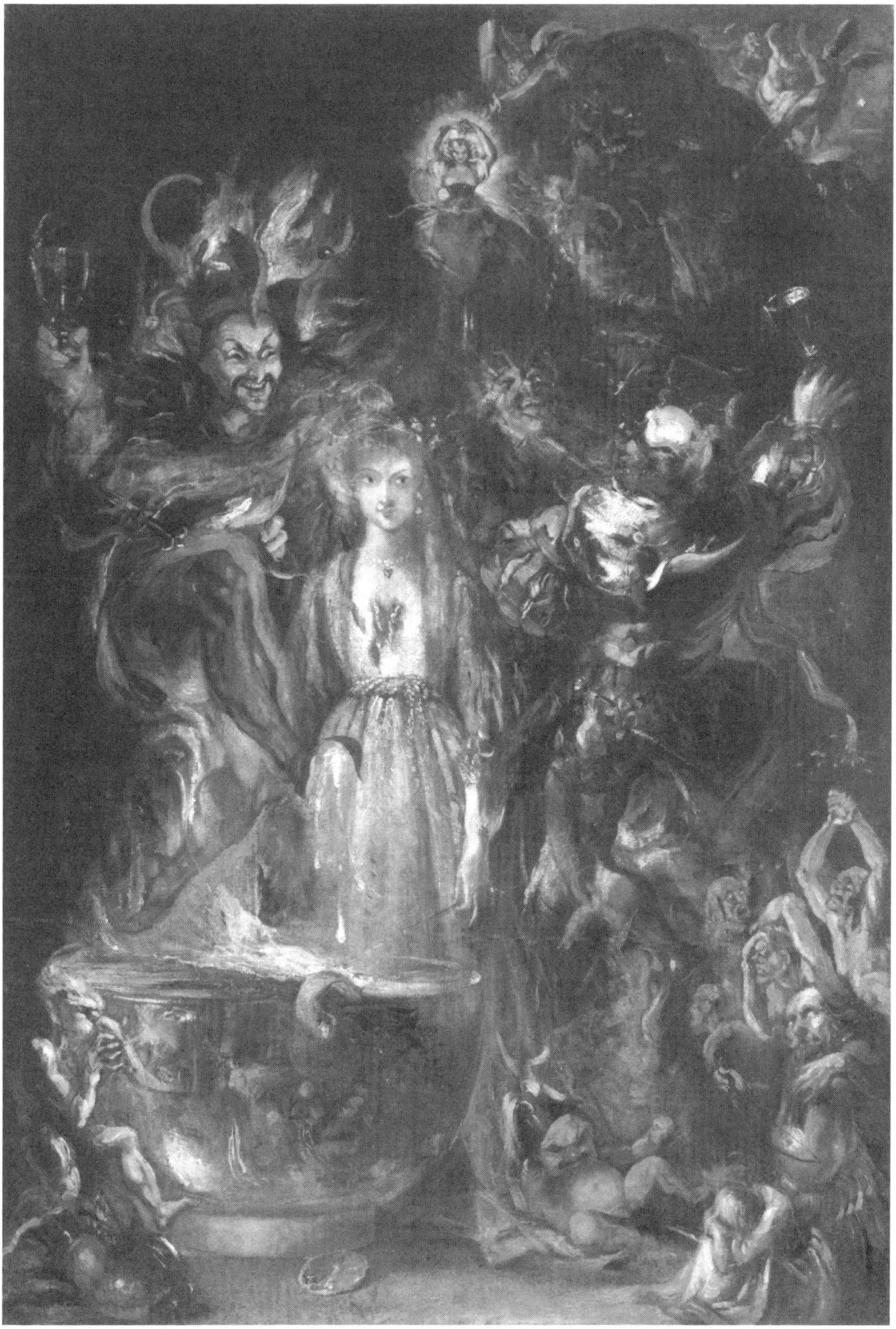

8
Theodor von Holst
Fantasy Based on Goethe's 'Faust', 1834
Oil on canvas 111.6 × 75.7 cm
Tate. Purchased 1990

1.10

Frankenstein

More than a novel, more the central, seemingly inexhaustible myth of the modern age, Mary Shelley's *Frankenstein* has been adapted, re-worked and transformed repeatedly since it was first published in 1818. It was first issued anonymously, and was assumed to be the product of Percy Bysshe Shelley (1792–1822), the husband of the still-teenaged Mary (1797–1851). The preface to the 1831 popular edition in which Mary Shelley acknowledged her authorship and accounted for the genesis of the novel, is reproduced elsewhere in this volume (see text 4.5).

The chapter excerpted here accounts for the generation of the monster by the brilliant but deluded scientist Victor Frankenstein in what modern readers, used to successive cinematic representations, may find surprisingly elusive terms. While far from graphic, the enduring potency of Shelley's imagery can hardly be in doubt, drawing together anxieties about science, nature, and the nature of man, and deeply-rooted psychological concerns about childbirth and sexuality.

1818

Mary Shelley 1797–1851
Frankenstein, Chapter 5

It was on a dreary night of November, that I beheld the accomplishment of my toils. With an anxiety that almost amounted to agony, I collected the instruments of life around me, that I might infuse a spark of being into the lifeless thing that lay at my feet. It was already one in the morning; the rain pattered dismally against the panes, and my candle was nearly burnt out, when, by the glimmer of the half-extinguished light, I saw the dull yellow eye of the creature open; it breathed hard, and a convulsive motion agitated its limbs.

How can I describe my emotions at this catastrophe, or how delineate the wretch whom with such infinite pains and care I had endeavoured to form? His limbs were in proportion, and I had selected his features as beautiful. Beautiful! — Great God! His yellow skin scarcely covered the work of muscles and arteries beneath; his hair was of a lustrous black, and flowing; his teeth of a pearly whiteness; but these luxuriances only formed a more horrid contrast with his watery eyes, that seemed almost of the same colour as the dun white sockets in which they were set, his shrivelled complexion, and straight black lips.

The different accidents of life are not so changeable as the feelings of human nature. I had worked hard for nearly two years, for the sole purpose of infusing life into an inanimate body. For this I had deprived myself of rest and health. I had desired it with an ardour that far exceeded moderation; but now that I had finished, the beauty of the dream vanished, and breathless horror and disgust filled my heart. Unable to endure the aspect of the being I had created, I rushed out of the room, and continued a long time traversing my bed-chamber, unable to compose my mind to sleep. At length lassitude succeeded to the tumult I had before endured; and I threw myself on the bed in my clothes, endeavouring to seek a few moments of forgetfulness. But it was in vain; I slept indeed, but I was disturbed by the wildest dreams. I thought I saw Elizabeth, in the bloom of health, walking in the streets of Ingolstadt. Delighted and surprised, I embraced her; but as I imprinted the first kiss on her lips, they became livid with the hue of death; her features appeared to change, and I thought that I held the corpse of my dead mother in my arms; a shroud enveloped her form, and I saw the grave-worms crawling in the folds of the flannel. I started from my sleep with horror; a cold dew covered my forehead, my teeth chattered, and every limb became convulsed; when, by the dim and yellow light of the moon as it forced its way through the window shutters, I beheld the wretch — the miserable monster whom I had created. He held up the curtain of the bed; and his eyes, if eyes they may be called, were fixed on me. His jaws opened, and he muttered some inarticulate sounds, while a grin wrinkled his cheeks. He might have spoken, but I did not hear; one hand was stretched out, seemingly to detain me, but I escaped and rushed down-stairs. I took refuge in the court-yard belonging to the house which I inhabited; where I remained during the rest of the night, walking up and down in the greatest agitation, listening attentively, catching and fearing each sound as if it were to announce the approach of the demoniacal corpse to which I had so miserably given life.

Oh! no mortal could support the horror of that countenance. A mummy again endued with animation could not be so hideous as that wretch. I had gazed on him while unfinished; he was ugly then; but when those muscles and joints were rendered capable of motion, it became a thing such as even Dante could not have conceived.

I passed the night wretchedly. Sometimes my pulse beat so quickly and hardly that I felt the palpitation of every artery; at others, I nearly sank to the ground through languor and extreme weakness. Mingled with this horror, I felt the bitterness of disappointment: dreams that had been my food and pleasant rest for so long a space, were now become a hell to me; and the change was so rapid, the overthrow so complete!

Morning, dismal and wet, at length dawned and discovered to my sleepless and aching eyes the church of Ingolstadt, its white steeple and clock, which indicated the sixth hour. The porter opened the gates of the court, which had that night been my asylum, and I issued into the streets, pacing them with quick steps, as if I sought to avoid the wretch whom I feared every turning of the street would present to my view. I did not dare return to the apartment which I inhabited, but felt impelled to hurry on, although wetted by the rain which poured from a black and comfortless sky.

I continued walking in this manner for some time, endeavouring, by bodily exercise, to ease the load that weighed upon my mind. I traversed the streets, without any clear conception of where I was, or what I was doing. My heart palpitated in the sickness of fear; and I hurried on with irregular steps, not daring to look about me:

> Like one who, on a lonely road,
> Doth walk in fear and dread,
> And, having once turned round, walks on,
> And turns no more his head;
> Because he knows a frightful fiend
> Doth close behind him tread.*

Continuing thus, I came at length opposite to the inn at which the various diligences and carriages usually stopped. Here I paused, I knew not why; but I remained some minutes with my eyes fixed on a coach that was coming towards me from the other end of the street. As it drew nearer, I observed that it was the Swiss diligence: it stopped just where I was standing; and, on the door being opened, I perceived Henry Clerval, who, on seeing me,

*Coleridge's Ancient Manner

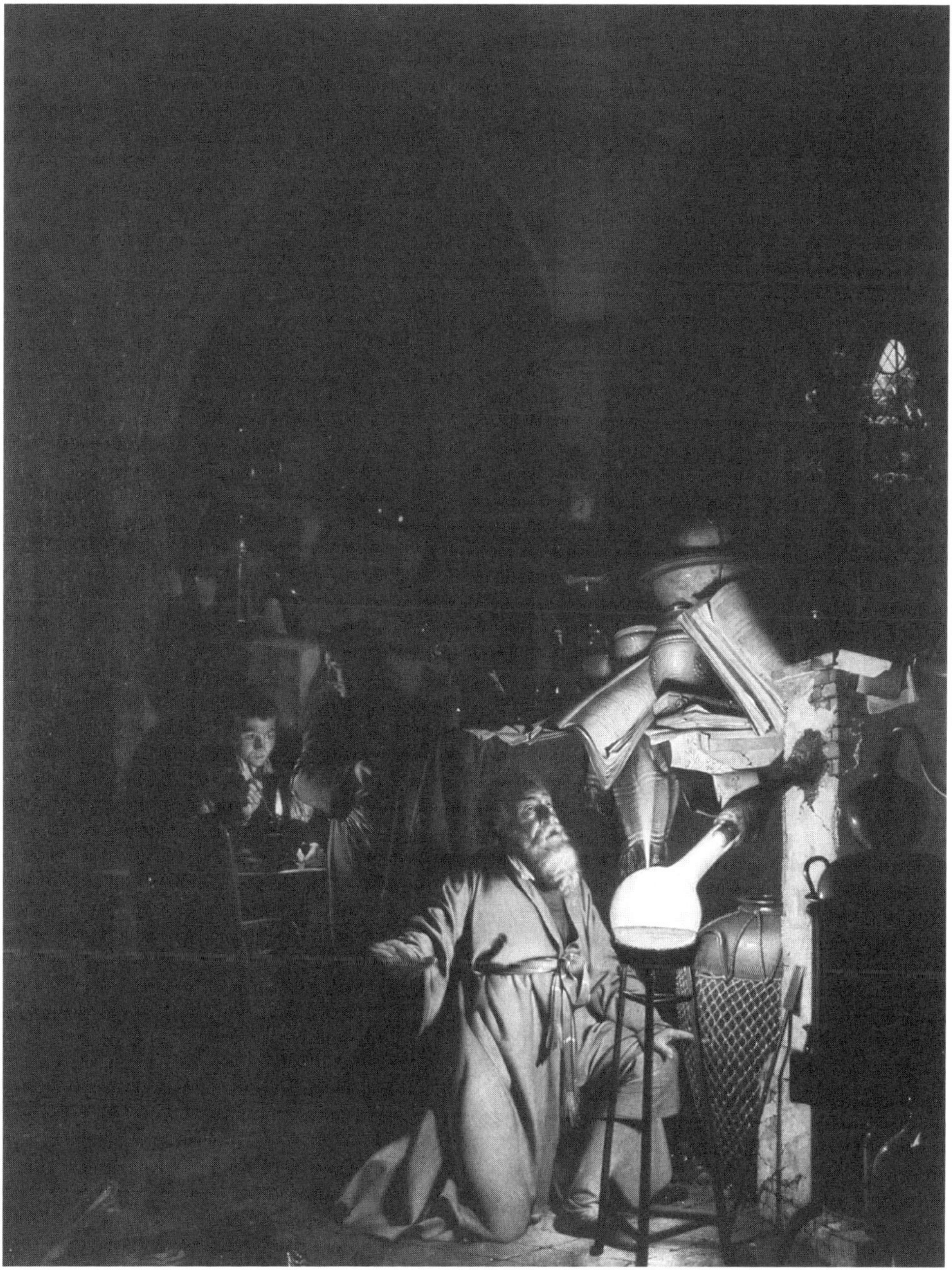

9
Joseph Wright of Derby
The Alchemist, 1771–95
Oil on canvas 127 × 101.6 cm
Derby Art Gallery

instantly sprung out. "My dear Frankenstein", exclaimed he, "how glad I am to see you! how fortunate that you should be here at the very moment of my alighting!"

Nothing could equal my delight on seeing Clerval; his presence brought back to my thoughts my father, Elizabeth, and all those scenes of home so dear to my recollection. I grasped his hand, and in a moment forgot my horror and misfortune; I felt suddenly, and for the first time during many months, calm and serene joy. I welcomed my friend, therefore, in the most cordial manner, and we walked towards my college. Clerval continued talking for some time about our mutual friends and his own good fortune in being permitted to come to Ingolstadt. 'You may easily believe,' said he, 'how great was the difficulty to persuade my father that it was not absolutely necessary for a merchant not to understand anything except bookkeeping; and, indeed, I believe I left him incredulous to the last, for his constant answer to my unwearied entreaties was the same as that of the Dutch schoolmaster in The Vicar of Wakefield: "I have ten thousand florins a year without Greek, I eat heartily without Greek." But his affection for me at length overcame his dislike of learning, and he has permitted me to undertake a voyage of discovery to the land of knowledge.'

'It gives me the greatest delight to see you; but tell me how you left my father, brothers, and Elizabeth.'

'Very well, and very happy, only a little uneasy that they hear from you so seldom. By the bye, I mean to lecture you a little upon their account myself. But, my dear Frankenstein,' continued he, stopping short and gazing full in my face— 'I did not before remark how very ill you appear; so thin and, pale; you look as if you had been watching for several nights.

'You have guessed right; I have lately been so deeply engaged in one occupation that I have not allowed myself sufficient rest, as you see; but I hope, I sincerely hope, that all these employments are now at an end and that I am at length free.'

I trembled excessively; I could not endure to think of, and far less to allude to, the occurrences of the preceding night. I walked with a quick pace, and we soon arrived at my college. I then reflected, and the thought made me shiver, that the creature whom I had left in my apartment might still be there, alive, and walking about. I dreaded to behold this monster, but I feared still more that Henry should see him. Entreating him therefore to remain a few minutes at the bottom of the stairs, I darted up towards my own room. My hand was already on the lock of the door before I recollected myself. I then paused, and a cold shivering came over me. I threw the door forcibly open, as children are accustomed to do when they expect a spectre to stand in waiting for them on the other side; but nothing appeared. I stepped fearfully in: the apartment was empty, and my bedroom was also freed from its hideous guest. I could hardly believe that so great a good fortune could have befallen me; but when I became assured that my enemy had indeed fled, I clapped my hands for joy and ran down to Clerval.

We ascended into my room, and the servant presently brought breakfast; but I was unable to contain myself. It was not joy only that possessed me; I felt my flesh tingle with excess of sensitiveness, and my pulse beat rapidly. I was unable to remain for a single instant in the same place; I jumped over the chairs, clapped my hands, and laughed aloud. Clerval at first attributed my unusual spirits to joy on his arrival; but when he observed me more attentively, he saw a wildness in my eyes for which he could not account; and my loud, unrestrained, heartless laughter frightened and astonished him.

'My dear Victor,' cried he, 'what, for God's sake, is the matter? Do not laugh in that manner. How ill you are! What is the cause of all this?'

'Do not ask me,' cried I, putting my hands before my eyes, for I thought I saw the dreaded spectre glide into the room; '*he* can tell. — Oh, save me! save me!' I imagined that the monster seized me; I struggled furiously and fell down in a fit.

Poor Clerval! what must have been his feelings? A meeting, which he anticipated with such joy, so strangely turned to bitterness. But I was not the witness of his grief; for I was lifeless and did not recover my senses for a long, long time...

Melmoth The Wanderer

Maturin's massive and convoluted novel *Melmoth the Wanderer* is now considered to be the central work of the latter phase of the Gothic novel, in its more restrictive definition. In a series of narratives-within-narratives, Maturin (1782–1824) gives every conceivable Gothic motif an airing, as he accounts for the deathless Melmoth's wanderings through history.

Maturin's novel is marked by a concentration on interior psychology, a tendency which was to dominate the Gothic and ghostly tales of the coming decades. The text has been productively considered in relation to the complex politics and psychology of early nineteenth-century Ireland — Maturin's homeland. The themes of containment and rebellion, familial disruption and religious superstition associated with the Gothic had particular resonance in this violently divided society. Here, Mautrin presents the contents of old and fragmented seventeenth century manuscript describing the horrific imprisonment of Stanton, and, here, the supernatural visit of the wicked Melmoth.

1820

Charles Maturin 1782–1824
Melmoth the Wanderer

On his first discovery of his situation, he had determined to take the utmost care of his health and intellect that the place allowed, as the sole basis of his hope of deliverance. But as that hope declined, he neglected the means of realizing it. He had at first risen early, walked incessantly about his cell, and availed himself of every opportunity of being in the open air. He took the strictest care of his person in point of cleanliness, and with or without appetite, regularly forced down his miserable meals; and all these efforts were even pleasant, as long as hope prompted them. But now he began to relax them all. He passed half the day in his wretched bed, in which he frequently took his meals, declined shaving or changing his linen, and, when the sun shone into his cell, he turned from it on his straw with a sigh of heartbroken despondency. Formerly, when the air breathed through his grating, he used to say, 'Blessed air of heaven, I shall breathe you once more in freedom! — Reserve all your freshness for that delicious evening when I shall inhale you, and be as free as you myself.' Now when he felt it, he sighed and said nothing. The twitter of the sparrows, the pattering of rain, or the moan of the wind, sounds that he used to sit up in his bed to catch with delight, as reminding him of nature, were now unheeded.

He began at times to listen with sullen and horrible pleasure to the cries of his miserable companions. He became squalid, listless, torpid, and disgusting in his appearance. * *

* * * *

It was one of those dismal nights, that, as he tossed on his loathsome bed, — more loathsome from the impossibility to quit it without feeling more 'unrest,' — he perceived the miserable light that burned in the hearth was obscured by the intervention of some dark object. He turned feebly toward the light, without curiosity, without excitement, but with a wish to diversify the monotony of his misery, by observing the slightest change made even accidentally in the dusky atmosphere of his cell. Between him and the light stood the figure of Melmoth, just as he had seen him from the first; the figure was the same; the expression of the face was the same, — cold, stony, and rigid; the eyes, with their infernal and dazzling luster, were still the same.

Stanton's ruling passion rushed on his soul; he felt this apparition like a summons to a high and fearful encounter. He heard his heart beat audibly, and could have exclaimed with Lee's unfortunate heroine, — 'It pants as cowards do before a battle; Oh the great march has sounded!'

Melmoth approached him with that frightful calmness that mocks the terror it excites. 'My prophecy has been fulfilled; — you rise to meet me rattling from your chains, and rustling from your straw — am I not a true prophet?' Stanton was silent. 'Is not your situation very miserable?' — Still Stanton was silent; for he was beginning to believe this an illusion of madness. He thought to himself, 'How could he have gained entrance here?' — 'Would you not wish to be delivered from it?' Stanton tossed on his straw, and its rustling seemed to answer the question. 'I have the power to deliver you from it.' Melmoth spoke very slowly and very softly, and the melodious smoothness of his voice made a frightful contrast to the stony rigor of his features, and the fiendlike brilliancy of his eyes. 'Who are you, and whence come you?' said Stanton, in a tone that was meant to be interrogatory and imperative, but which, from his habits of squalid debility, was at once feeble and querulous. His intellect had become affected by the gloom of his miserable habitation, as the wretched inmate of a similar mansion, when produced before a medical examiner, was reported to be a complete Albino.—His skin was bleached, his eyes turned white; he could not bear the light; and, when exposed to it, he turned away with a mixture of weakness and restlessness, more like the writhings of a sick infant than the struggles of a man.

Such was Stanton's situation. He was enfeebled now, and the power of the enemy seemed without a possibility of opposition from either his intellectual or corporeal powers. * *

* * * *

Of all their horrible dialogue, only these words were legible in the manuscript, 'You know me now.' — 'I always knew you.' — 'That is false; you imagined you did, and that this has been the cause of all the wild * * * *

* * * * *

of the * * *

* * * of your finally being lodged in this mansion of misery, where only I would seek, where only I can succor you.' — 'You, demon!' — 'Demon! — Harsh words! — Was it a demon or a human being placed you here? — Listen to me, Stanton; nay, wrap not yourself in that miserable blanket, — that cannot shut out my words. Believe me, were you folded in thunder clouds, you must hear *me*! Stanton, think of your misery. These bare walls — what do they present to the intellect or to the senses? — White-wash, diversified with the scrawls of charcoal or red chalk, that your happy predecessors have left for you to trace over. You have a taste for drawing, — I trust it will improve. And here's a grating, through which the sun squints on you like a stepdame, and the breeze blows, as if it meant to tantalize you with a sigh from that sweet mouth, whose kiss you must never enjoy. And where's your library, — intellectual man, — travelled man?' he repeated in a tone of bitter derision; 'where be your companions, your peaked men of countries, as your favorite Shakespeare has it? You must be content with the spider and the rat, to crawl and scratch round your flock-bed! I have known prisoners in the Bastile to feed them for companions, — why don't you begin your task? I have known a spider to descend at the tap of a finger, and a rat to come forth when the daily meal was brought, to share it with his fellow

prisoner! — How delightful to have vermin for your guests! Aye, and when the feast fails them, they make a meal of their entertainer! -You shudder. — Are you, then, the first prisoner who has been devoured alive by the vermin that infested his cell? — Delightful banquet, not 'where you eat, but where you are eaten!' Your guests, however, will give you one token of repentance while they feed; there will be gnashing of teeth, and you shall hear it, and feel it too perchance! — And then for meals — Oh you are daintily off! — The soup that the cat has lapped; and (as her progeny has probably contributed to the hell broth) why not? — Then your hours of solitude, deliciously diversified by the yell of famine, the howl of madness, the crash of whips, and the broken-hearted sob of those who, like you, are supposed, or *driven* mad by the crimes of others! — Stanton, do you imagine your reason can possibly hold out amid such scenes? — Supposing your reason was unimpaired, your health not destroyed, — suppose all this, which is, after all, more than fair supposition can grant, guess the effect of the continuance of these scenes on your senses alone. A time will come, and soon, when, from mere habit, you will echo the scream of every delirious wretch that harbors near you; then you will pause, clasp your hands on your throbbing head, and listen with horrible anxiety whether the scream proceeded from *you* or *them*. The time will come, when, from the want of occupation, the listless and horrible vacancy of your hours, you will feel as anxious to hear those shrieks, as you were at first terrified to hear them, — when you will watch for the ravings of your next neighbor, as you would for a scene on the stage. All humanity will be extinguished in you. The ravings of these wretches will become at once your sport and your torture. You will watch for the sounds, to mock them with the grimaces and bellowings of a fiend. The mind has a power of accommodating itself to its situation, that you will experience in its most frightful and deplorable efficacy. Then comes the dreadful doubt of one's own sanity, the terrible announcer that *that* doubt will soon become fear, and *that* fear certainty. Perhaps (still more dreadful) the *fear* will at last become a *hope*, — shut out from society, watched by a brutal keeper, writhing with all the impotent agony of an incarcerated mind, without communication and without sympathy, unable to exchange ideas but with those whose ideas are only the hideous specters of departed intellect, or even to hear the welcome sound of the human voice, except to mistake it for the howl of a fiend, and stop the ear desecrated by its intrusion, — then at last your fear will become a more fearful hope; you will wish to become one of them, to escape the agony of consciousness. As those who have long leaned over a precipice, have at last felt a desire to plunge below, to relieve the intolerable temptation of their giddiness*, you will hear them laugh amid their wildest paroxysms; you will say, 'Doubtless those wretches have some consolation, but I have none; my sanity is my greatest curse in this abode of horrors. They greedily devour their miserable meals, while I loathe mine. They sleep sometimes

*A fact, related to me by a person who was near committing suicide in a similar situation, to escape what he called 'the excruciating torture of giddiness'.

soundly, while my sleep is — worse than their waking. They are revived every morning by some delicious illusion of cunning madness, soothing them with the hope of escaping, baffling or tormenting their keeper; my sanity precludes all such hope. *I know I never can escape*, and the preservation of my faculties is only an aggravation of my sufferings. I have all their miseries, — I have none of their consolations. They laugh, — I hear them; would I could laugh like them.' You will try, and the very effort will be an invocation to the demon of insanity to come and take full possession of you from that moment forever.

(There were other details, both of the menaces and temptations employed by Melmoth, which are too horrible for insertion. One of them may serve for an instance.)

'You think that the intellectual power is something distinct from the vitality of the soul, or, in other words, that if even your reason should be destroyed, (which it nearly is), your soul might yet enjoy beatitude in the full exercise of its enlarged and exalted faculties, and all the clouds which obscured them be dispelled by the Sun of Righteousness, in whose beams you hope to bask forever and ever. Now, without going into any metaphysical subtleties about the distinction between mind and soul, experience must teach you, that there can be no crime into which madmen would not, and do not, precipitate themselves; mischief is their occupation, malice their habit, murder their sport, and blasphemy their delight. Whether a soul in this state can be in a hopeful one, it is for you to judge; but it seems to me, that with the loss of reason (and reason cannot long be retained in this place) you lose also the hope of immortality. — Listen,' said the tempter, pausing, 'listen to the wretch who is raving near you, and whose blasphemies might make a demon start. — He was once an eminent puritanical preacher. Half the day he imagines himself in a pulpit, denouncing damnation against Papists, Arminians, and even Sublapsarians (he being a Supra-lapsarian himself). He foams, he writhes, he gnashes his teeth; you would imagine him in the hell he was painting, and that the fire and brimstone he is so lavish of were actually exhaling from his jaws. At night his *creed retaliates on him*; he believes himself one of the reprobates he has been all day denouncing, and curses God for the very decree he has all day been glorifying Him for.

'He, whom he has for twelve hours been vociferating 'is the loveliest among ten thousand,' becomes the object of demoniac hostility and execration. He grapples with the iron posts of his bed, and says he is rooting out the cross from the very foundations of Calvary; and it is remarkable, that in proportion as his morning exercises are intense, vivid, and eloquent, his nightly blasphemies are outrageous and horrible.—Hark! Now he believes himself a demon; listen to his diabolical eloquence of horror!'

Stanton listened, and shuddered...

1.12

The Raven

The American writer Edgar Allan Poe (1809–49) was the most original re-interpreter of the Gothic in the mid-nineteenth century. His tales and poems are considered to have set the standard for narrative concision and effective literary horror, and have been adapted for cinema (generally rather loosely) many times. 'The Raven', first published anonymously in 1845, was repeatedly printed in his own lifetime and since. Bringing together Poe's preoccupations with beauty, tragedy and the melancholic, it presents the death of a beautiful woman, 'unquestionably, the most poetical topic in the world', as Poe put it in an essay reflecting on the nature of this composition.

1845

Edgar Allan Poe 1809–49
The Raven

Once upon a midnight dreary, while I pondered, weak and weary,
Over many a quaint and curious volume of forgotten lore —
While I nodded, nearly napping, suddenly there came a tapping,
As of some one gently rapping, rapping at my chamber door.
''Tis some visitor,' I muttered, 'tapping at my chamber door —
Only this, and nothing more.'

Ah, distinctly I remember it was in the bleak December,
And each separate dying ember wrought its ghost upon the floor.
Eagerly I wished the morrow; — vainly I had sought to borrow
From my books surcease of sorrow — sorrow for the lost Lenore —
For the rare and radiant maiden whom the angels named Lenore —
Nameless here for evermore.

And the silken sad uncertain rustling of each purple curtain
Thrilled me — filled me with fantastic terrors never felt before;
So that now, to still the beating of my heart, I stood repeating
''Tis some visitor entreating entrance at my chamber door —
Some late visitor entreating entrance at my chamber door; —
This it is, and nothing more.'

Presently my soul grew stronger; hesitating then no longer,
'Sir,' said I, 'or Madam, truly your forgiveness I implore;
But the fact is I was napping, and so gently you came rapping,
And so faintly you came tapping, tapping at my chamber door,
That I scarce was sure I heard you' — here I opened wide the door; —
Darkness there, and nothing more.

Deep into that darkness peering, long I stood there wondering, fearing,
Doubting, dreaming dreams no mortal ever dared to dream before;
But the silence was unbroken, and the darkness gave no token,
And the only word there spoken was the whispered word, 'Lenore?'
This I whispered, and an echo murmured back the word, 'Lenore!'
Merely this and nothing more.

Back into the chamber turning, all my soul within me burning,
Soon again I heard a tapping somewhat louder than before.
'Surely,' said I, 'surely that is something at my window lattice;
Let me see then, what thereat is, and this mystery explore —
Let my heart be still a moment and this mystery explore; —
'Tis the wind and nothing more.'

Open here I flung the shutter, when, with many a flirt and flutter,
In there stepped a stately Raven of the saintly days of yore.
Not the least obeisance made he; not a minute stopped or stayed he;
But, with mien of lord or lady, perched above my chamber door —
Perched upon a bust of Pallas just above my chamber door —
Perched, and sat, and nothing more.

Then this ebony bird beguiling my sad fancy into smiling,
By the grave and stern decorum of the countenance it wore,
'Though thy crest be shorn and shaven, thou,' I said, 'art sure no craven.
Ghastly grim and ancient raven wandering from the Nightly shore —
Tell me what thy lordly name is on the Night's Plutonian shore!'
Quoth the Raven, 'Nevermore.'

Much I marvelled this ungainly fowl to hear discourse so plainly,
Though its answer little meaning-little relevancy bore;
For we cannot help agreeing that no living human being
Ever yet was blessed with seeing bird above his chamber door —
Bird or beast above the sculptured bust above his chamber door,
With such name as 'Nevermore.'

But the Raven, sitting lonely on the placid bust, spoke only
That one word, as if his soul in that one word he did outpour.
Nothing further then he uttered; not a feather then he fluttered —
Till I scarcely more than muttered 'Other friends have flown before —
On the morrow will *he* leave me, as my Hopes have flown before.'
Then the bird said, 'Nevermore.'

Startled at the stillness broken by reply so aptly spoken,
'Doubtless,' said I, 'what it utters is its only stock and store,
Caught from some unhappy master whom unmerciful Disaster
Followed fast and followed faster till his songs one burden bore —
Till the dirges of his Hope that melancholy burden bore
Of "Never-nevermore."'

But the Raven still beguiling all my sad soul into smiling,
Straight I wheeled a cushioned seat in front of bird and bust and door;
Then, upon the velvet sinking, I betook myself to linking
Fancy unto fancy, thinking what this ominous bird of yore —
What this grim, ungainly, ghastly, gaunt, and ominous bird of yore
Meant in croaking 'Nevermore.'

This I sat engaged in guessing, but no syllable expressing
To the fowl whose fiery eyes now burned into my bosom's core;
This and more I sat divining, with my head at ease reclining
On the cushion's velvet violet lining that the lamp-light gloated o'er,
But whose velvet violet lining with the lamp-light gloating o'er,
She shall press, ah, nevermore!

Then, methought, the air grew denser, perfumed from an unseen censer
Swung by Seraphim whose foot-falls tinkled on the tufted floor.
'Wretch,' I cried, 'thy God hath lent thee — by these angels he has sent thee
Respite — respite and nepenthe from thy memories of Lenore!
Quaff, oh quaff this kind nepenthe, and forget this lost Lenore!'
Quoth the raven, 'Nevermore.'

'Prophet!' said I, 'thing of evil! — prophet still, if bird or devil! —
Whether tempter sent, or whether tempest tossed thee here ashore,
Desolate yet all undaunted, on this desert land enchanted —
On this home by Horror haunted — tell me truly, I implore —
Is there — is there balm in Gilead? — tell me — tell me, I implore!'
Quoth the Raven, 'Nevermore.'

'Prophet!' said I, 'thing of evil! — prophet still, if bird or devil!
By that Heaven that bends above us — by that God we both adore —
Tell this soul with sorrow laden if, within the distant Aidenn,
It shall clasp a sainted maiden whom the angels named Lenore —
Clasp a rare and radiant maiden, whom the angels named Lenore?'
Quoth the Raven, 'Nevermore.'

'Be that word our sign of parting, bird or fiend!' I shrieked, upstarting —
'Get thee back into the tempest and the Night's Plutonian shore!
Leave no black plume as a token of that lie thy soul hath spoken!
Leave my loneliness unbroken! — quit the bust above my door!
Take thy beak from out my heart, and take thy form from off my door!'
Quoth the Raven, 'Nevermore.'

And the raven, never flitting, still is sitting, still is sitting
On the pallid bust of Pallas just above my chamber door;
And his eyes have all the seeming of a demon's that is dreaming,
And the lamp-light o'er him streaming throws his shadow on the floor;
And my soul from out that shadow that lies floating on the floor
Shall be lifted — nevermore!

Dracula

Bram Stoker's *Dracula* (1897) is only matched by Mary Shelley's *Frankenstein* in establishing a central horror-myth for modern times. The blood-sucking fiend of European folklore had been a popular literary theme in the previous decades, starting with John Polidori's *The Vampyre* (1819). Stoker's text remains remarkable for its powerfully weird imagery and, particularly, its strong sense of eroticism, both of which are highlighted in the excerpts here from chapter Three. The narrator is the Englishman Jonathan Harker, who finds himself imprisoned in Count Dracula's castle in mysterious eastern Europe.

The Irish writer and theatrical manager Stoker (1847–1912) produced a number of fictions whose thematic concern with sexual and ethnic violation have been variously related to the precarious state of Anglo-Irish political relations, Stoker's personal psychology and the sexual hypocrisy of the era. For his part, Stoker became rather reticent about the appearance of sexually explicit literature, as an excerpt from his later essay 'The Censorship of Fiction' testifies (see p.307).

1897

Bram Stoker 1847–1912
Dracula

When I found that I was a prisoner a sort of wild feeling came over me. I rushed up and down the stairs, trying every door and peering out of every window I could find; but after a little the conviction of my helplessness overpowered all other feelings. When I look back after a few hours I think I must have been mad for the time, for I behaved much as a rat does in a trap. When, however, the conviction had come to me that I was helpless I sat down quietly — as quietly as I have ever done anything in my life — and began to think over what was best to be done. I am thinking still, and as yet have come to no definite conclusion. Of one thing only am I certain: that it is no use making my ideas known to the Count. He knows well that I am imprisoned; and as he has done it himself, and has doubtless his own motives for it, he would only deceive me if I trusted him fully with the facts. So far as I can see, my only plan will be to keep my knowledge and my fears to myself, and my eyes open. I am, I know, either being deceived, like a baby, by my own fears, or else I am in desperate straits; and if the latter be so, I need, and shall need, all my brains to get through. I had hardly come to this conclusion when I heard the great door below shut, and knew that the Count had returned. He did not come at once into the library, so I went cautiously to my own room and found him making the bed. This was odd, but only confirmed what I had all along thought — that there are no servants in the house. When later I saw him through the chink of the hinges of the door laying the table in the dining-room, I was assured of it; for if he does himself all these menial offices, surely it is proof that there is no one else to do them. This gave me a fright, for if there is no-one else in the castle, it must have been the Count himself who was the driver of the coach that brought me here. This is a terrible thought, for if so, what does it mean that he could control the wolves, as he did, by only holding up his hand for silence? How was it that all the people at Bistritz and on the coach had some terrible fear for me? What meant the giving of the crucifix, of the garlic, of the wild rose, of the mountain ash?

[...]

Later. — I endorse the last words written, but this time there is no doubt in question. I shall not fear to sleep in any place where he is not. I have placed the crucifix over the head of my bed — I imagine that my rest is thus freer from dreams, and there it shall remain.

When he left me I went to my room. After a little while, not hearing any sound, I came out and went up the stone stair to where I could look out towards the south. There was some sense of freedom in the vast expanse, inaccessible though it was to me, as compared with the narrow darkness of the courtyard. Looking out on this, I felt that I was indeed in prison, and I seemed to want a breath of fresh air, though it were of the night. I am beginning to feel this nocturnal existence tell on me. It is destroying my nerve. I start at my own shadow, and am full of all sorts of horrible imaginings. God knows that there is ground for my terrible fear in this accursed place! I looked out over the beautiful expanse, bathed in soft yellow moonlight till it was almost as light as day. In the soft light the distant hills became melted, and the shadows in the valleys and gorges of velvety blackness. The mere beauty seemed to cheer me. There was peace and comfort in every breath I drew. As I leaned from the window my eye was caught by something moving a storey below me, and somewhat to my left, where I imagined, from the order of the rooms, that the windows of the Count's own room would look out. The window at which I stood was tall and deep, stone — mullioned, and though weather-worn, was still complete. But it was evidently many a day since the case had been there. I drew back behind the stonework, and looked carefully out.

What I saw was the Count's head coming out from the window. I did not see the face, but I knew the man by the neck and the movement of his back and arms. In any case I could not mistake the hands which I had had some many opportunities of studying. I was at first interested and somewhat amused, for it is wonderful how small a matter will interest and amuse a man when he is a prisoner. But my very feelings changed to repulsion and terror when I saw the whole man slowly emerge from the window and begin to crawl down the castle wall over the dreadful abyss, *face down*, with his cloak spreading out around him like great wings. At first I could not believe my eyes. I thought it was some trick of the moonlight, some weird effect of shadow; but I kept looking, and it could be no delusion. I saw the fingers and toes grasp the corners of the stones, worn clear of the mortar by the stress of years, and by thus using every projection and inequality move downwards with considerable speed, just as a lizard moves along a wall.

What manner of man is this, or what manner of creature, is it in the semblance of man? I feel the dread of this horrible place overpowering me; I am in fear, in awful fear, and there is no escape for me; I am encompassed about with terrors that I dare not think of...

[...]

Later: the morning of 16 May. — God preserve my sanity, for to this I am reduced. Safety and the assurance of safety are things of the past. Whilst I live on here there is but one thing to hope for, that I may not go mad, if, indeed, I be not mad already. If I be sane, then surely it is maddening to think that of all the foul things that lurk in this hateful place the Count is the least dreadful to me; that to him alone I can look for safety, even though this be only whilst I can serve his purpose. Great God! merciful God! Let me be calm, for out of that way lies madness indeed. I begin to get new lights on certain things which have puzzled me. Up to now I never quite knew what Shakespeare meant when he made Hamlet say,

> 'My tablets! quick, my tablets!
> 'Tis meet that I put it down,'

for now, feeling as though my own brain were unhinged or as if the shock had come which must end in its undoing, I turn to my diary for repose. The habit of entering accurately must help to soothe me.

The Count's mysterious warning frightened me at the time; it frightens me more not when I think of it, for in the future he has a fearful hold upon me. I shall fear to doubt what he may say!

When I had written in my diary and had fortunately replaced the book and pen in my pocket I felt sleepy. The Count's warning came into my mind, but I took pleasure in disobeying it. The sense of sleep was upon me, and with it the obstinacy which sleep brings as outrider. The soft moonlight soothed, and the wide expanse without gave a sense of freedom which refreshed me. I determined not to return to-night to the gloom-haunted rooms, but to sleep here, where, of old ladies had sat and sung and lived sweet lives whilst their gentle breasts were sad for their menfolk away in the midst of remorseless wars. I drew a great couch out of its place near the corner, so that as I lay, I could look at the lovely view to east and south, and unthinking of and uncaring for the dust, composed myself for sleep.

I suppose I must have fallen asleep; I hope so, but I fear, for all that followed was startlingly real — so real that now sitting here in the broad, full sunlight of the morning, I cannot in the least believe that it was all sleep.

I was not alone. The room was the same, unchanged in any way since I came into it; I could see along the floor, in the brilliant moonlight, my own footsteps marked where I had disturbed the long accumulation of dust. In the moonlight opposite me were three young women, ladies by their dress and manner. I thought at the time that I must be dreaming when I saw them, far, though the moonlight was behind them, they threw no shadow on the floor. They came close to me, and looked at me for some time, and then whispered together. Two were dark, and had high aquiline noses, like the Count, and great dark, piercing eyes, that seemed to be almost red when contrasted with the pale yellow moon. The other was fair, as fair as can be, with great wavy masses of golden hair and eyes like pale sapphires. I seemed somehow to know her face, and to know it in connection with some dreamy fear, but I could not recollect at the moment how or where. All three had brilliant white teeth that shone like pearls against the ruby of their voluptuous lips. There was something about them that made me uneasy, some longing and at the same time some deadly fear. I felt in my heart a wicked, burning desire that they would kiss me with those red lips. It is not good to note this down, lest some day it should meet Mina's eyes and cause her pain, but it is the truth. They whispered together, and then they all three laughed — such a silvery, musical laugh, but as hard as though the sound never could have come through the softness of human lips. It was like the intolerable, tingling sweetness of water glasses when played on by a cunning hand. The fair girl shook her head coquettishly, and the other two urged her on. One said:— 'Go on! You are first, and we shall follow; yours' is the right to begin.' The other added:— 'He is young and strong. There are kisses for us all.' I lay quiet, looking out from under my eyelashes in an agony of delightful anticipation. The fair girl advanced and bent over me till I could feel the movement of her breath upon me. Sweet it was in one sense, honey-sweet, and sent the same tingling through the nerves as her voice, but with a bitter underlying the sweet, a bitter offensiveness, as one smells in blood.

I was afraid to raise my eyelids, but looked out and saw perfectly under the lashes. The girl went on her knees, and bent over me, fairly gloating. There was a deliberate voluptuousness which was both thrilling and repulsive, and as she arched her neck she actually licked her lips like an animal, till I could see in the moonlight the moisture shining on the scarlet lips and on the red tongue as it lapped the white sharp teeth. Lower and lower went her head as the lips went below the range of my mouth and chin and seemed to fasten on my throat. Then she paused, and I could hear the churning sound of her tongue as it licked her teeth and lips, and I could feel the hot breath on my neck. Then the skin of my throat began to tingle as one's flesh does when the hand that is to tickle it approaches nearer — nearer. I could feel the soft, shivering touch of the lips on the supersensitive skin of my throat, and the hard dents of two sharp teeth, just touching and pausing there. I closed my eyes in languorous ecstasy and waited — waited with beating heart.

But at that instant, another sensation swept through me as quick as lightning. I was conscious of the presence of the Count, and of his being as if lapped in a storm of fury. As my eyes opened involuntarily I saw his strong hand grasp the slender neck of the fair woman and with giant's power draw it back, the blue eyes transformed with fury, the white teeth champing with rage, and the fair cheeks blazing red with passion. But the Count! Never did I imagine such wrath and fury, even to the demons of the pit. His eyes were positively blazing. The red light in them was lurid, as if the flames of hell-fire blazed behind them. His face was deathly pale, and the lines of it were hard like drawn wires; the thick eyebrows that met over the nose now seemed like a heaving bar of white-hot metal. With a fierce sweep of his arm, he hurled the woman from him, and then motioned to the others, as though he were beating them back; it was the same imperious gesture that I had seen used to the wolves. In a voice which, though low and almost in a whisper, seemed to cut through the air and then ring in the room he said:—

'How dare you touch him, any of you? How dare you cast eyes on him when I had forbidden it? Back, I tell you all! This man belongs to me! Beware how you meddle with him, or you'll have to deal with me.' The fair girl, with a laugh of ribald coquetry, turned to answer him:—

'You yourself never loved; you never love!' On this the other women joined, and such a mirthless, hard, soulless laughter rang through the room that it almost made me faint to hear. It seemed like the pleasure of fiends. Then the Count turned, after looking at my face attentively, and said in a soft whisper:—

'Yes, I too can love; you yourselves can tell it from the past. Is it not so? Well, now I promise you that when I am done with him you shall kiss him at your will. Now go! go! I must awaken him, for there is work to be done.'

'Are we to have nothing to-night?' said one of them, with a low laugh, as she pointed to the bag which he had thrown upon the floor, and which moved as though there were some living thing within it. For answer he nodded his head. One of the women jumped forward and opened it. If my ears did not deceive me there was a gasp and a low wail, as of a half smothered child. The women closed round, whilst I was aghast with horror; but as I looked, they disappeared, and with them the dreadful bag. There was no door near them, and they could not have passed me without my noticing. They simply seemed to fade into the rays of the moonlight and pass out through the window, for I could see outside the dim, shadowy forms for a moment before they entirely faded away.

Then the horror overcame me, and I sank down unconscious.

The Psychological and Aesthetic Functions of Horror and the Fantastic

Can we, should we, how do we find pleasure in reading about or looking at images of horror, fantasy and the supernatural?

These questions have been posed repeatedly among critics, philosophers and practitioners since antiquity. Within the classical tradition of criticism, deriving from ancient authors and codified to a greater or lesser degree in the seventeenth century, horrible and fantastical scenes were not the proper province of art. Or, rather, if the horrible was represented, it would be regulated and made acceptable; if the fantastic was an element in a piece of art, it would be made to seem reasonable and realistic; the eccentric would be made regular, and the ugly given a makeover. The weird and outlandish would be expelled from the purview of the true artist, and from that of the men of good taste who appreciated his art.

There were always alternatives and complexities in this line of argument. In particular, the Greek critic Longinus (first century AD), in his work 'On the Sublime', gave licence to more wildly imaginative and grandiose efforts. His work was known and translated in the eighteenth century; and it was this old concept of the Sublime that was elaborated — most influentially by Edmund Burke — into the dominant aesthetic framework of the era. The Sublime allowed for the idea of the extreme and excessive in art, and for the possibility of terror having a valuable social and psychological function.

A number of the excerpts here reflect the potency of the Sublime as an idea. But the selection as a whole, incorporating later texts by writers, psychoanalysts and critics, suggests the variety of responses to the supernatural in art, and a more general, and recurring, desire to connect the fantastic to the primal desires of mankind.

2.1

The Traditional Functions of Ghost Stories

The following excerpts suggest the role of ghostly and fantastic tales in traditional village culture. In the urbane, basically urban literary culture developed through the early part of the eighteenth century, rural life was treated both with a degree of disdain and a certain fascination. The accounts by Joseph Addison (1672–1719) and Mark Akenside (1721–70) here reveal the attraction felt by modern authors for the supernatural tales that formed an entertainment among working people.

Henry Bourne's pioneering *Antiquitates Vulgares* was an isolated attempt to document the beliefs and traditions of the working people of the British Isles. In his accounts of folk beliefs, Bourne (1694–1733) documents the stock materials of the supernatural Gothic — the Devil, ghosts and apparitions, haunted houses. He takes every opportunity he might to condemn ignorance and gullibility, tendencies that are a sort of hangover from the reign of the pre-Reformation church which needed to be regulated in this more enlightened age.

14 March 1711

Joseph Addison 1672–1719
The Spectator, no.12

I remember last Winter there were several young Girls of the Neighbourhood sitting about the Fire with my Land-lady's Daughters, and telling Stories of Spirits and Apparitions. Upon my opening the Door the young Women broke off their Discourse, but my Land-lady's Daughters telling them that it was no Body but the Gentleman (for that is the Name which I go by in the Neighbourhood as well as in the Family) they went on without minding me. I seated my self by the Candle that stood on a Table at one End of the Room; and pretending to read a Book that I took out of my Pocket, heard several dreadful Stories of Ghosts as pale as Ashes that had stood at the Feet of a Bed, or walked over a Church-yard by Moon-light: And of others that had been conjured into the *Red-Sea*, for disturbing People's Rest, and drawing their Curtains at Midnight; with many other old Womens Fables of the like Nature. As one Spirit raised another, I observed that at the End of every Story the whole Company closed their Ranks and crouded about the Fire: I took Notice in particular of a little Boy, who was so attentive of every Story, that I am mistaken if he ventures to go to bed by himself this Twelvemonth. Indeed they talked so long, that the Imaginations of the whole Assembly were manifestly crazed, and I am sure will be the worse for it as long as they live. I heard one of the Girls, that had looked upon me over her Shoulder, asking the Company how long I had been in the Room, and whether I did not look paler than I used to do. This put me under some Apprehensions that I should be forced to explain my self if I did not retire; for which Reason I took the Candle in my Hand, and went up into my Chamber, not without wondering at this unaccountable Weakness in reasonable Creatures, who love to astonish and terrify one another. Were I a Father, I should take a particular Care to preserve my Children from these little Horrours of Imagination, which they are apt to contract when they are young, and are not able to shake off when they are in Years. I have known a Soldier that has enter'd a Breach, affrighted at his own Shadow; and look pale upon a little scratching at his Door, who the Day before had march'd up against a Battery of Cannon. There are Instances of Persons, who have been terrify'd, even to Distraction, at the Figure of a Tree or the shaking of a Bull-rush. The Truth of it is, I look upon a sound Imagination as the greatest Blessing of Life, next to a clear Judgment and a good Conscience. In the mean Time, since there are very few whose Minds are not more or less subject to these dreadful Thoughts and Apprehensions, we ought to arm our selves against them by the Dictates of Reason and Religion, *to pull the old Woman out of our Hearts* (as *Persius* expresses it in the Motto of my Paper,) and extinguish those impertinent Notions which we imbibed at the Time that we were not able to judge of their Absurdity. Or if we believe, as many wise and good Men have done, that there are such Phantoms and Apparitions as those I have been speaking of, let us endeavour to establish to our selves an Interest in him who holds the Reins of the whole Creation in his Hand, and moderates them after such a Manner, that it is impossible for one Being to break loose upon another without his Knowledge and Permission.

For my own Part, I am apt to join in Opinion with those whose believe that all the Regions of Nature swarm with Spirits; and that we have Multitudes of Spectators on all our Actions, when we think our selves most alone: But instead of terrifying my self with such a Notion, I am wonderfully pleased to think that I am always engaged with such an innumerable Society in searching out the Wonders of the Creation, and joining in the same Consort of Praise and Adoration.

1725

Henry Bourne 1696–1733

Antiquitates Vulgares; Or, The Antiquities of the Common People

Chapter X: 'Of the Country Conversation in a Winter's Evening: Their Opinions of Spirits and Apparitions; of the Devil's appearing with a cloven foot; of Fairies and Hobgoblins; of the walking Places of Spirits; and of haunted Houses'

Nothing is commoner in *Country Places*, than for a whole Family in a *Winter's Evening*, to sit around the Fire, and tell Stories of Apparitions and Ghosts. And no Question of it, but this adds to the natural Fearfulness of Men, and makes them many Times imagine they see Things, which really are nothing, but their own Fancy. From this, and seldom any other Cause, it is, that *Herds* and *Shepherds* have all of them seen *frequent Apparitions*, and are generally so well stock'd with Stories of their own Knowledge. Some of them have seen *Fairies*, some *Spirits* in the Shapes of *Cows* and *Dogs* and *Horses*; and some have seen even the *Devil* himself, with a *cloven Foot*. All which, is either *Hearsay* or a *strong Imagination*. Not that there have not been, or may not be Apparitions; we know that there have undoubtedly been such Things, and that there still are, upon particular Occasions; but that almost all the Stories of Ghosts and Spirits, are grounded on no other Bottom, than the Fears and Fancies, and weak Brains of Men.

In their Account of the Apparition of the Devil, they always describe him with a *cloven Foot*: That is always his distinguishing Badge, whatever Shape he appears in; whether it be in Beauty or Deformity, he never appears without it. Such is the old Tradition they have received of his appearing, and such is their Belief of it.

Indeed it must be confess'd, that this is not so improbable and ridiculous as many Things they hold. For tho' perhaps few of them have ought else for this Opinion, but *old Wives Fables*, or the Picture of the Devil, which they have always observed drawn with a cloven Foot, yet there seems to be some Truth in it. For in the Times of frequent Apparitions, the Devil was wont to appear so, if we may believe in Antiquity; and there is also some Reason for it, considering the Circumstances of the fallen Angels.

[...]

Another Tradition they hold, and which is often talk'd of, is, that there are particular Places alotted to Spirits to walk in. Thence it was formerly, such frequent Reports were abroad of this and that particular Place being haunted by a Spirit, and that the common People say now and then, such a Place is dangerous to be pass'd though at Night, because a Spirit walks there. Nay, they'll further tell you, that some Spirits have lamented the Hardness of their Condition, in being obliged to walk in cold and uncomfortable Places, and have therefore desir'd the Person who was so hardy as to speak to them, to gift them with a warmer Walk, by some well grown *Hedge*, or in some *shady Vale*, where they might be shelter'd from the Rain and Wind.

The Stories, that Apparitions have seen oftner than once in the same Place, have no Doubt been the Rise and Spring of the walking Place of Spirits; but why they are said sometimes to cry out for Places that are more comfortable, is not so certainly known. It is however highly probable, that when the Ignorance and Superstition of the *Romish* Church, had filled the World with *Apparitions* and *Ghosts*, that this also was invented among them. For they seem to have the most *Right* to an Invention of this Nature, whose Brains were so fruitful of Folly, as to invent that *Dunstan* took the Devil by the Nose, with a Pair of hot *Tongs* till he roar'd again. For if the Devil may be burnt, he may also be starv'd; if he took such Pains to get his Nose out of the *Pincers*, without Doubt in a frosty Night, he would wish to be as warm as possible. He that believes the one, must necessarily believe the other. And therefore it very near amounts to a Demonstration, who were the Authors of this Opinion, *viz.* The *Monks*. We are sure they invented the one, and need little question but they invented the other.

[...]

The last Topick of this Conversation I shall take Notice of, shall be the Tales of *haunted* Houses. And indeed it is not to be wonder'd at, that this is never omitted. For formerly almost every Place had a House of this Kind. If a House was seated on some melancholy Place, or built in some old Romantick manner, or if any particular Accident had happen'd in it, such as Murder, sudden Death, or the like, to be sure that House had a mark set on it, and was afterwards esteemed the Habitation of a Ghost. In talking upon this Point, they generally show how the Occasion of the House's being *haunted*, the merry Pranks of the Spirit, and

10
Richard Newton
Resurrection Men
Published 1 October 1792
Handcoloured etching and aquatint 31.8 × 23 cm
The British Museum, London

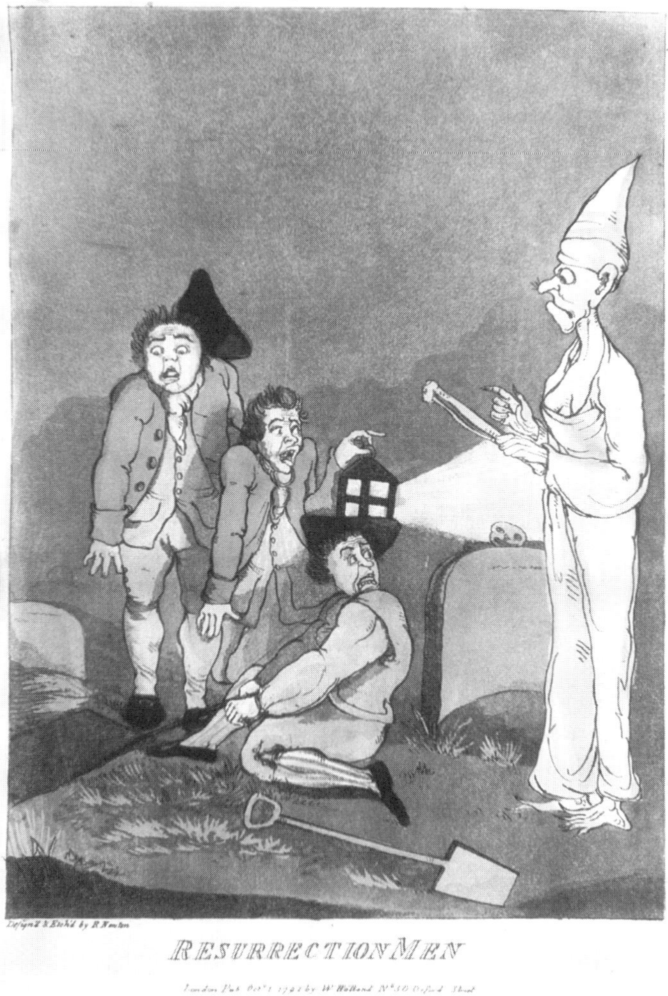

how it was laid. Stories of this Kind are infinite, and there are few *Villages*, which have not either had such a House in it, or near it.

And indeed there are Men of good Learning and Knowledge, who are as far as others from Superstition, who are inclinable to believe, that such Things have been upon particular Emergencies; tho', amongst the Stories that are told, they believe not one in a thousand. They know that Spirits have frequently appeared to Men out of Houses, and they can see no Reason why they may not have appeared in them: They know nothing in an House more than in another Place, to prevent an Apparition, but an equal Help to its Visibility. The Air, which a Ghost is supposed to be wrapped in, when it becomes visible to Men, is there to be found, and they know of nothing else that may be an Argument against it. An Author of good Credit tells us, That when he was at *Rome*, he was taken with Illness, and obliged to keep his Bed: As he lay in this Condition, he observed, as he was once awake, a *Woman* of a very beautiful Person coming towards him. Upon this he was silent some Time, and very thoughtful, weighing all the while with himself, whether it was not rather a *deceptio visus* than a real Being. But when he perceived his Senses sound and intire, and the Object still continued; he asked, What she was? In Answer to which, she repeated the very Words he had spoke to her, in a sneering and disdainful Manner. After he had taken a good View of him, she departed.

The Commentator upon this Place, says, He looks upon this Story, and the rest which are mentioned along with it, to be nothing but Dreams and Fancies. And for ought that I know to the contrary, they may be so; but whatever it must be confes'd, this Story in particular is well attested, being told by the Man himself, who was a great and learned Man, and who, if we may believe himself, seems to be as sure that he had his Eyes open, as the Commentator can be of the contrary.

But whatever Truth there may be in it, it is certain that in the Church of *Rome* they are perswaded of the Truth of it, to a Fault. For they are so sure of it, that they have particular Forms of *exorcising* such Houses; which because they have often been heard of, but seldom seen; and are those very Things, which raised, in the Vulgar formerly, such an Opinion of their ignorant Priests, as to make them be esteemed Men of the greatest Faith and Learning; and because also the Opinion has reached even our Days, and 'tis common for the present Vulgar to say, none can lay a Spirit but a *Popish Priest*; it shall be the Business of the next Chapter, to give one of those Forms of *exorcising* an House; not that they are envied for their Art of *conjuring*, but that it may be seen, how well they deserve the Character they go under.

*c.*1730

Round about our Coal Fire: Or, Christmas Entertainments

'Treating of Hobgoblins, Raw-heads, and Bloody-bones, Buggy-bows, Tom-pokers, Bull-beggars; and such like horrible Bodies'

One of the great Amusements, when the Country-folks begin to repose themselves, is to relate the direful Account of the above Monsters, which their Nurses or Mothers have described to them, under the most terrible Shapes; I confess I was a long time before I could get over it, for my Nurse had so imprest them in my Mind, that many a Time I had none of the best Smells in the Bed where I lay; and then I as surely felt the smart of the Rod the next Morning, just as you see them in the Picture. So I imagin'd them, one was to Bite, another to Scratch, another to Bully, &c, but since I am grown tall enough, and one about coming to years of Discretion, I have had the Advantage of an honest Friend, who has led me as he used to do by his startled Horse, to see them, and know what they are; I found them then to be all of the human

Race, one a poor starv'd snarling Critic, another a Man who had Impudence enough to Pyrate the Works of other Men; a third who valued himself more for his Guts than his Brains, and could only say Bo! — Another a little squirting Fellow, who aim'd at being a Flea in a Man's Ear; another a Bite and Scandal-bearer, and so on; such Cabals as I speak of are in many Corners of the Earth, and in full Club make their Chairman pronounce the Doom of all before them; but they are not any longer to appear as Bugbears either to Men, Women, or Children; for when we know them, the Enchantment is broke, and their Gang perishes.

1744

Mark Akenside 1721–70
The Pleasures of The Imagination, Book I, II, 255–70

... Hence finally, by night
The village-matron, round the blazing hearth,
Suspends the infant-audience with her tales,
Breathing astonishment! of witching rhimes,
And evil spirits: of the death-bed call
To him who robb'd the widow, and devour'd
The orphan's portion: of unquiet souls
Ris'n from the grave to ease the heavy guilt
Of deeds in life conceal'd; of shapes that walk
At dead of night, and clank their chains, and wave
The torch of hell around the murd'rer's bed.
At ev'ry solemn pause the croud recoil
Gazing each other speechless, and congeal'd
With shiv'ring sighs: till eager for th' event,
Around the beldame all arrect they hang,
Each trembling heart with grateful terrors quell'd.

New Aesthetic Frameworks for Horror and Fantasy

The first half of the eighteenth century saw the transformation of the nature of literary criticism and aesthetic discourse. With a growing middle-class audience for culture, the rather rarefied old standards of taste and judgement, hide-bound to classical values, were examined anew. With this re-examination came a new appreciation of the possibilities of horror, fantasy and the supernatural. Such a reappraisal was always imminent in classical literary criticism, by virtue of the examples laid down by the Greek author on the 'sublime', Longinus.

The essayist Joseph Addison stands at the head of modern English criticism. With Richard Steele he co-authored *The Spectator*, which set out an urban, urbane ideal of literary culture, aside from the court, aside from the stuffy rituals of officialdom, the aesthetic co-relative of this ideal was laid out in a series of essays published in 1712, known collectively as 'The Pleasures of the Imagination'. Here, Addison proposed a visual, sensual and pleasurable foundation for the work of art, which might encompass, as here, elements of pain and horror. In this, and in casting aside 'cold' rules as foreign to British cultural tradition, Addison helped pave the way to the imaginative and subjective innovations of the Gothic as a literary mode. Paper no.419 heralded precisely that development, looking back to Shakespeare as the exemplar of the imaginative writer, and the representative figure of a peculiarly national tradition of the fantastic. Hume's text 'On Tragedy' indicates the extension of new critical ideas into a more rigorous philosophical context.

23 June 1712

Joseph Addison 1672–1719
The Spectator, no.412

I shall first consider those Pleasures of the Imagination, that arise from the actual View and Survey of outward Objects: And these, I think, all proceed from the Sight of what is Great, *Uncommon*, or *Beautiful*. There may, indeed, be something so terrible or offensive, that Horrour or Loathsomness of an Object may over-bear the pleasure which results from its Greatness, *Novelty* or *Beauty*; but still there will be such a Mixture of Delight in the very Disgust it gives us, as any these three Qualifications are most conspicuous and prevailing.

By *Greatness*, I do not only mean the Bulk of any single Object, but the Largeness of a whole View, considered as one entire Piece. Such are the Prospects of an open Champian Country, a vast uncultivated Desart, of huge Heaps of Mountains, high Rocks, and Precipices, or a wide Expanse of Waters, where we are not struck with the Novelty or Beauty of the Sight, but with that rude kind of Magnificence which appears in many of these stupendous Works of nature. Our Imagination loves to be filled with an Object, or to grasp at anything that is too big for its Capacity. We are flung into a pleasing Astonishment at such unbounded Views, and feel a delightful Stillness and Amazement in the Soul at the a Apprehension of them. The mind of man naturally hates every-thing that looks like a Restraint upon it, and is apt to fancy itself under sort of Confinement, when the sight is pent up in a arrow Compass, and shortened on every side by the Neighborhood of Walls or Mountains. On the contrary, a spacious Horizon is an Image of Liberty, where the Eye has Room to range abroad, to expatiate at large on the Immensity of its Views, and to lose it self amidst the Variety of Objects that offer themselves to its Observation. Such wide and undetermined Prospects are as pleasing to the Fancy, as the Speculations of Eternity or Infinitude are to the Understanding. But if there be a Beauty or Uncommonness joyned with this Grandeur, as in a troubled Ocean, a Heaven adorned with Stars and Meteors, or a spacious Landskip cut out into Rivers, Woods, Rocks, and Meadows, the Pleasure still grows upon us, as it arises from more than a single Principle.

Every thing that is *new* or *uncommon* raises a Pleasure in the Imagination, because it fills the Soul with an agreeable Surprise, gratifies its Curiosity, and gives it an Idea of which it was not before possessed. We are indeed so often conversant with one Sett of Objects, and tired out with so many repeated Shows of the same Things, that whatever is *new* or *uncommon* contributes a little to vary Human Life, and to divert our Minds, for a while with the Strangeness of its Appearance: It serves us for a kind of Refreshment, and takes off from that Satiety we are apt to complain of in our usual and ordinary Entertainments. It is this that bestows Charms on a Monster, and makes even the Imperfections of Nature please us. It is this that recommends Variety, where the Mind is every Instant called off to something new, and the Attention not suffered to dwell too long, and waste itself on any particular Object. It is this, likewise, that improves what is great or beautiful, and makes it afford the Mind a double Entertainment. Groves, Fields, and Meadows, are at any season of the year pleasant to look upon, but never so much as in the opening of the Spring, when they are all new and fresh, with their first Gloss upon them, and not yet too much accustomed and familiar to the Eye. For this reason there is nothing that more enlivens a prospect than Rivers, Jetteaus, or Falls of Water, where the Scene is perpetually shifting, and entertaining the Sight every moment with something that is new. We are quickly tired with looking upon Hills and Valleys, where every thing continues fixed and settled in the same Place and Posture, but find our Thoughts a little agitated and relieved at the sight of such Objects as are ever in Motion and sliding away from beneath the Eye of the Beholder.

But there is nothing that makes its way more directly to the Soul than *beauty*, which immediately diffuses a secret Satisfaction and Complacency thro' the Imagination, and gives a Finishing to any thing that is Great or Uncommon. The very first Discovery of it strikes the Mind with an inward Joy, and spreads a Chearfulness and Delight through all its Faculties. There is not perhaps any real Beauty or Deformity more in one piece of Matter than Another, because we might have been so made, that whatsoever now appears loathsom to us, might have shown itself agreeable; but we find by Experience, that there are several Modifications of Matter which the Mind, without any previous Consideration, pronounces at first sight Beautiful or Deformed. Thus we see that every different Species of sensible Creatures has its different Notions of Beauty, and that each of them is most affected with the Beauties of its own kind. This is no where more remarkable than in Birds of the same Shape and Proportion, where, we often see the Male determined in his Courtship by the single Grain or Tincture of a Feather, and never discovering any Charms but in the Colour of its Species.

[...]

As the Fancy delights in every thing that is Great, Strange, or Beautiful, and is still more pleased the more it finds of these Perfections in the same Object, so it is capable of receiving a new Satisfaction by the Assistance of another Sense. Thus any continued Sound, as the Musick of Birds, or a Fall of Water, awakens every moment the Mind of the Beholder, and makes him more attentive to the several Beauties of the Place that lie before him. Thus if there arises a Fragrancy of Smells or Perfumes, they heighten the Pleasures of the Imagination, and make even the Colours and Verdure of the Landskip appear more agreeable; for the Ideas of both Senses recommend each other, and are pleasanter together than when they enter the Mind separately: As the different Colours of a Picture, when they are well disposed, set off one another, and receive an additional Beauty from the Advantage of their Situation.

1 July 1712

Joseph Addison 1672–1719
The Spectator, no.419

There is a kind of Writing, wherein the Poet quite loses sight of Nature, and entertains his Reader's Imagination with the Characters and Actions of such Persons as have many of them no Existence, but what he bestows on them. Such are Fairies, Witches, Magicians, Demons, and departed Spirits. This Mr *Dryden* calls *the Fairie way of Writing*, which is, indeed, more difficult than any other that depends on the Poet's Fancy, because he has no Pattern to follow in it, and must work altogether out of his own Invention.

There is a very odd turn of Thought required for this sort of Writing, as it is impossible for a Poet to succeed in it, who has not a particular Cast of Fancy, and an Imagination naturally fruitful and superstitious. Besides this, he ought to be very well versed in Legends and Fables, antiquated Romances, and the Traditions of Nurses and old Women, that he may fall in with our natural Prejudices, and humour those Notions which we have imbibed in our Infancy. For, otherwise, he will be apt to make his Fairies talk like People of his own Species, and not like other Setts of Beings, who converse with different Objects, and think in a different manner from that of Mankind ... I do not say with Mr *Bays* in the *Rehearsal*, that Spirits must not be confined to speak Sense, but it is certain their Sense ought to be a little discoloured, that it may seem particular, and proper to the Person and the Condition of the Speaker.

These Descriptions raise a pleasing kind of Horrour in the Mind of the Reader, and amuse his Imagination with the Strangeness and Novelty of the Persons who are represented in them. They bring up into our Memory the Stories we have heard in our Child-hood, and favour those secret Terrours and Apprehensions to which the Mind of Man is naturally subject. We are pleased with surveying the different Habits and Behaviours of Foreign Countries, how much more delighted and surprised when we are led, as it were, into a new Creation, and see the Persons and Manners of another Species? Men of cold Fancies, and Philosophical Dispositions, object to this kind of Poetry, that it has not Probability enough to affect the Imagination. But to this it may be answered, that we are sure, in general, there are many Intellectual Beings in the World besides our selves, and several Species of Spirits, who are subject to different Laws and Oeconomies from those of Mankind; when we see, therefore, any of these represented naturally, we cannot look upon the Representation as altogether impossible; nay, many are prepossest with such false Opinions, as dispose them to believe these particular Delusions; at least, we have all heard so many pleasing Relations in favour of them, that we do not care for seeing through the Falshood, and willingly give our selves up to so agreeable an Imposture.

The Ancients have not much of this Poetry among them, for, indeed, almost the whole Substance of it owes its Original to the Darkness and Superstition of later Ages, when pious Frauds were made us of to amuse Mankind, and frighten them into a Sense of their Duty. Our Forefathers looked upon Nature with more Reverence and Horrour, before the World was enlightened by Learning and Philosophy, and loved to astonish themselves with the Apprehensions of Witchcraft, Prodigies, Charms and Enchantments. There was not a Village in *England* that had not a Ghost in it, the Church-yards were all haunted, every large Common had a Circle of Fairies belonging to it, and there was scarce a Shepherd to be met with who had not seen a Spirit.

Among all the Poets of this Kind our *English* are much the best, by what I have yet seen, whether it be that we abound with more Stories of this Nature, of that the Genius of our Country is fitter for this sort of Poetry. For the *English* are naturally Fanciful, and very often disposed by that Gloominess and Melancholly of Temper, which is so frequent in our Nation, to many wild Notions and Visions, to which others are not so liable.

Among the *English*, *Shakespear* has incomparably excelled all others. That noble Extravagance of Fancy, which he had in so great Perfection, thoroughly qualified him to touch this weak superstitious Part of his Reader's Imagination; and made him capable of succeeding, where he had nothing to support him besides the Strength of his own Genius. There is something so wild and yet so solemn in the Speeches of his Ghosts, Fairies, Witches, and the like Imaginary Persons, that we cannot forbear thinking them natural, tho' we have no Rule by which to judge of them, and must confess, if there are such Beings in the World, it looks highly probable they should talk and act as he has represented them.

1757

David Hume 1711–76
'Of Tragedy'

It seems an unaccountable pleasure, which the spectators of a well-wrote tragedy receive from sorrow, terror, anxiety, and other passions, which are in themselves disagreeable and uneasy. The more they are touched and affected, the more are they delighted with the spectacle, and as soon as the uneasy passions cease to operate, the piece is at an end. One scene of full joy and contentment and security is the utmost, that any composition of this kind can bear; and it is sure always to be the concluding one. If in the texture of the piece, there be interwoven any scenes of satisfaction, they afford only faint gleams of pleasure, which are thrown in by way of variety, and in order to plunge the actors into deeper distress, by means of that contrast and disappointment. The whole art of the poet is employed, in rouzing and supporting the compassion and indignation, the anxiety and resentment of his audience. They are pleased in proportion as they are afflicted, and never are so happy as when they employ tears, sobs, and cries to give vent to their sorrow, and relieve their heart, swollen with the tenderest sympathy and compassion.

The few critics who have had some tincture of philosophy, have remarked this singular phenomenon, and have endeavoured to account for it.

L'Abbe *Dubos*, in his reflections on poetry and painting, asserts, that nothing is in general so disagreeable to the mind as the languid, listless state of indolence, into which it falls upon the removal of all passion and occupation. To get rid of this painful situation, it seeks every amusement and pursuit; business, gaming, shows, executions; whatever will rouze the passions, and take its attention from itself. No matter what the passion is: Let it be disagreeable, afflicting, melancholy, disordered; it is still better than that insipid languor, which arises from perfect tranquility and repose.

It is impossible not to admit this account, as being, at least, in part satisfactory. You may observe, when there are several tables of gaming, that all the company run to those, where the deepest play is, even though they find not there the best players. The view, or at least, imagination of high passions, arising from great loss or gain, affects the spectators by sympathy, gives him some touches of the same passions, and serves them for a momentary entertainment. It makes the time pass the easier with them, and is some relief to that oppression, under which men commonly labour, when left entirely to their own thoughts and meditations.

We find, that common lyars always magnify, in their narrations, all kinds of danger, pain, distress, sickness, deaths, murders, and cruelties; as well as joy, beauty, mirth, and magnificence. It is an absurd secret, which they have for pleasing their company, fixing their attention, and attaching them to such marvelous relations, by the passions and emotions, which they excite.

There is, however, a difficulty in applying to the present subject, in its full extent, this solution, however ingenious and satisfactory it may appear. It is certain, that the same object of distress, which pleases in a tragedy, were it really set before us, would give the most unfeigned uneasiness; tho' it be then the most effectual cure to languor and indolence. Monsieur *fontenelle* seems to have been sensible to this difficulty; and accordingly attempts another solution of the phænomenon; at least makes some addition to the theory aboveforementioned*.

'Pleasure and pain,' says he, 'which are two sentiments so different in themselves, differ not so much in their cause. From the instance of tickling, it appears, that the movement of

*Reflexions sur la poetique.536

pleasure, pushed a little too far, becomes pain; and that the movement of pain, a little moderated, becomes pleasure. Hence it proceeds, that there is such a thing as a sorrow, soft and agreeable: It is a pain weakened and diminished. The heart likes naturally to be moved and affected. Melancholy objects suit it, and even disastrous and sorrowful, provided they are softened by some circumstance. It is certain, that on the theatre the representation has almost the effect of reality; but yet it has not altogether that effect. However we may be hurried away by the spectacle; whatever dominion the senses and imagination may usurp over the reason, there still lurks at the bottom a certain idea of falshood in the whole of what we see. This idea, tho' weak and disguised, suffices to diminish the pain which we suffer from the misfortunes of those whom we love, and to reduce that affliction to such a pitch as converts it into a pleasure. We weep for the misfortune of a hero, to whom we are attached: In the same instant we comfort ourselves, by reflecting, that it is nothing but a fiction: And it is precisely, that mixture of sentiments, which composes an agreeable sorrow, and tears that delight us. But as that affliction, which is caused by exterior and sensible objects, is stronger than the consolation which arises from an internal reflection, they are the effects and symptoms of sorrow, that ought to predominate in the composition.'

This solution seems just and convincing; but perhaps it wants still some new addition, in order to make it answer fully the phænomenon, which we here examine. All the passions, excited by eloquence, are agreeable in the highest degree, as well as those which are moved by painting and the theatre. The epilogues of *cicero* are, on this account chiefly, the delight of every reader of taste; and it is difficult to read some of them without the deepest sympathy and sorrow. His merit as an orator, no doubt, depends much on his success in this particular. When he had raised tears in his judges and all his audience, they were then the most highly delighted,' and expressed the greatest satisfaction with the pleader. The pathetic description of the butchery, made by *verres* of the *sicilian* captains, is a masterpiece of this kind: But I believe none will affirm, that the being present at a melancholy scene of that nature would afford any entertainment. Neither is the sorrow here softened by fiction: For the audience were convinced of the reality of every circumstance. What is it then, which in this case raises a pleasure from the bosom of uneasiness, so to speak; and a pleasure, which still retains all the features and outward symptoms of distress and sorrow?

I answer: This extraordinary effect proceeds from that very eloquence, with which the melancholy scene is represented. The genius required to paint objects in a lively manner, the art employed in collecting all the pathetic circumstances, the judgment displayed in disposing them: the exercise, I say, of these noble talents, together with the force of expression, and beauty of oratorial numbers, diffuse the highest satisfaction on the audience, and excite the most delightful movements. By this means, the uneasiness of the melancholy passions is not only overpowered and effaced by something stronger of an opposite kind; but the whole movement of those passions is converted into pleasure, and swells the delight which the eloquence raises in us. The same force of oratory, employed on an uninteresting subject, would not please half so much, or rather would appear altogether ridiculous; and the mind, being left in absolute calmness and indifference, would relish none of those beauties of imagination or expression, which, if joined to passion, give it such exquisite entertainment. The impulse or vehemence, arising from sorrow, compassion, indignation, receives a new direction from the sentiments of beauty. The latter, being the predominant emotion, seize the whole mind, and convert the former into themselves, tincture them so strongly as totally to alter their nature: And the soul, being, at the same time, roused by passion, and charmed by eloquence, feels on the whole a strong movement, which is altogether delightful.

The same principle takes place in tragedy; with this addition, that tragedy is an imitation; and imitation is always of itself agreeable. This circumstance serves still farther to smooth the motions of passion, and convert the whole feeling into one uniform and strong enjoyment. Objects of the greatest terror and distress please in painting, and please more than the most beautiful objects, that appear calm and indifferent.* The affection, rouzing the mind, excites a large stock of spirit and vehemence; which is all transformed into pleasure by the force of the prevailing movement. It is thus the fiction of tragedy softens the passion, by an infusion of a new feeling; not merely by weakening or diminishing the sorrow. You may by degrees weaken a real sorrow, till it totally disappears; yet in none of its gradations will it ever give pleasure; except, perhaps, by accident, to a man sunk under lethargic indolence, whom it rouses from that languid state...

* Painters make no scruple of representing distress and sorrow as well as any other passion; But they seem not to dwell so much on these melancholy affections as the poets, who, tho' they copy every emotion of the human breast, yet pass very quickly over the agreeable sentiments. A painter represents only one instant; and if that be passionate enough, it is sure to affect and delight the spectator: But nothing can furnish the poet a variety of scenes and incidents and sentiments, except distress, terror, or anxiety. Compleat joy and satisfaction is attended with security, and leaves no farther room for action.

2.3

The Sublime

Edmund Burke's treatise on the physical and psychological effects of beauty, horror and terror was perhaps the key aesthetic text of the late eighteenth century. Complexly articulating a series of anxieties about gender, social authority and Anglo-Irish ethnicity, Burke proposed that the sources of the most powerful experiences lay in the encounter with the immense, overwhelming and terrible: in a word, the 'Sublime'. Fundamentally antithetical to the Sublime was the objects and experiences that Burke classifies as 'Beautiful'. Where the Sublime moves, invigorates and exercises the mind and the moral faculties, the Beautiful is trivial, facile and ultimately corrupting.

The passages selected here demonstrate Burke's sophisticated articulation of a subtle relationship between horror and pleasure, pain and fulfilment. Modern commentators have elaborated on the complexity and richness of Burke's text. For contemporaries, it served as a validation for horror and the fantastic in art, an alibi for eccentricity, and a potent framework for artists, critics and consumers to explore the subjective dimensions of the aesthetic experience.

Anna Barbauld's text is now recognised as among the most important documents in the development of a critical framework for understanding the Gothic in the late eighteenth century. Barbauld (née Aikin, 1743–1825) establishes that there is pleasure to be found in horror because of its invigorating novelty — an idea which had precedents in Addison and Burke. But she also establishes a simple principle: the more horrible and fantastic a literary scene may be, the greater the pleasure arising from it.

The Scottish poet and critic James Beattie (1735–1803) provides, with his 'Illustrations on Sublimity', an important shift away from the more strictly philosophical and physiological preoccupations of Burke, to attend to the literal embodiment of the Sublime. Here, Beattie first considers how a character in literature or art may embody the sublime; and how, importantly, in so doing the need for a clear moral narrative or allegorical purpose falls away. Incidentally, Beattie opens the way to an amoral kind of heroic representation. The latter part of the extract elaborates on the paradoxical appeal of horror, making use of Burkean notions of aesthetic distance.

1757
Second edition
1759

Edmund Burke 1729–97
Philosophical Enquiry into the Origin of our Ideas of the Sublime and Beautiful

PAIN and PLEASURE
It seems then necessary towards moving the passions of people advanced in life to any considerable degree, that the objects designed for that purpose, besides their being in some measure new, should be capable of exciting pain or pleasure from other causes. Pain and pleasure are simple ideas, incapable of definition. People are not liable to be mistaken in their feelings, but they are very frequently wrong in the names they give them, and in their reasonings about them. Many are of the opinion, that pain arises necessarily from the removal of some pleasure; as they think pleasure does from the ceasing or diminution of some pain. For my part, I am rather inclined to imagine, that pain and pleasure, in their most simple and natural manner of affecting, are each of a positive nature, and by no means necessarily dependent on each other for their existence. The human mind is often, and I think it is for the most part, in a state neither of pain nor pleasure, which I call a state of indifference. When I am carried from this state into a state of actual pleasure, it does not appear necessary that I should pass through the medium of any sort of pain. If in such a state of indifference, or ease, or tranquillity, or call it what you please, you were to be suddenly entertained with a concert of music; or suppose some object of a fine shape, and bright, lively colours, to be presented before you; or imagine your smell is gratified with the fragrance of a rose; or if without any previous thirst you were to drink of some pleasant kind of wine, or to taste of some sweetmeat without being hungry; in all the several senses, of hearing, smelling and tasting, you undoubtedly find a pleasure; yet if I inquire into the state of your mind previous to these gratifications, you will hardly tell me that they found you in any kind of pain; or, having satisfied these several senses with their several pleasures, will you say that any pain has succeeded, though the pleasure is absolutely over? Suppose on the other hand, a man in the same state of indifference, to receive a violent blow, or to drink of some bitter potion, or to have his ears wounded with some harsh and grating sound; here is no removal of pleasure; and yet here is felt in every sense which is affected, a pain very distinguishable. It may be said, perhaps, that the pain in these cases had its rise from the removal of the pleasure which the man enjoyed before, though that pleasure was of so low a degree as to be perceived only by the removal. But this seems to me a subtilty that is not discoverable in nature. For if, previous to the pain, I do not feel any actual pleasure, I have no reason to judge that any such thing exists; since pleasure is only pleasure as it is felt. The same may be said of pain, and with equal

reason. I can never persuade myself that pleasure and pain are mere relations, which can only exist as they are contrasted; but I think I can discern clearly that there are positive pains and pleasures, which do not at all depend upon each other. Nothing is more certain to my own feelings than this. There is nothing which I can distinguish in my mind with more clearness than the three states, of indifference, of pleasure, and of pain. Every one of these I can perceive without any sort of idea of its relation to anything else. Caius is afflicted with a fit of the colic; this man is actually in pain; stretch Caius upon the rack, he will feel a much greater pain; but does this pain of the rack arise from the removal of any pleasure? or is the fit of the colic a pleasure or a pain, just as we are pleased to consider it?

Of the SUBLIME

Whatever is fitted in any sort to excite the ideas of pain, and danger, that is to say, whatever is in any sort terrible, or is conversant about terrible objects, or operates in a manner analogous to terror, is a source of the *sublime*; that is, it is productive of the strongest emotion which the mind is capable of feeling. I say the strongest emotion, because I am satisfied the ideas of pain are much more powerful than those which enter on the part of pleasure. Without all doubt, the torments which we may be made to suffer are much greater in their effect on the body and mind, than any pleasure which the most learned voluptuary could suggest, or than the liveliest imagination, and the most sound and exquisitely sensible body, could enjoy. Nay, I am in great doubt whether any man could be found, who would earn a life of the most perfect satisfaction, at the price of ending it in the torments, which justice inflicted in a few hours on the late unfortunate regicide in France. But as pain is stronger in its operation than pleasure, so death is in general a much more affecting idea than pain; because there are very few pains, however exquisite, which are not preferred to death: nay, what generally makes pain itself, if I may say so, more painful, is, that it is considered as an emissary of this king of terrors. When danger or pain press too nearly, they are incapable of giving any delight, and are simply terrible; but at certain distances, and with certain modifications, they may be, and they are, delightful, as we every day experience. The cause of this I shall endeavour to investigate hereafter.

The Effects of SYMPATHY in the Distresses of Others

To examine this point concerning the effect of tragedy in a proper manner, we must previously consider how we are affected by the feelings of our fellow-creatures in circumstances of real distress. I am convinced we have a degree of delight, and that no small one, in the real misfortunes and pains of others; for let the affection be what it will in appearance, if it does not make us shun such objects, if on the contrary it induces us to approach them, if it makes us dwell upon them, in this case I conceive we must have a delight or pleasure of some species or other in contemplating objects of this kind. Do we not read the authentic histories of scenes of this nature with as much pleasure as romances or poems, where the incidents are fictitious? The prosperity of no empire, nor the grandeur of no king, can so agreeably affect in the reading, as the ruin of the state of Macedon, and the distress of its unhappy prince. Such a catastrophe touches us in history as much as the destruction of Troy does in fable. Our delight, in cases of this kind, is very greatly heightened, if the sufferer be some excellent person who sinks under an unworthy fortune. Scipio and Cato are both virtuous characters; but we are more deeply affected by the violent death of the one, and the ruin of the great cause he adhered to, than with the deserved triumphs and uninterrupted prosperity of the other; for terror is a passion which always produce delight when it does not press too closely; and pity is a passion accompanied with pleasure, because it arises from love and social affection. Whenever we are formed by nature to any active purpose, the passion which animates us to it is attended with delight, or a pleasure of some kind, let the subject-matter be what it will; and as our Creator has designed that we should be united by the bond of sympathy, he has strengthened that bond by a proportionable delight; and there most where our sympathy is most wanted,—in the distresses of others. If this passion was simply painful, we would shun with the greatest care all persons and places that could excite such a passion; as some, who are so far gone in indolence as not to endure any strong impression, actually do. But the case is widely different with the greater part of mankind; there is no spectacle we so eagerly pursue, as that of some uncommon and grievous calamity; so that whether the misfortune is before our eyes, or whether they are turned back to it in history, it always touches with delight. This is not an unmixed delight, but blended with no small uneasiness. The delight we have in such things, hinders us from shunning scenes of misery; and the pain we feel prompts us to relieve ourselves in relieving those who suffer; and all this antecedent to any reasoning, by an instinct that works us to its own purposes, without our concurrence.

OBSCURITY

To make anything very terrible, obscurity seems in general to be necessary. When we know the full extent of any danger, when we can accustom our eyes to it, a great deal of the apprehension vanishes. Every one will be sensible of this, who considers how greatly night adds to our dread, in all cases of danger, and how much the notions of ghosts and goblins, of which none can form clear ideas, affect minds, which give credit to the popular tales concerning such sorts of beings. Those despotic governments, which are founded on the passions of men, and principally upon the passion of fear, keep their chief as much as may be from the public eye. The policy has been the same in many cases of religion. Almost all the heathen temples were dark. Even in the

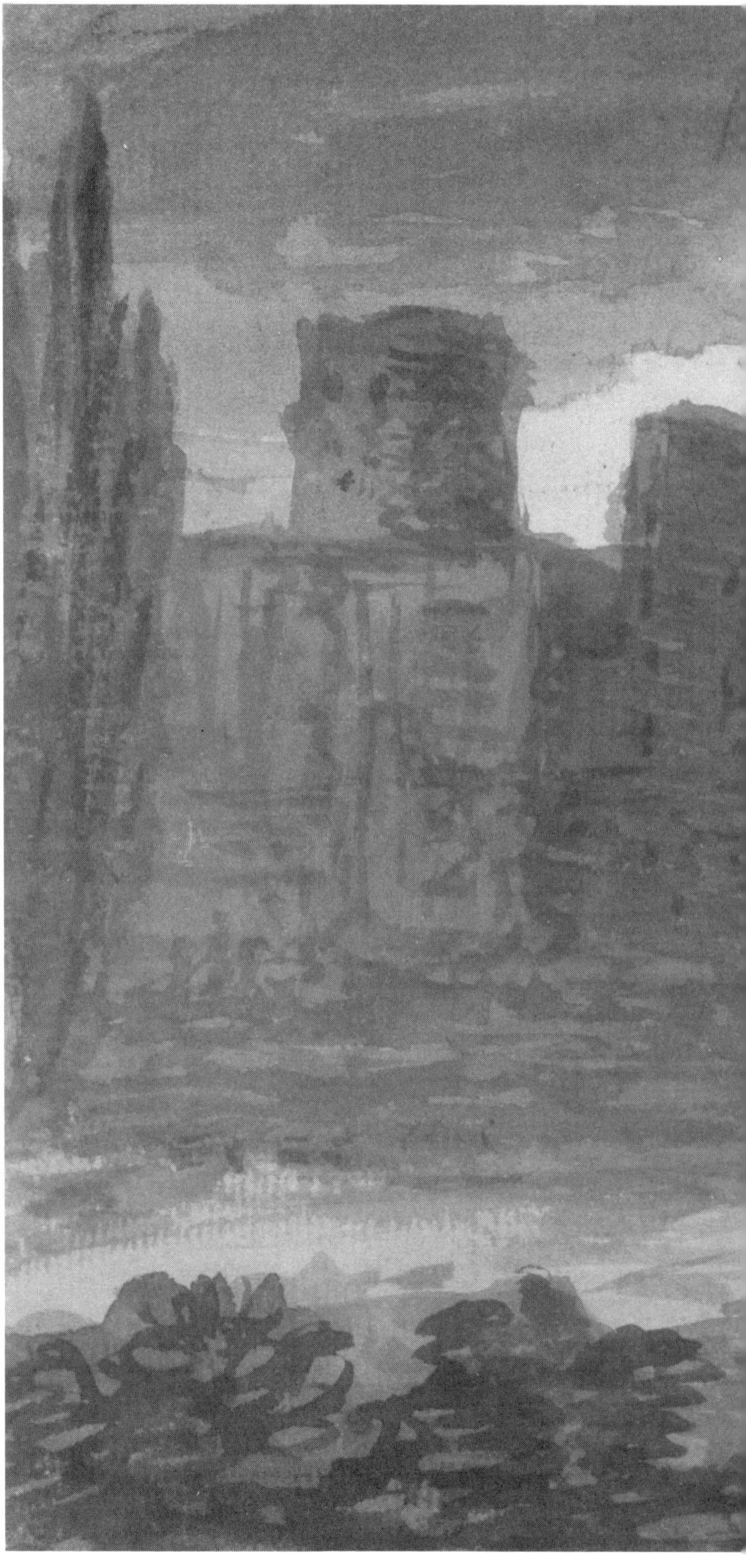

11
Alexander Cozens
The Enchanted Castle, 1780s
Watercolour and pencil on paper 15.5 × 18.5 cm
Tate. Purchased as part of the Oppé Collection with assistance from the National Lottery through the Heritage Lottery Fund 1996

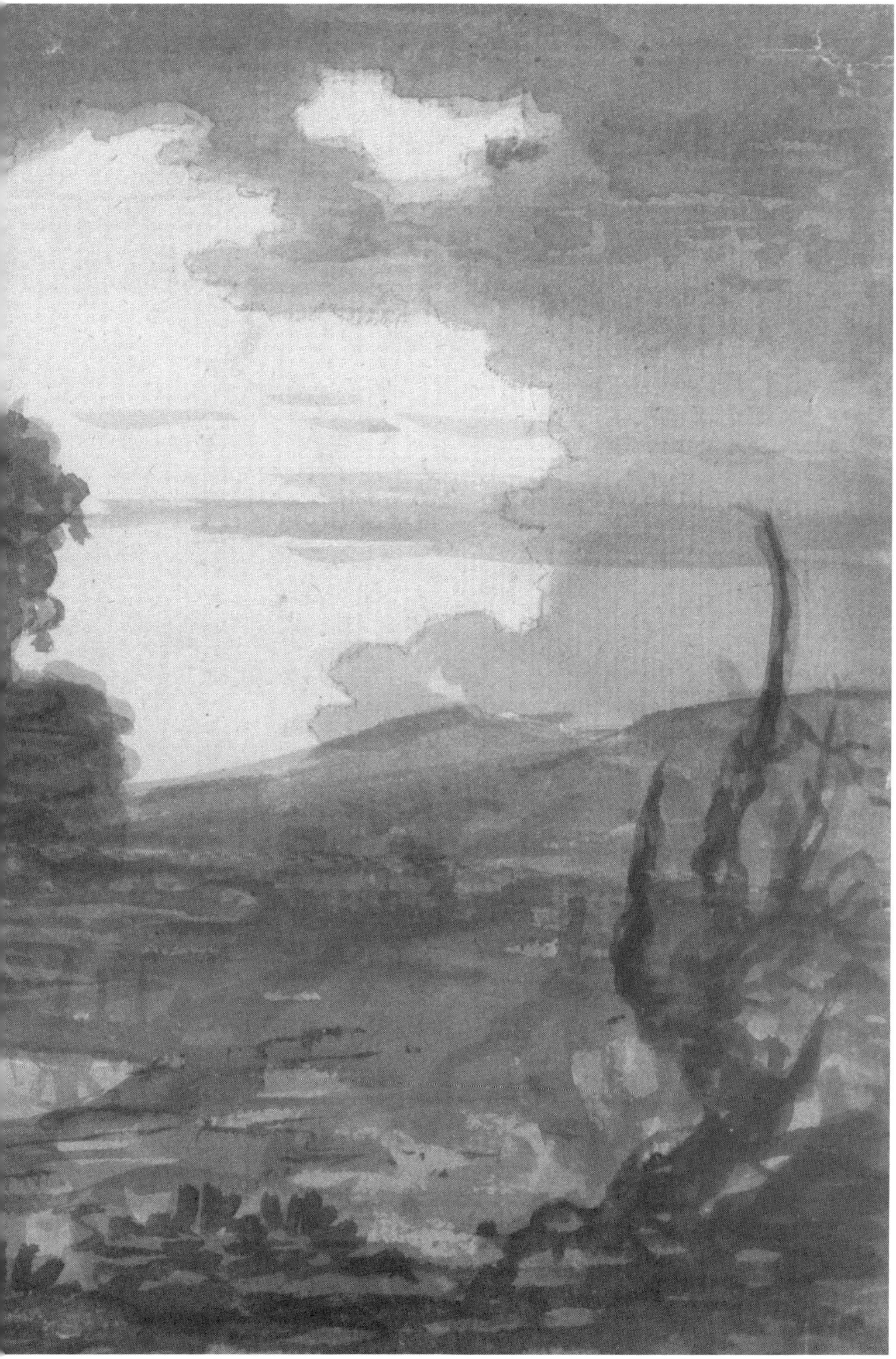

barbarous temples of the Americans at this day, they keep their idol in a dark part of the hut, which is consecrated to his worship. For this purpose too the Druids performed all their ceremonies in the bosom of the darkest woods, and in the shade of the oldest and most spreading oaks. No person seems better to have understood the secret of heightening, or of setting terrible things, if I may use the expression, in their strongest light, by the force of a judicious obscurity, than Milton. His description of Death in the second book is admirably studied; it is astonishing with what a gloomy pomp, with what a significant and expressive uncertainty of strokes and colouring, he has finished the portrait of the king of terrors:

> *—The other shape,*
> *If shape it might be called that shape had none*
> *Distinguishable, in member, joint, or limb;*
> *Or substance might be called that shadow seemed;*
> *For each seemed either; black he stood as night;*
> *Fierce as ten furies; terrible as hell;*
> *And shook a deadly dart. What seemed his head*
> *The likeness of a kingly crown had on.*

In this description all is dark, uncertain, confused, terrible, and sublime to the last degree.

Of the difference Between CLEARNESS and OBSCURITY with regard to the passions

It is one thing to make an idea clear, and another to make it *affecting* to the imagination. If I make a drawing of a palace, or a temple, or a landscape, I present a very clear idea of those objects; but then (allowing for the effect of imitation, which is something) my picture can at most affect only as the palace, temple, or landscape would have affected in the reality. On the other hand, the most lively and spirited verbal description I can give, raises a very obscure and imperfect *idea* of such objects; but then it is in my power to raise a stronger *emotion* by the description than I could do by the best painting. This experience constantly evinces. The proper manner of conveying the *affections* of the mind from one to another, is by words; there is a great insufficiency in all other methods of communication; and so far is a clearness of imagery from being absolutely necessary to an influence upon the passions, that they may be considerably operated upon, without presenting any image at all, by certain sounds adapted to that purpose; of which we have a sufficient proof in the acknowledged and powerful effects of instrumental music. In reality, a great clearness helps but little towards affecting the passions, as it is in some sort an enemy to all enthusiasms whatsoever.

POWER

Besides those things which *directly* suggest the idea of danger, and those which produce a similar effect from a mechanical

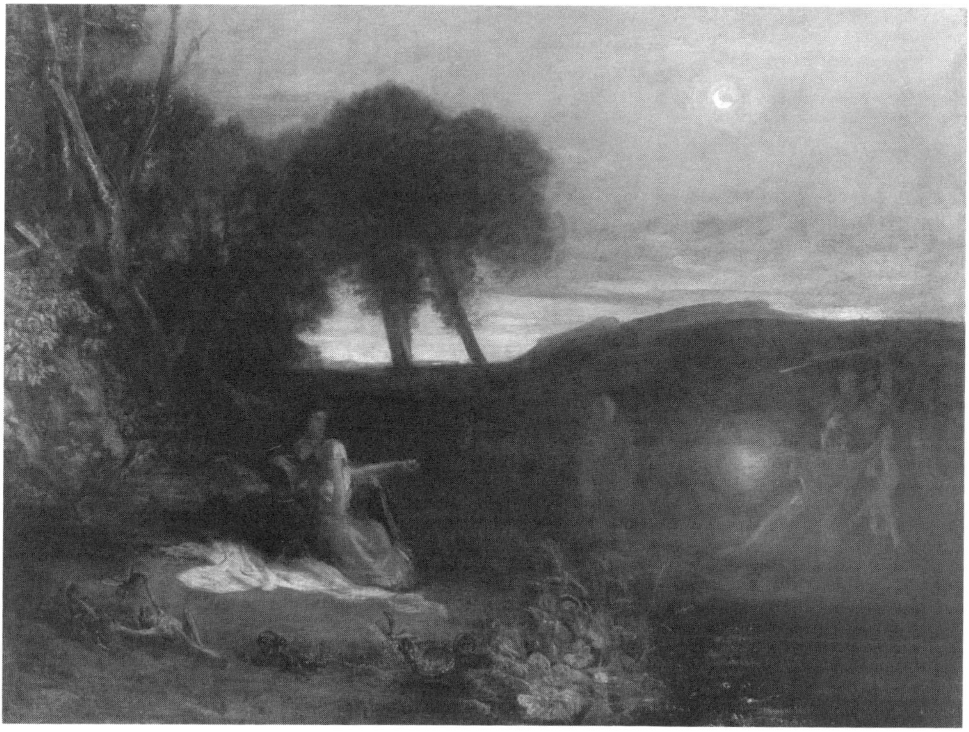

12
J.M.W. Turner
A Subject from the Runic Superstitions, exh. 1808
Oil on canvas 92.1 × 121.9 cm
Tate. Bequeathed by the artist 1856

cause, I know of nothing sublime, which is not some modification of power. And this branch rises, as naturally as the other two branches, from terror, the common stock of everything that is sublime. The idea of power, at first view, seems of the class of those indifferent ones, which may equally belong to pain or to pleasure. But in reality, the affection, arising from the idea of vast power, is extremely remote from that neutral character. For first, we must remember, that the idea of pain, in its highest degree, is much stronger than the highest degree of pleasure; and that it preserves the same superiority through all the subordinate gradations. From hence it is, that where the chances for equal degrees of suffering or enjoyment are in any sort equal, the idea of the suffering must always be prevalent. And indeed the ideas of pain, and, above all, of death, are so very affecting, that whilst we remain in the presence of whatever is supposed to have the power of inflicting either, it is impossible to be perfectly free from terror. Again, we know by experience, that, for the enjoyment of pleasure, no great efforts of power are at all necessary; nay, we know, that such efforts would go a great way towards destroying our satisfaction: for pleasure must be stolen, and not forced upon us; pleasure follows the will; and therefore we are generally affected with it by many things of a force greatly inferior to our own. But pain is always inflicted by a power in some way superior, because we never submit to pain willingly. So that strength, violence, pain, and terror, are ideas that rush in upon the mind together. Look at a man, or any other animal of prodigious strength, and what is your idea before reflection? Is it that this strength will be subservient to you, to your ease, to your pleasure, to your interest in any sense? No; the emotion you feel is, lest this enormous strength should be employed to the purposes of rapine and destruction. That power derives all its sublimity from the terror with which it is generally accompanied, will appear evidently from its effect in the very few cases, in which it may be possible to strip a considerable degree of strength of its ability to hurt. When you do this, you spoil it of everything sublime, and it immediately becomes contemptible. An ox is a creature of vast strength; but he is an innocent creature, extremely serviceable, and not at all dangerous; for which reason the idea of an ox is by no means grand. A bull is strong too: but his strength is of another kind; often very destructive, seldom (at least amongst us) of any use in our business; the idea of a bull is therefore great, and it has frequently a place in sublime descriptions, and elevating comparisons. Let us look at another strong animal, in the two distinct lights in which we may consider him. The horse in the light of a useful beast, fit for the plough, the road, the draft; in every social, useful light, the horse has nothing sublime: but is it thus that we are affected with him, *whose neck is clothed with thunder, the glory of whose nostrils is terrible, who swalloweth the ground with fierceness and rage, neither believeth that it is the sound of the trumpet?* In this description, the useful character of the horse entirely disappears, and the terrible and sublime blaze out together. We have continually about us animals of a strength that is considerable, but not pernicious. Amongst these we never look for the sublime; it comes upon us in the gloomy forest, and in the howling wilderness, in the form of the lion, the tiger, the panther, or rhinoceros. Whenever strength is only useful, and employed for our benefit or our pleasure, then it is never sublime: for nothing can act agreeably to us, that does not act in conformity to our will; but to act agreeably to our will, it must be subject to us, and therefore can never be the cause of a grand and commanding conception.

1773

Anna Barbauld 1743–1825
‘On the Pleasure Derived from Objects of Terror’

That the exercise of our benevolent feelings, as called forth by the view of human afflictions, should be a source of pleasure, cannot appear wonderful to one who considers that relation between the moral and natural system of man, which has connected a degree of satisfaction with every action or emotion productive of the general welfare. The painful sensation immediately arising from a scene of misery, is so much softened and alleviated by the reflex sense of self-approbation on attending virtuous sympathy, that we find, on the whole, a very exquisite and refined pleasure remaining, which makes us desirous of again being witnesses to such scenes, instead of flying from them with disgust and horror. It is obvious how greatly such a provision must conduce to the ends of mutual support and assistance. But the apparent delight with which we dwell upon objects of pure terror, where our moral feelings are not in the least concerned, and no passion seems to be excited but the depressing one of fear, is a paradox of the heart, much more difficult of solution.

The reality of this source of pleasure seems evident from daily observation. The greediness with which the tales of ghosts and goblins, of murders, earthquakes, fires, shipwrecks, and all the most terrible disasters attending human life, are devoured by every ear, must have been generally remarked. Tragedy, the most favourite work of fiction, has taken a full share of those scenes; 'it has supt full with horrors'— and has, perhaps, been more indebted to its tender and pathetic parts. The ghost of Hamlet, Macbeth descending into the witches' cave, and the tent scene in Richard, command as forcibly the attention of our souls as the parting of Jasseir and Belvidera, the fall of Wolsey, or the death of Shore. The inspiration of *terror* was by the antient critics assigned as the peculiar province of tragedy; and the Greek and Roman tragedians have introduced some extraordinary personages for this purpose: not only the shades of the dead, but the furies and other fabulous inhabitants of the infernal regions. Collins, in his most poetical ode to Fear, has finely enforced this idea.

> Tho' gentle Pity claims her mingled part,
> Yet all the thunders of the scene are thine.

The old Gothic romance and the Eastern tale, with their genii, giants, enchantments, and transformations, however a refined critic may censure them as absurd and extravagant, will ever retain a most powerful influence on the mind, and interest the reader independently of all perculiarity of taste. Thus the great Milton, who had a strong bias to these wildnesses of the imagination, has with striking effect made the stories 'of forests and enchantments drear,' a favourite subject with his *Penseroso*; and had undoubtedly their awakening images strong upon his mind when he breaks out,

> Call up him that left half-told
> The story of Cambuscan bold; &c.

How are we then to account for the pleasure derived from such objects? I have often been led to imagine that there is a deception in these cases; and that the avidity with which we attend is not a proof of our receiving real pleasure. The pain of suspense, and the irresistible desire of satisfying curiosity, when once raised, for our eagerness to go quite through an adventure, though we suffer actual pain during the whole course of it. We rather chuse to suffer the smart pang of a violent emotion than the uneasy craving of an unsatisfied desire. That this principle, in many instances, may involuntarily carry us through what we dislike, I am convinced from experience. This is the impulse which renders the poorest and most insipid narrative interesting when once we get fairly into it; and I have frequently felt it with regard to our modern novels, which, if lying on my table, and taken up in an idle hour, have led me through the most tedious and disgusting pages, while, like Pistol eating his leek, I have swallowed and execrated to the end. And it will not only force us through dullness, but through actual torture — through the relation of a Damien's execution, or an inquisitor's act of faith. When children, therefore, listen with pale and mute attention to the frightful stories of apparitions, we are not, perhaps, to imagine that they are in a state of enjoyment, any more than the poor bird which is dropping into the mouth of the rattlesnake — they are chained by the ears, and fascinated by curiosity. This solution, however, does not satisfy me with respect to the well-wrought scenes of aritificial terror which are formed by a sublime and vigorous imagination. Here, though we know before-hand what to expect, we enter into them with eagerness, in quest of a pleasure already experienced. This is the pleasure constantly attached to the excitement of surprise from new and wonderful objects. A strange and unexpected event awakens the mind, and keeps it on the stretch; and where the agency of invisible beings is introduced, of 'forms unseen, and mightier far than we,' our imagination, darting forth, explores with rapture the new world which is laid open to its view, and rejoices in the expansion of its powers. Passion and fancy cooperating elevate the soul to its highest pitch; and the pain of terror is lost in amazement.

Hence, the more wild, fanciful, and extraordinary are the circumstance of a scene of horror, the more pleasure we receive from it; and where they are too near common nature, though violently borne by curiosity through the adventure, we cannot repeat it or reflect on it, without an over-balance of pain. In the *Arabian nights* are many most striking examples of the terrible joined with the marvellous: the story of Aladin and the travels of Sinbad are particularly excellent. The *Castle of Otranto* is a very spirited modern attempt upon the same plan of mixed terror, adapted to the model of Gothic romance. The best conceived, and most strongly worked-up scene of mere natural horror that I recollect, is in Smollett's *Ferdinand count Fathom*; where the hero, entertained in a lone house in a forest, finds a corpse just slaughtered in the room where he is sent to sleep, and the door of which is locked upon him. It may be amusing for the reader to compare his feelings upon these, and from thence form his opinion of the justness of my theory.

1783

James Beattie 1735–1803
'Illustrations on Sublimity'

When great qualities prevail in any person, they form what is called a sublime character. Every good man is a personage of this order: but a character may be sublime, which is not completely good, nay, which is upon the whole very bad. For the test of sublimity is not moral approbation, but that pleasurable astonishment werewith certain things strike the beholder … even in Satan, as Milton has represented him in *Paradise Lost*, though there are no qualities than can be called good in a moral view; nay, though every purpose of that wicked spirit is bent to evil, and to that only; yet there is the grandeur of a ruined archangel: there is force able to contend with the most boisterous elements; and there is boldness, which no power, but what is Almighty, can intimidate. These qualities are astonishing: and, though we always detest his malignity, we are often compelled to admire that very greatness by which we are confounded and terrified.

And be not surprised, that we sometimes admire what we cannot approve. These two emotions may, and frequently do, coincide; Sarpedon and Hector, Epaminondas and Aristides, David and Jonathan, we both approve and admire. But they do not necessarily coincide: for goodness calls forth the one, and greatness the other; and that which is great is not always good, and that may be good which is not great. Troy in flames, Palmyra in ruins, the ocean in a storm, and Etna in thunder and conflagration, are magnificent appearances, but do not immediately impress our minds with the idea of good: and a clear fountain is not a grand object, though in many parts of the world it would be valued above all treasures …

There is a kind of horror, which may be infused into the mind both by natural appearances, and by verbal description; and which, though it makes the blood seem to run cold, and produce a momentary fear, is not unpleasing, but may be even agreeable: and therefore, the objects that produce it are justly denominated sublime. Of natural appearances that affect the mind in this manner, are vast caverns, deep and dark woods, overhanging precipices, the agitation of the sea in a storm: and some of the sounds aboveforementioned have the same effect, as those of cannon and thunder. Verbal descriptions infusing sublime horror are such as convey lively ideas, of the objects of superstition, as ghosts and enchantments; or of the thoughts that haunt the imaginations of the guilty; or of those external things, which are pleasingly terrible, as storms, conflagrations, and the like.

It may seem strange, that horror of any kind should give pleasure. But the fact is certain. Why do people run to see battles, executions, and shipwrecks? Is it, as an Epicurian would say, to compare themselves with others, and exult in their own security while they see the distress of those who suffer? No, surely: good minds are swayed by different motives. It is, that they may be at hand, to give every assistance in their power to their unhappy brethren? This would draw the benevolent, and even the tender-hearted, to a shipwreck; but to a battle, or to an execution, could not bring spectators, because there the humanity of individuals is of no use. It must be, because a sort of gloomy satisfaction, or terrifick pleasure, accompanies the gratification of that curiosity, which events of this nature are apt to raise in minds of a certain frame.

No parts of Tasso are read with greater relish, than where he describes the darkness, silence, and other horrors, of the enchanted forest: and the poet himself is so sensible of the captivating influence of such ideas over the human imagination, that he makes the catastrophe of the poem in some measure depend upon them. Milton is not less amoured 'of forests and enchantments drear:' as appears from the use to which he applies them in *Comus*: the scenery whereof charms us the more, because it affects our minds, as it did the bewildered lady, and causes 'a thousand fantasies' —

> to throng into the memory,
> Of calling shapes, and beckoning shadows dire,
> And aery tongues, that syllable men's names
> On sands, and shores, and desert wildernesses.

Forests in every age must have had attractive horrors: otherwise so many nations would not have resorted thither, to celebrate the rites of superstition. And the inventors of what is called the Gothick, but perhaps should rather be called the Saracen, architecture, must have been enraptured with the same imagery, when, in forming and arranging the pillars and aisles of their churches, they were so careful to imitate the rows of lofty trees in a deep grove.

Observe how a few children assembled about a fire, and listening to tales of apparitions and witchcraft. You may see them grow pale, and crowd closer and closer through fear: while he who is snug in the chimney corner, and at the greatest distance from the door, considers himself as peculiarly fortunate; because he thinks that, if the ghost should enter, he has a better chance to escape, than if he were in a more exposed situation. And yet, notwithstanding their present, and their apprehension of future, fears, you could not perhaps propose any amusement that would at this time be more acceptable. The same love of such horrors as are not attended with sensible inconvenience continues with us through life: and Aristotle has affirmed, that the end of tragedy is to purify the soul by the operations of pity and terror.

The mind and body of man are so constituted, that without action, neither can the one be healthy, nor the other happy. And as bodily exercises, though attended with fatigue, as Dancing, or with some degree of danger, as Hunting, are not on that account the less agreeable; so those things that give delight, which rouse the soul, even when they bring along with them horror, anxiety, or sorrow, provided these passions be transient, and their causes rather imaginary than real.

2.4

Gothic Romance

The interplay between realism and fantasy, historical truth and the imagination was a central concern to later eighteenth-century criticism on the novel. The Gothic texts that appeared through the last third of the century seemed to some critics to be an appalling abuse of the facts of history, and a too-insecure foundation for mounting any narrative of moral value; for others, the liberties taken with historical truth were a means of accessing deeper ideas, and were all the more expressive; others, too, argued that the finest Gothic novels did present a finely-drawn picture of history. The following excerpts, relating to Walpole's *The Castle of Otranto*, illustrate some of the terms of such arguments.

1765

Horace Walpole 1717–97
Preface to the Second Edition of *The Castle of Otranto*

The favourable manner in which this little piece has been received by the public, calls upon the author to explain the grounds on which he composed it. But before he opens those motives, it is fit that he should ask pardon of his readers for having offered his work to them under the borrowed personage of a translator. As diffidence of his own abilities, and the novelty of the attempt, were the sole inducements to assume that disguise, he flatters himself he shall appear excusable. He resigned his performance to the impartial judgment of the public; determined to let it perish in obscurity, if disapproved; nor meaning to avow such a trifle, unless better judges should pronounce that he might own it without a blush.

It was an attempt to blend the two kinds of Romance, the ancient and the modern. In the former, all was imagination and improbability: in the latter, nature is always intended to be, and sometimes has been, copied with success. Invention has not been wanting; but the great resources of fancy have been dammed up, by a strict adherence to common life. But if in the latter species Nature has cramped imagination, she did but take her revenge, having been totally excluded from old Romances. The actions, sentiments, conversations, of the heroes and heroines of ancient days were as unnatural as the machines employed to put them in motion.

The author of the following pages thought it possible to reconcile the two kinds. Desirous of leaving the powers of fancy at liberty to expatiate through the boundless realms of invention, and thence of creating more interesting situations, he wished to conduct the mortal agents in his drama according to the rules of probability; in short, to make them think, speak, and act, as it might be supposed mere men and women would do in extraordinary positions. He had observed, that in all inspired writings, the personages under the dispensation of miracles and witnesses to the most stupendous phenomena, never lose sight of their human character: whereas in the productions of romantic story, an improbable event never fails to be attended by an absurd dialogue. The actors seem to lose their senses, the moment the laws of Nature have lost their tone. As the public have applauded the attempt, the author must not say he was entirely unequal to the task he had undertaken: yet if the new route he has struck out shall have paved a road for men of brighter talents, he shall own with pleasure and modesty, that he was sensible the plan was capable of receiving greater embellishments than his imagination or conduct of the passions could bestow on it.

1778

Clara Reeve 1729–1807
Preface to *The Old English Baron*

As this Story is of a species which, tho' not new, is out of the common track, it has been thought necessary to point out some circumstances to the reader, which will elucidate the design, and, it is hoped, will induce him to form a favourable, as well as a right judgment of the work before him.

This Story is the literary offspring of the Castle of Otranto, written upon the same plan, with a design to unite the most attractive and interesting circumstances of the ancient Romance and modern Novel, at the same time it assumes a character and manner of its own, that differs from both; it is distinguished by the appellation of a Gothic Story, being a picture of Gothic times and manners. Fictitious Stories have been the delight of all times and all countries, by oral tradition in barbarous, by writing in more civilized ones; and altho' some persons of wit and learning have condemned them indiscriminately, I would venture to affirm, that even those who so much affect to despise them under one form, will receive and embrace them under another.

Thus, for instance, a man shall admire and almost adore the Epic poems of the Ancients, and yet despise and execrate the ancient Romances, which are only Epics in prose.

History represents human nature as it is in real life; — alas, too often a melancholy retrospect! — Romance displays only the amiable side of the picture; it shews the pleasing features, and throws a veil over the blemishes: Mankind are naturally pleased with what gratifies their vanity; and vanity, like all passions of the human heart, may be rendered subservient to good and useful purposes.

I confess that it may be abused, and become an instrument to corrupt the manners and morals of mankind; so may poetry, so may plays, so may every kind of composition; but that will prove nothing more than the old saying lately revived by the philosophers the most in fashion, 'that every earthly thing has two handles.'

The business of Romance is, first, to excite the attention; and, secondly, to direct it to some useful, or at least innocent, end; Happy the writer who attains both these points, like Richardson! and not unfortunate, or undeserving praise, he who gains only the latter, and furnishes out an entertainment for the reader!

Having, in some degree, opened my design, I beg leave to conduct my reader back again, till he comes within view of the Castle of Otranto; a work which, as already has been observed, is an attempt to unite the various merits and graces of the ancient Romance and modern Novel. To attain this end, there is required a sufficient degree of the marvellous, to excite the attention; enough of the manners of real life, to give an air of probability to the work; and enough of the pathetic, to engage the heart in its behalf.

13
Henry Fuseli
Percival Delivering Belisane from the Enchantment of Urma, exh.1783
Oil on canvas 99.1 × 125.7cm
Tate. Presented by the National Art Collections Fund 1941

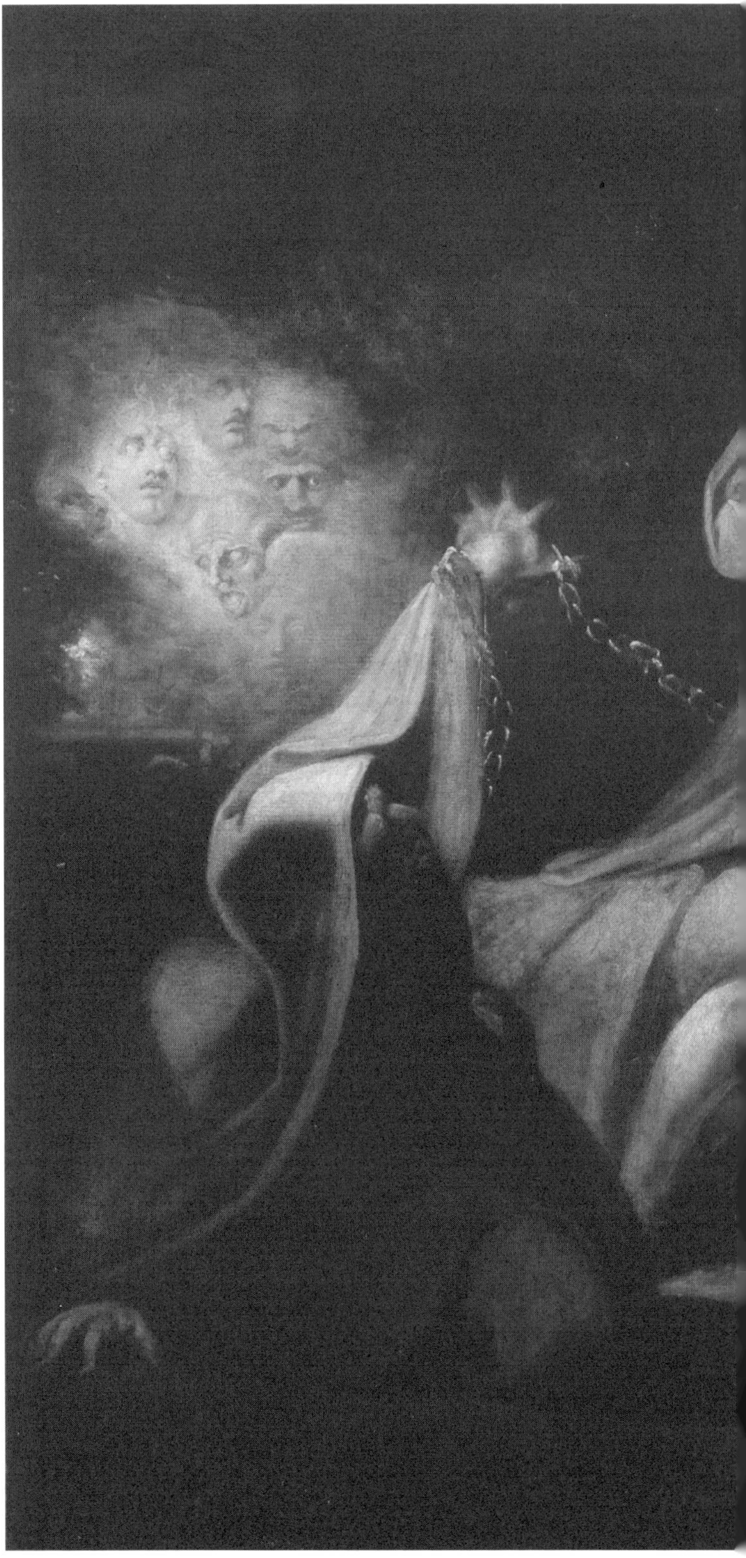

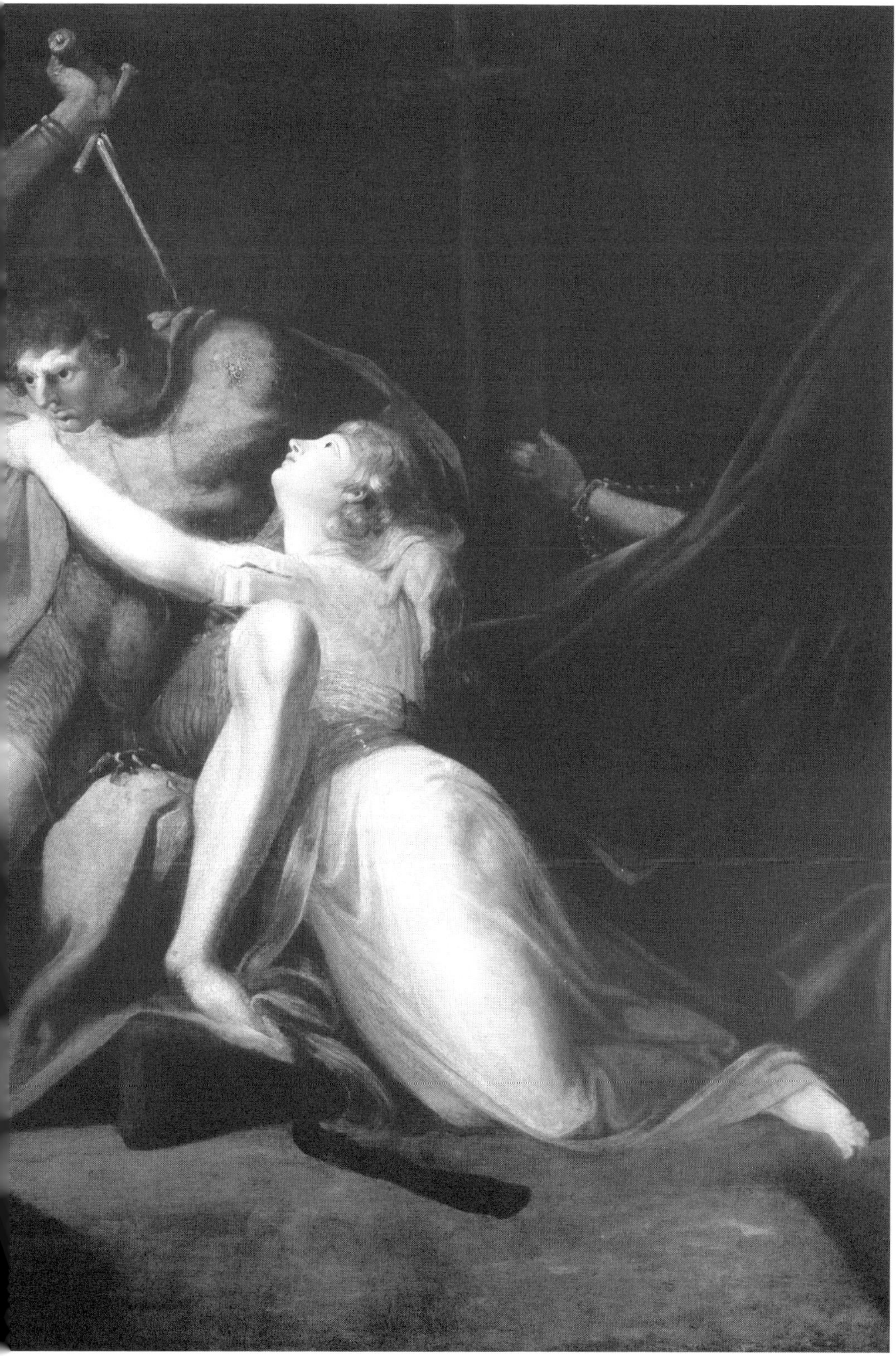

The book we have mentioned is excellent in the two last points, but has a redundancy in the first; the opening excites the attention very strongly; the conduct of the story is artful and judicious; the characters are admirably drawn and supported; the diction polished and elegant; yet, with all these brilliant advantages, it palls upon the mind (though it does not upon the ear); and the reason is obvious, the machinery is so violent, that it destroys the effect it is intended to excite. Had the story been kept within the utmost *verge* of probability, the effect had been preserved, without losing the least circumstance that excites or detains the attention.

For instance, we can conceive, and allow of, the appearance of a ghost; we can even dispense with an enchanted sword and helmet; but then they must keep within certain limits of credibility: A sword so large as to require an hundred men to lift it; a helmet that by its own weight forces a passage through a court-yard into an arched vault, big enough for a man to go through; a picture that walks out of its frame; a skeleton ghost in a hermit's cowl: — When your expectation is wound up to the highest pitch, these circumstances take it down with a witness, destroy the work of imagination, and, instead of attention, excite laughter. I was both surprised and vexed to find the enchantment dissolved, which I wished might continue to the end of the book; and several of its readers have confessed the same disappointment to me: The beauties are so numerous, that we cannot bear the defects, but want it to be perfect in all respects.

In the course of my observations upon this singular book, it seemed to me that it was possible to compose a work upon the same plan, wherein these defects might be avoided; and the *keeping*, as in *painting*, might be preserved.

But then I began to fear it might happen to me as to certain translators, and imitators of Shakespeare; the unities may be preserved, while the spirit is evaporated. However, I ventured to attempt it; I read the beginning to a circle of friends of approved judgment, and by their approbation was encouraged to proceed, and to finish it.

By the advice of the same friends I printed the first Edition in the country, where it circulated chiefly, very few copies being sent to London, and being thus encouraged, I have determined to offer a second Edition to that public which has so often rewarded the efforts of those, who have endeavoured to contribute to its entertainment.

The work has lately undergone a revision and correction, the former Edition being very incorrect; and by the earnest solicitation of several friends, for whose judgment I have the greatest deference, I have consented to a change of the title from the *Champion of Virtue* to the *Old English Baron*: — as that character is thought to be the principal one in the story.

I have also been prevailed upon, though with extreme reluctance, to suffer my name to appear in the title-page; and I do now, with the utmost respect and diffidence, submit the whole to the candour of the Public.

1811

Walter Scott 1771–1832
Introduction to *The Castle of Otranto*

It is doing injustice to Mr Walpole's memory to allege, that all which he aimed at in *The Castle of Otranto* was 'the art of exciting surprise and horror'; or, in other words, the appeal to that secret and reserved feeling of love for the marvellous and supernatural, which occupies a hidden corner in almost every one's bosom. Were this all which he had attempted, the means by which he sought to attain his purpose might, with justice, be termed both clumsy and puerile. But Mr Walpole's purpose was both more difficult of attainment, and more important when attained. It was his object to draw such a picture of domestic life and manners, during the feudal times, as might actually have existed, and to paint it chequered and agitated by the action of supernatural machinery, such as the superstition of the period received as matter of devout credulity. The natural parts of the narrative are so contrived, that they associate themselves with the marvellous occurrences; and, by the force of that association, render those *speciosa miracula* striking and impressive, although our cooler reason admits their impossibility. Indeed to produce, in a well-cultivated mind, any portion of that surprise and fear which is founded on supernatural events, the frame and tenor of the whole story must be adjusted in perfect harmony with the mainspring of the interest. He who, in early youth, has happened to pass a solitary night in one of the few ancient mansions which the fashion of more modern times has left undespoiled of their original furniture, has probably experienced, that the gigantic and preposterous figures dimly visible in the defaced tapestry, the remote clang of the distant doors which divide him from living society, the deep darkness which involves the high and fretted roof of the apartment, the dimly-seen pictures of ancient knights, renowned for their valour, and perhaps for their crimes, the varied and indistinct sounds which disturb the silent desolation of a half-deserted mansion; and, to crown all, the feeling that carries us back to ages of feudal power and papal superstition, join together to excite a corresponding sensation of supernatural awe, if not of terror. It is in such situations, when superstition becomes contagious, that we listen with respect, and even with dread, to the legends which are our sport in the garish light of sunshine, and amid the dissipating sights and sounds of every-day life. Now it seems to have been Walpole's object to attain, by the minute accuracy of the fable, sketched with singular attention to the costume of the period in which the scene was laid, that same association which might prepare his reader's mind for the reception of prodigies congenial to the creed and feelings of the actors. His feudal tyrant, his distressed damsel, his resigned, yet dignified, churchman — the Castle itself, with its feudal arrangement of dungeons, trap-doors, oratories, and galleries, the

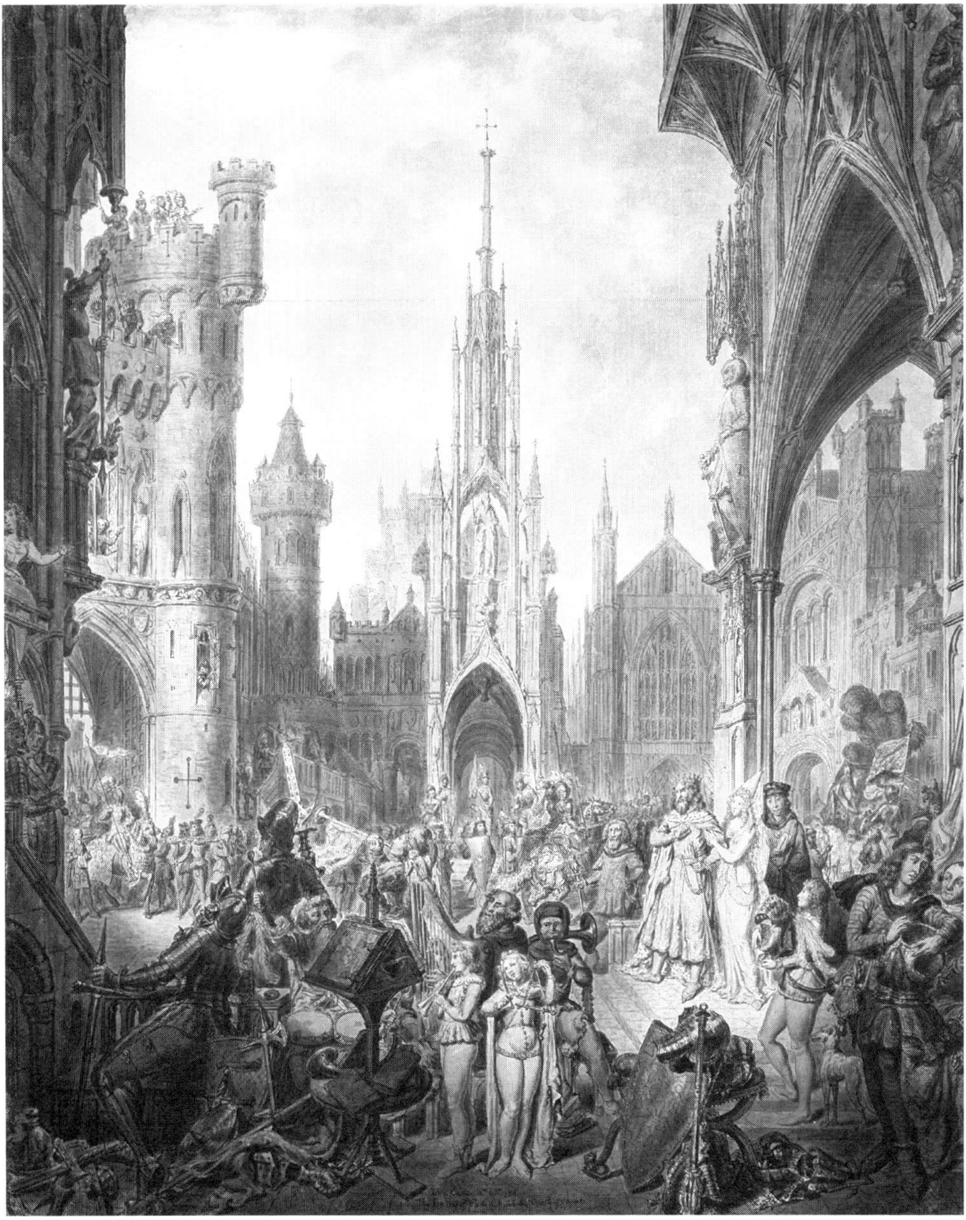

14
John Carter
The Entry of Prince Frederick into the Castle of Otranto, 1790
Watercolour on paper
Lewis Walople Library,
Farmington CT

incidents of the trial, the chivalrous procession, and the combat—in short, the scene, the performers, and action, so far as it is natural, form the accompaniments of his spectres and his miracles, and have the same effect on the mind of the reader that the appearance and drapery of such a chamber as we have described may produce upon that of a temporary inmate. This was a task which required no little learning, no ordinary, degree of fancy, no common portion of genius, to execute. The association of which we have spoken is of a nature peculiarly delicate, and subject to be broken and disarranged. It is, for instance, almost impossible to build such a modern Gothic structure as shall impress us with the feelings we have endeavoured to describe. It may be grand, or it may be gloomy; it may excite magnificent or melancholy ideas; but it must fail in bringing forth the sensation of supernatural awe, connected with halls that have echoed to the sounds of remote generations, and have been pressed by the footsteps of those who have long since passed away. Yet Horace Walpole has attained in composition, what, as an architect, he must have felt beyond the power of his art. The remote and superstitious period in which his scene is laid, the art with which he has furnished forth its Gothic decoration, the sustained, and, in general, the dignified tone of feudal manners, prepare us gradually for the favourable reception of prodigies which, though they could not really have happened at any period, were consistent with the belief of all mankind at that in which the action is placed. It was, therefore, the author's object not merely to excite surprise and terror, by the introduction of supernatural agency, but to wind up the feelings of his reader till they became for a moment identified with those of a ruder age, which

> Held each strange tale devoutly true.

The difficulty of attaining this nice accuracy of delineation may be best estimated by comparing *The Castle of Otranto* with the less successful efforts of later writers; where, amid all their attempts to assume the tone of antique chivalry, something occurs in every chapter so decidedly incongruous, as at once reminds us of an ill-sustained masquerade, in which ghosts, knight-errants, magicians, and damsels gent, are all equipped in hired dresses from the same warehouse in Tavistock-street.

2.5

Henry Fuseli's Ghostly Horror

Henry Fuseli's painting of Hamlet's first encounter with the ghost of his father, from Shakespeare's play, was the most famous visual representation of a ghost of the age, and was known and admired for decades afterwards. The original painting was created for John Boydell, the London entrepreneur who set up a gallery of modern pictures illustrating Shakespeare in 1789. But it was the engraving after this painting (which is now lost) that spread Fuseli's fame as a master of the supernatural.

It is in relation to Fuseli's supernatural scenes, and his Hamlet above all others of this kind, that we find critics working out the terms for a specifically visual form of the Gothic sublime, deriving from Burke a line of aesthetic argument that he did not himself pursue. For Burke the Sublime was something that could arise in nature, or in the works of God, but not through the simple craft of men other than in ersatz form.

1789

Humphrey Repton 1752–1818
The Bee

The spirit which dictated the Scene here represented, seems to have guided the enthusiastic pencil of the Artist: the whole Picture is in a great style of sublimity and horror: the sombre colouring freezes the blood with awe: in the *Ghost* we see

——- 'that fair and warlike form,
In which the Majesty of buried Denmark
Did some time march.—-'

The struggle of *Hamlet* to break free from *Horatio*, has given opportunity by displaying the Painter's knowledge in Anatomy: even through the drapery, the exertion of every limb seems to confirm the words of *Hamlet*, where he says,

——- 'My fate cries out,
And makes each petty artery in this body
As hardy as the Nemean lion's nerve.
Still I am call'd — Unhand me, gentlemen —
By heaven, I'll make a ghost of him that lets me.—'

From the ingenious position of the Moon behind the helmet, we are delighted with its beams, whether dimly playing on the distant waves, or glittering with strong catching lights on the armour of the Ghost.

May 1789

Fuseli on his *Hamlet*, from *The Analytical Review*
The uniform sweep of gloom, that quietly diffuses itself over this picture, seems in unison with the still horror of impatient curiosity, which reflection had sharpened and puzzled.

The ardour of rational courage braces Hamlet's nerves; his eyes already have flown to the shade, who strides with majestic dignity, and looks a king.

The position of the moon preserves the prevailing tone, and prevents the playfulness of its beams from disturbing the harmony of the whole, by introducing the tranquil yet cheerful sensations, they usually produce. This is a happy effort of genius to cut a gordian knot, and substitute a beauty for a defect.

8 May 1789

The Gazetteer
The more we contemplate this very interesting collection of pictures, the more entertaining and interesting they do appear. The dialogue of Shakespeare *comes home to all mens business and bosoms*; we are all conversant with his language, and have fixed in our minds some good ideas of the appearances of his characters. Until the opening of this Gallery the Theatre was the only place in which we could see them repeated, and there the poet was

sometimes misconceived. But, here, the Ghost, clad in compleat steel, gives that awe-struck appearance, which is so wonderfully described in the poet, and we are almost tempted to ask why he

> *Revisits thus the glimpses of the moon,*
> *Making night hideous?*

18 May 1789

The Diary; or, Woodfall's Register

This picture is an address to the mind: it exhibits the Ghost described by Shakespeare

> '*There is* no *speculation* in *those eyes*
> *Which* he *doeth glare withal.*'

The figure is colossal; it reaches from Earth to Heaven; from the waves to the Moon, which being very judiciously placed behind the helmet of the Kings, gives that kind of beamy, misty hue, that (notwithstanding its magnitude) seems impalpable to the touch. The colouring has that *sombre*, solemn cast, which is peculiarly appropriate to the scene, and the figures of Hamlet and Horatio, are drawn with great spirit, correctness, and taste.

18 May 1789

The Star

Here the Critic is swallowed up in the mute admiration of Genius. This is, indeed, a Ghost such as SHAKESPEARE alone could evoke in verse, and only FUSELI call forth upon canvas. — These *unspeculating* eye-balls which yet rest upon HAMLET their fixed significance — that thin but majestic form which shews to the pale glimmering of the moon its blue evanescency — are beauties which the pencil of Genius alone can reach, and to which the Critic has no rules to apply.

15 (opposite above)
Robert Thew after Henry Fuseli
Hamlet, Horatio, Marcellus and the Ghost, published 29 September 1796
Engraving 44.1 × 59.6 cm
The British Museum, London

16 (opposite below)
James Gillray
Magagrida & Conspirators, Consulting the Ghost of Oliver Cromwell,
published June 1782
Engraving 22.5 × 32.7 cm
The British Museum, London

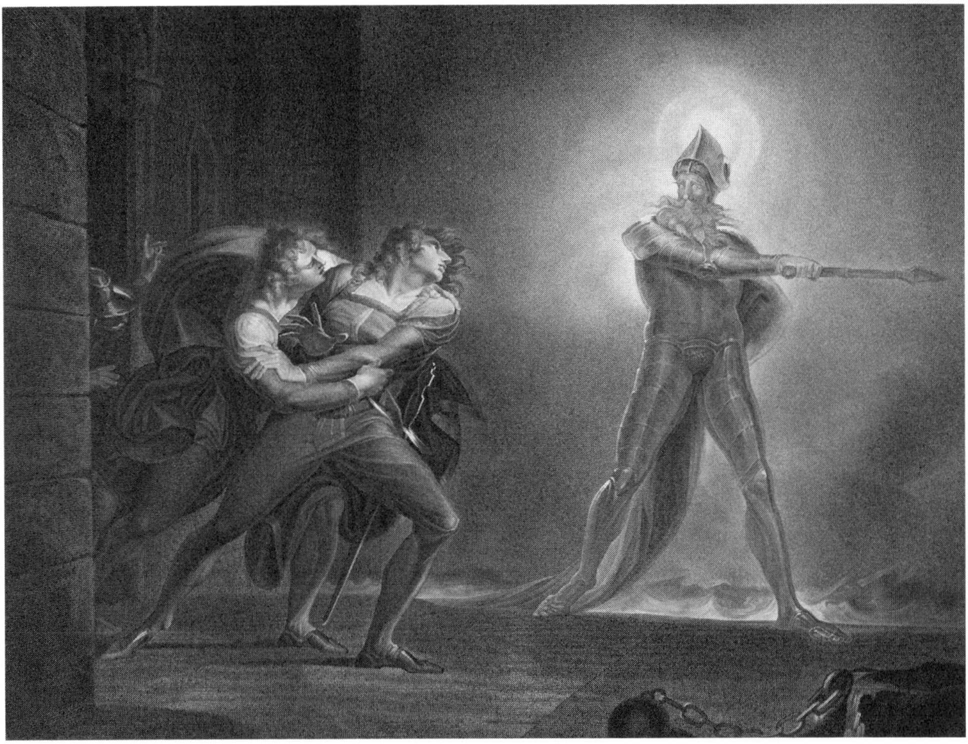

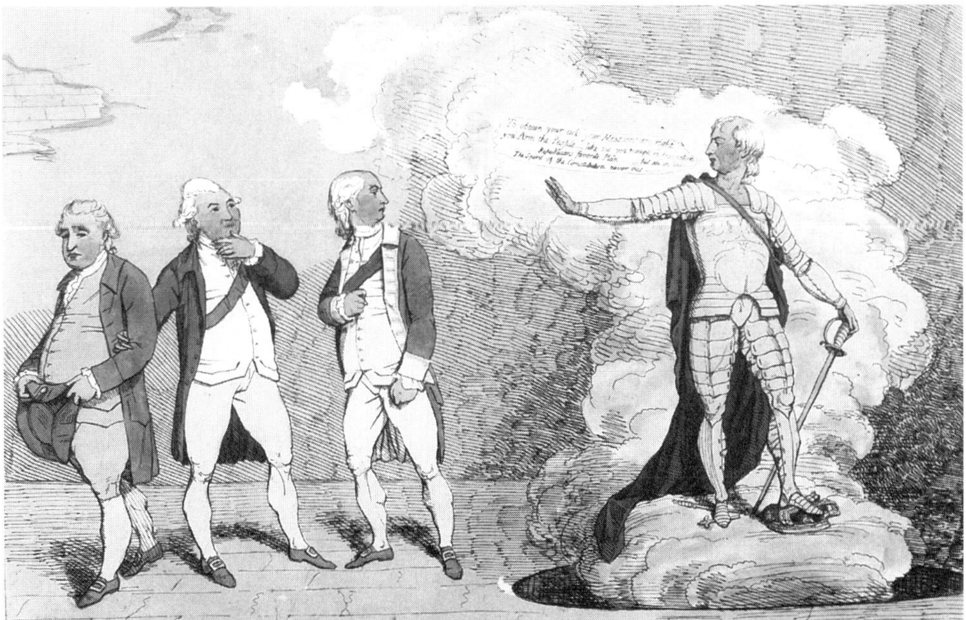

2.6

Mary Shelley and Sir Walter Scott on the Subject of The Supernatural

The ascent of a taste for the supernatural and horrific coincided quite precisely with a vast transformation of the basic conditions of life for a large sector of the British population. Between 1760 and 1840 a succession of technological, commercial and political innovations established a recognisably modern world, more comfortable, convenient and even perhaps more democratic than had ever been known. Yet these changes were accompanied by a sense of anxiety, fragility and distance (in part, what Karl Marx would identify at the end of this period as the effect of 'alienation'). It was, after all, only some portion of society that benefited, and they did so on the basis of the (willing, or unwilling) labour of others here and abroad; and if Britain achieved now a level of wealth and imperial power which was approached only by ancient Rome, it could also suffer a similar fate, descending into immoral luxury.

The writers and critics of the period were not unconscious of the paradoxes apparent in the rise of the Gothic. The theory of the Sublime offered a means of explaining the desire for terror; nostalgia for a lost way of life might give a clue to the appeal of old ghost-stories; a desire for child-like wonder might also inspire a taste for the fantastic. Here, Shelley and Scott reflect on the nature of superstitious beliefs in a self-consciously reasoning age, in two of the earliest, sustained accounts of this kind.

March 1824

Mary Shelley 1797–1851
'On Ghosts'

I look for ghosts — but none will force
Their way to me; 'tis falsely said
That there was ever intercourse
Between the living and the dead — *Wordsworth*

What a different earth do we inhabit from that on which our forefathers dwelt! The antediluvian world, strode over by mammoths, preyed upon by the megatherion, and peopled by the offspring of the Sons of God, is a better type of the earth of Homer, Herodotus, and Plato, than the hedged-in cornfields and measured hills of the present day. The globe was then encircled by a wall which paled in the bodies of men, whilst their feathered thoughts soared over the boundary; it had a brink, and in the deep profound which it overhung, men's imaginations, eagle-winged, dived and flew, and brought home strange tales to their believing auditors. Deep caverns harboured giants; cloudlike birds cast their shadows upon the plains; while far out at sea lay islands of bliss, the fair paradise of Atlantis or El Dorado sparkled with untold jewels. Where are they now? The Fortunate Isles have lost the glory that spread a halo round them; for who deems himself nearer to the golden age, because he touches at the interior of New Holland, our only terra incognita; and our sole mare incognitum, the north-west passage. But these are tame wonders, lions in leash; we do not invest Mungo Park, or the Captain of the Hecla, with divine attributes; no one fancies that the waters of the unknown river bubble up from hell's fountain, no strange and weird power is supposed to guide the ice-berg, nor do we fable that a stray pick pocket from Botany Bay has found the gardens of the Hesperides within the circuit of the Blue Mountains. What have we left to dream about? The clouds are no longer the charioted servants of the sun, nor does he any more bathe his glowing brow in the bath of Thetis; the rainbow has ceased to be the messenger of the Gods, and thunder is no longer their awful voice, warning man of that which is to come. We have the sun which has been weighed and measured, but not understood; we have the assemblage of the plants, the congregation of the stars, and yet the unshackled ministration of the winds: — such is the list of our ignorance.

Nor is the empire of the imagination less bounded in its own proper creations, than in those which were bestowed on it by the poor blind eyes of our ancestors. What has become of enchantresses with their palaces of crystal and dungeons of palpable darkness? What of fairies and their wands? What of witches and their familiars? and last, what of ghosts, with beckoning hands and fleeting shapes, which quelled the soldier's brave heart, and made the murderer disclose to the astonished noon the veiled work of midnight? These which were realities to our forefathers, in our wiser age —

> ——Characterless are grated
> To dusty nothing

Yet is it true that we do not believe in ghosts? There used to be several traditionary tales repeated, with their authorities, enough to stagger us when we consigned them to that place where that is which 'is as though it had never been.' But these are gone out of fashion. Brutus's dream has become a deception of his overheated brain, Lord Lyttleton's vision of called a cheat; and one by one these inhabitants of deserted houses, moonlight glades, misty mountain tops, and midnight church-yards, have been ejected from their immemorial seats, and small thrill is felt when the dead majesty of Denmark blanches the cheek and unsettles the reason of his philosophic son.

But do none of us believe in ghosts? If this question be read at noon-day, when —

> Every little corner, nook, and hole,
> Is penetrated with the insolent light —

at such a time derision is seated on the features of my reader. But let it be twelve at night in a lone house; take up, I beseech you, the story of the Bleeding Nun; or of the Statue, to which the bridegroom gave the wedding ring, and she came into the dead of night to claim him, tall, white, and cold; or of the Grandsire, who with shadowy form and breathless lips stood over the couch and kissed the foreheads of his sleeping grandchildren, and thus doomed them to their fated death; and let all these details be assisted by solitude, flapping curtains, rushing wind, a long and dusky passage, an half open door — O, then truly, another answer may be given, and many will request leave to sleep upon it, before they decide whether there be such a thing as a ghost in the world, or out of the world, if that phraseology be more spiritual. What is the meaning of this feeling?

For my own part, I never saw a ghost except once in a dream. I feared it in my sleep; I awoke trembling, and lights and the speech of others could hardly dissipate my fear. Some years ago I lost a friend, and a few months afterwards visited the house where I had last seen him. It was deserted, and though in the midst of a city, its vast halls and spacious apartments occasioned the same sense of loneliness as if it had been situated on an uninhabited heath. I walked through the vacant chambers by twilight, and one save I awakened to echoes of their pavement. The far mountains (visible from the upper windows) had lost their tinge of sunset; the tranquil atmosphere grew leaden coloured as the golden stars appeared in the firmament; no wind ruffled the shrunk-up river which crawled lazily through the deepest channel of it wide and empty bed; the chimes of the Ave Maria had ceased, and the bell hung moveless in the open belfry: beauty invested a reposing world, and awe was inspired by beauty only. I walked through the rooms filled with sensations of the most poignant grief. He had been there; his living frame had been caged by those walls, his breath had mingled with that atmosphere, his step had been on those stones, I thought: — the earth is a tomb, the gaudy sky a vault, we but walking corpses. The wind rising in the east rushed through the open casements, making them shake; — methought, I heard, I felt — I know not what — but I trembled. To have seen him but for a moment, I would have knelt until the stones had been worn by the impress, so I told myself, and so I knew a moment after, but then I trembled, awe-struck and fearful. Wherefore? There is something beyond us of which we are ignorant. The sun drawing up the vaporous air makes a void, and the wind rushes in to fill it, — thus beyond our soul's ken there is an empty space; and our hopes and fears, in gentle gales or terrific whirlwinds, occupy the vacuum; and if it does no more, it bestows on the feeling heart a belief that influences do exist to watch and guard us, though they be impalpable to the coarser faculties.

I have heard that when Coleridge was asked if he believed in ghosts, — he replied that he had seen too many to put any trust in their reality; and the person of the most livery imagination that I ever knew echoed this reply. But these were not real ghosts (pardon, unbelievers, my mode of speech) that they saw; they were shadows, phantoms unreal; that while they appalled the senses, yet carried no other feeling to the mind of others than delusion, and were viewed as we might view an optical deception which we see to be true with our eyes, and know to be false with our understandings. I speak of other shapes. The running bride, who claims the fidelity of her betrothed; the murdered man who shakes to remorse the murderer's heart; ghosts that lift the curtains at the foot of your bed as the clock chimes one, who rise all pale and ghastly from the church-yard and haunt their ancient abodes; who, spoken to, reply; and whose cold unearthly touch makes the hair stand stark upon the head; the true old-fashioned, foretelling, flitting, gliding ghost, — who has seen such a one?

I have known of two persons who at broad daylight have owned that they believe in ghosts, for that they had seen one ...

1830

Sir Walter Scott 1771–1832
Letters on Demonology and Witchcraft

I may, however, add, that the charm of the tale depends much upon the age of the person to whom it is addressed; and that the vivacity of fancy which engages us in youth to pass over much that is absurd, in order to enjoy some single trait of imagination, dies within us when we obtain the age of manhood, and the sadder and graver regions which lie beyond it. I am the more conscious of this, because I have been myself at two periods of my life, distant from each other, engaged in scenes favourable to that degree of superstitious awe which my countrymen expressively call being *eerie*.

On the first of these occasions, I was only nineteen or twenty years old, when I happened to pass a night in the magnificent old baronial castle of Glammis, the hereditary seat of the Earls of Strathmore. The hoary pile contains much in its appearance, and in the traditions connected with it, impressive to the imagination. It was the scene of the murder of a Scottish king of great antiquity; not, indeed, the gracious Duncan, with whom the name naturally associates itself, but Malcolm the Second. It contains also a curious monument of the peril of feudal times, being a secret chamber, the entrance of which, by the law or custom of the family, must only be known to three persons at once, viz., the Earl of Strathmore, his heir apparent, and any third person whom they may take into their confidence. The extreme antiquity of the building is vouched by the immense thickness of the walls, and the wild and straggling arrangement of the accommodation within doors. As the late Earl of Strathmore seldom resided in that ancient mansion, it was, when I was there, but half-furnished, and that with movables of great antiquity, which, with the pieces of chivalric armour hanging upon the walls, greatly contributed to the general effect of the whole. After a very hospitable reception from the late Peter Proctor, Esq., then seneschal of the castle, in Lord Strathmore's absence, I was conducted to my apartment in a distant corner of the building. I must own, that as I heard door after door shut, after my conductor had retired, I began to consider myself too far from the living, and somewhat too near the dead. We had passed through what is called 'The King's Room,' a vaulted apartment, garnished with stags' antlers, and similar trophies of the chase, and said by tradition to be the spot of Malcolm's murder, and I had an idea of the vicinity of the castle chapel.

In spite of the truth of history, the whole night scene in Macbeth's castle rushed at once upon my mind, and struck my imagination more forcibly than even when I have seen its terrors represented by the late John Kemble and his inimitable sister. In a word, I experienced sensations which, though not remarkable either for timidity or superstition, did not fail to affect me to the point of being disagreeable, while they were mingled at the same time with a strange and indescribable kind of pleasure, the recollection of which affords me gratification at this moment.

In the year 1814 accident placed me, then past middle life, in a situation somewhat similar to that which I have described.

I had been on a pleasure voyage with some friends around the north coast of Scotland, and in that course had arrived in the salt-water lake under the Castle of Dunvegan, whose turrets, situated upon a frowning rock, rise immediately above the waves of the loch. As most of the party, and I myself in particular, chanced to be well known to the Laird of Macleod, we were welcomed to the castle with Highland hospitality, and glad to find ourselves in polished society, after a cruise of some duration. The most modern part of the castle was founded in the days of James VI.; the more ancient is referred to a period 'whose birth tradition notes not.' Until the present Macleod connected by a drawbridge the site of the castle with the mainland of Skye, the access must have been extremely difficult. Indeed, so much greater was the regard paid to security than to convenience, that in former times the only access to the mansion arose through a vaulted cavern in a rock, up which a staircase ascended from the sea-shore, like the buildings we read of in the romances of Mrs. Radcliffe.

Such a castle in the extremity of the Highlands was of course furnished with many a tale of tradition, and many a superstitious legend, to fill occasional intervals in the music and song, as proper to the halls of Dunvegan as when Johnson commemorated them. We reviewed the arms and ancient valuables of this distinguished family — saw the dirk and broadsword of Rorie Mhor, and his horn, which would drench three chiefs of these degenerate days. The solemn drinking-cup of the Kings of Alan must not be forgotten, nor the fairy banner given to Macleod by the Queen of Fairies; that magic flag, which has been victorious in two pitched fields, and will still float in the third, the bloodiest and the last, when the Elfin Sovereign shall, after the fight is ended, recall her banner, and carry off the standard-bearer.

Amid such tales of ancient tradition I had from Macleod and his lady the courteous offer of the haunted apartment castle, about which, as a stranger, I might be supposed interested. Accordingly, I took possession of it about the witching hour. Except perhaps some tapestry hangings, and the extreme thickness of the walls, which argued great antiquity, nothing could have been more comfortable than the interior of the apartment; but if you looked from the windows the view was such as to correspond with the highest tone of superstition. An autumnal blast, sometimes clear, sometimes driving mist before it, swept along the troubled billows of the lake, which it occasionally concealed, and by fits disclosed. The waves rushed in wild disorder on the shore, and covered with foam the steep piles of rock, which, rising from the sea in forms something resembling the human figure, have obtained the name of Macleod's Maidens, and in such a night seemed no bad representatives of the Norwegian goddesses called Choosers of the Slain, or Riders of the Storm. There was something of the dignity of danger in the scene; for on a platform beneath the windows lay an ancient battery of cannon, which had sometimes been used against privateers even of late years. The distant scene was a view of that part of the Quillan mountains which are called, from their form, Macleod's Dining-Tables. The voice of an angry cascade, termed the Nurse of Rorie Mhor, because that chief slept best in its vicinity, was heard from time mingling its notes with those of wind and wave. Such was the haunted room at Dunvegan, and as such, it well deserved a less sleepy inhabitant. In the language of Dr Johnson, who has stamped his memory on this remote place, ' I looked around me, and wondered that I was not more affected; but the mind is not at all times equally ready to be moved.' In a word, it is necessary to confess, that of all I heard or saw, the most engaging spectacle was the comfortable bed, in which I hoped to make amends for some nights on ship-board, and where I slept accordingly thinking of ghost or goblin till I was called by my servant in the morning.

From this I am taught to infer, that tales of ghosts and demonology are out of date at forty years and upwards; that it is only in the morning of life that this feeling of superstition 'comes o'er us like a summer cloud,' affecting us with fear which is solemn and awful rather than painful; and I am tempted to think that, if I were to write on the subject at all, it should have been during a period of life when I could have treated it with more interesting vivacity, and might have been at least amusing if I could not be instructive. Even the present fashion of the world seems to be ill suited for studies of this fantastic nature; and the most ordinary mechanic has learning sufficient to laugh at the figments which in former times were believed by far advanced in the deepest knowledge of the age.

I cannot, however, in conscience carry my opinion of my countrymen's good sense so far as to exculpate them entirely from the charge of credulity. Those who are disposed to look for them may, without much trouble, see such manifest signs, both of superstition and the disposition to believe in its doctrines, as may render it no useless occupation to compare the follies of our fathers with our own. The sailors have a proverb that every man in his lifetime must eat a peck of impurity; and it seems yet more clear that every generation of the human race must swallow a certain measure of nonsense. There remains hope, however, that the grosser faults of our ancestors are now out of date; and that whatever follies the present race may be guilty of, the sense of humanity is too universally spread to permit them to think of tormenting wretches till they confess what is impossible, and then burning them for their pains.

2.7

Poe on the Imagination

Edgar Allan Poe's stories and poems have a pivotal role in the transmutation of the Gothic conventions of the late eighteenth and early nineteenth centuries into the new generic forms of the modern era: the horror tale, science-fiction, fantasy adventure and the detective novel. His preoccupation with the psychology of fear retains something of the philosophical and physiological temper of the earlier period, while looking forward to the cosmic and psychoanalytic tendencies to come.

Poe dedicated a number of essays to exploring the nature of poetic composition and the creative urge towards the fantastic. His tale *The Imp of the Perverse* tackles a subject familiar since Burke — the subconscious impulses which lead to a fascination with danger, horror and the wicked. Poe's attention to sustained psychological experiences, rather than incident, and his eschewal of more conventional supernatural forces in favour of inexplicable influences and paranoia, attracted considerable interest from contemporary writers (especially in France) and proved profoundly influential in the coming decades.

1845

Edgar Allan Poe 1809–49
The Imp of the Perverse

In the consideration of the faculties and impulses — of the *prima mobilia* of the human soul, the phrenologists have failed to make room for a propensity which, although obviously existing as a radical, primitive, irreducible sentiment, has been equally overlooked by all the moralists who have preceded them. In the pure arrogance of the reason, we have all overlooked it. We have suffered its existence to escape our senses, solely through want of belief — of faith; — whether it be faith in Revelation, or faith in the Kabbala. The idea of it has never occurred to us, simply because of its supererogation. We saw no *need* of the impulse — for the propensity. We could not perceive its necessity. We could not understand, that is to say, we could not have understood, had the notion of this *primum mobile* ever obtruded itself; — we could not have understood in what manner it might be made to further the objects of humanity, either temporal or eternal. It cannot be denied that phrenology and, in great measure, all metaphysicianism, have been concocted *à priori*. The intellectual or logical man, rather than the understanding or observant man, set himself to imagine designs — to dictate purposes to God. Having thus fathomed to his satisfaction, the intentions of Jehovah, out of these intentions he built his innumerable systems of mind. In the matter of phrenology, for example, we first determined, naturally enough, that it was the design of the Deity that man should eat. We then assigned to man an organ of alimentiveness, and this organ is the scourge with which the Deity compels man, will-I nill-I, into eating. Secondly, having settled it to be God's will that man should continue his species, we discovered an organ of amativeness, forthwith. And so with combativeness, with ideality, with causality, with constructiveness, — so, in short, with every organ, whether representing a propensity, a moral sentiment, or a faculty of the pure intellect. And in these arrangements of the *principia* of human action, the Spurzheimites, whether right or wrong, in part, or upon the whole, have but followed, in principle, the footsteps of their predecessors; deducing and establishing every thing from the preconceived destiny of man, and upon the ground of the objects of his Creator.

It would have been wiser, it would have been safer, to classify, (if classify we must,) upon the basis of what man usually or occasionally did, and was always occasionally doing, rather than upon the basis of what we took it for granted the Deity intended him to do. If we cannot comprehend God in his visible works, how then in his inconceivable thoughts, that call the works into being? If we cannot understand him in his objective creatures, how then in his substantive moods and phases of creation?

Induction, *à posteriori*, would have brought phrenology to admit, as an innate and primitive principle of human action, a paradoxical something, which we may call *perverseness*, for want of a more characteristic term. In the sense I intend, it is, in fact, a *mobile* without motive, a motive not *motivirt*. Through its promptings we act without comprehensible object; or, if this shall be understood as a contradiction in terms, we may so far modify the proposition as to say, that through its promptings we act, for the reason that we should *not*. In theory, no reason can be more unreasonable, but, in fact, there is none more strong. With certain minds, under certain conditions, it becomes absolutely irresistible. I am not more certain that I breathe, than that the assurance of the wrong or error of any action is often the one unconquerable *force* which impels us, and alone impels us to its prosecution. Nor will this overwhelming tendency to do wrong for the wrong's sake, admit of analysis, or resolution into ulterior elements. It is a radical, a primitive impulse elementary. It will be said, I am aware, that when we persist in acts because we feel we should *not* persist in them, our conduct is but a modification of that which ordinarily springs from the *combativeness* of phrenology. But a glance will show the fallacy of this idea. The phrenological combativeness has for its essence, the necessity of self-defence. It is our safeguard against injury. Its principle regards our well-being; and thus the desire to be well, is excited simultaneously with its development. It follows, that the desire to be well must be excited simultaneously with any principle which shall be merely a modification of combativeness, but in the case of that something which I term *perverseness*, the desire to be well is not only not aroused, but a strongly antagonistical sentiment exists.

An appeal to one's own heart is, after all, the best reply to the sophistry just noticed. No one who trustingly consults and thoroughly questions his own soul, will be disposed to deny the entire radicalness of the propensity in question. It is not more incomprehensible than distinctive. There lives no man who at some period has not been tormented, for example, by an earnest desire to tantalize a listener by circumlocution. The speaker is aware that he displeases; he has every intention to please; he is usually curt, precise, and clear, the most laconic and luminous language is struggling for utterance upon his tongue, it is only with difficulty that he restrains himself from giving it flow; he dreads and deprecates the anger of him whom he addresses; yet, the thought strikes him, that by certain involutions and parentheses this anger may be engendered. That single thought is enough. The impulse increases to a wish, the wish to a desire, the desire to an uncontrollable longing, and the longing, (to the deep regret and mortification of the speaker, and in defiance of all consequences,) is indulged.

We have a task before us which must be speedily performed. We know that it will be ruinous to make delay. The most important crisis of our life calls, trumpet-tongued, for immediate energy and action. We glow, we are consumed with eagerness to commence the work, with the anticipation of whose glorious result our whole souls are on fire. It must, it shall be undertaken to-day, and yet we put it off until to-morrow, and why? There is no answer, except that we feel perverse, using the word with no comprehension of the principle. To-morrow arrives, and with it a more impatient anxiety to do our duty, but with this very increase of anxiety arrives, also, a nameless, a positively fearful, because unfathomable, craving for delay. This craving gathers strength as the moments fly. The last hour for action is at hand. We tremble with the violence of the conflict within us, — of the definite with the indefinite — of the substance with the shadow. But, if the contest have proceeded thus far, it is the shadow which prevails, — we struggle in vain. The clock strikes, and is the knell of our welfare. At the same time, it is the chanticleer — note to the ghost that has so long overawed us. It flies — it disappears — we are free. The old energy returns. We will labor *now*. Alas, it is *too late*!

We stand upon the brink of a precipice. We peer into the abyss — we grow sick and dizzy. Our first impulse is to shrink from the danger. Unaccountably we remain. By slow degrees our sickness and dizziness, and horror, become merged in a cloud of unnameable feeling. By gradations, still more imperceptible, this cloud assumes shape, as did the vapor from the bottle out of which arose the genius in the Arabian Nights. But out of this *our* cloud upon the precipice's edge, there grows into palpability, a shape, far more terrible than any genius or any demon of a tale, and yet it is but a thought, although a fearful one, and one which chills the very marrow of our bones with the fierceness of the delight of its horror. It is merely the idea of what would be our sensations during the sweeping precipitancy of a fall from such a height. And this fall — this rushing annihilation — for the very reason that it involves that one most ghastly and loathsome of all the most ghastly and loathsome images of death and suffering which have ever presented themselves to our imagination — for this very cause do we now the most vividly desire it. And because our reason violently deters us from the brink, *therefore*, do we the most impetuously approach it. There is no passion in nature so demoniacally impatient, as that of him who, shuddering upon the edge of a precipice, thus meditates a plunge. To indulge, for a moment, in any attempt at *thought*, is to be inevitably lost; for reflection but urges us to forbear, and *therefore* it is, I say, that we *cannot*. If there be no friendly arm to check us, or if we fail in a sudden effort to prostrate ourselves backward from the abyss, we plunge, and are destroyed.

Examine these similar actions as we will, we shall find them resulting solely from the spirit of the *Perverse*. We perpetrate them because we feel that we should *not*. Beyond or behind this there is no intelligible principle; and we might, indeed, deem this perverseness a direct instigation of the arch-fiend, were it not occasionally known to operate in furtherance of good.

I have said thus much, that in some measure I may answer your question — that I may explain to you why I am here — that I may assign to you something that shall have at least the faint aspect of a cause for my wearing these fetters, and for my tenanting this cell of the condemned. Had I not been thus prolix, you might either have misunderstood me altogether, or, with the rabble, have fancied me mad. As it is, you will easily perceive that I am one of the many uncounted victims of the Imp of the Perverse.

It is impossible that any deed could have been wrought with a more thorough deliberation. For weeks, for months, I pondered upon the means of the murder. I rejected a thousand schemes, because their accomplishment involved a *chance* of detection. At length, in reading some French memoirs, I found an account of a nearly fatal illness that occurred to Madame Pilau, through the agency of a candle accidentally poisoned. The idea struck my fancy at once. I knew my victim's habit of reading in bed. I knew, too, that his apartment was narrow and ill-ventilated. But I need not vex you with impertinent details. I need not describe the easy artifices by which I substituted, in his bed-room candle-stand, a wax-light of my own making for the one which I there found. The next morning he was discovered dead in his bed, and the coroner's verdict was, — 'Death by the visitation of God.'

Having inherited his estate, all went well with me for years. The idea of detection never once entered my brain. Of the remains of the fatal taper, I had myself carefully disposed. I had left no shadow of a clew by which it would be possible to convict, or even to suspect me of the crime. It is inconceivable how rich a sentiment of satisfaction arose in my bosom as I reflected upon my absolute security. For a very long period of time, I was accustomed to revel in this sentiment. It afforded me more real delight than all the mere worldly advantages, accruing from my sin. But there arrived at length an epoch, from which the pleasurable feeling grew, by scarcely perceptible gradations, into a haunting and harassing thought. It harassed because it haunted. I could scarcely get rid of it for an instant. It is quite a common thing to be thus annoyed with the ringing in our ears, or rather in our memories, of the burthen of some ordinary song, or some unimpressive snatches from an opera. Nor will we be the less tormented if the song in itself be good, or the opera air meritorious. In this manner, at last, I would perpetually catch myself pondering upon my security, and repeating, in a low undertone, the phrase, 'I am safe.'

One day, whilst sauntering along the streets, I arrested myself in the act of murmuring, half aloud, these customary syllables. In a fit of petulance, I remodelled them thus: — 'I am safe — I am safe — yes — if I be not fool enough to make open confession!'

No sooner had I spoken these words, than I felt an icy chill creep to my heart. I had had some experience in these fits of perversity, (whose nature I have been at some trouble to explain,) and I remembered well, that in no instance, I had successfully resisted their attacks. And now my own casual self-suggestion that I might possibly be fool enough to confess the murder of which I had been guilty, confronted me, as if the very ghost of him whom I had murdered — and beckoned me on to death.

At first, I made an effort to shake off this nightmare of the soul. I walked vigorously — faster — still faster — at length I ran. I felt a maddening desire to shriek aloud. Every succeeding wave of thought overwhelmed me with new terror, for, alas! I well, too well understood that to *think*, in my situation, was to be lost. I still quickened my pace. I bounded like a madman through the crowded thoroughfares. At length, the populace took the alarm, and pursued me. I felt *then* the consummation of my fate. Could I have torn out my tongue, I would have done it, but a rough voice resounded in my ears — a rougher grasp seized me by the shoulder. I turned — I gasped for breath. For a moment I experienced all the pangs of suffocation; I became blind, and deaf, and giddy; and then some invisible fiend, I thought, struck me with his broad palm upon the back. The long-imprisoned secret burst forth from my soul.

They say that I spoke with a distinct enunciation, but with marked emphasis and passionate hurry, as if in dread of interruption before concluding the brief but pregnant sentences that consigned me to the hangman and to hell.

Having related all that was necessary for the fullest judicial conviction, I fell prostrate in a swoon.

But why shall I say more? To-day I wear these chains, and am *here*! To-morrow I shall be fetterless! — *but where*?

2.8

Gothic Curiosities

Andrew Lang (1844–1912) was an anthropologist, classicist and historian, and a founding member of the Folk-Lore Society (1878). His recollections of reading Mrs Radcliffe are not free from a certain shame-facedness, but are interesting for suggesting the status of this author among sober-minded people of the end of the nineteenth century. The enthusiasm of the literary scholar Montague Summers (1880–1948), by contrast, helped found the modern study of the Gothic. The vast scholarly achievements of *The Gothic Bibliography* (1940) and *The Gothic Quest* (1938) are foundation-stones of modern work into the field. His was not simply an academic interest, however: he dressed in an eighteenth-century style, and was a committed occultist and Catholic who held genuine supernatural beliefs.

July 1900

Andrew Lang 1844–1912
'Mrs Radcliffe's Novels'

Does any one now read Mrs Radcliffe, or am I the only wanderer in her windy corridors, listening timidly to groans and hollow voices, and shielding the flame of a lamp, which, I fear, will presently flicker out, and leave me in darkness? People know the name of 'The Mysteries of Udolpho;' they know that boys would say to Thackeray, at school, 'Old fellow, draw us Vivaldi in the Inquisition.' But have they penetrated into the chill galleries of the Castle of Udolpho? Havc they shuddered for Vivaldi in face of the sable-clad and masked Inquisition? Certainly Mrs Radcliffe, within the memory of man, has been extremely popular. The thick double-columned volume in which I peruse the works of the Enchantress belongs to a public library. It is quite the dirtiest, greasiest, most dog's-eared, and most bescribbled tome in the collection. Many of the books have remained, during the last hundred years, uncut, even to this day, and I have had to apply the paper knife to many an author, from Alciphron (1790) to Mr Max Müller, and Dr Birkbeck Hill's edition of Bozzy's 'Life of Dr Johnson.' But Mrs Radcliffe has been read diligently, and copiously annotated.

1938

Montague Summers 1880–1948
Introduction to *The Gothic Quest*

My love for the romances of Mrs Radcliffe dates from my very first years. Among my earliest recollections is an edition of her Works in one rather formidable fat volume, double-columned — which offered no difficulties then — and embellished with woodcuts that were a perpetual delight, not least because of their close affinity to the plays of Webb and Pollock of which one was giving nightly performances. Bound in bull black morocco, gilt-tooled, Mrs Radliffe lived on the summit of the highest shelves in a sombre and shadowy but by no means large old library, where the books stood ranged in very neat rows in tall mahogany cases behind heavy glass doors. Most sections were locked and keyless, but the particular bookcase whence Mrs Radcliffe would be reached by mounting upon a chair and stretching rather far was always left unfastened, as I suppose containing standard literature and works approved for general and uncensored perusal, Scott, Dickens, Thackeray, Trollope, Marryat, Fenimore Cooper, Lignard, Miss Strickland, Prescott, and the more sober historians. *Tom Jones*, I remember, was banished to the remotest altitudes, and jailed beyond all hope of release. What a day it was — diem numera meliore lapillo, as old Persius bids — that day when I discovered how an alien key would fit the bookcase locks!

I now recognise that I began my acquaintance with Mrs Radcliffe — an acquaintance that was soon to warm into affection and them to love — from Limbard's edition of 1824. A schoolboy friend — we were not in our 'teens — lent me a copy of *The Bravo of Venice* he had picked up on some twopenny stall. *The Monk* was not to follow until some years later. Next I was attracted by a title, *Manfroné; or, The One-Handed Monk*, the four volumes of which I espied in a dingy little shop, and soon proudly possessed for one shilling. Thus I may be said to have been fairly started on my Gothic career. Very early too do I remember *Horrid Mysteries*, to which I did not make my way viâ Jane Austen, for when I came to read *Northanger Abbey*, how delighted I was to find the recommendation of sweet Miss Andrews. [...]

The Gothic Novel with its romantic unrealities, its strange beauties, its very extravagances — if you will — was to a great extent the Novel of Escape from the troubles and carking cases of everyday life. Men wearied of fiction which, clever and pointed as the strokes might be, presented too nearly the world almost as they saw it around them. Sidney Bidulph and Lady Barton were found to be distressing; the heroines of Mrs Lennox, Henrietta and Euphemia; Mrs Gibbes' Sukey Thorby; George Walker's Cinthelia; were all voted ordinary. The novel of real life to achieve complete success must have mingled with it something of surprise, something of romance ... if served with Gothic sauce the domestic novel was generally considered far more appetizing fare.

The explanation is that both at home and abroad dark shadows were lowering; the times were difficult, full of anxiety and unrest; there was a sense of dissatisfaction to-day and of apprehension for the morrow; there were wars and rumours of wars. Readers sought some counter-excitement, and to many the novel became the precious anodyne. There is something in this which may be closely paralleled at the present time, and never before than now were readers so greedy for 'fictional anæsthetics'.

1931

Montague Summers 1880–1948
'Introduction' to *The Supernatural Omnibus*

The ghost story should be short, simple and direct. Who told the first ghost story? I do not know, but I am sure that it was simple enough and that it sufficiently thrilled the hearers. Some son of Adam, I suppose, far back in dimmest antiquity, housed in a cave, as he looked up at the vast endless spaces of heaven powdered with nightly stars, as he wondered at the mysterious darkness, the depths of shadow, the remoteness of shapes familiar by day but which took on strange forms at the approach of evening: marvelled and told his children how he seemed to see the shadow of their grandsire who had gone from them so short a while, who had lain stark and motionless and cold. The old hunter had returned, yet he brought terror in his train, for now he had something of the night and the wind, of the great untrammelled forces of Nature with which man contended daily for his right to live. And his brood listened with awe; they trembled, they scarce knew why, and were afraid.

2.9

The Nightmare-Touch

The writer of fantastic tales and translator of Oriental ghost stories, Lafcadio Hearn (1850–1904) has one of the more exotic biographies to be found among authors in this genre. Born in the Greek islands to Greek and Irish parents, Hearn grew up in Ireland and was educated among Jesuits in France and England (losing an eye along the way as the result of being violently bullied at school). Following periods of homelessness, he ended up working in journalism in America, where he specialised in gruesome crime reports. He subsequently moved to Japan, eventually taking up Japanese citizenship. His modern reputation arises mainly from his translations of Chinese and Japanese supernatural tales, but his own weird and horrific stories, reflected in this autobiographical essay, reflect a cosmic conception of horror which reaches out to the vast distances of space, but also deep into into personal psychology.

1900

Lafcadio Hearn 1850–1904
'Nightmare-Touch'

What is the fear of ghosts among those who believe in ghosts?
All fear is the result of experience — experience of the individual or of the race, — experience either of the present life or of lives forgotten. Even the fear of the unknown can have no other origin. And the fear of ghosts must be a product of past pain.

Probably the fear of ghosts, as well as the belief in them, had its beginning in dreams. It is a peculiar fear. No other fear is so intense; yet none is so vague. Feelings thus voluminous and dim are super-individual mostly, — feelings inherited, — feelings made within us by the experience of the dead.

What experience?
Nowhere do I remember reading a plain statement of the reason why ghosts are feared. Ask any ten intelligent persons of your acquaintance, who remember having once been afraid of ghosts, to tell you exactly why they were afraid, — to define the fancy behind the fear; — and I doubt whether even one will be able to answer the question. The literature of folk-lore — oral and written — throws no clear light upon the subject. We find, indeed, various legends of men torn asunder by phantoms; but such gross imaginings could not explain the peculiar quality of ghostly fear. It is not a fear of bodily violence. It is not even a reasoning fear, — not a fear that can readily explain itself, — which would not be the case if it were founded upon definite ideas of physical danger. Furthermore, although primitive ghosts may have been imagined as capable of tearing and devouring, the common idea of a ghost is certainly that of a being intangible and imponderable.

Now I venture to state boldly that the common fear of ghosts is *the fear of being touched by ghosts*, — or, in other words, that the imagined Supernatural is dreaded mainly because of its imagined power to touch. Only to *touch*, remember! — not to wound or kill.

But this dread of the touch would itself be the result of experience — chiefly, I think, of prenatal experience stored up in the individual by inheritance, like the child's fear of darkness. And who can ever have had the sensation of being seized by ghosts? The answer is simple: — *Everyone who has been seized by phantoms in a dream.*

Elements of primeval fears — fears older than humanity — doubtless enter into the child-terror of darkness. But the more definite fears of ghosts may very possibly be composed with inherited result of dream-pain, — ancestral experience of nightmare. And the intuitive terror of supernatural touch can thus be evolutionally explained...

Psychological Perspectives

Sigmund Freud (1856–1939) hardly needs any introduction. While his theories of the unconscious, in their technical detail, remain challenging and controversial, his basic arguments about the suppression of sexual desire being the shaping motivation of human culture and personal psychology have entered the wider realm. His 1919 essay 'The Uncanny' has been particularly influential in literary and cultural studies. His argument about the power of horror and the supernatural arising, paradoxically, not from the alien qualities of such effects, but in their manifestation of repressed or forgotten realities has proved as important for the modern age as, perhaps, Burke's theory of the Sublime was to an earlier era.

Ernest Jones (1879–1958) was a central figure in the early history of British psychoanalysis, and instrumental in seeing Freud's works translated into English. His 1931 book *On the Nightmare* offers a vast historical survey of the key nightmare-motifs of the vampire, the werewolf, the devil, the incubus and the witch, tracing these in myth, legend, folklore and literature, and exploring the relationship of these to the deep-rooted sexual motives shaping human culture.

1919

Sigmund Freud 1856–1939
The Uncanny
trans. Alix Strachey 1925

It is only rarely that a psycho-analyst feels impelled to investigate the subject of aesthetics even when aesthetics is understood to mean not merely the theory of beauty, but the theory of feeling. He works in other planes of mental life and has little to do with those subdued emotional activities which, inhibited in their aims and dependent upon a multitude of concurrent factors, usually furnish the material for the study of aesthetics. But it does occasionally happen that he has to interest himself in some particular province of that subject; and then it usually proves to be a rather remote region of it and one that has been neglected in standard works.

The subject of the 'uncanny' is a province of this kind. It undoubtedly belongs to all that is terrible — to all that arouses dread and creeping horror; it is equally certain, too, that the word is not always used in a clearly definable sense, so that it tends to coincide with whatever excites dread. Yet we may expect that it implies some intrinsic quality which justifies the use of a special name. One is curious to know what this peculiar quality is which allows us to distinguish as 'uncanny' certain things within the boundaries of what is 'fearful'...

... if psycho-analytic theory is correct in maintaining that every emotional effect, whatever its quality, is transformed by repression into morbid anxiety, then among such cases of anxiety there must be a class in which the anxiety can be shown to come from something repressed which *recurs*. This class of morbid anxiety would then be no other than what is uncanny, irrespective of whether it originally aroused dread or some other affect. In the second place, if this is indeed the secret nature of the uncanny, we can understand why the usage of speech has extended *das Heimliche* into its opposite *das Unheimliche*; for this uncanny is in reality nothing new or foreign, but something familiar and old-established in the mind that has been estranged only by the process of repression. This reference to the factor of repression allows us, furthermore, to understand Schelling's definition of the uncanny as something which ought to have been kept concealed but which has nevertheless come to light.

It only remains for us to test our new hypothesis on one or two more examples of the uncanny.

Many people experience the feeling in the highest degree in relation to death and dead bodies, to the return of the dead, and to spirits and ghosts. As we have seen, many languages in use to-day can only render the German expression 'an *unheimliches* house' by 'a *haunted* house'. We might indeed have begun our investigations with this example, perhaps the most striking of all, of something uncanny, but we refrained from doing so because the uncanny in it is too much mingled with and in part covered by what is purely gruesome. There is scarcely any other matter, however, upon which our thoughts and feelings have changed so little since the very earliest times, and in which discarded forms have been so completely preserved under a thin disguise, as that of our relation to death. Two things account for our conservatism: the strength of our original emotional reaction to it, and the insufficiency of our scientific knowledge about it. Biology has not yet been able to decide whether death is the inevitable fate of every living being or whether it is only a regular but yet perhaps avoidable event in life. It is true that the proposition 'All men are mortal' is paraded in text-books of logic as an example of a generalization, but no human being really grasps it, and our unconscious has as little use now as ever for the idea of its own mortality. Religions continue to dispute the undeniable fact of death of each one of us and to postulate a life after death; civil governments still believe that they cannot maintain moral order among the living if they do not uphold this prospect of a better life after death as a recompense for earthly existence. In our great cities, placards announce lectures which will tell us how to get into touch with the souls of the departed; and it cannot be denied that many of the most able and penetrating minds among our scientific men have come to the conclusion, especially towards the close of their lives, that a contact of this kind is not entirely impossible. Since practically all of us still think as savages do on this topic, it is not matter for surprise that the primitive fear of the dead is still so strong within us and always ready to come to the surface at any opportunity. Most likely our fear still contains the old belief that the deceased becomes the enemy of the survivor and wants to carry him off to share his new life with him. Considering our unchanged attitude towards death, we might rather inquire what has become of the repression, that necessary condition for enabling a primitive feeling to recur in the shape of an uncanny effect. But repression is there, too. All so-called educated people have ceased to believe, officially at any rate, that the dead can become visible as spirits, and have hedged round any such appearances with improbable and remote circumstances; their emotional attitude towards their dead, moreover, once a highly dubious and ambivalent one, has been toned down in the higher strata of the mind into a simple feeling of reverence.

We have now only a few more remarks to add, for animism, magic and witchcraft, the omnipotence of thoughts, man's attitude of death, involuntary repetition and the castration-complex comprise practically all the factors which turn something fearful into an uncanny thing.

We all call a living person uncanny, usually when we ascribe evil motives to him. But that is not all; we must not only credit him with bad intentions but must attribute these intentions capacity to achieve their aim in virtue of certain special powers. A good instance of this is the 'Gettatore', that uncanny figure of

Roman superstition which Schaeffer, with intuitive poetic feeling and profound psycho-analytic knowledge, has transformed into a sympathetic figure in his *Josef Montfort*. But the question of these secret powers brings us back again to the realm of animism. It is her intuition that he possesses secret power of this kind that makes Mephistopheles so uncanny to the pious Gretchen. 'She divines that I am certainly a spirit, even the devil himself perchance'.

The uncanny effect of epilepsy and of madness has the same origin. The ordinary person sees in them the workings of forces hitherto unsuspected in his fellow-man but which at the same time he is dimly aware of in a remote corner of his own being. The Middle Ages quite consistently ascribed all such maladies to daemonic influences, and in this their psychology was not so far out. Indeed, I should not be surprised to hear that psycho-analysis, which is concerned with laying bare these hidden forces, has itself become uncanny to many people for that very reason. In one case, after I had succeeded — though none too rapidly — in effecting a cure which had lasted many years in a girl who had been an invalid, the patient's own mother confessed to this attitude long after the girl's recovery.

Dismembered limbs, a severed head, a hand cut off at the wrist, feet which dance by themselves — all these have something peculiarly uncanny about them, especially when, as in the last instance, they prove able to move of themselves in addition. As we already know, this kind of uncanniness springs from its association with the castration-complex. To many people the idea of being buried alive while appearing to be dead is the most uncanny thing of all. And yet psycho-analysis has taught us that this terrifying phantasy is only a transformation of another phantasy which had nothing terrifying about it at all, but was filled with a certain lustful pleasure, I mean, of intra-uterine existence.

*****

There is one more point of general application I should like to add, though, strictly speaking, it has been included in our statements about animism and mechanisms in the mind that have been surmounted; for I think it deserves special mention. This is that an uncanny effect is often and easily produced by effacing the distinction between imagination and reality, such as when something that we have hitherto regarded as imaginary appears before us in reality, or when a symbol takes over the full functions and significance of the thing is symbolizes, and so on. It is this element which contributes not a little to the uncanny effect attaching to magical practices. The infantile element in this, which also holds sway in the minds of neurotics, is the over-accentuation of psychical reality in comparison with physical reality — a feature closely allied to the belief in the omnipotence of thoughts. In the midst of the isolation of war-time a number of the English *Strand Magazine* fell into my hands; and, amongst other not very interesting matter, I read a story about a young married couple, who move into a furnished flat in which there is a curiously shaped table with carvings of crocodiles on it. Towards evening they begin to smell an intolerable and very typical odour that pervades the whole flat; things begin to get in their way and trip them up in the darkness; they seem to see a vague form gliding up the stairs — in short, we are given to understand that the presence of the table causes ghostly crocodiles to haunt the place, or that the wooden monsters come to life in the dark, or something of that sort. It was a thoroughly silly story, but the uncanny feeling it produced was quite remarkable.

To conclude this collection of examples, which is certainly not complete, I will relate an instance taken from psycho-analytical experience; if it does not rest upon mere coincidence, it furnishes a beautiful confirmation of our theory of the uncanny. It often happens that male patients declare that they feel there is something uncanny about the female genital organs. This *unheimlich* place, however, is the entrance to the former *heim* [home] of all human beings, to the place where everyone dwelt once upon a time and in the beginning. There is a humorous saying: 'Love is home-sickness'; and whenever a man dreams of a place or a country and says to himself, still in the dream, 'this place is familiar to me, I have been there before', we may interpret this place as being his mother's genitals or her body. In this case, too, the *unheimlich* is what was once *heimlich*, home-like, familiar; the prefix 'un' is the token of repression.

1931

Ernest Jones 1879–1958
On the Nightmare

The interest men have at all ages taken in dreams and the far-reaching significance that has been attributed to them make it very probable that the phenomena there experienced have greatly influenced the forming of waking thoughts. If this, as I have shown elsewhere, can still happen among educated people, it must have done so on a far more extensive scale in past ages when the general importance attaching to dreams was much greater than to-day.

The vividness of dreams is so intense at times that even educated people may find it hard or actually impossible to distinguish them from real events. I have, for example, mentioned the case of a physician whose mistaking a dream for a real memory led to disagreeable consequences. In fact, this confusion with reality characterizes all intense emotional experiences, not only in dreams, but also in other rarer expressions of the imagination such as ecstatic trances, visions and so on...

The difficulty of distinguishing dreams from the experiences of waking life is naturally greater in less tutored minds, such as those of children and savages. Numerous observers have remarked on the extraordinary clearness with which dreams impose themselves on the minds of savages as indubitable reality. Herbert Spencer lays special stress on this point and adduces a mass of material in illustration of it. Im Thurn gives many striking examples of it at the present day: one Indian threatened to leave the traveller because the latter, so he said, had inconsiderately made him work all night dragging his canoe up a series of difficult cataracts; another nearly killed a comrade on the ground that his master had ordered him to inflict a severe chastisement on him (it turned out that he had dreamt this).

That dreams must have exercised a considerable influence in moulding men's beliefs needs, therefore, no further demonstration, and there is also in several important respects unanimity of the further questions of the extent of this influence and the details of the process itself.

[...]

It would seem worth while now to review the characteristic features common to the five groups of phenomena considered above [vampires, ghosts, werewolves, the incubus, the devil]. In the first place — and this is one of the main theses of this book — they all represent constructions built out of numerous elements which not only had an independent existence among the beliefs of European peoples, but which are still to be found to-day in widely separated parts of the world. For the fusing of the constituents into a composite belief the Christian Church bears in every case the prime responsibility, in four cases the Roman Catholic and in one the Orthodox Greek Church. It is worthy of note that leading authorities of the Church had repeatedly, previous to the twelfth century, denied the truth of popular beliefs in these constituents, particularly sorcery, lewd intercourse with Incubi, transformation of human beings into animals, night journeys with demons and witchcraft, and they insisted on the dream origin of these beliefs: it was reserved for the Middle Ages to plunge into an obscurantism that the so-called Dark Ages had rejected. The composite beliefs in question endured approximately three hundred years; after their course was run they did not vanish, but dissolved once more into their original elements. Even the fully developed beliefs have lasted on among the uneducated portions of society, and that this is far from rare may be illustrated by the fact that the present writer has personally met with people who were as convinced of the truths of these beliefs as the general population was in the Middle Ages: belief in the constituent elements themselves is far more widely spread and may at times be encountered even among the educated. During the Middle Ages and later belief in these five superstitions tended to assume epidemic proportions and then gave rise to frightful suffering and an outbreak of persecutory mania almost without parallel.

The five superstitions were closely interwoven together, and in many respects even passed over into one another. The psychological meaning of them is even more closely connected than their outward appearance. All the elements out of which the five supertitious beliefs were built were projections of unconscious and repressed sexual material. In this material two features are above all noteworthy, the prominence of incestuous wishes and of infantile forms of sexuality.

The actual formulation of the superstitions after they had been fully developed was influenced by a variety of factors, principally of a social and religious nature; the analysis of them is thus an historical problem. The most important were two features in the attitude of the Christian Church: the fear and hate it displayed towards unorthodox worship, which to it was equivalent to disobedience against God; and the abnormally exaggerated effort it expended in the service of sexual repression, particularly in its horror of incest. It cannot be chance that these two features, which evoked as savage emotions and conduct as human beings are capable of, represent the two sides of the fundamental Oedipus complex, revolt against the father and sexual love towards the mother.

The relations the five superstitions bear to the Nightmare are especially close. The superstitions themselves may psychologically be designated as phobias the latent content of which represents repressed incestuous wishes. In the intensity of the dread accompanying them they are surpassed by no other experience than that of the Nightmare and allied anxiety dreams. In many of their features they contain a symbolism highly characteristic of anxiety dreams. Other features common to both are: the sudden transformation of one person into another or into some animal; the occurrence of phantastic and impossible animal forms; the alternation of the imagined object between extreme attractiveness and the most intense disgust; the apparently simultaneous existence of the same person in two different places; the idea of flying or riding through the air; and the apprehension of sexual acts as torturing assaults. The central point of the latent content both of the Nightmare and the five superstitions here examined is composed of repressed incestuous wishes relating to coitus. In four out of the five there are also present other sexual wishes, various perversions of infantile origin, just as there are with the anxiety dreams that do not belong to the classical Nightmare type. Nightmares have even shown at times the tendency, so prominent with the superstitions, to assume epidemic form. The extensive record obtaining between the Nightmare and these superstitions, not only in their essential psychological signification but also in many points in their manifest structure, makes it probable that actual dream experiences were of considerable importance in making the elaboration of them possible.

[...]

If by 'scientific' materialism is meant the tendency to discount the significance of mental and spiritual experiences, to displace the psychical by the physical, then the history of the

Nightmare affords one of the most impressive examples of its darkening counsel. Until this tendency manifested itself, in relatively recent times, no sharp distinction had been drawn between the voluptuous and the fearful experiences of sleep. Both were equally ascribed to the activity of supernatural beings, and even in medical circles, the same names, Incubus, Ephialtes, were used to designate both. Writers had repeatedly observed that the series of voluptuous — voluptuous-fearful — fearful in dream life was of an unbroken graduation, and daily clinical experience amply confirms this. The typical Nightmare is merely one extreme member of this series. It was Freud who first demonstrated the inherent connection between intra-psychic dread and repressed sexual impulses, and we can now understand the Nightmare as an event in which such impulses have been overwhelmed, and shrouded, by extreme fear. The intensity of the fear is proportionate to the guilt of the repressed incestuous wishes that are striving for imaginary gratification, the physical counterpart of which is an orgasm — often provoked by involuntary masturbation. If the wish were not in a state of repression, there would be no fear, and the result would be a simple erotic dream. The real cause of the Nightmare has thus two essential attributes: (1) it arises from within, (2) it is of mental origin, a sexual wish in a state of repression. Except for the repression this statement is true also of erotic dreams.

M.R. James on The Supernatural

Cambridge don, and author of highly admired supernatural fictions, Montague Rhodes James (1862–1936) is considered a major figure in modern Gothic writing. Eschewing the extravagant or fantastic in favour of an unsettling of reality, his fictions are admired for their narrative concision and psychological penetration. Although a distinguished scholar and antiquarian, James was determinedly evasive about the nature and function of the supernatural tale. His comments, quoted here, arguably represent an archetypically English style of fuzzy thinking and equivocation, while as equally typically laying down a deeply restrictive formula. James would elsewhere priggishly dismiss sex and horror as legitimate elements in the supernatural tale (see p.310).

1924

M.R. James 1862–1936
'Introduction' to V.H. Collins (ed.), *Ghosts and Marvels: A Selection of Uncanny Tales from Daniel Defoe to Algernon Blackwood*

Often I have been asked to formulate my views about ghost stories and tales of the marvellous, the mysterious, the supernatural. Never had I been able to find out whether I had any views that could be formulated. The truth is, I suspect, that the *genre* is too small and special to bear the imposition of far-reaching principles. Widen the question, and ask what governs the general construction of short stories in general, and a great deal might be said, and has been said. There are, of course, instances of whole novels in which the supernatural governs the plot; but among them are few successes. The ghost story is, at its best, only a particular sort of short story, and is subject to the same broad rules as the whole mass of them. Those rules, I imagine, no writer ever consciously follows. In fact, it is absurd to talk of them as rules; they are qualities which have been observed to accompany success.

Some such qualities I have noted, and while I cannot undertake to write about broad principles, something more concrete is capable of being recorded. Well, then: two ingredients most valuable in the concocting of a ghost story are, to me, the atmosphere and the nicely managed crescendo. I assume, of course, that the writer will have got his central idea before he undertakes the story at all. Let us, then, be introduced to the actors in a placid way; let us see them going about their ordinary business, undisturbed by forebodings, pleased with their surroundings; and into this calm environment let the ominous thing put out its head, unobtrusively at first, and then more insistently, until it holds the stage. It is not amiss sometimes to leave a loophole for a natural explanation; but I would say, let the loophole be so narrow as not to be quite practicable. Then, for the setting. The detective story cannot be too much up-to-date: the motor, the telephone, the aeroplane, the newest slang, are all in place there. For the ghost story a slight haze of distance is desirable. 'Thirty years ago,' 'Not long before the war,' are very proper openings. If a really remote date be chosen, there is more than one way of bringing the reader in contact with it. The findings of documents about it can be made plausible; or you may begin with your apparition and go back over the years to tell the cause of it; or (as in 'Schalken the Painter') you may set the scene directly in the desired epoch, which I think is hardest to do with success. On the whole (though not a few instances might be quoted against me) I think that a setting so modern that the ordinary reader can judge of its naturalness for himself is preferable to anything antique. For some degree of actuality is the charm of the best ghost stories; not a very insistent actuality, but one strong enough to allow the reader to identify himself with the patient; while it is almost inevitable that the reader of an antique story should fall into the position of a mere spectator.

These are personal impressions. Many other views are current, and have been justified in practice ...

17 April 1931

M.R. James 1862–1936
'Ghosts — Treat them Gently!'
Evening News

What first interested me in ghosts? This I can tell you quite definitely. In my childhood I chanced to see a toy Punch and Judy set, with figures cut out in cardboard. One of these was The Ghost. It was a tall figure habited in white with an unnaturally long and narrow head, also surrounded with white, and a dismal visage.

Upon this my conceptions of a ghost were based, and for years it permeated my dreams.

Other questions — why I like ghost stories, or what are the best, or why they are the best, or a recipe for writing such things — I have never found them easy to be so positive about. Clearly, however, the public likes them. The recrudescence of ghost stories in recent years is notable: it corresponds, of course, with the vogue of the detective tale.

The ghost story can be supremely excellent in its kind, or it may be deplorable. Like other things, it may err by excess or defect. Bram Stoker's *Dracula* is a book with very good ideas in it, but — to be vulgar — the butter is spread far too thick. Excess is the fault here: to give an example of erring by defect is difficult, because the stories that err in that way leave no impression in the memory.

I am speaking of the literary ghost story here. The story that claims to be 'vericidal' (in the language of the Society of Psychical Research) is a very different affair. It will probably be quite brief, and will conform to one of several familiar types. This is but reasonable, for, if there be ghosts — as I am quite prepared to believe — the true ghost story need do no more than illustrate the normal habits (if normal is the right word), and may be as mild as milk.

The literary ghost, on the other hand, has to justify his existence by some startling demonstration, or, short of that, must be furnished with a background that will throw him into full relief and make him the central feature.

Since then things which the ghost can effectively do are very limited in number, ranging about death and madness and the discovery of secrets, the setting seems to me all-important, since it is there that there is the greatest opportunity for variety.

It is upon this and upon the first glimmer of the appearance of the supernatural that pains must be lavished. But we need not, we should not, use all the colours in the box. In the infancy of the art we needed the haunted castle on a beetling rock to put us in the right frame: the tendency is not yet extinct, for I have just read a story with a mysterious mansion on a desolate height in Cornwall and a gentleman practising the worst sort of magic. How often, too, have ruinous old houses been described or shown to me as fit scenes for stories!

'Can't you imagine some old monk or friar wandering about this long gallery?' No, I can't.

[...]

But, though the subject has its fascinations, I see no use in being pontifical about it. These stories are meant to please and amuse us. If they do so, well: but, if not, let us relegate them to the top shelf and say no more about it.

H.P. Lovecraft on Cosmic Horror

The American writer Howard Phillips Lovecraft (1890–1937) has some claim to be the most important writer of the fantastic and horrific in the modern era. Working originally in distinctly cultish circles — publishing in amateur and pulp magazines and attracting the passionate support of a network of writers and collaborators — he is now admired as a classic, perhaps to be accepted into the canon of modern literature. The extravagant weirdness of his imagery, the cultish nature of his following, and the conservative (sometimes racist) vein to his thought have attracted critical reservations: his work triumphantly traverses the divide between 'trash' and 'literature', and the 'amateur' and the 'professional'.

Despite the distinctively modern science-fiction and cosmic elements, Lovecraft's work has an important relationship with the early Gothic tradition. Lovecraft felt himself to be an eighteenth-century figure in some sense, distinctly out of time and out of place in modern America. His views on the literary tradition of horror were laid out in *Supernatural Horror in Literature*, first published in an amateur magazine and latterly as a short book.

1927
Revised edition
1939

H.P. Lovecraft 1890–1937
Supernatural Horror in Literature

The oldest and strongest emotion of mankind is fear, and the oldest and strongest kind of fear is fear of the unknown. These facts few psychologists will dispute, and their admitted truth must establish for all time the genuineness and dignity of the weirdly horrible tales as a literary form. Against it are discharged all the shafts of a materialistic sophistication which clings to frequently felt emotions and external events, and of a naively inspired idealism which deprecates the aesthetic motive and calls for a didactic literature to 'uplift' the reader toward a suitable degree of smirking optimism. But in spite of all this opposition the weird tale has survived, developed, and attained remarkable heights of perfection; founded as it is on a profound and elementary principle whose appeal, if not always universal, must necessarily be poignant and permanent to minds of the requisite sensitiveness.

The appeal of the spectrally macabre is generally narrow because it demands from the reader a certain degree of imagination and a capacity for detachment from everyday life. Relatively few are free enough from the spell of the daily routine to respond to rappings from outside, and tales of ordinary feelings and events, or of common sentimental distortions of such feelings and events, will always take first place in the taste of the majority; rightly, perhaps, since of course these ordinary matters make up the greater part of human experience. But the sensitive are always with us, and sometimes a curious streak of fancy invades an obscure corner of the hardest head; so that no amount of rationalisation, reform, or Freudian analysis can quite annul the thrill of the chimney-corner whisper or the lonely wood. There is here involved psychological pattern or tradition as real and as deeply grounded in mental experience as any other pattern or tradition of mankind; coeval with the religious feeling and closely related to many aspects of it, and too much a part of our innermost biological heritage to lose keen potency over a very important, though not numerically great, minority of our species.

Man's first instincts and emotions formed his response to the environment in which he found himself. Definite feelings based on pleasure and pain grew up around the phenomena whose causes and effects he understood, whilst around those which he did not understand — and the universe teemed with them in the early days — were naturally woven such personifications, marvelous interpretations, and sensations of awe and fear as would be hit upon by a race having few and simple ideas and limited experience. The unknown, being likewise the unpredictable, became for our primitive forefathers a terrible and omnipotent source of boons and calamities visited upon mankind for cryptic and wholly extra-terrestrial reasons, and thus clearly belonging to spheres of existence whereof we know nothing and wherein we have no part. The phenomenon of dreaming likewise helped to build up the notion of an unreal or spiritual world; and in general, all the conditions of savage dawn-life so strongly conducted toward a feeling of the supernatural, that we need not wonder at the thoroughness with which man's very hereditary essence has become saturated with religion and superstition. That saturation must, as a matter of plain scientific fact, be regarded as virtually permanent so far as the subconscious mind and inner instincts are concerned; for though the area of the unknown has been steadily contracting for thousands of years, an infinite reservoir of mystery still engulfs most of the outer cosmos, whilst a vast residuum of powerful inherited associations clings round all the objects and processes that were once mysterious, however well they may now be explained. And more than this, there is an actual physiological fixation of the old instincts in our nervous tissue, which would make them obscurely operative even were the conscious mind to be purged of all sources of wonder.

Because we remember pain and the menace of death more vividly than pleasure, and because our feelings toward the beneficent aspects of the unknown have from the first been captured and formalised by conventional religious rituals, it has fallen to the lot of the darker and more maleficent side of cosmic mystery to figure chiefly in our popular supernatural folklore. This tendency, too, is naturally enhanced by the fact that uncertainty and danger are always closely allied; thus making any kind of an unknown world a world of peril and evil possibilities. When to this sense of fear and evil the inevitable fascination of wonder and curiosity is superadded, there is born a composite body of keen emotion and imaginative provocation whose vitality must of necessity endure as long as the human race itself. Children will always be afraid of the dark, and men with minds sensitive to hereditary impulse will always tremble at the thought of the hidden and fathomless worlds of strange life which may pulsate in the gulfs beyond the stars, or press hideously upon our own globe in unholy dimensions which only the dead and the moonstruck can glimpse.

With this foundation, no one need wonder at the existence of a literature of cosmic fear. It has always existed, and always will exist ...

Part 3

Rediscovering the Gothic

The relationship between the Gothic Revival in architecture and design, and the Gothic as a literary genre is a complex one, neither directly causal nor wholly incidental. The 'Gothic' may have a medieval setting, but it may not; artists and writers promoting the 'Gothic Revival' may address questions of imagination and the fantastic associated with the literary genre, but they may not. This selection draws out these issues, focusing on materials that appeared when both the Gothic and the Gothic Revival were at their height.

It is not the purpose of these extracts to demonstrate in any technical or very detailed way the ascent of Gothic motifs and structures in architecture, nor the development of architectural history, with its elaboration of increasingly comprehensive and precise periodisations and stylistic vocabularies, although both of these themes are, perforce, alluded to in passing among the excerpts appearing here. The focus is, rather, on the emotional and psychological potency of the Gothic style, as it appeared to enthusiasts through the later eighteenth and nineteenth centuries, and the shifting structures of aesthetic judgement that allowed these aberrant resonances a place in the realm of taste.

3.1

The Case Against the Gothic

The dominant view of medieval architecture through the first half of the eighteenth century was that it was artless, barbaric, and, by virtue of its apparently indissoluble associations with the Roman Catholic Church, too full of superstitious feeling to be legitimately appreciated by the modern Briton. The classical style of ancient Greece and Rome represented, instead, the rationalism and artful grandeur to which such clear-minded and sophisticated Protestant citizens were meant to aspire.

The texts from Addison and Hume presented here demonstrate the assertion of this standard of taste on the part of an urban and urbane educated elite, while the short article from *The Builder's Magazine* sums up the more technical complaint about the illogic and ill-proportions of the style. The section from Smollett's comic novel *The Expedition of Humphrey Clinker* more ironically lays out the case against Gothic, while conveniently outlining some of the dominant theories about the cultural origins of the architectural style (theories that were already rather old-fashioned). The correspondent is the bluff and prejudiced Matthew Bramble.

The cultural critics of the 1750s and 1760s became concerned, as part of a continuing critique of modern manners stemming from *The Spectator* and its ilk, to attack the frivolous and irrational character of fashion. The appearance of the 'Gothic', along with the 'Chinese', in contemporary design registered the decay of taste as a consequence of material luxury, moral corruption and the introduction of feminine or effeminated influences. The excerpt from *The Connoisseur*, an essay-journal edited and largely written by Bonnell Thornton and George Colman, exemplifies this perspective, which helped define a bluff, masculine, patriotic opposition to modern innovations.

26 June 1712

Joseph Addison 1679–1719
The Spectator, no.415

Let any one reflect on the Disposition of Mind he finds in himself, at his first Entrance into the *Pantheon* at *Rome*, and how his Imagination is filled with something Great and Amazing; and, at the same time, how little, in proportion, he is affected with the Inside of a *Gothick* Cathedral, tho' it be five times larger than the other; which can arise from nothing else, but the Greatness of the Manner of the one, and the Meanness of the other.

1742

David Hume 1711–78
'Of Simplicity and Refinement'

... Productions, which are merely surprising, without being natural, can never give any lasting Entertainment to the Mind. To draw Chimeras is not, properly speaking, to copy or imitate. The Justness of the Representation is lost, and the Mind is displeas'd to find a Picture, which bears no Resemblance to any Original. Nor are such excessive Refinements more agreeable in the epistolary or philosophic stile, than in the Epic or Tragic. Too much Ornament is a fault in every Kind of Production. Uncommon Expressions, strong Flashes of Wit, pointed Similies, and epigrammatic Turns, especially when laid too thick, are a Disfigurement, rather than any Embellishment of Discourse. As the Eye, in surveying a *Gothic* Building, is distracted by the Multiplicity of Ornaments, and loses the whole by its minute Attention to the Parts'; so the Mind, in perusing a Work overstock'd with Wit, is fatigu'd and disgusted with the constant Endeavour to shine and surprize.

13 May 1758

Bonnell Thornton 1724–68 and George Colman 1732–94
The Connoisseur, no.120

TASTE is at present the darling idol of the polite world, and the world of letters; and, indeed, seems to be considered as the quintessence of almost all the arts and sciences. The fine ladies and gentlemen dress with Taste; the architects, whether Gothic or Chinese, build with Taste; the painters paint with Taste; the poets write with Taste; and, in short, fiddlers, players, singers, dancers, and mechanics themselves, are all the sons and daughters of

Taste. Yet, in this amazing superabundancy of Taste, few can say what it really is, or what the word itself signifies.

... The first species of Taste, which gives a loose to the imagination, indulges itself in caprice, and is perpetually striking new notes, is the chief regulator of fashion. In dress, it has put hunting poles into the hands of our gentlemen, and erected coaches and windmills on the heads of our ladies. In equipage, it has built chariots of *papier maché*, and, by putting spotted Danish horses, into harness, has made our beaux look like Bacchus in his car drawn by leopards. The ornaments, both on the outside and inside of our houses, are all Gothic or Chinese; and whoever makes a pagod of his parlour, throws a plank or two with an irregular cross-barred paling over a dirty ditch, or places battlements on a roof-house or a stable, fits up his house and garden entirely in Taste.

1771

Tobias Smollett 1721–71
The Expedition of Humphrey Clinker

To Dr LEWIS.

I have not found all the benefit I expected at Scarborough, where I have been these eight days — From Harrigate we came hither by the way of York, where we stayed only one day to visit the Castle, the Minster, and the Assembly-room. The first, which was heretofore a fortress, is now converted to a prison, and is the best, in all respects, I ever saw, at home or abroad — It stands in a high situation, extremely well ventilated; and has a spacious area within the walls, for the health and convenience of all the prisoners except those whom it is necessary to secure in close confinement — Even these last have all the comforts that the nature of their situation can admit. Here the assizes are held, in a range of buildings erected for that purpose.

As for the Minster, I know not how to distinguish it, except by its great size and the height of its spire, from those other ancient churches in different parts of the kingdom, which used to be called monuments of Gothic architecture; but it is now agreed, that this stile is Saracen rather than Gothic; and, I suppose, it was first imported into England from Spain, great part of which was under the dominion of the Moors. Those British architects, who adopted this stile, don't seem to have considered the propriety of their adoption. The climate of the country, possessed by the Moors or Saracens, both in Africa and Spain, was so exceedingly hot and dry, that those who built places of worship for the multitude, employed their talents in contriving edifices that should be cool; and, for this purpose, nothing could be better adopted than those buildings, vast, narrow, dark, and lofty, impervious to the sun-beams, and having little communication with the scorched external atmosphere; but ever affording a refreshing coolness, like subterranean cellars in the heats of summer, or natural caverns in the bowels of huge mountains. But nothing could be more preposterous, than to imitate such a mode of architecture in a country like England, where the climate is cold, and the air eternally loaded with vapours; and where, of consequence, the builder's intention should be to keep the people dry and warm — For my part, I never entered the Abbey church at Bath but once, and the moment I stept over the threshold, I found myself chilled to the very marrow of my bones — When we consider, that in our churches, in general, we breathe a gross stagnated air, surcharged with damps from vaults, tombs, and charnel-houses, may we not term them so many magazines of rheums, created for the benefit of the medical faculty? and safely aver, that more bodies are lost, than souls saved, by going to church, in the winter especially, which may be said to engross eight months in the year. I should be glad to know, what offence it would give to tender consciences, if the house of God was made more comfortable, or less dangerous to the health of valetudinarians; and whether it would not be an encouragement to piety, as well as the salvation of many lives, if the place of worship was well floored, wainscotted, warmed, and ventilated, and its area kept sacred from the pollution of the dead. The practice of burying in churches was the effect of ignorant superstition, influenced by knavish priests, who pretended that the devil could have no power over the defunct if he was interred in holy ground; and this, indeed, is the only reason that can be given for consecrating all cemeteries, even at this day.

The external appearance of an old cathedral cannot be but displeasing to the eye of every man, who has any idea of propriety and proportion, even though he may be ignorant of architecture as a science; and the long slender spire puts one in mind of a criminal impaled with a sharp stake rising up through his shoulder — These towers, or steeples, were likewise borrowed from the Mahometans; who, having no bells, used such minarets for the purpose of calling the people to prayers — They may be of further use, however, for making observations and signals; but I would vote for their being distinct from the body of the church, because they serve only to make the pile more barbarous, or Saracenical.

[...]

Yours, Matt. Bramble
Scarborough, July 4

1774

The Builder's Magazine: Or Monthly Companion for Architects, Carpenters, Masons, Bricklayers, &c

Gothic *Architecture*, is that which deviates from the proportions, characters, &c. of the antique. It is frequently very solid, heavy and massive; and sometimes, on the contrary, exceedingly light, delicate, and rich. The abundance of little, whimsical, wild, and chimerical ornaments, are its most usual characters. The profiles of this are generally very incorrect. Gothic architecture is distinguished into two kinds, ancient and modern. The ancient is that which was brought by the Goths into Germany in the fifth century. The edifices built in this manner were exceedingly massive, heavy, and coarse. Those of the modern Gothic run into the other extreme, being light, delicate, and rich to excess. All the ancient cathedrals are of this kind. It is not to be doubted, but that the inventors of the Gothic architecture thought they had far surpassed the Greek architects. A Greek building has not one ornament, but what adds beauty to the whole. No daring out-of-the-way strokes, nothing quaint to impose on the eye. The proportions are so just, that nothing appears very grand in itself, although the whole is striking and noble. On the contrary, in the Gothic architecture, we see large vaults raised on slender pillars, which one would expect every minute to tumble down, though they will stand for many ages. Every thing is crammed with windows, roses, crosses, figures, &c.

3.2

Gothic Meditations

With Addisons's essay in issue no.26 of *The Spectator*, representing the reflections of the fictitious character Sir Roger de Coverley in Westminster Abbey, we may sense a more sensitive appreciation of the Gothic, if not as an architectural style, at least as a fittingly numinous setting for philosophical meditation.

The mid-eighteenth century saw the production of a number of poetic texts dwelling on the theme of melancholy reflection. Robert Blair (1699–1746), Thomas Gray (1716–71) and others, known as the 'Graveyard Poets', take a cue from the solitary contemplation of graveyards or ruined abbeys to meditate on mortality, time and fate. Although not intended to inspire horror, in the sensationalist sense, and rather meant as philosophical and sentimental, these texts anticipate some important aspects of the Gothic novel of later decades. Widely republished and enthusiastically read by generations, the 'Graveyard Poets' continued as a major point of reference for many decades.

30 March 1711

Joseph Addison 1672–1719
The Spectator, no.26

When I am in a serious Humour, I often walk by my self in *Westminster* Abbey; where the Gloominess of the Place, and the Use to which it is applied, with the Solemnity of the Building, and the Condition of the People who lye in it, are apt to fill the Mind with a kind of Melancholy, or rather Thoughtfulness, that is not disagreeable. I Yesterday pass'd a while Afternoon in the Churchyard, the Cloysters, and the Church, amusing myself with the Tomb-stones and Inscriptions that I met with in those several Regions of the Dead. Most of them recorded nothing else of the buried Person, but that he was born upon one Day, and died upon another: The whole History of his Life, being comprehended in those two Circumstances that are common to all Mankind. I could not but look upon these Registers of Existence, whether of Brass or Marble, as a kind of Satyr upon the departed Persons; who had left no other Memorial of them, but that they were born and that they died ...

Upon my going into the Church, I entertain'd myself with the digging of a Grave; and saw in every shovel-full of it that was thrown up, the Fragment of a Bone or Skull intermixt with a kind of fresh mouldering Earth, that some time or other had a Place in the Composition of a humane Body. Upon this I began to consider with myself what innumerable Multitudes of People lay confus'd together under the Pavement of that ancient Cathedral; how Men and Women, Friends and Enemies, Priests and Soldiers, Monks and prebendaries, were crumbled against one another, and blended together in the same common Mass; how Beauty, Strength, and Youth, with Old-age, Weakness, and Deformity, lay undistinguish'd in the same promiscuous Heap of Matter.

[...]

I have left the Repository of our English kings for the Contemplation of another Day, when I shall find my Mind disposed for so serious an Amusement. I know that Entertainments of this Nature, are apt to raise dark and dismal Thoughts in timorous Minds and gloomy Imaginations; but for my own Part, though I am always serious, I do not know what it is to be melancholy; and can therefore take a View of Nature in her deep and solemn Scenes, with the same Pleasure as her most gay and delightful ones. By this Means I can improve my self with those Objects which others consider with Terrour. When I look upon the Tombs of the Great, every Emotion of Envy dies in me; when I read the Epitaphs of the Beautiful, every inordinate Desire goes out; when I meet with the Grief of Parents upon a Tomb-stone, my Heart melts with Compassion; when I see the Tomb of the Parents themselves, I consider the Vanity of grieving for those whom we must quickly follow; when I see kings lying by those who deposed them, when I consider rival wits placed side by side, or the holy men that divided the world with their contests and disputes, I reflect with sorrow and astonishment on the little competitions, factions, and debates of mankind. When I read the several dates of the tombs, of some that died yesterday, and some six hundred years ago, I consider that great day when we shall all of us be contemporaries, and make our appearance together.

1743

Robert Blair 1699–1746
The Grave (ll. 1–44)

Whilst some affect the Sun, and some the Shade,
Some flee the City, some the Hermitage;
Their Aims as various, as the Roads they take
In Journeying thro' Life; — the Task be mine,
To paint the gloomy Horrors of the *Tomb*;
Th' appointed Place of Rendezvous, where all
These Travellers meet. Thy Succours I implore,
Eternal King! whose potent Arm sustains
The Keys of Hell and Death. THE GRAVE, dread Thing!
Men shiver, when thou'rt nam'd: Nature appall'd
Shakes off her wonted Firmness. Ah ! how dark
The long-extended Realms, and rueful Wastes!
Where nought but Silence reigns, and Night, dark Night,
Dark as was Chaos, 'ere the Infant Sun
Was roll'd together, or had try'd his Beams
Athwart the Gloom profound! The sickly Taper
By glimm'ring thro' thy low-brow'd misty Vaults,
(Furr'd round with mouldy Damps, and ropy Slime)
Lets fall a supernumerary Horror,
And only serves to make thy Night more irksome.
Well do I know thee by thy trusty *ew*,
Cheerless, unsocial Plant! that loves to dwell
'Midst Sculls and Coffins, Epitaphs and Worms:
Where light-heel'd Ghosts, and visionary Shades,
Beneath the wan, cold Moon (as Fame reports)
Embody'd thick, perform their Mystick Rounds,
No other merriment, dull tree! is thine.

See yonder Hallow'd Fane! the pious Work
Of Names once fam'd, now dubious or forgot,
And buried' midst the Wreck of Things which were:
There lie interr'd the more illustrious Dead.
The Wind is up: Hark! how it howls! Methinks
Till now, I never heard a Sound so dreary:
Doors creak, and Windows clap, and Night's foul Bird,
Rook'd in the Spire screams loud; the gloomy Isles
Black plaster'd, and hung round with Shreds of
'Scutcheons,
And tatter'd Coats of Arms, send back the Sound,
Laden with heavier Airs, from the low Vaults,
The Mansions of the Dead. Rous'd from their Slumbers,
In grim Array the grisly Spectres rise,
Grin horrible, and, obstinately sullen
Pass and repass, hush'd as the Foot of Night.
Again! the Screech-Owl shrieks! Ungracious Sound!
I'll hear no more; it makes one's Blood run chill ...

1751

Thomas Gray 1716–71
Elegy Written in a Country Churchyard

The *Curfeu* tolls the Knell of parting Day,
The lowing Herd wind slowly o'er the Lea,
The Plow-man homeward plods his weary Way,
And leaves the World to Darkness, and to me.
  Now fades the glimmering Landscape on the Sight,
And all the Air a solemn Stillness holds;
Save where the Beetle wheels his droning Flight,
And drowsy Tinklings lull the distant Folds.
  Save that from yonder Ivy-mantled Tow'r
The moping Owl does to the Moon complain
Of such, as wand'ring near her secret Bow'r,
Molest her ancient solitary Reign.
  Beneath those rugged Elms, that Yew-Tree's Shade,
Where heaves the Turf in many a mould'ring Heap,
Each in his narrow Cell for ever laid,
The rude Forefathers of the Hamlet sleep.
  The breezy Call of Incense-breathing Morn,
The Swallow twitt'ring from the Straw-built Shed,
The Cock's shrill Clarion, or the echoing Horn,
No more shall wake them from their lowly Bed.
  For them no more the blazing Hearth shall burn,
Or busy Houswife ply her Evening Care:
No Children run to lisp their Sire's Return,
Or climb his Knees the envied Kiss to share.
  Oft did the Harvest to their Sickle yield,
Their Furrow oft the stubborn Glebe has broke;

How jocund did they drive their Team Afeld!
How bow'd the Woods beneath their sturdy Stroke!
Let not Ambition mock their useful Toil,
Their homely Joys, and Destiny obscure;
Nor Grandeur hear with a disdainful Smile
The short and simple Annals of the Poor.
The Boast of Heraldry, the Pomp of Pow'r,
And all that Beauty, all that Wealth e'er gave,
Awaits alike th' inevitable Hour.
The Paths of Glory lead but to the Grave.
Forgive, ye Proud, th' involuntary Fault,
If memory to these no Trophies raise,
Where thro' the long-drawn Isle and fretted Vault
The pealing Anthem swells the Note of Praise.
Can storied Urn or animated Bust
Back to its Mansion call the fleeting Breath?
Can Honour's Voice provoke the silent Dust,
Or Flatt'ry soothe the dull cold Ear of Death!
Perhaps in this neglected Spot is laid
Some Heart once pregnant with celestial Fire;
Hands, that the Reins of Empire might have sway'd,
Or wak'd to Extacy the living Lyre.
But Knowledge to their Eyes her ample Page
Rich with the Spoils of Time did ne'er unroll;
Chill Penury repress'd their noble Rage,
And froze the genial Current of the Soul.
Full many a Gem of purest Ray serene,
The dark unfathom'd Caves of Ocean bear:
Full many a Flower is born to blush unseen,
And waste its Sweetness on the desart Air.
Some village — *Hampden*, that with dauntless Breast
The little Tyrant of his Fields withstood;
Some mute inglorious *Milton* here may rest,
Some *Cromwell* guiltless of his Country's Blood.
Th' Applause of list'ning Senates to command,
The Threats of Pain and Ruin to despise,
To scatter Plenty o'er a smiling Land,
And read their Hist'ry in a Nation's Eyes,
Their Lot forbad: nor circumscrib'd alone
Their growing Virtues, but their Crimes confin'd;
Forbad to wade through Slaughter to a Throne,
And shut the Gates of Mercy on Mankind,
The struggling Pangs of conscious Truth to hide,
To quench the Blushes of ingenuous Shame,
Or heap the Shrine of Luxury and Pride
With Incense, kindled at the Muse's Flame.
Far from the madding Crowd's ignoble Strife,
Their sober Wishes never learn'd to stray;
Along the cool sequester'd Vale of Life
They kept the noiseless Tenor of their way.
Yet ev'n these Bones from Insult to protect,
Some frail Memorial still erected nigh,
With uncouth Rhimes and shapeless Sculpture deck'd,
Implores the passing Tribute of a Sigh.
Their Name, their Years, spelt by th' unletter'd Muse,
ThePlace of Fame and Elegy supply:
And many a holy Text around she strews,
That teach the rustic Moralist to dye.
For who to dumb Forgetfulness a Prey,
This pleasing anxious Being e'er resign'd,
Left the warm Precincts of the chearful Day,
Nor cast one longing ling'ring Look behind!
On some fond Breast the parting Soul relies,
Some pious Drops the closing Eye requires;
Ev'n from the Tomb the Voice of Nature cries,
Awake, and faithful to her wanted Fires.
For thee, who mindful of th' unhonour'd Dead
Dost in these Lines their artless Tale relate;
If chance, by lonely Contemplation led,
Some hidden Spirit shall inquire thy Fate,
Haply some hoary-headed Swain may say,
'Oft have we seen him at the Peep of Dawn
Brushing with hasty Steps the Dews away
To meet the sun upon the upland lawn.
'There at the Foot of yonder nodding Beech
That wreathes its old fantastic Roots so high,
His listless Length at Noontide wou'd he stretch,
And pore upon the Brook that babbles by.
'Hard by yon Wood, now smiling as in Scorn,
Mutt'ring his wayward Fancies he wou'd rove,
Now drooping, woeful wan, like one forlorn,
Or craz'd with Care, or cross'd in hopeless Love.
'One Morn I miss'd him on the custom'd hill,
Along the Heath and near his fav'rite Tree;
Another came; nor yet beside the Rill,
Nor up the Lawn, nor at the Wood was he;
'The next with Dirges due in sad Array
Slow thro' the Church-way Path we saw him born.
Approach and read (for thou can'st read) the Lay,
Grav'd on the Stone beneath yon aged Thorn.'

THE EPITAPH

Here rests his Head upon the Lap of Earth
A Youth to Fortune and to Fame unknown:
Fair Science frown'd not on his humble Birth,
And Melancholy mark'd him for her own.
Large was his Bounty, and his Soul sincere,
Heav'n did a Recompense as largely send:
He gave to Mis'ry all he had, a Tear,
He gain'd from Heav'n ('twas all he wish'd) a Friend.
No farther seek his Merits to disclose,
Or draw his Frailties from their dread Abode,
(There they alike in trembling Hope repose)
The Bosom of his Father and his God.

17
Philip James de Loutherbourg
A Philosopher in a Moonlit Churchyard, 1790
Oil on canvas 86.3 × 68.5 cm
Paul Mellon Collection, Yale Center for British Art, New Haven

18
Thomas Gainsborough
Wooded Landscape with Peasant Reading Tombstone, Rustic Lovers and Ruined Church
1779–80, reprinted 1797
Soft-ground etching
29.8 × 39.4 cm
Tate. Presented by A.E. Anderson 1910

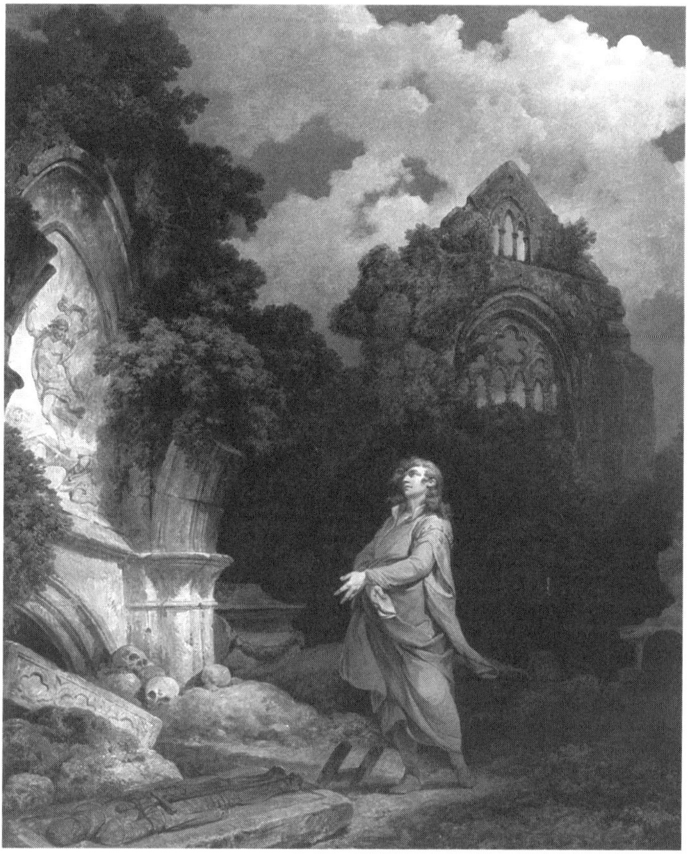

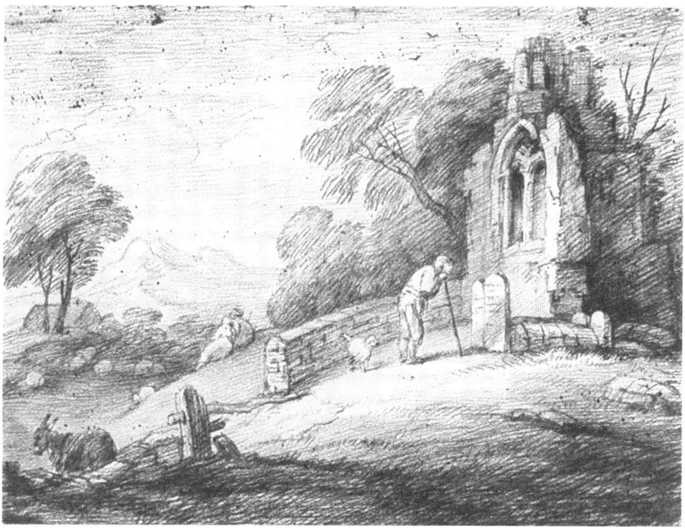

3.3

The Case for Gothic: Relativist Perspectives

The mid-eighteenth century was a seminal moment in the development of aesthetics as a philosophical discipline. The consideration of the value and nature of works of art became removed from wider societal considerations and from purely technical contexts, to become a debate in its own right. The judgement of taste emerged as a means of asserting social authority and personal quality in more subtle and elusive ways than previously; the unconscious tendencies which informed such judgements were given a new emphasis, partly undermining the idea that a work of art or literature could be explained with reference to an established set of rules.

In this context, the possibility that unconventional literary or artistic forms could be reappraised emerged with vigour. Edmund Spenser, Shakespeare and Gothic architecture were each subjected to novel interpretations, which did not seek to excuse their deviations from the orderly rules and symmetry of classical literature and design, and sought instead to evaluate them in relation to the standards of their own times and in relation to specific cultural contexts. The texts excerpted here give a flavour of these new relativist approaches, and the implications of these for the taste for the Gothic, in the widest sense.

1715

John Hughes 1677–1720
Preface to Spenser's *Fairie Queene*

The want of Unity in the Story makes it difficult for the Reader to carry it in his Mind, and distracts too much his Attention to the several Parts of it; and indeed the whole Frame of it wou'd appear monstrous, if it were to be examin'd by the Rules of Epick Poetry, as they have been drawn from the Practice of *Homer* and *Virgil*. But as it is plain the Author never design'd it by those Rules, I think it ought rather to be consider'd as a Poem of a particular kind, describing in a Series of Allegorical Adventures or Episodes the most noted Virtues and Vices: to compare it therefore with the Models of Antiquity, wou'd be like drawing a Parallel between the *Roman* and the *Gothick* Architecture. In the first there is doubtless a more natural Grandeur and Simplicity: in the latter, we find great Mixtures of Beauty and Barbarism, yet assisted by the Invention of a Variety of interior Ornaments; and tho the former is more majestick as a whole, the latter may be very surprizing and agreeable in its Parts.

1753

William Hogarth 1697–1764
The Analysis of Beauty

Westminster Abbey is a good contrast to St Paul's, with regard to simplicity and distinctness, the great number of its filligrean ornaments, and small divided and subdivided parts appear confused when nigh, and are totally lost at a moderate distance; yet there is nevertheless such a consistency of parts altogether in a good gothic taste, and such propriety relative to the gloomy ideas, they were calculated to convey, that they have at length acquir'd an establish'd and distinct character in building. It would be looked upon as an impropriety and as a kind of provocation to build places for mirth and entertainment in the same taste.

1762

Horace Walpole 1717–97
Anecdotes of Painting, vol.1

It is difficult for the noblest Grecian temple to convey half so many impressions to the mind, as a cathedral does of the best Gothic taste — a proof of skill in the architects and of address in the priests who erected them. The latter exhausted their knowledge of the passions in composing edifices whose pomp, mechanism, vaults, tombs, painted windows, gloom and perspectives infused such sensations of romantic devotion;

and they were happy in finding artists capable of executing such machinery.

One must have taste to be sensible to the beauties of Grecian architecture; one only wants passions to feel Gothic. In St Peter's one is convinced that it was built by great princes — In Westminster Abbey, one thinks not of the builder; the religion of the place makes its first impression — and though stripped of its altars and shrines, it is nearer converting one to popery than all the regular pageantry of Roman domes. Gothic churches infuse superstition; Grecian, admiration. The papal see amassed its wealth by Gothic cathedrals, and displays it in Grecian temples.

I certainly do not mean by this little contrast to make any comparison between the rational beauties of regular architecture, and the unrestrained licentiousness of that which is called Gothic. Yet I am clear that the persons who executed the latter, had much more knowledge of their art, more taste, more genius, and more propriety than we chuse to imagine. There is a magic hardiness in the execution of some of their works which could not have sustained themselves if dictated by mere caprice. There is a tradition that Sir Christopher Wren went once a year to survey the roof of the chapel of King's college, and said that if any man would show him where to place the first stone, he would engage to build such another. That there is in great grace in several places even in their clutter of slender pillars, and in the application of their ornaments, though the principles of the latter are so confined that they may almost all be reduced to the trefoil, extended and varied, I shall not appeal to the edifices themselves — It is sufficient to observe, that Inigo Jones, Sir Christopher Wren and Kent, who certainly understood beauty, blundered into the heaviest and clumsiest composition whenever they aimed at imitations of the Gothic — Is an art despicable in which a great master cannot shine?

1762

Richard Hurd 1720–1808
Letters on Chivalry and Romance

When an architect examines a Gothic structure by Grecian rules, he finds nothing but deformity. But the Gothic architecture has it's own rules, by which when it comes to be examined, it is seen to have it's merit, as well as the Grecian. The question is not, which of the two is conducted in the simplest or truest taste: but, whether there be not sense and design in both, when scrutinized by the laws on which each is projected.

1767

William Duff 1732–1815
An Essay on Original Genius

A Genius for Architecture truly ORIGINAL, will, by the native force and plastic power of Imagination, strike out for itself new and surprising Models in this Art; and, by its combining faculty, will select out of the infinite variety of ideal forms that float in the mind, those of the Grand and Beautiful, which it will unite in one consummate as well as uncommon design. We have already observed, that every original Genius, whether in Architecture or in any other of the liberal Arts, is peculiarly distinguished by a powerful bias to INVENTION. It was this bias which we may call the instinctive, insuppressible Impulse of Genius, whose spontaneous efforts designed those stupendous Gothic structures, that appear so magnificent in their ruins. The Architects, who first planned those edifices, though unacquainted with the polite Arts, or with the *Grecian* and *Roman* Architecture, were doubtless great Originals in their profession, since they planned them by the unaided strength of their own Genius. Their untutored imaginations prompted them to aspire to the Solemn, the Vast, and the Wonderful; and allowing an unbounded scope to the exercise of this faculty, they were enabled to give to their buildings that awful, though irregular grandeur, which elevates the mind, and produces the most pleasing astonishment. These Gothic edifices shew the inventive power of the human mind in a striking light, and are sufficient to convince us, that excellence in Architecture was not confined to the *Greeks* and *Romans*, but may be sometimes displayed among a people in other respects barbarous.

1780

Horace Walpole 1717–97
Preface to vol.4 of *Anecdotes of Painting*

This delicate redundance of ornament growing into our architecture might perhaps be checked, if our artists would study the sublime dreams of Piranesi, who seems to have conceived visions of Rome beyond what it boasted even in the meridian of its splendour. Savage as Salvator Rosa, fierce as Michael Angelo, and exuberant as Rubens, he has imagined scenes that would startle geometry, and exhaust the Indies to realize. He piles palaces on bridges, and temples on palaces, and scales Heaven with mountains of edifices. Yet what taste in his boldness! what grandeur in his wildness! what labour and thought both in his rashness and details! Architecture, indeed, has in a manner two sexes; its masculine dignity can only exert its muscles in public works and at public expense; its softer beauties come better within the compass of private residence and enjoyment.

19 (below)
Giovanni Battista Piranesi
Title page to Invenzioni Capric. ai Carceri (Fanciful Images of Prisons), c.1749–50
Etching 54.5 × 41 cm
The British Museum, London

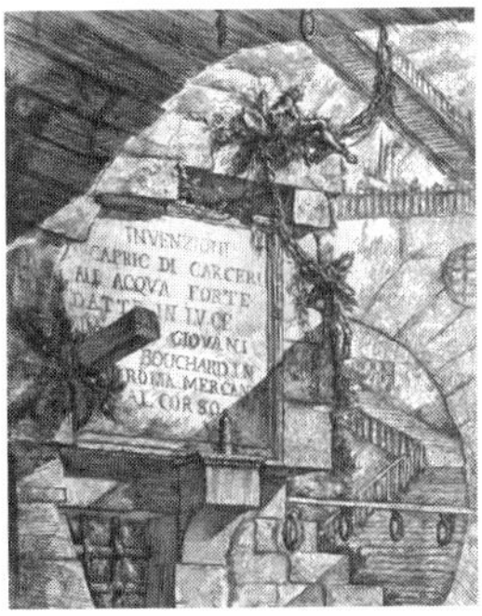

1786

Joshua Reynolds 1723–92
Discourses on Art, XIII

There is in Architecture, as in Painting, an inferior branch of art, in which the imagination appears to have no concern. It does not however acquire the name of a polite and liberal art, from its usefulness, or administering to our wants or necessities, but from some higher principle: we are sure that in the hands of a man of genius it is capable of inspiring sentiment, and of filling the mind with great and sublime ideas.

It may be worth the attention of Artists, to consider in what materials are in the hands, that may contribute to this end; and whether this art has it not in its power to address itself to the imagination with effect, by more ways than are generally employed by Architects.

To pass over the effect produced by that general sympathy and proportion, by which the eye is delighted, as the ear is with musick, Architecture certainly possesses many principles in common with Poetry and Painting. Among those which may be reckoned as the first, is, that of affecting the imagination by means of association of ideas. Thus, for instance, as we have naturally a veneration for antiquity, whatever building brings to our remembrance ancient custom and manners, such as the Castles of the Barons of ancient Chivalry, is sure to give this delight. Hence it is that towers and battlements are so often selected by the Painter and the Poet, to make a part of the composition of their ideal Landskip; and it is from hence in a good degree, that in the buildings of Vanbrugh, who was a poet as well as an Architect, there is a greater display of imagination, than we shall find perhaps in any other; and this is the ground and the effect which we feel in many of his works, notwithstanding the faults with which many of them are justly charged. For this purpose, Vanbrugh appears to have had recourse to some principles of Gothick Architecture; which, though not so ancient as the Grecian, is more so to our imagination, with which the Artist is more concerned than with absolute truth.

1788–1818

Henry Fuseli 1741–1825
Aphorisms on Art, no. 105

We are more impressed by Gothic than by Greek mythology, because the bands are not yet rent which tie us to its magic; he has a powerful hold on us who holds by our superstition or by a theory of honour.

3.4

The Possibilities of the Sublime

As conceived by Edmund Burke, the Sublime was pre-eminently evident in works of nature and acts of God. The works of man could, in effect, be only a pale imitation of the true grandeur manifested in these. Yet his evocative descriptions of the psychological and physiological effects of the Sublime held the possibility of finding these qualities in architecture and art. Such was certainly explored by the architectural critics of the rising generation, whose reappraisal of the Gothic as an historical style often rested on the evoking of the spiritual and emotional effects which were most effectively explained with reference to Burkean notions. The Catholic priest and religious controversialist John Milner (1752–1826) is excerpted here; his pioneering efforts in the field of architectural history contained within them a profound sense of spiritual need. His rejection of classical styles — so long associated with rational, clear-headed Protestantism — was necessarily politically loaded in a period when Catholicism was still effectively outlawed.

1757
2nd edition 1759

Edmund Burke 1729–97
A Philosophical Enquiry into the Origin of our Ideas of the Sublime and Beautiful

SUCCESSION **and** UNIFORMITY

Succession and uniformity of parts are what constitute the artificial infinite. 1. *Succession*; which is requisite that the parts may be continued so long and in such a direction, as by their frequent impulses on the sense to impress the imagination with an idea of their progress beyond their actual limits. 2. *Uniformity*; because if the figures of the parts should be changed, the imagination at every change finds a check; you are presented at every alteration with the termination of one idea, and the beginning of another; by which means it becomes impossible to continue that uninterrupted progression, which alone can stamp on bounded objects the character of infinity. It is in this kind of artificial infinity, I believe, we ought to look for the cause why a rotund has such a noble effect. For in a rotund, whether it be a building or a plantation, you can nowhere fix a boundary; turn which way you will, the same object still seems to continue, and the imagination has no rest. But the parts must be uniform, as well as circularly disposed, to give this figure its full force; because any difference, whether it be in the disposition, or in the figure, or even in the color of the parts, is highly prejudicial to the idea of infinity, which every change must check and interrupt, at every alteration commencing a new series. On the same principles of succession and uniformity, the grand appearance of the ancient heathen temples, which were generally oblong forms, with a range of uniform pillars on every side, will be easily accounted for. From the same cause also may be derived the grand effect of the aisles in many of our own old cathedrals. The form of a cross used in some churches seems to me not so eligible as the parallelogram of the ancients; at least, I imagine it is not so proper for the outside. For, supposing the arms of the cross every way equal, if you stand in a direction parallel to any of the side walls, or colonnades, instead of a deception that makes the building more extended than it is, you are cut off from a considerable part (two-thirds) of its *actual* length; and to prevent all possibility of progression, the arms of the cross, taking a new direction, make a right angle with the beam, and thereby wholly turn the imagination from the repetition of the former idea. Or suppose the spectator placed where he may take a direct view of such a building, what will be the consequence? the necessary consequence will be, that a good part of the basis of each angle formed by the intersection of the arms of the cross, must be inevitably lost; the whole must of course assume a broken, unconnected figure; the lights must be unequal, here strong, and there weak; without that noble gradation which the perspective always effects on parts disposed uninterruptedly in a right line. Some or all of these objections will lie against every figure of a cross, in whatever view you take it. I exemplified them in the Greek cross, in which these faults appear the most strongly; but they appear in some degree in all sorts of crosses. Indeed there is nothing more prejudicial to the grandeur of buildings, than to abound in angles; a fault obvious in many; and owing to an inordinate thirst for variety, which, whenever it prevails, is sure to leave very little true taste.

Magnitude in BUILDING

To the sublime in building, greatness of dimension seems requisite; for on a few parts, and those small, the imagination cannot rise to any idea of infinity. No greatness in the manner can effectually compensate for the want of proper dimensions. There is no danger of drawing men into extravagant designs by this rule; it carries its own caution along with it. Because too great a length in buildings destroys the purpose of greatness, which it was intended to promote; the perspective will lessen it in height as it gains in length; and will bring it at last to a point; turning the whole figure into a sort of triangle, the poorest in its effect of almost any figure that can be presented to the eye. I have ever observed, that colonnades and avenues of trees of a moderate length, were, without comparison, far grander, than when they were suffered to run to immense distances. A true artist should put a generous deceit on the spectators, and effect the noblest designs by easy methods. Designs that are vast only by their dimensions, are always the sign of a common and low imagination. No work of art can be great, but as it deceives; to be otherwise is the prerogative of nature only. A good eye will fix the medium betwixt an excessive length or height, (for the same objection lies against both), and a short or broken quantity; and perhaps it might be ascertained to a tolerable degree of exactness, if it was my purpose to descend far into the particulars of any art.

1808

John Milner 1752–1826
'Observations on the Means Necessary for Further Illustrating the Ecclesiastical Architecture of the Middle Ages', in *Essays on Gothic Architecture*

The most curious and interesting fact, however, in my opinion, for the investigation of architectural antiquaries, is, to ascertain the true principles of *the Sublime and Beautiful*, as applied to those sacred fabrics which are the undoubted masterpieces and glory of the pointed order. It is in vain that Sir Christopher Wren and Mr Evelyn ... stigmatize these structures, as being 'congestions of heavy, dark, melancholy, monkish piles, without any just proportion, use, or beauty.' For it is confessedly true, that every man who has an eye to see, and a soul to feel, on entering into York minster and Chapter-house, or into King's college or Windsor chapel, or into the cathedrals of Lincoln or Winchester, is irresistibly struck with mingled impressions of awe and pleasure, which no other buildings are capable of producing; and however he may approve of the Grecian architecture for the purposes of civil and social life, yet he instinctively experiences in the former a frame of mind that fits him for prayer and contemplation, which all the boasted regularity and magnificence of Sir Christopher's and the nation's pride, I mean St Paul's cathedral, cannot communicate, at least in the same degree.

To explain in detail the principles on which the above-mentioned effects are produced, would be to describe the whole structure of an ancient cathedral; and, at the same time, to form the best panegyric on the architects who raised them. This, however, it is not my intention to do, but merely to enumerate a few of those principles which are more obvious. In the first place, then, it is well known that height and length are amongst the primary sources of *the Sublime*: it is equally agreed that these are the proportions which our ancient architects chiefly affected in their religious structures. But besides the real effect of these proportions, which were generally carried as far as they were capable of, the mind was farther impressed by an artificial height and length, which were the natural produce of the style employed. For the aspiring form of the pointed arches, the lofty pediments, and the tapering pinnacles with which our cathedrals are adorned, contribute perhaps still more to give an idea of height than their real elevation. In like manner, the perspective of uniform columns, ribs, and arches, repeated at equal distances, as they are seen in the aisles of those fabrics, produces an artificial infinite in the mind of the spectator, when the same extent of plain surface would perhaps hardly affect it at all. For a similar reason, I think the effect of the ancient cathedrals is greatly helped by the variety of the constituent parts and ornaments, though I suppose them all to be executed in one uniform style. The eye is quickly satisfied by any object, however great and magnificent, which it can take in all at once, as the mind is with what it can completely comprehend; but when the former, having wandered through the intricate and interminable length of a pointed vault in an ancient cathedral, discovers two parallel aisles of equal length and richness with it; thence proceeding, discovers the transepts, the side chapels, the choir, the sanctuary, and the Lady chapel, all equally interesting for their design and execution, and all of them calculated for different purposes, the eye, I say, in these circumstances, is certainly much more entertained, and the mind more dilated and gratified, than can

20
Thomas Girtin
Guisborough Priory, Yorkshire, 1801
Watercolour on paper
62.9 × 50.8 cm
Tate. Presented by the National Art Collections Fund (Herbert Powell Bequest) 1967

21
J.M.W. Turner
The Chancel and Crossing of Tintern Abbey, Looking towards the East Window, 1794
Pencil and watercolour on paper 35.8 × 25.5 cm
Tate. Bequeathed by the artist 1856

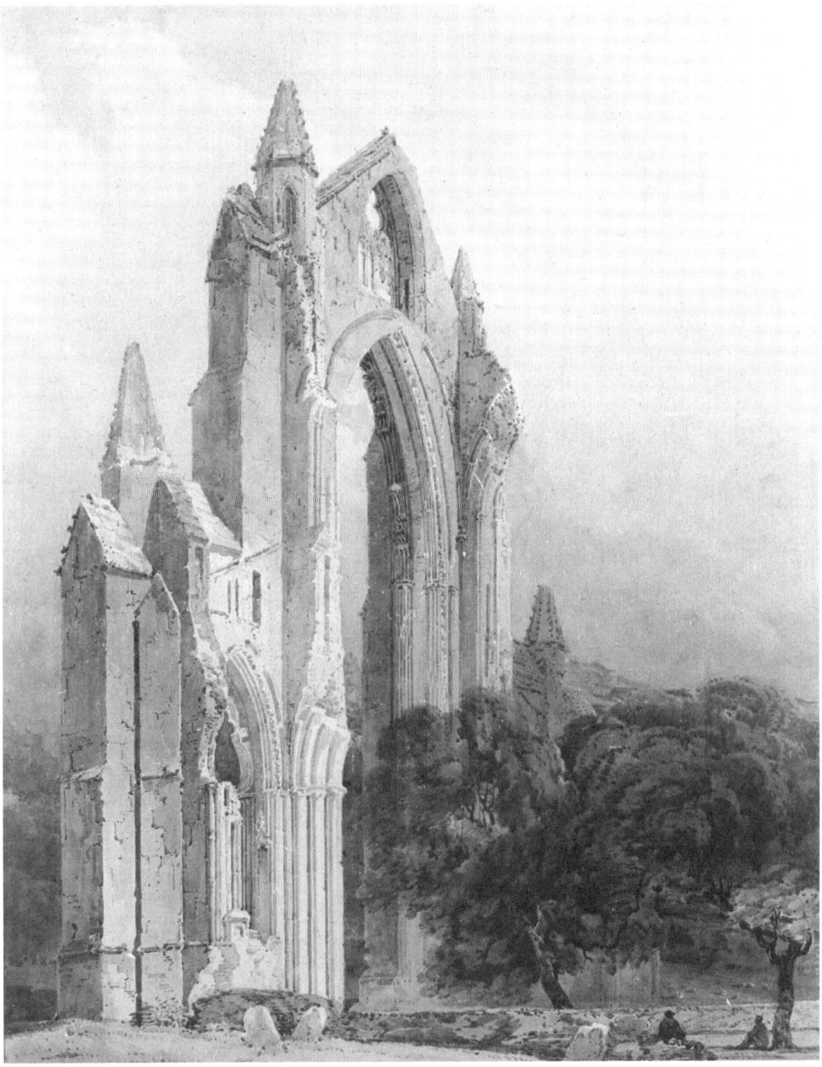

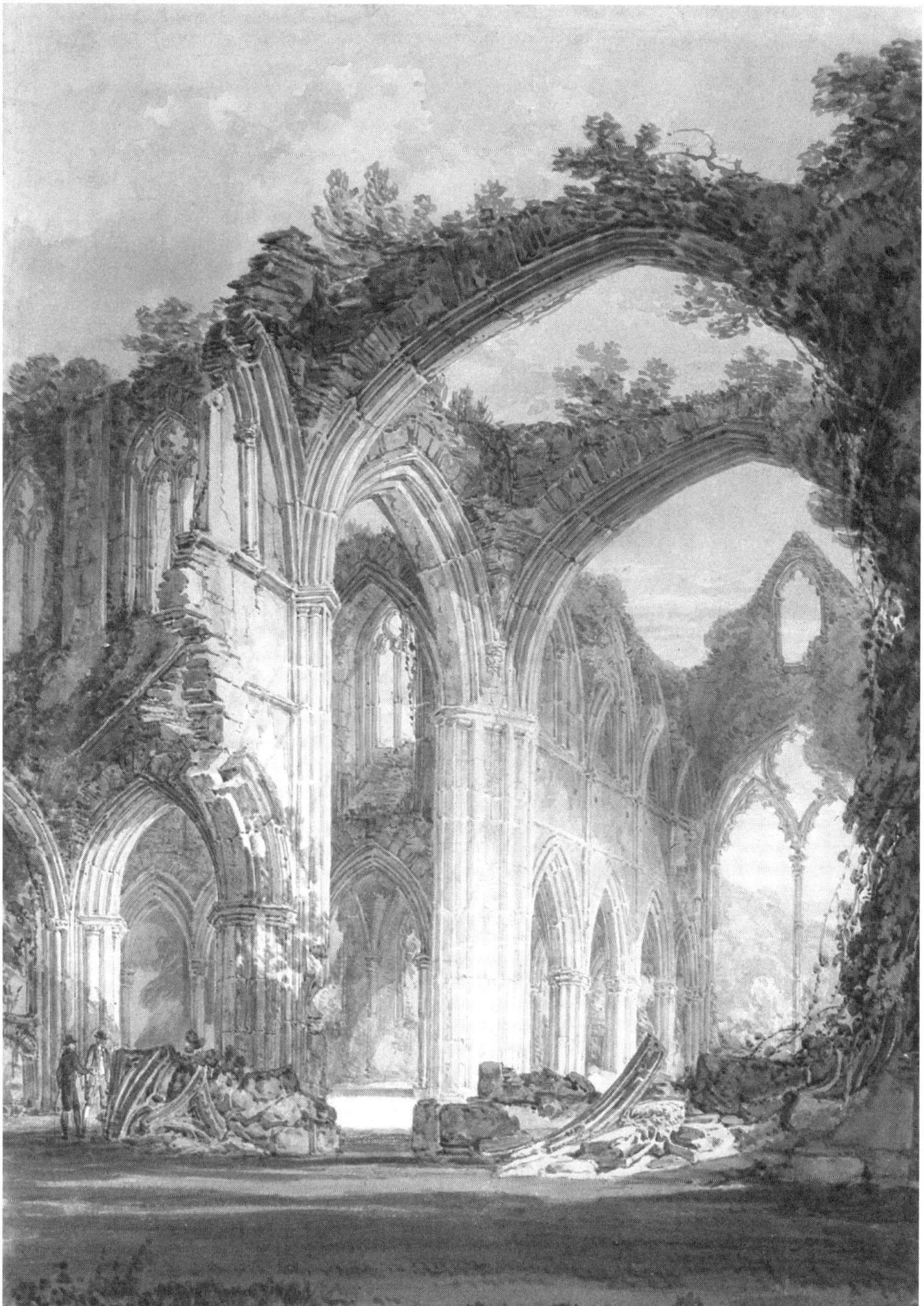

possibly be effected by any single view, even though our modern architects should succeed in their attempts to make one entire sweep of the contents of a cathedral, in order to shew it all at a single view, and to make one vast empty room of the whole.

It is not necessary for me to dwell upon the effects of that solemn gloom which reigns in these venerable structures, from the studied exclusion of too glaring a light, or upon that glowing effect produced by appropriate painting and carving of the windows, and other parts of them, or upon the essential beauty and just proportions in which they are raised, where the infinite variety of ribs, arches, bosses, and other ornaments, all grow out of the main columns, with the regularity of Nature in the vegetable kingdom, and also with her wise contrivance to combine strength with beauty; I say, it is not necessary for me to dwell upon these points, because, however they may be carped at by interested men, they are obvious of themselves, and admitted by all persons of candour and sentiment.

3.5

The Picturesque

The 'picturesque' was one of the key cultural terms of the late eighteenth and early nineteenth centuries. Referring, in its strict definition, to the suitability or susceptibility of a scene to pictorial representation, the 'picturesque' evoked a complex sense of the psychological, historical and emotional response to the landscape. While the Sublime landscape terrified and excited, the Picturesque view had more gentle, but no less potent effects. As theorised by William Gilpin, Uvedale Price, the poet William Mason and the connoisseur Richard Payne Knight, such scenes evoked, in their rugged variety, naturalness, asymmetry and bounty, a sense of profound, reflective pleasure. The buildings most suitable to the Picturesque — humble cottages, run-down working buildings and, above all, ruined abbeys and castles — enhanced such meditations by putting them in relation to human history. The conventions of the Picturesque encouraged, then, a new appreciation of medieval architecture, for its rich historical and emotional associations.

1783

William Mason 1724–97
The English Garden: A Poem, Bk. IV (ll. 65–109)

Crowning a gradual hill his Mansion rose
In antient English grandeur: Turrets, Spires,
And Windows, climbing high from base to roof
In wide and radient rows, bespoke its birth
Coëval with those rich cathedral fanes,
(Gothic ill-nam'd) where harmony results
From disunited parts; and shapes minute,
At once distinct and blended, boldly form
One vast majestic whole. No modern art
Had marr'd with misplac'd symmetry the Pile.
ALCANDER held it sacred: On a height,
Which westering to its site the front survey'd,
He first his taste employ'd: for there a line
Of thinly scatter'd Beech too tamely broke
The blank Horizon. 'Draw we round yon knowl,'
ALCANDER cry'd, 'in stately Norman mode,
A wall embattled; and within its guard
Let every structure needful for a Farm
Arise in Castle-semblance; the huge Barn
Shall with a mock Portcullis arm the gate,
Where Ceres entering, o'er the flail-proof floor
In golden triumph rides; some Tower rotund
Shall to the Pigeons and their callow young
Safe roost afford; and ev'ry buttress broad,
Whose proud projection seems a mass of stone,
Give space to stall the heifer, and the steed.
So shall each part, tho' turn'd to rural use,
Deceive the eye with those bold feudal forms
That Fancy loves to gaze on.' This achiev'd
Now nearer home he calls returning Art
To hide the structure rude where Winter pounds
In conic pit his congelations hoar,
That Summer may his tepid beverage cool
With the chill luxury; his Dairy too
There stands of form unsightly; both to veil,
He builds of old disjointed moss-grown stone
A time-struck Abbey*. An impending grove
Screens it behind with reverential shade;
While bright in front the stream reflecting spreads,
Which winds a mimic River o'er his Lawn.
The Fane conventual there is dimly seen,
The mitred Window, and the Cloister pale,
With many a mouldering Column; Ivy soon
Round the rude chinks her net of foliage spreads;
Its verdant meshes seem to prop the wall.

1794

Richard Payne Knight 1750–1824
The Landscape: A Didactic Poem, Bk. 2 (ll. 280–93)

Bless'd is the man in whose sequester'd glade,
Some ancient abbey's walls diffuse their shade;
With mouldering windows pierced, and turret's crown'd,
And pinnacles with clinging ivy bound.
Bless'd too is he, who, 'midst his tufted trees,
Some ruin'd castle's lofty towers sees;
Imbosom'd high upon the mountain's brow,
Or nodding o'er the stream that glides below.
Nor yet unenvy'd, to whose humbler lot
Falls the retired and antiquated cot; —
Its roof with weeds and mosses cover'd o'er,
And honeysuckles climbing round the door;
While mantling vines along its walls are spread,
And clustering ivy decks the chimney's head.

* It was said in the first Book, ver. 384, that of those architectural Objects which improved a fine natural English prospect, the two principal ones were a Castle and an Abbey. In conformity with this Idea, Alcander first begins to exercise his taste, by forming a resemblance of those two capital artificial features, uniting them, however, with utility. The precept is here meant to be conveyed by description, which had before been given more directly in Book II, ver. 21.

Beauty scorns to dwell
Where Use is exil'd.

1786

William Gilpin 1724–1804
Observations Relative Chiefly to Picturesque Beauty

To these natural features, which are, in a great degree, peculiar to the landscape of England, we may lastly add another, of the artificial kind — the ruins of abbeys; which, being naturalized to the soil, might indeed, without much impropriety, be classed among its natural beauties.

Ruins are commonly divided into two kinds; castles, and abbeys. Of the former few countries perhaps can produce so many, as this island; for which various causes may be assigned. The feudal system, which lasted long in England, and was carried high, produced a number of castles in every part. King Stephen's reign contributed greatly to multiply them. And in the northern counties, the continued wars with Scotland had the same effect. Many of these buildings, now fallen into decay, remain objects of great beauty.

In the ruins of castles however, other countries may compare with ours. But in the remains of abbeys no country certainly can.

Where popery prevails, the abbey is still intire and inhabited; and of course less adapted to landscape.

But it is the mode of architecture, which gives such excellence to these ruins. The Gothic style, in which they are generally composed, is, I apprehend, unrivalled among foreign nations; and may be called a peculiar feature in English landscape.

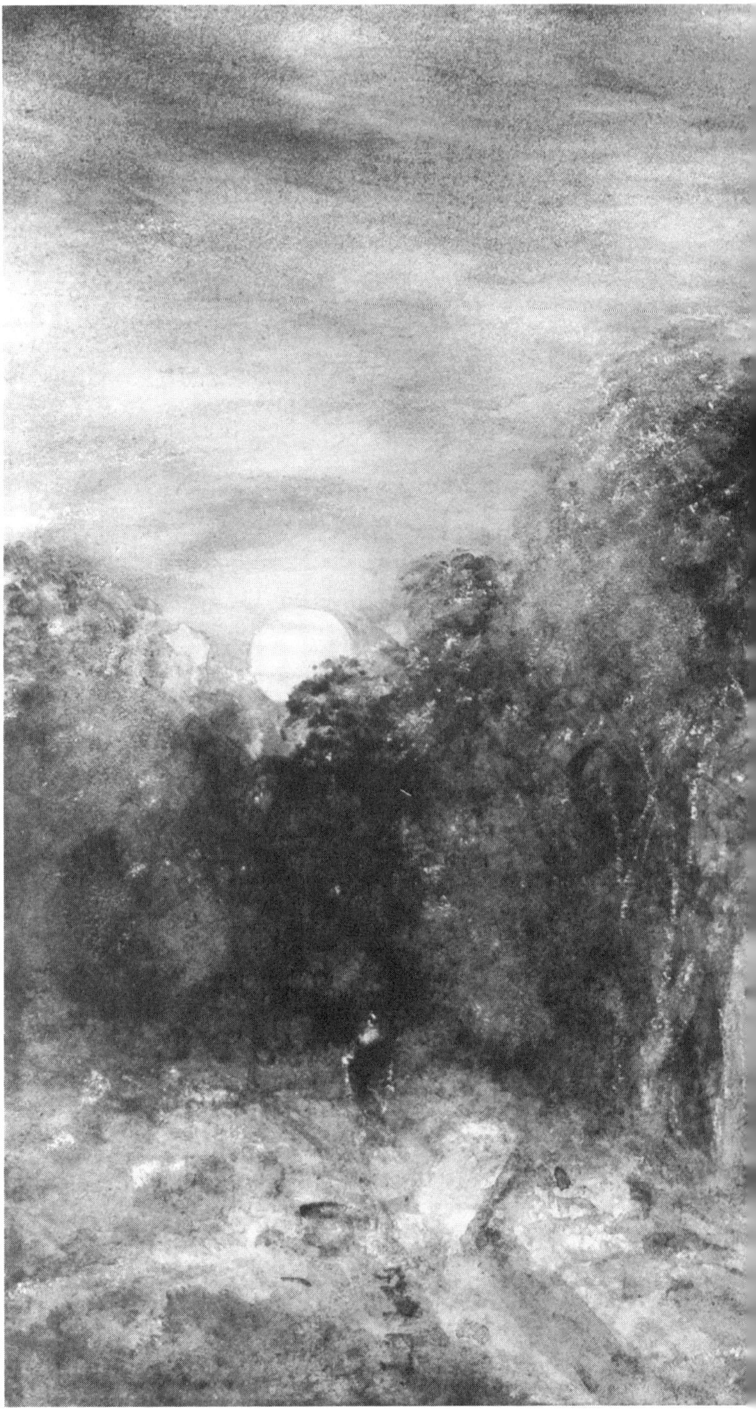

22
John Constable
Netley Abbey by Moonlight, *c.*1833
Watercolour and pencil on paper 14.6 × 20 cm
Tate. Purchased 1969

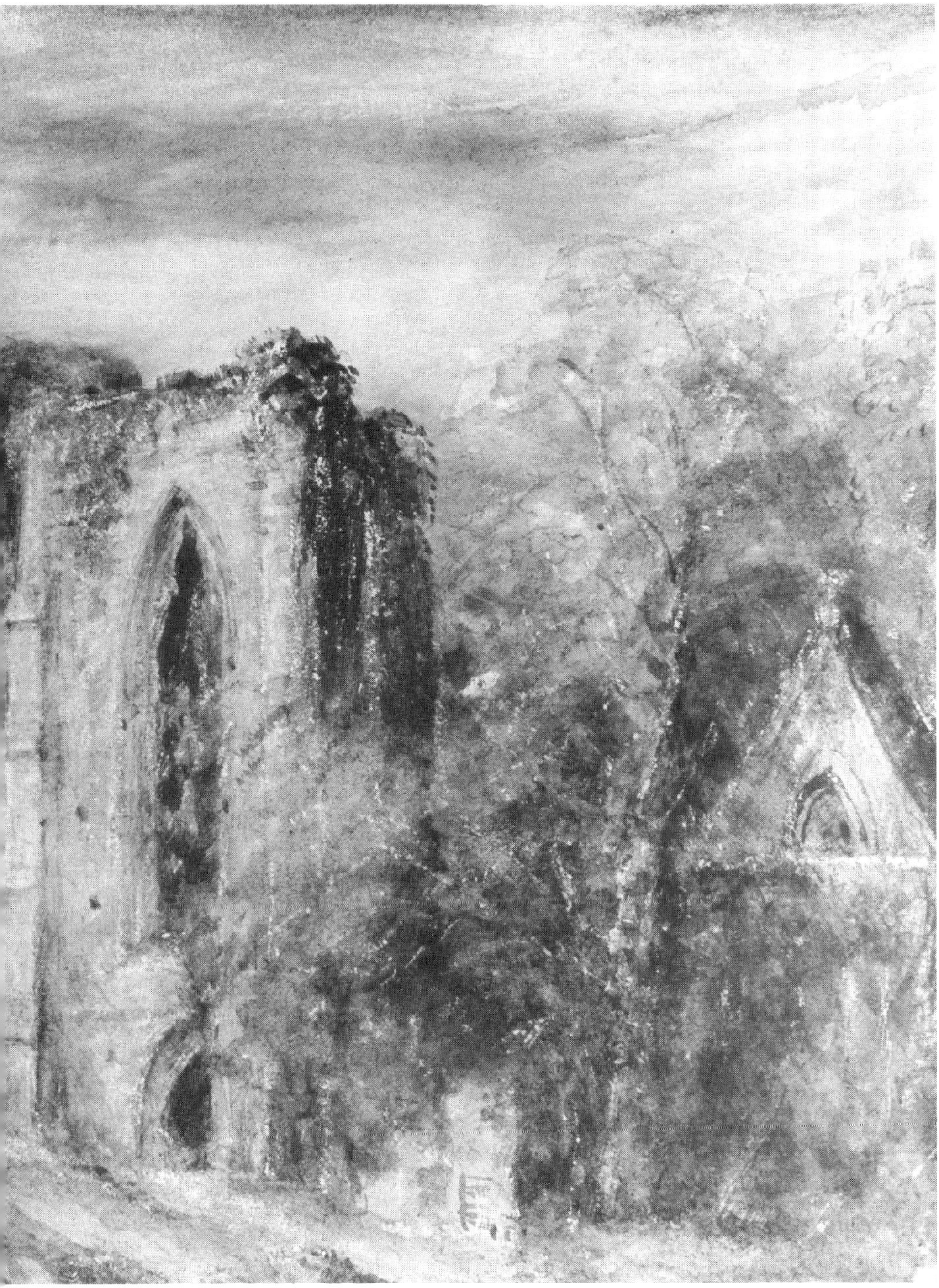

3.6

William Blake

The visionary artist and poet William Blake (1757–1827) held medieval art and architecture in high esteem, and drew from it in his works in original ways. As a young pupil of the reproductive engraver James Basire, he had been sent while still in his teens to draw the monuments in Westminster Abbey. While that project was dryly antiquarian in its intentions, the combined influences of new aesthetic theories and poetic ideals, and Blake's religious and spiritual leanings soon encouraged a more imaginative relationship with the previously neglected resources of the medieval past. Those early studies proved to be a decisive influence. While 'official' art theory, represented by Sir Joshua Reynolds at the Royal Academy, still held the over-complicated and evocative forms of the Gothic style in low esteem, Blake saw in them the expression of a purer ideal of the spiritual life than was to be found in the conventionally more highly considered classical forms. In his own art, we can find a recurring use of the attenuated forms and stylised repetitions of Gothic architecture and sculpture. This tendency recurs in the art of his followers, including Samuel Palmer (1805–91).

c.1810

William Blake 1757–1827
On Virgil

Sacred Truth has pronounced that Greece & Rome as Babylon & Egypt: so far from being parents of Arts & Sciences as they pretend: were destroyers of all Art. Homer Virgil & Ovid confirm this opinion & make us reverence The Word of God, the only light of antiquity that remains unperverted by War. Virgil in the Eneid Book VI. line 848 says Let others study Art: Rome has somewhat better to do, namely War & Dominion.

Rome & Greece swept Art into their maw & destroyd it a Warlike State never can produce Art. It will Rob & Plunder & accumulate into one place, & Translate & Copy & Buy & Sell & Criticise, but not Make.

Mathematic Form is Eternal in the Reasoning Memory. Living Form is Eternal Existence.

Grecian is Mathematic Form
Gothic is Living Form

c.1808

William Blake 1757–1827
Annotation to Sir Joshua Reynolds, *Discourses on Art*

'would, probably, have been one of the first painters of his age, (and he lived in all era of great artists,) had he been initiated into those great principles ...'

What does this mean 'Would have been one of the first Painters of his Age' Albert Durer Is! Not would have been! Besides. let them look at Gothic Figures & Gothic Buildings, & not talk of Dark Ages or of Any Age! Ages are All Equal. But Genius is Always Above The Age

23
Samuel Palmer
Coming from Evening Church, 1830
Mixed media on gesso on paper 30.2 × 20 cm
Tate. Purchased 1922

24
William Blake
Christ in the Sepulchre, Guarded by Angels, c.1805
Pencil, pen and ink and watercolour on paper
43.2 × 31.7 cm
The Victoria and Albert Museum, London

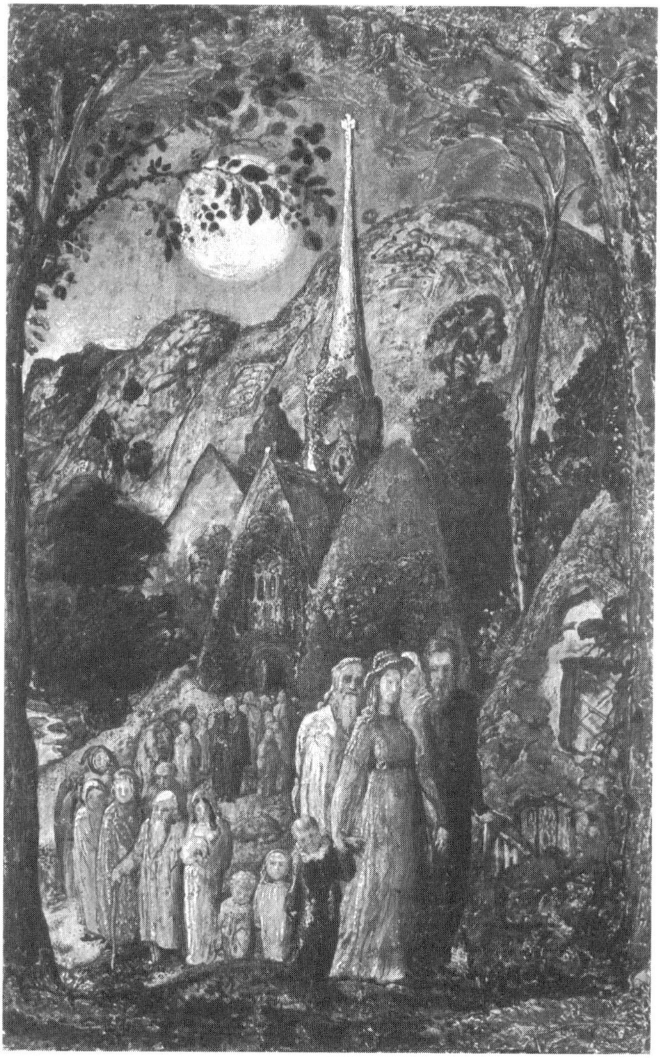

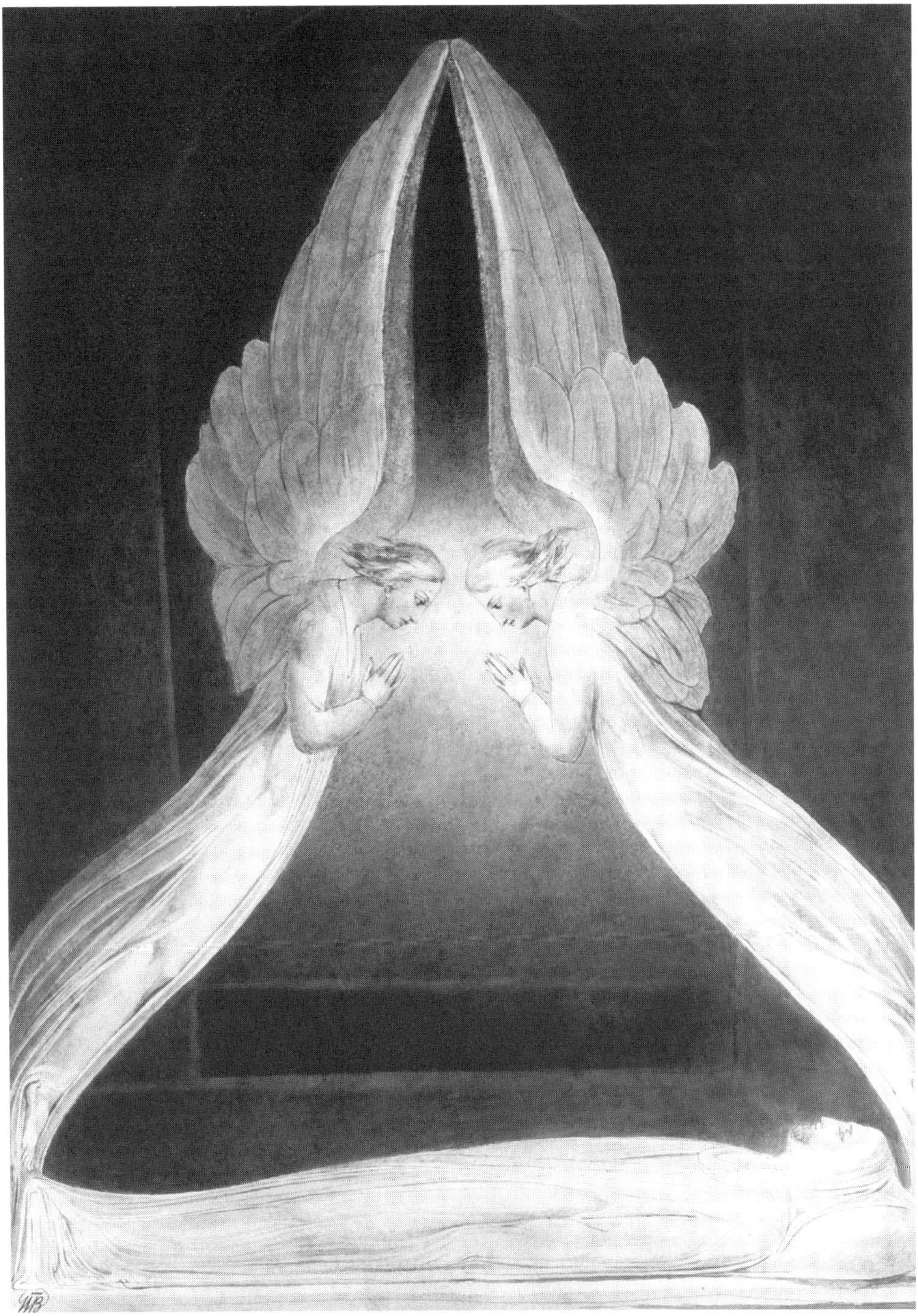

John Carter

The architectural draughtsman John Carter (1748–1817) waged a long war against the innovations of modern architecture and the abuses of historical monuments in *The Gentleman's Magazine*, well-established as the leading periodical publication for gentlemen with antiquarian and historical interests. In the first excerpt here, Carter dramatises a visit to the ruined abbey at Neath in Wales, now used as an iron forge. He conjures a remarkable scene of post-apocalyptic horror, where pallid workers are damned to repetitious industry, like Radcliffian monks hypnotised by their mysterious, and no less wicked, rituals.

The second excerpt, a Gothic evocation of the horrible state of of St David's in Wales, followed an attack in *The Gentleman's Magazine* on Carter from a correspondent, who dismissed Carter as a 'rhapsodist' and wondered 'what Historian, some centuries hence ... would have patience enough to wade through the wild effusions of his fancy, for such morsels of description as he gives?'

1804

John Carter 1748–1817
'An Architect'
The Gentleman's Magazine, vol.74

A clear and ambient air I leave; and pestilential vapours, smoke, and noxious mists, now avail me as I forward march. Baleful invitation to proceed! The horizon once more begins to be discernible; and I see before me the town of *Neath*, dark and sulphureous. The ground was covered with a black dust, which, like the passing natives, I strove not to behold; and kept a middle way between the wretched hovel and their attendant accumulations, as though some dire contamination awaited my perilous passage. The bourn once passed in Resolutions folds, could I know aught of dread; my promise to pursue the 'flying furor' beckoning in the van? No. Antiquity bleeds at every pore. Sound, sound to the conflict, let me heal her wounded honours, or cease to be!

Neath Abbey

Ye Powers! How horrid, how infernal, was all before me! Deep in the very centre of the sacred walls were set the furnaces wherein the poisonous ore becomes a prey to fusion. What dreadful crash or mighty engines! what oaths, what imprecations! With flames and smoke the scene was filled, the sad prototype of that place of 'outer darkness' which the wicked alone must know. A belle is tolled, and see the brotherhood come forth. Their vestments are fable, it is true; their visages pale and wan; but not through the austerities of religious observances, as of the old sojourners in this devoted ground, but through the rage of heat, metallic effluvia, and ungovernable inebriety. What a disorderly procession is pressing on, wild and ungovernable, noisy and tumultuous! Ha! was it so in former days, when solemn pomp drew on the pious throng to thread these paths among?

Standing within the verge of the grand gateway to the Abbey, an absolute ruin, alike bearing the marks of pestiferous exhalations, I found it impossible to approach the Abbey; I therefore noted down from this station these remarks. The walls came on my sight as making out the Cloisters, Nave, the Abbey buildings, &c. The Architecture is in the Pointed style; the structures lofty, and the decorations grand: yet all unroofed, despoiled, and left a prey to the present race of inmates, unknowing where they tread, on whom they tread! I flew from the stagnant stream which erst so clearly flowed by the surrounding mounds, the hideous din, the 'vale of darkness,' nd turned not. I saw the blasted objects no more. Yet Memory, at times the curse of retrospective thought, even now intrudes upon my secluded state, bearing hard on those few comforts which this life bestows.

St David's

So reduced is this City, both in the mansions and consequence of the inhabitants, so changed are these people from their ancient customs, so lost to such a character as that of a Pilgrim, or so far forgetful that there still exists among them the shrine of their Patron Saint to attract the devotions of such a *Wanderer*; that when I entered the *High-street*, which I forsooth took for a few straggling huts in the suburbs of so celebrated a place, I began to enquire the distance I had to go to my desired haven; when I should meet with the wealthy and courteous Citizens; and how soon I might expect to behold the lofty towers and spires of the splendid Cathedral. I quickly found what a train of errors I had fallen into; the renowned City had me then within its vortex: the town's folk were honest, to be sure, but unintelligible, and barbarous in their reception; and as for decrying the sacred piles, the hovels hid them entirely from my sight or those who only might take their 'walk' about the few poor streets remaining. Feeling most uncomfortable, a thousand doubts and surmises clinging round my heart, as I made my way into the inn, a shocking shelter for my fatigued body, though the host and his family had something of human kindness about them; I concluded that little time was to be lost before I claimed the protection of the Dignitary presiding over the holy piles sacred to St David. He, good man, was every thing my hope had raised; he soon perceived my agitated frame, and instantly accounted for my perturbed manner of behaviour, gave me his hand, and bid my fears have rest. Reciting the cause of my visitation, he gave me full liberty to pursue my purpose, declaring, he himself would conduct me to the several Antiquities; and, whatever assistance or comfort I might require, I had but to name them, and he would procure the same. What could I covet more? My spirits recruited by these assurances, I returned towards my hostelry; when, approaching the house, good stars! my soul was again filled with alarm; the population of the place was assembled before the door, and, with violent outcries and menacing arms, seemed to prognosticate some shocking outrage. Entering, I encountered a company of poor Pilgrims, who, like myself, had trod the toilsome way to pay their orisons at St David's shrine. Surprise and dread on either part prevented our associating together in one common cause, to dare the threatening multitude, and to visit the object of our vows and prayers. How unfriendly, how suspicious this, for countrymen thus to meet, and then to fly each other's sight! But they went cheerless, and without protection, and we saw each other, alas, no more!

The Close surrounding the religious fabrics is in compass more than a mile, the encircling wall of which remains on many parts of the line: it was decorated with four grand Gateways; one still is left to the East, leading from the City, and a noble one it is, having two lofty Towers and the entrance between them. Passing through this inlet, the scene opened in a most wonderful manner. Below lies the Cathedral, and beyond the ruined walls of the

Bishop's Palace peer upon the sight: in the distance rise black and ragged mountains, altogether giving emotions that cannot be described, and which can never be obliterated from my imagination. After standing some time in this situation, I descended the steep of the church-yard, and commenced my labour by surveying

The Bishop's Palace

A small stream divides this structure from the Cathedral; and it is rather remarkable, the general plan (a regular square) is laid out in contradict line to that of the Church, being fronted South-west, South-east, North-east, and North-west. The North-east front shews little more than the return of the South-east front, and the entrance Tower. The North-west front, nearly gone. North-east front, perfect. South-west front, perfect. I wish it to be understood in the present instance, that by the word *perfect* I mean the meer upright of the walls; as all the roofs, groins, or other covering over-head, are utterly destroyed. The dimensions of the buildings are prodigious, the decorations superb, and shew the early Pointed Style of architecture. Among the windows, which are lofty, and finely disposed, is a curious circular one, filled with rich mullions and tracery. The finishing line or parapet to the work is one of the most majestic decorations I ever witnessed; and it is to be remembered, that there is but one other example of this sort to be met with in Wales (in England nothing of this kind exists), and that is at Swansea. This parapet is made out by a succession of arches supported by octangular columns, with ornamented capitals, &c. The arches are perforated, serving not only to impart an appearance of grandeur, but to admit of defensive operations in the same way as used in the interstices of battlements.

Being now come into the Great Court, the scene at first appeared more than the work of mortal hands; a visionary fabric drawn to the eye of a heated Professionalist, like me, whose mind is bound under the dominion of Antiquity; but I soon found it was reality, and I could not reconcile all I saw with the fantastic, and common erections of modern times, raised in my native country, and constructed with plaster and other perishable materials, under the presumption that they adorn the land. On my left ran the Bishop's Hall, and other apartments, the stair-case porch belonging thereto, &c. Before me, King John's Hall, Chapel, and a stair-case porch communicating to these places likewise. The arcaded parapet is carried also round the walls of this court. The basement story, or crypt, is vaulted with curious groins, and shews many other architectural particulars appertaining to such a place; but its condition is deplorable …

At the conclusion of my notes and sketches of these buildings, I gave into many an embittered reflection; and, like the intelligent and feeling author who has produced to the publick of late his impartial sentiments on the state of St David's, I called to mind the former splendour of this Palace, its princely entertainments, its sacred councils; commented on the exalted minds of the Episcopal Founders, who raised up at a moment's notice, as it were, by saying 'Thus we will, and thus let it be,' a range of apartments fit to contain a Royal Guest; and ruminated on the majesty of those who had here sojourned. Now, sad reverse! the walls are unroofed, the chambers unprotected, and the Crypt turned into receptacles for the most wretched therein to shelter them, who had indeed no other homes. Tell me of dungeons, horrid for the miserable maniac, or the unfortunate mendicant, for criminals vile, or those left to undergo the sentence of the law; I go with the reciter, a man who seeks for human woes, to pity and relieve; for here was much of this, and endured by those who had no other crime but that of being poor. To behold them crawling from out these desolated cells, hung round with damps and ouzy vegetation; the rising springs inundating their clay cold bed; and, when the thunders roll and lightnings fly, the trembling superstructures threatening destruction on their devoted heads! Indeed their fate was piteous and full of sorrow. Fearful I saw them crowd around me like spectres, lean and wan. 'A little charity for Jesus his sake,' they cried; 'or else we starve, we die!'

Was it possible, in a scene like this, to close my Architectural memoranda with a cold phlegmatic detail of 'expected technical terms,' with a callous indifference, and be silent of those who were thus suffering? No. Many there are I trust, who can listen to a tale of other things than about a string of heights, and widths, lengths, and breadths, openings, columns, groins, and galleries, and say, 'let the Architect tell us what we are to expect to meet with to affect our senses, other than the buildings themselves.' If we are content to hear of the present state of our Antiquities, let us hear also what attached sensations are thereunto belonging; not alone to impart information, but to inspire a wish to preserve them from further harm, and to raise a dread toward turning them over to calamitous purposes, or entire destruction.

3.8

Gothic Taste

Horace Walpole's suburban villa Strawberry Hill and William Beckford's massive Wiltshire home Fonthill Abbey are the two greatest and most influential achievements of the early Gothic revival in architecture. The buildings and their contents were subject to extensive commentary, criticism and imitation. In both cases the owners were closely involved in the design and decoration of their homes, finding an opportunity to craft a complete personal vision aside from the realm of public life, which both found troublesome and, to a greater or lesser degree, painful.

Walpole bought the relatively modest Strawberry Hill in Twickenham in 1747. In the early 1750s it was subjected to a thoroughgoing, but basically superficial, refurbishment, with the addition of battlements and an overhaul of the interiors in a style that combined (or juxtaposed) a genuine and scholarly passion for the past with a superficiality of decorative effect. As Scott's commentary of the villa presented here states, Strawberry Hill stood at the head of the modern taste for the Gothic as an historically evocative mode of interior design. And as the comments at the end of 'W.G's' discussion of Fonthill suggest, the combination of domestic comfort and antiquarian atmosphere was deeply appealing. Jane Austen's satirical comments on the taste for Gothic architecture from *Northanger Abbey* (1818), the second excerpt here, play on the contrast between a fashionable passion for the Gothic past, and domestic realities.

William Beckford's gargantuan house, Fonthill Abbey, was his preoccupation for over twenty years, after returning in 1796 from exile on the Continent. The long period of its design and building was a subject of tremendous fascination for contemporaries; his architect, James Wyatt, presented outlandishly ambitious designs at the Royal Academy exhibitions in 1797 and 1798. Public interest came to a head in 1822 when it was finally announced complete. The report from *The Gentleman's Magazine* reproduced here outlines the debates that arose at that point, and also usefully reminds us of all that had changed between the period of Walpole's Gothic pursuits and this later date, in the way of preservationist thinking, architectural history and revivalism.

1811

Walter Scott 1771–1832
Introduction to *The Castle of Otranto*

Mr Walpole's domestic occupations, as well as his studies, bore evidence of his taste for English antiquities, which was then uncommon. He loved, as a satirist has expressed in, 'to gaze on Gothic toys through Gothic glass'; and the villa at Strawberry-Hill, which he chose for his abode, gradually swelled into a feudal castle, by the addition of turrets, towers, galleries, and corridors, whose fretted roofs, carved panels, and illuminated windows, were garnished with the appropriate furniture of scutcheons, armorial-bearings, shields, tilting lances, and all the panoply of chivalry. The Gothic order of architecture is now so generally, and, indeed, indiscriminately used, that we are rather surprised if the country-house of a tradesman retired from business does not exhibit lanceolated windows, divided by stone shafts, and garnished by painted glass, a cupboard in the form of a cathedral-stall, and a pig-house with a front borrowed from the façade of an ancient chapel. But, in the middle of the eighteenth century, when Mr Walpole began to exhibit specimens of the Gothic style, and to show how patterns, collected from cathedrals and monuments, might be applied to chimney-pieces, ceilings, windows, and balustrades, he did not comply with the dictates of a prevailing fashion, but pleased his own taste, when he realised his own visions, in the romantic cast of the mansion which he erected.

1818

Jane Austen 1775–1817
Northanger Abbey

As they drew near the end of their journey, her impatience for a sight of the abbey — for some time suspended by his conversation on subjects very different — returned in full force, and every bend in the road was expected with solemn awe to afford a glimpse of its massy walls of grey stone, rising amidst a grove of ancient oaks, with the last beams of the sun playing in beautiful splendour on its high Gothic windows. But so low did the building stand, that she found herself passing through the great gates of the lodge into the very grounds of Northanger, without having discerned even an antique chimney.

She knew not that she had any right to be suprized, but there was a something in this mode of approach which she certainly had not expected. To pass between lodges of a modern appearance, to find herself with such ease in the very precincts of the abbey, and driven so rapidly along a smooth, level road of fine gravel, without obstacle, alarm, or solemnity of any kind, struck her as odd and inconsistent. She was not long at leisure, however, for such considerations. A sudden scud of rain, driving full in her face, made it impossible for her to observe anything further, and fixed all her thoughts on the welfare of her new straw bonnet:— and she was actually under the Abbey walls, was springing, with Henry's assistance, from the carriage, was beneath the shelter of the old porch, and had even passed on to the hall, where her friend and the general were waiting to welcome her, without feeling one awful foreboding of future misery to herself, or one moment's suspicion of any past scenes of horror being acted within the solemn edifice. The breeze had not seemed to waft the sighs of the murdered to her; it had wafted nothing worse than a thick mizzling rain; and having given a good shake to her habit, she was ready to be shown into the common drawing-room, and capable of considering where she was.

An abbey! —yes, it was delightful to be really in an abbey! — but she doubted, as she looked round the room, whether anything within her observation would have given her the consciousness. The furniture was in all the profusion and elegance of modern taste. The fire-place, where she had expected the ample width and ponderous carving of former times, was contracted to a Rumford, with slabs of plain though handsome marble, and ornaments over it of the prettiest English china. The windows, to which she looked with peculiar dependence, from having heard the general talk of his preserving them in their Gothic form with reverential care, were yet less what her fancy had portrayed. To be sure, the pointed arch was preserved — the form of them was Gothic — they might be even casements — but every pane was so large, so clear, so light! To an imagination which had hoped for the smallest divisions, and the heaviest stone-work, for painted glass, dirt, and cobwebs, the difference was very distressing...

1822

William Lisle Bowles 1762–1850
'Lines on a First View of Fonthill Abbey, Aug. 21st, 1822'

The mighty master wav'd his wand, and lo!
On the astonish'd eye the glorious show
Bursts, like a vision; SPIRIT OF THE PLACE,
Has the Arabian wizard, with his mace
Smitten the barren downs far onward spread,
And bade th' enchanted Palace tower instead?
Bade the dark woods their solemn shades extend?
High to the clouds yon spiry tow'r ascend?
And, starting from th' umbrageous avenue,
Spread the rich pile magnificent to view?
Enter — from this arch'd portal, look again,
Back, on the lessening woods and distant plain.
Ascend the steps — the high and fretted roof
Is woven by some Elfin hand aloof,
Whilst from the painted windows' long array,
A mellow'd light is shed, as not of day.
How gorgeous all! Oh never may the spell
Be broken, that array'd those radiant forms so well.

1822

'Candid Critique of the Architecture of Fonthill Abbey'

The curiosity so long and so ardently excited by the unexampled exclusion, not only of strangers, but of almost every individual (not employed in its construction) from inspecting the edifice called Fonthill Abbey is at length in part satisfied.

Amongst the multitude of persons so suddenly admitted to gaze upon this novel and extensive structure, with its precious contents and surrounding beauties, it is natural to expect that by far the greater number will view the varied scene with enthusiastic delight, while others will express a more qualified degree of approbation, and some an affectation of indifference. We are accordingly prepared to hear many 'applaud with fashioned pomp of phrase;' but when we find panegyric heightened with bombast, and '*a descriptive Guide*' spun into a political disquisition, we are involuntarily led to suspect that even Books may be '*made to sell*.'

It is truly curious to observe the expression of different opinions and different feelings upon this subject, which is now become a public theme; some who consider the design and its accomplishments as the *acmé* of perfection, are disposed to divide the merit between the taste of the proprietor and the skill of the architect; some are anxious to impress the idea that the whole design was digested and arranged before the unfortunate decease of the late Mr Wyatt, and that the execution of the whole has since been conducted by his original plans; while others not entertaining so exalted an opinion of this extraordinary effort of munificence, taste, and skill, are disposed to believe that a more perfect specimen of what is called 'Gothic Architecture' would have been produced if the late Mr Wyatt had been allowed to form the design upon his own judgement. But however this may be, and without noticing in this place the hackneyed observation, that the styles of various periods are indiscriminately blended together, it may be proper to observe, that the legitimate object of criticism, is to improve the future, rather than to cast ill-natured censure upon the past; and that the venial errors of taste should not be visited with the severity necessarily tolerated in the reprehension of immorality or vice. If we view the edifice in question under the guidance of this principle, although we may find some essential errors, we may also find some real beauties, even in parts which psuedo-critics may condemn, as deviations from their abstract notions of correct and congruous style ...

In forming a candid opinion upon the whole, it should not be forgotten that the erection of this edifice was an effort to revive a style of architecture which there are strong reasons to believe was never practiced under definite rules: commenced at a period when little progress had been made in producing correct graphic representations of buildings and ornamental buildings in the style called Gothic. The admirers of this style are, however, since that period, much indebted to the enthusiastic and indefatigable exertions of Mr Britton, who has selected and presented to the public eye, in his 'Architectural' and 'Cathedral Antiquities,' very many elegant specimens of the ingenuity and taste of our ancestors, which for correctness of drawing and effect of engraving, far surpass any preceding works of the same description, and have excited a degree of emulation that must lead to the development of data calculated to correct the taste of the Architectural Student.

It should also be recollected, that actual practice is much more necessary for the requirement of a complete knowledge of this intricate subject than the mere study of doubtful theories.

There are probably architects of the present day who would erect a Gothic structure of equal magnitude, with less faults than are to be found at Fonthill; if it were not so, the benefit of experience, which might have been acquired in thirty years, would be lost; for within that period much more has been done towards the restoration of our ancient Ecclesiastical Edifices, and a disposition to cultivate a correct taste has been evinced.

It is, however, too frequently forgotten, that the improved conveniences of modern times prevent in a great degree the adoption of ancient models, without incurring the charge of innovation. This was felt by Lord Orford himself at Strawberry Hill, of which he found it necessary to observe, that he did not wish to make his house so Gothic as to be unfit to live in; and this, it must be presumed, was felt by Mr Beckford: it must therefore be pretty obvious, that the most fastidious architectural critic of the present age would be as little pleased to inhabit a mansion built after the exact model of one of the fourteenth century, as the most discontented political reformer would be with the precise constitution of the same period. When all these circumstances are duly considered, it must remain for ever questionable, whether any other person would have conducted the same undertaking with greater success than the deceased Architect of Fonthill.

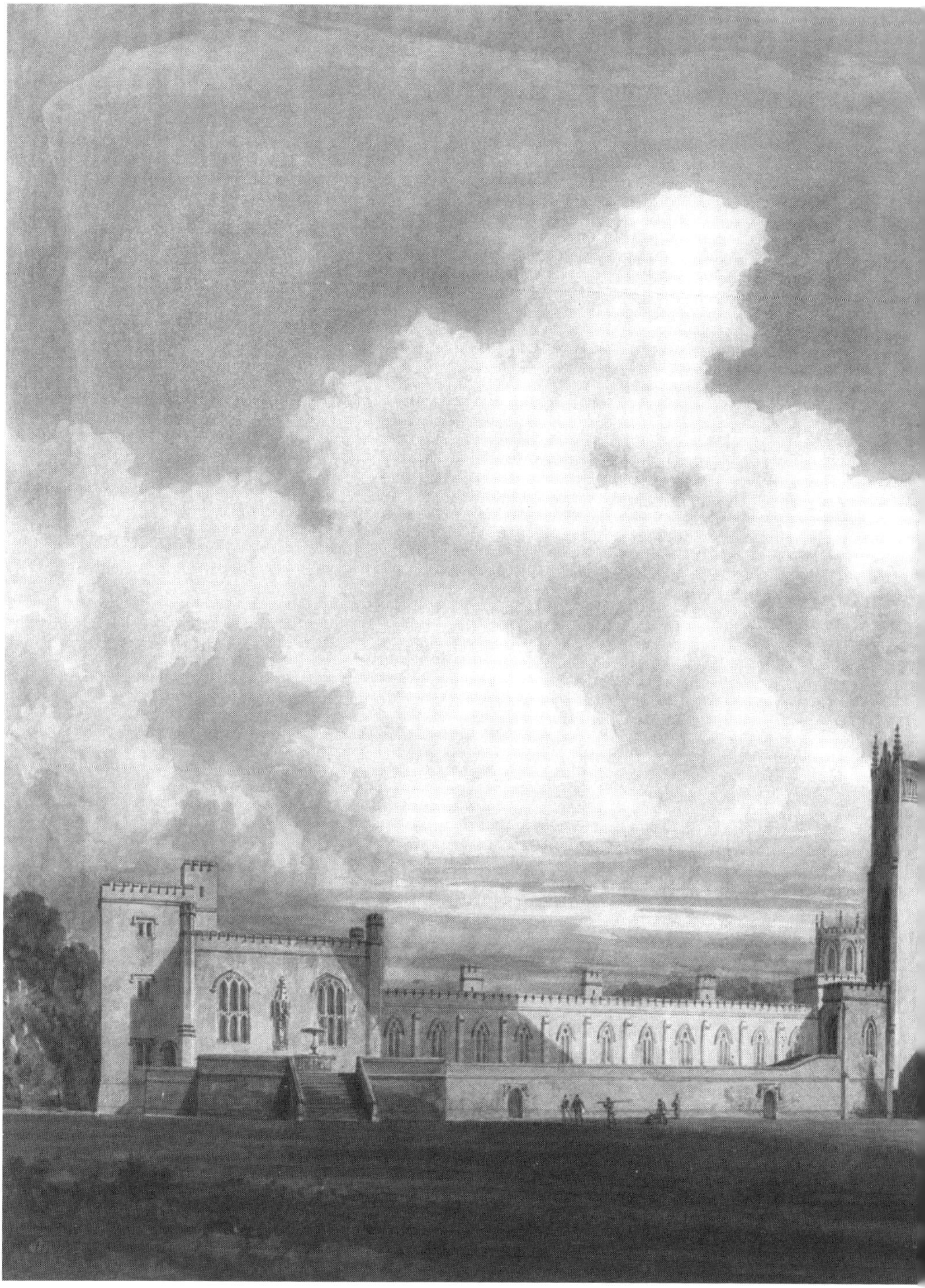

25
J.M.W. Turner and James Wyatt
Projected Design for Fonthill Abbey, Wiltshire, 1798

Watercolour on wove paper backed with linen 67 × 105.4 cm
The Paul Mellon Collection, Yale Center for British Art, New Haven

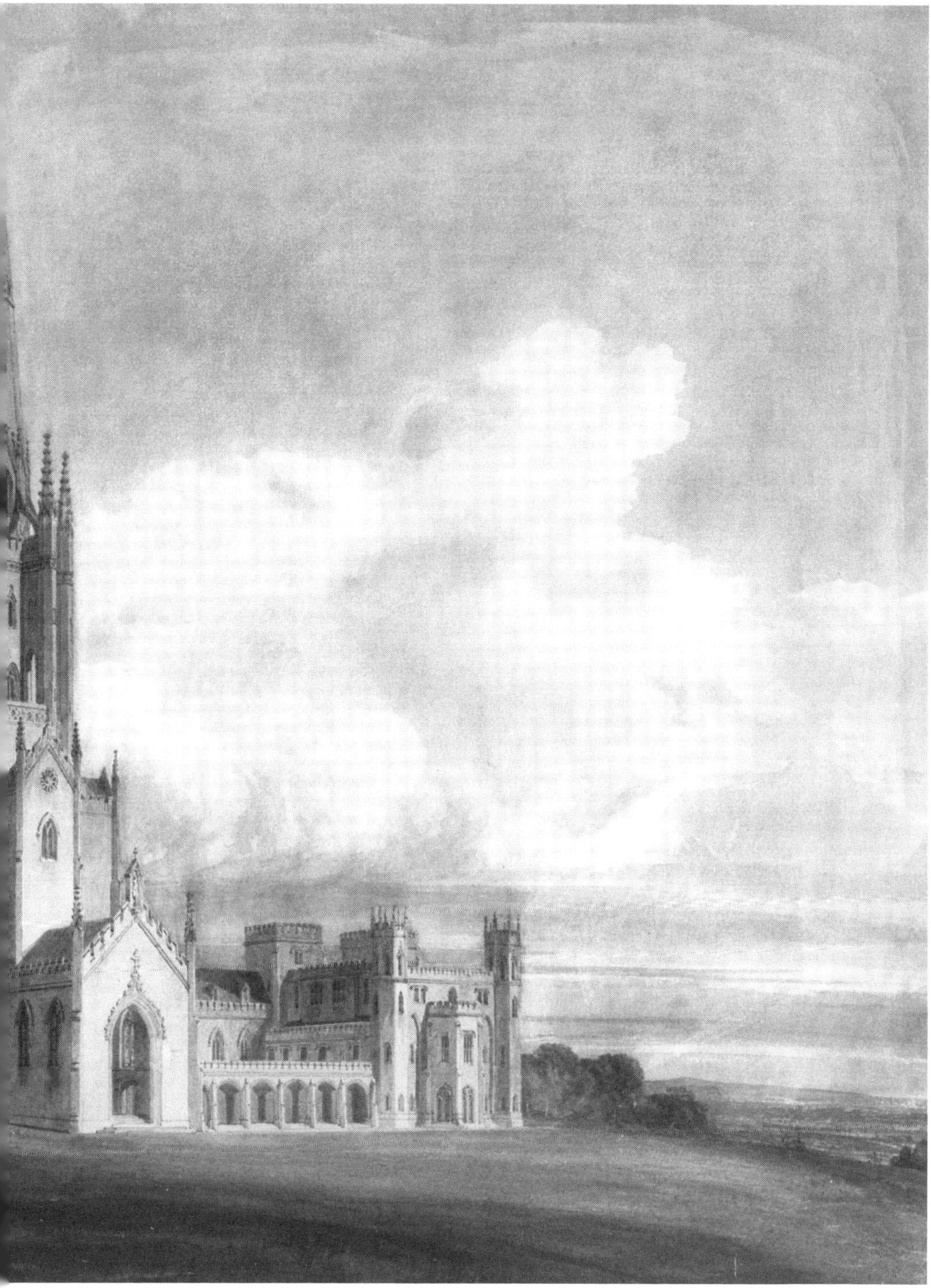

Gothic Horror

The Gothic revivalists of the nineteenth century had sought recurrently to retrieve the Gothic from the stigma of dark irrationalism and horror, which had only been compounded by the aesthetics of the Sublime, and the writings of Walpole, Radcliffe and their ilk. Here, however, the writer and translator Lafcadio Hearn relishes such associations, belatedly bringing the themes of horror, the fantastic and the stylistic traits of the Gothic back into provocative association. At once cosmic and personal, mystical and sensationalist, joyful and full of awe, Hearn's little essay evokes a whole, rich history of shifting perceptions of Gothic architecture.

1900

Lafcadio Hearn 1850–1904
'Gothic Horror'

1 Long before I had arrived at what catechisms call the age of reason, I was frequently taken, much against my will, to church. The church was very old; and I can see the interior of it at this moment just as plainly as I saw it forty years ago, when it appeared to me like an evil dream. There I first learned to know the peculiar horror that certain forms of Gothic architecture can inspire ... I am using the word 'horror' in a classic sense, — in its antique meaning of ghostly fear.

On the very first day of this experience, my child-fancy could place the source of the horror. The wizened and points shapes of the windows immediately terrified me. In their outline I found the form of apparitions that tormented me in sleep; — and at once I began to imagine some dreadful affinity between goblins and Gothic churches. Presently, in the tall doorways, in the archings of the aisles, in the ribbings and groinings of the roof, I discovered other and wilder suggestions of fear. Even the façade of the organ, — peaking high into the shadow above its gallery, — seemed to me a frightful thing ... Had I been then suddenly obliged to answer the question, 'What are you afraid of?' I should have whispered, '*Those points!*' I could not otherwise have explained the matter: I only knew that I was afraid of the 'points.'

Of course the real enigma of what I felt in that church could not present itself to my mind while I continued to believe in goblins. But long after the age of superstitious terrors, other Gothic experiences severally revived the childish emotion in so startling a way as to convince me that childish fantasy could not account for the feeling. Then my curiosity was aroused; and I tried to discover some rational cause for the horror. I read many books, and asked many questions; but the mystery seemed only to deepen.

Books about architecture were very disappointing. I was much less impressed by what I could find in them than by reference in pure fiction to the awfulness of Gothic art, — particularly by one writer's confession that the interior of a Gothic church, seen at night, gave him the idea of being inside the skeleton of some monstrous animal; and by a far-famed comparison of the windows of a cathedral to eyes, and of its door to a great mouth, 'devouring the people.' These imaginations explained little; they could not be developed beyond the phase of vague intimation: yet they stirred such emotional response that I felt sure they had touched some truth. Certainly the architecture of a Gothic cathedral offers strange resemblances to the architecture of bone; and the general impression that it makes upon the mind is an impression of life. But this impression or sense of life I found to be indefinable, — not a sense of any life organic, but of a life latent and dæmonic. And the manifestation of that life I felt to be in the *pointing* of the structure.

Attempts to interpret the emotion by effects of altitude and gloom and vastness appeared to me of no worth; for buildings loftier and larger and darker than any Gothic cathedral, but of a different order of architecture, — Egyptian, for instance, — could not produce a like impression. I felt certain that the horror was made by something altogether peculiar to Gothic construction, and that this something haunted the tops of the arches.

'Yes, Gothic architecture is awful,' said a religious friend, 'because it is the visible expression of the Christian faith. No other religious architecture expresses spiritual longing; but the Gothic embodies it. Every part climbs or leaps; every supreme detail soars and points like fire ...' 'There may be considerable truth in what you say,' I replied; — 'but it does not relate to the riddle that baffles me. Why should shapes that symbolize spiritual longing create horror? What should any expression of Christian ecstasy inspire alarm? ... '

Other hypotheses in multitude I tested without avail; and I returned to the simple and savage conviction that the secret of the horror somehow belonged to the points of the archings. But for years I could not find it. At last, at last, in the early hours of a certain tropical morning, it revealed itself quite unexpectedly, while I was looking at a glorious group of palms.

Then I wondered at my stupidity in not having guessed the riddle before.

II The characteristics of many kinds of palm have been made familiar by pictures and photographs. But the giant palms of the American tropics cannot be adequately represented by the modern methods of pictorial illustration: they must be seen. You cannot draw or photograph a palm two hundred feet high.

The first sight of a group of such forms, in their natural environment of tropical forest, is a magnificent surprise, — a surprise that strikes you dumb. Nothing seen in temperate zones, — not even the huger growths of the Californian slope, — could have prepared your imagination for the weird solemnity of that mighty colonnade. Each stone-grey trunk is a perfect pillar, — but a pillar of which the stupendous grace has no counterpart in the works of man. You must strain your head well back to follow the soaring of the prodigious column, up, up, up through the abysses of green twilight, till at last — far beyond a break in that infinite interweaving of limbs and lianas which is the roof of the forest — you can catch one dizzy glimpse of the capital: a parasol of emerald feathers outspread in a sky so blinding as to suggest the notion of azure electricity.

Now what is the emotion that such a vision excites, — and emotion too powerful to be called wonder, too weird to be called delight? Only when the first shock is passed, — when the several elements that were combined in it have begun to set in motion widely different groups of ideas, — can you comprehend how very complex it much have been. Many impressions belonging to personal experience were doubtless revived in it, but also with them a multitude of sensations more shadowy, — accumulations of organic memory; possibly even vague feelings older than man, — for the tropical shapes that aroused the emotion have a history more ancient than our race.

One of the first elements of the emotion to become clearly distinguishable is the æsthetic; and this, in its general mass, might be termed the sense of terrible beauty. Certainly the spectacle of that unfamiliar life, — silent, tremendous, springing to the sun in colossal aspiration, striving for light against Titans, and heedless of man in the gloom beneath as of a groping beetle, — thrills like the rhythm of some single marvellous verse that is learned in a glance and remembered forever. Yet the delight, even at its vividest, is shadowed by a queer disquiet. The aspect of that monstrous, pale, naked, smooth-stretching column suggests a life as conscious as the serpent's. You stare at the towering lines of the shape, — vaguely fearing to discern some sign of stealthy movement, some beginning of undulation. Then sight and reason combine to correct the suspicion. Yes, motion is there, and life enormous — but a life seeking only sun, — life, rushing like the jet of a geyser, straight to the giant day.

III During my own experience I could perceive that certain feelings commingled in the wave of delight, — feelings related to ideas of power and slendor and triumph, — were accompanied by a faint sense of religious awe. Perhaps our modern æsthetic sentiments are so interwoven with various inherited elements of religious emotionalism that the recognition of beauty cannot arise independently of reverential feeling. Be this as it may, such a feeling defined itself while I gazed; — and at once the great grey trunks were changed to the pillars of a mighty aisle; and from attitudes of dream there suddenly descended upon me the old dark thrill of Gothic horror.

Even before it died away, I recognized that it must have been due to some old cathedral-memory revived by the vision of those giant trunks uprising into gloom. But neither the height nor the gloom could account for anything beyond the memory. Columns tall as those palms, but supporting a classic entablature, could evoke no sense of disquiet resembling the Gothic horror. I felt sure of this, — because I was able, without any difficulty, to shape immediately the imagination of such a façade. But presently the mental picture distorted. I saw the architrave elbow upward in each of the spaces between the pillars, and curve and point itself into a range of prodigious arches; — and again the sombre thrill descended upon me. Simultaneously there flashed to me the solution of the mystery. I understood that the Gothic horror was *a horror of monstrous motion*, — and that it had seemed to belong to the points of the arches because the idea of such motion was chiefly suggested by the extraordinary angle at which the curves of the arching touched.

To any experienced eye, the curves of Gothic arching offers a striking resemblance to certain curves of vegetal growth; — the curves of the palm-branch being, perhaps, especially suggested. But observe that the architectural form suggests more than any vegetal comparison could illustrate! The meeting of two palm-crests would indeed form a kind of Gothic arch; yet the effect of so short an arch would be insignificant. For nature to repeat the strange impression of the real Gothic arch, it were necessary that the branches of the touching crests should vastly exceed, both in length of curve and strength of spring, anything of their kind existing in the vegetable world. The effect of the Gothic arch depends altogether upon the intimation of energy. An arch formed by the intersection of two short sprouting lines could suggest only a feeble power of growth; but the lines of the tall mediæval arch seemed to express a crescent force immensely surpassing that of nature. And the horror of Gothic architecture is not in the mere suggestion of a growing life, but in the suggestion of an energy tremendous and tremendous.

Of course the child, oppressed by the strangeness of Gothic forms, is yet incapable of analyzing the impression received: he is frightened without comprehending. He cannot divine that the points and the curves are terrible because they represent the prodigious exaggeration of a real law of vegetal growth. He dreads the shapes because they seem alive; yet he does not know how to express this dread. Without suspecting why, he feels that this silent manifestation of power, everywhere pointing and piercing upward, is not natural. To his startled imagination, the building stretches itself like a phantasm of sleep, — makes itself tall and taller with intent to frighten. Even though built by hands of men, it has ceased to be a mass of dead stone: it is infused with Something that thinks and threatens; — it has become a shadowing malevolence, a multiple goblinry, a monstrous fetish!

Part 4

Fantastic Artists and Writers

The idea of the creative artist being an outsider or eccentric has roots in antiquity and was elaborated into a substantial and powerful myth with the rise of artistic biography in the Renaissance. But in the late eighteenth and early nineteenth centuries, the anti-social dimensions of the painter or writer's persona assumed a new significance, as the audience for art and literature expanded to a degree — and reached into social sectors — that could never have been imagined, by virtue of the new technologies for print and reproduction and public exhibitions.

The tradition of the wild, inspired artist was taken to a new level in the nineteenth century, as artistic eccentricity and social rebellion were consolidated as defining features of the modern artist. This selection shows how the fantasy artist became, in himself, the subject of fantasy, whether in confessional autobiography, or as figures in the sickly and decadent fictions of Poe and Lovecraft.

4.1

Horace Walpole on the Writing of The Castle of Otranto

Horace Walpole's voluminous correspondence is one of the greatest documents of late eighteenth-century literary, cultural and political life. Full of gossip and waspish wit, Walpole occasionally reflects on his character as an author. In the first, famous letter quoted here, he lays claim to a dream-inspiration for *The Castle of Otranto*. When he wrote the second letter excerpted below, he had only recently heard of a French translation of his novel, *Le Château d'Otrante* (Paris and Amsterdam, 1767). His comments reveal his self-identification as a wildly inspired writer, and his bullish rejection of established taste.

9 March 1765

Horace Walpole 1717–97
to William Cole

I had time to write but a short note with *The Castle of Otranto*, as your messenger called on me at four o'clock as I was going to dine abroad. Your partiality to me and Strawberry had I hope inclined you to excuse the wildness of the story. You will even have found some traits to put you in mind of this place. When you read of the picture quitting its panel, did not you recollect the portrait of Lord Falkland all in white in my gallery? Shall I even confess to you what was the origin of this romance? I waked one morning in the beginning of last June from a dream, of which all I could recover was, that I had thought myself in an ancient castle (a very natural dream for a head filled like mine with Gothic story) and that on the uppermost bannister of a great staircase I saw a gigantic hand in armour. In the evening I sat down and began to write, without knowing in the least what I intended to say or relate. The work grew on my hands, and I grew fond of it — add that I was very glad to think of anything rather than politics — In short I was so engrossed with my tales, which I completed in less than two months, that one evening I wrote from the time I had drunk my tea, about six o'clock, till half an hour after one in the morning, when my hand and fingers were so weary, that I could not hold the pen to finish the sentence, but left Matilda and Isabella talking, in the middle of a paragraph. You will laugh at my earnestness, but if I have amused you by retracing with any fidelity the manners of ancient days, I am content, and give you leave to think me as idle as you please.

13 March 1767

Horace Walpole 1717–97
to Madame Deffand

So they have translated by my Castle of Otranto, probably in ridicule of the author. So be it; — however, I beg you will let their raillery pass in silence. Let the critics have their own way; they give me no uneasiness. I have not written the book for the present age, which will endure nothing but *cold common sense*. I confess to you, my dear friend, (and you will think me madder than ever) that this is the only one of my works with which I am myself pleased; I have given reins to my imagination till I became on fire with the visions and feelings which it excited. I have composed it in defiance of rules, of critics, and of philosophers; and it seems to me just so much the better for that very reason. I am even persuaded, that some time hereafter, when taste shall resume the place which philosophy now occupies, my poor Castle will find admirers...

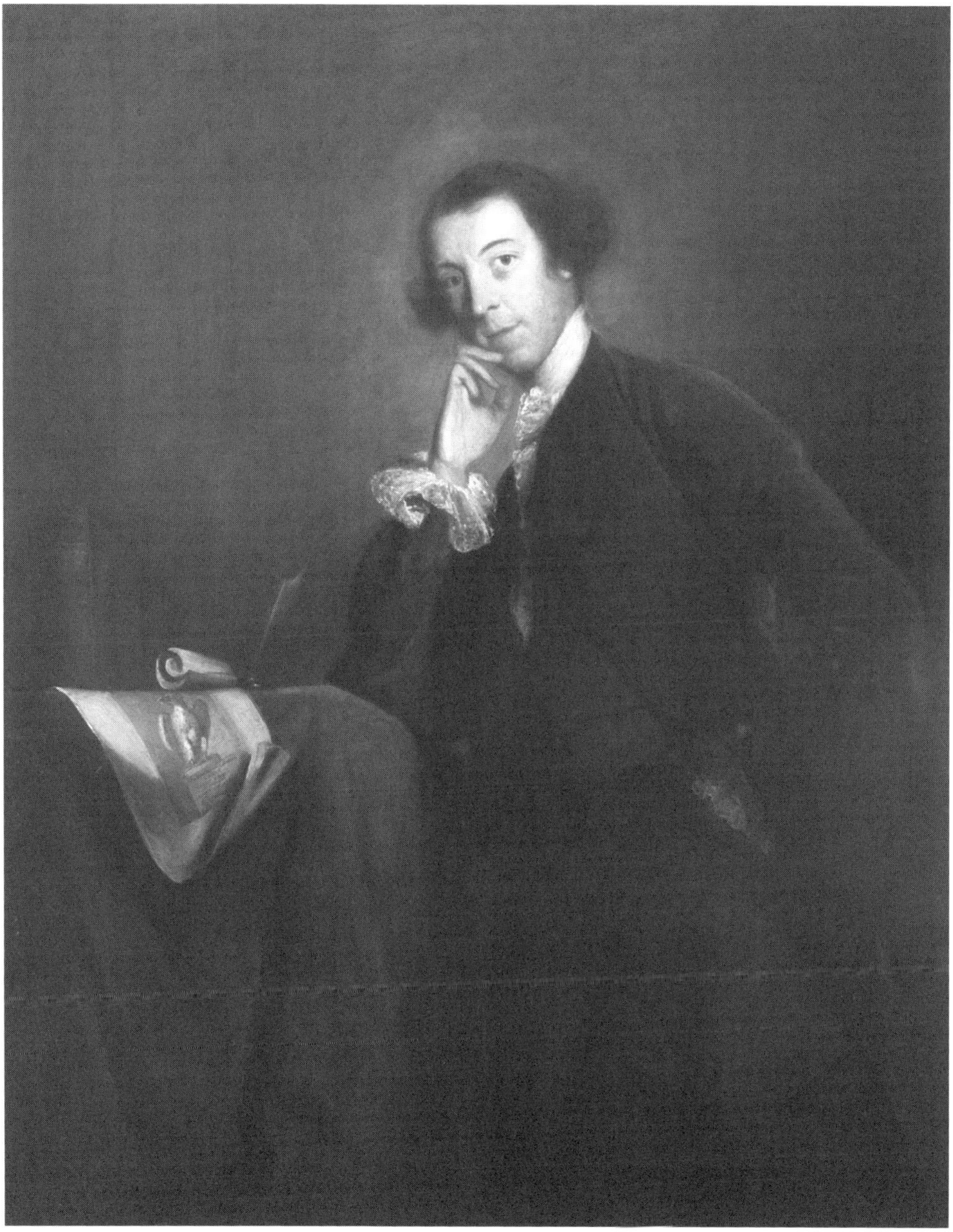

26
Joshua Reynolds
Portrait of Horace Walpole,
*c.*1756–7
Oil on canvas
127.2 × 101.8 cm
The National Portrait
Gallery, London

Beckford's Fantastic Artist

William Beckford's pampered youth saw him exposed to several important Gothic and exotic influences. His friendship with his tutors the artist Alexander Cozens and the architect William Chambers — both of whom were distinctly cosmopolitan in their backgrounds — brought to his attention the power of Oriental styles and kept him informed of advanced art and architectural theory. Such influences were apparent in his flippant but knowledgeable collection of imaginary artists' lives, printed in 1780. His tale of 'Blunderbussiana' evokes particularly the myths around the Italian artist Salvator Rosa (1615–73), whose paintings of savage landscapes and romantic 'banditti' were said to have been inspired by his first-hand experience of life as an outlaw. In Beckford's time, the ideal of the recklessly Sublime artist was resurrected particularly with the figure of John Hamilton Mortimer — the 'English Salvator' — and, mockingly, in relation to the painter Maria Cosway.

1780

William Beckford 1759–1844
"Blunderbussiana"

It was with difficulty we can ascertain the place or even the country where this artist was born; but we have most reason to imagine it was Dalmatia, towards the confines of Croatia. Rouzinski Blunderbussiana, father of him whose adventures will be the subject of the following pages, was captain of some banditti, for many years the terror of Dalmatia and the neighbouring countries. This formidable band exercised the most unlimited depradations, and as they were very numerous, nothing but an army could oppose them. Finding, however, security in defiles amongst the mountains, known but to themselves, the Venetian and Hungarian soldiery attempted their extirpation in vain. Rouzinski, their leader, was one of the haughtiest of mankind; his uncommon stature, matchless intrepidity, and wonderful success, had raised him to the despotic command of these brave savages, to whom no enterprize seemed impossible, and who executed their projects almost as soon as they were conceived. The caves in which they resided were hollowed in the rocks, forming the summit of a mountain in the wild province of the Morlakes, which they had in a manner subdued; no one daring to approach the spot they had established their habitations. The peak of this mountain, seen from afar, was regarded by the Dalmations with horror. Had they known what scenes it concealed, they would have trembled indeed. The plan of this work will not admit a particular description of this mountain and its caves, or else I should certainly have lain before my readers some particulars concerning the residence of these banditti, which, perhaps, might have been worthy of their attention; but at present I must confine myself merely to what relates to the life of Blunderbussiana. His father returning with a rich booty from Turkey, brought with him a lady of some distinction, who had fallen unfortunately into his hands. He conveyed her to his cave, attempted to amuse her with the sight of those magazines (immense grottoes) which contained his treasures, and by degrees falling deeply in love with her, laid them all at her feet.

The young Turk, who had seen but little of the world, was charmed with the manly aspect of her admirer, and dazzled by his liberality, after some time forgot the disgust his savage profession inspired. She at length consented to make him happy; and our hero sprung from this connection, which was celebrated with tumultuous festivity throughout all the subterraneous empire. Blunderbussiana's first ideas, caught from the objects around, cannot be supposed of the gentlest nature. He beheld gloomy caverns hollowed in craggy rocks, which threatened every instant to fall upon his head. He heard each night dreadful relations of combats which had happened in the day, and often, when

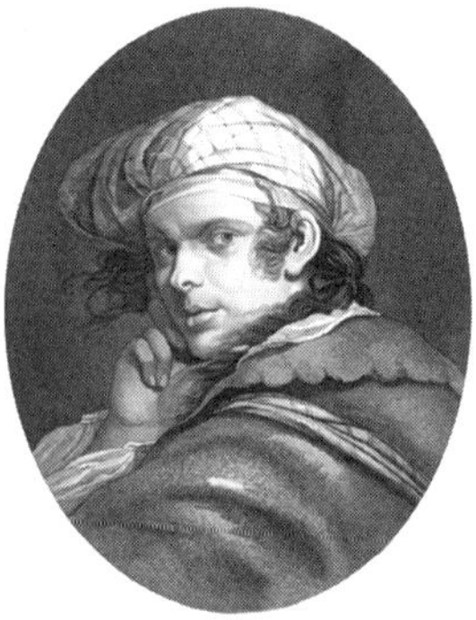

27
Robert Blyth after John Hamilton Mortimer
Self-Portrait in the Character of a Banditti, published 19 September 1782
Etching, on sheet 43 × 32 cm
The National Portrait Gallery, London

wandering about the entrance of the caves, he spied his father and his companions stripping the slain, and letting down their bodies into pits and fissures which had never been fathomed. Being long inured to such ghastly sights, he by degrees grew pleased with them, and his inclination for painting first manifested itself in the desire he had of imitating the figures of his father's warriors.

Rouzinski, as soon as his son was able to dart a javelin or bear a musket, led him to the chace, and exulted in the activity with which he pursued the boar, and the alacrity with which he murdered the trembling stag. After he had spent a year in these sanguinary amusements, his father thought him worthy to partake his expeditions, and led him first to the rencounter of a pretty large body of Turks, who escorted some Hungarian merchants. 'Such for the future must be your game,' said the ruthless robber to his son, who performed prodigies of cruelty and valour. But let me draw a veil over such frightful pictures. Though the truth forbids me entirely to conceal them, humanity pleads strongly for the abridgement of their relation. Two summers passed away in continual rapines and eternal scenes of active oppression. The winter was the season of repose, and the young Rouzinski employed it in recollecting the adventures of the summer months and fixing them by his pencil. Sometimes he read a treatise upon painting, finding it among the spoils of some Italians, which assisted him infinitely. They much recommended the study of anatomy, and he did not hesitate to follow the advice they gave. His father's band frequently bringing bodies to their caves, he amused himself with dissecting and imitating the several parts, till he attained such a perfection in muscular expression as is rarely seen in the works of the greatest masters. His application was surprizing; for his curiosity to examine the structures of the human frame being inflamed, he pursued the study with such eagerness as those who are not *amateurs* cannot easily imagine. Every day discovered some new artery, or tendon to his view; every hour produced some masterly design, and though without any person to guide him, he made a progress which would have done credit to the most eminent artists. He now began to put his figures together in a great manner, and to group them with judgment; but colours were wanting, and without materials, Michael Angelo would have conceived the dome of St Peter's in vain. He had read in his treatise of the works of Italian painters, which he languished to behold, and was determined, if possible, in the ensuing summer, to escape from his father and fly to a country, where he might indulge his inclinations; however, for the present he was charmed with the opportunities of perfecting himself in anatomy, and that occupation diverted his intention of taking flight for some time. In the spring he used early in the morning to quit his cave, and frequently trussing a body over his shoulders, repaired to a wood, and delighted himself in exploring it. Instead of carrying with him, in his walks, a nice pocket edition of some Elzevir classic, he was never without a leg or an arm, which he went slicing along, and generally accompanied his operations with a melodious whistling; for he was of a cheerful disposition, and, if he had had a different education, would have been an ornament to society.

Summer came, and he was called to attend his father, and a select detachment of the band, on an expedition into the Hungarian territories; but some regular troops being aware of their attentions, lay in ambush for their coming, sallied upon them, and left old Rouzinski, with thirty of his comrades, dead upon the field. Blunderbussiana escaped, and made the best of his way thro' forests deemed impenetrable, and mountains, where he subsisted on wild fruit and the milk of goats. When he reached the borders of cultivation, his savage mien and the barbarous roll of his eyes, frighted every villager that beheld him; and so strange was his appearance, that some said he could be nothing but the Antichrist, and others believed him to be the Wandering Jew. After having experienced numerable hardships, which none but those accustomed from their infancy to fatigues could have sustained, he arrived at Friuli; where he was employed in cutting wood, by a Venetian surgeon, who had retired there to enjoy an estate which had been lately bequeathed him. One day, after he had worked very hard, he seized a cat that was frisking about near him, and, by way of recreation, dissected the animal with such skill, that his master, who happened to pass by, was quite surprized, and mentioned this circumstance to several of his friends at dinner, amongst whom the famous Joseph Porta chanced to be present. This painter, who was a great admirer of anatomy, wished to see the young proficient, and being struck with his uncouth figure, began to sketch out his portrait on some tablets he carried about him. Blunderbussiana was in raptures during the performance, and begging earnestly to examine it more narrowly, snatched the pencil from Porta's hand, and in a few strokes corrected some faults in the anatomy with such boldness and veracity, as threw the painter into amazement. Happening to want a servant at this time, Porta desired his friend to permit Blunderbussiana's returning with him to Venice; a request he granted without delay, and the young man joyfully accompanied him. He did not long remain with his master as a servant, being soon considered in the light of a disciple. All possible advantages were procured him, and after a year's study he gave several pieces to the public, in which the *clair obscure* was finely observed. The scenes of his former life were still fresh in his memory, and his pictures almost always represented vast perspective caverns red with the lights of fires, around which banditti were carousing; or else dark valleys between shaggy rocks strewed with the spoils of murder'd travellers. His father, leaning on his spear, and giving orders to his warriors, was generally the principal object in these pieces, characterised by a certain horror, which those ignorant of such dreadful scenes fancied imaginary. If he represented waters, they were dark and troubled; if trees, deformed and withered. His skies were

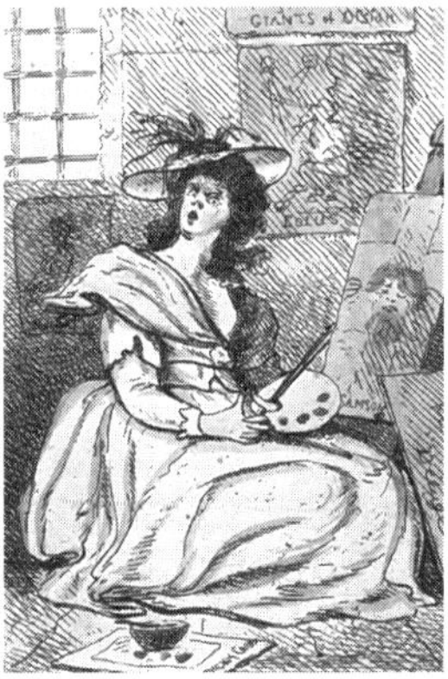

28
Anon.
Maria Costive. At her Studies (caricature of Maria Cosway), published 29 April 1786
Engraving 15 × 23.5 cm
The British Museum, London

lowering, and his *clair obscure* in that style the Italians call *sgraffito* (a greyish melancholy tint) which suited the gloominess of his subjects. It might be conjectured from this choice of subjects, that Blunderbussiana was a very dismal personage. On the contrary, he was, as we hinted before, of a social disposition, and much relished by those with whom he spent the hours he dedicated to amusement. His pleasures, to be sure, were singular, and probably will not be styled such by many of our readers. For example; after a cheerful repast, which he never failed to enliven by his sallies, he would lead some of his friends to ramble about at midnight, and leading them slily to some burying ground, entice them, by way of frolick, to steal some of the bodies, which he bore off with the greatest glee; exulting more than if he had carried in his arms the fairest ladies in the environs. This diversion proved fatal to him at length; for he caught a violent fever in consequence of a drinking match, which was to precede one of these delicious excursions. The disorder, attacking his robust constitution, reduced him in two days to a very critical situation; and, burning with heat, he plunged into a cold bath, out of which he was taken delirious, and being conveyed to his bed, began to rave in a frightful manner. Every minute he seemed to behold the mangled limbs of those he had anatomized, quivering in his apartment. 'Haste, give me my instruments,' cried he, 'that I may spoil the gambols of three cursed legs, that are just stalked into the room, and are going to jump on me. Help! help! or they will kick me out of bed. There again; only see those ugly heads, that do nothing but roll over me! — Hark! what a lumbering noise they make! now they glide along as smoothly as if on a bowling-green. — Mercy defend me from those gogling eyes! — Open all the windows, set wide the doors, — let those grim cats out that spit fire at me and lash me with their tails. O how their bones rattle! — Help! — Mercy! — O!' — The third day released him from his torments, and his body, according to his desire, was delivered, with all his anatomical designs, to the college of surgeons. Such was the end of the ingenious Blunderbussiana, whose skeleton the faculty have canonized, and whose paintings, dispersed in most of the Venetian palaces, still terrify the tender-hearted.

4.3

Henry Fuseli: Hobgoblin Painter

The career of Henry Fuseli (1741–1825) illustrates in a striking fashion the curiously ambivalent attitude towards eccentricity, extravagance and the fantastic in the late eighteenth and early nineteenth centuries. Adopting an outspoken persona that seemed to match the outrageous and fantastical nature of his art, Fuseli might be assumed to be a prototype for the bohemian or decadent artists of a later period. Certainly, the myths about his eating raw pork to inspire visionary dreams have proved resilient. But at the same time, he enjoyed in the later part of his life a high degree of establishment approval. He was Professor of Painting and Keeper of the Royal Academy of Arts, and in these capacities was responsible for the education of a whole generation of British artists. Fuseli's own writings on art reflect this divided identity, and expose a degree of ambivalence around the relationship of individual imagination to cultural tradition, of the creative will to the rules of art; the commentaries of Fuseli's sometime acolyte Benjamin Robert Haydon (1786-1846) reveal a sense of disillusion or scepticism around this unstable conception of the visionary artist.

1801

Henry Fuseli 1741–1825
Lectures on Painting, 'Invention'

Before we proceed to the process and methods of invention, it is not superfluous to advert to a question which has often been made, and by some has been answered in the negative; *whether it be within the artist's province or not, to find or to combine a subject from himself, without having recourse to tradition or the stores of history and poetry?* Why not, if the subject be within the limits of art and the combinations of nature, though it should have escaped observation? Shall the immediate avenues of the mind, open to all its observers, from the poet to the novelist, be shut only to the artist? Shall he be reduced to receive as alms from them what he has a right to share as common property? Assertions like this, say in other words, that the Laocoon owes the impression he makes on us to his name alone, and that if tradition had not told a story and Pliny fixed it to that work, the artist's conception of a father with his sons, surprised and entangled by two serpents within the recesses of a cavern or lonesome dell, was inadmissible and transgressed the laws of invention. I am much mistaken, if, so far from losing its power over us with its traditional sanction, it would not rouse our sympathy more forcibly, and press the subject closer to our breast, were it considered only as the representation of an incident common to humanity. The ancients were so convinced of their right that they assigned it its own class, and Theon the Samian is mentioned by Quintilian, whom none will accuse or suspect of confounding the limits of the arts, in his list of primary painters, as owing his celebrity to that intuition into the moments of sudden movements of nature, which the Greeks call φαντασιας, the Romans *visiones*, and we might circumscribe by the phrase of 'unpremeditated conceptions' the reproduction of associated ideas.

1788–1818

Henry Fuseli 1741–1825
Aphorisms on Art

9 The fiery sets his subject in a blaze, and mounts its vapours; the melancholy cleaves the rock, or gropes through thorns for his; the sanguine deluges all, and seizes none; the phlegmatic sucks one, and drops off with repletion.

10 Some enter the gates of art with golden keys, and take their seats with dignity among the demi-gods of fame; some burst the doors and leap into a niche with savage power; thousands consume their time in chinking useless keys, and aiming feeble pushes against the inexorable doors.

11 Heaven and earth, advantages and obstacles, conspire to educate genius.

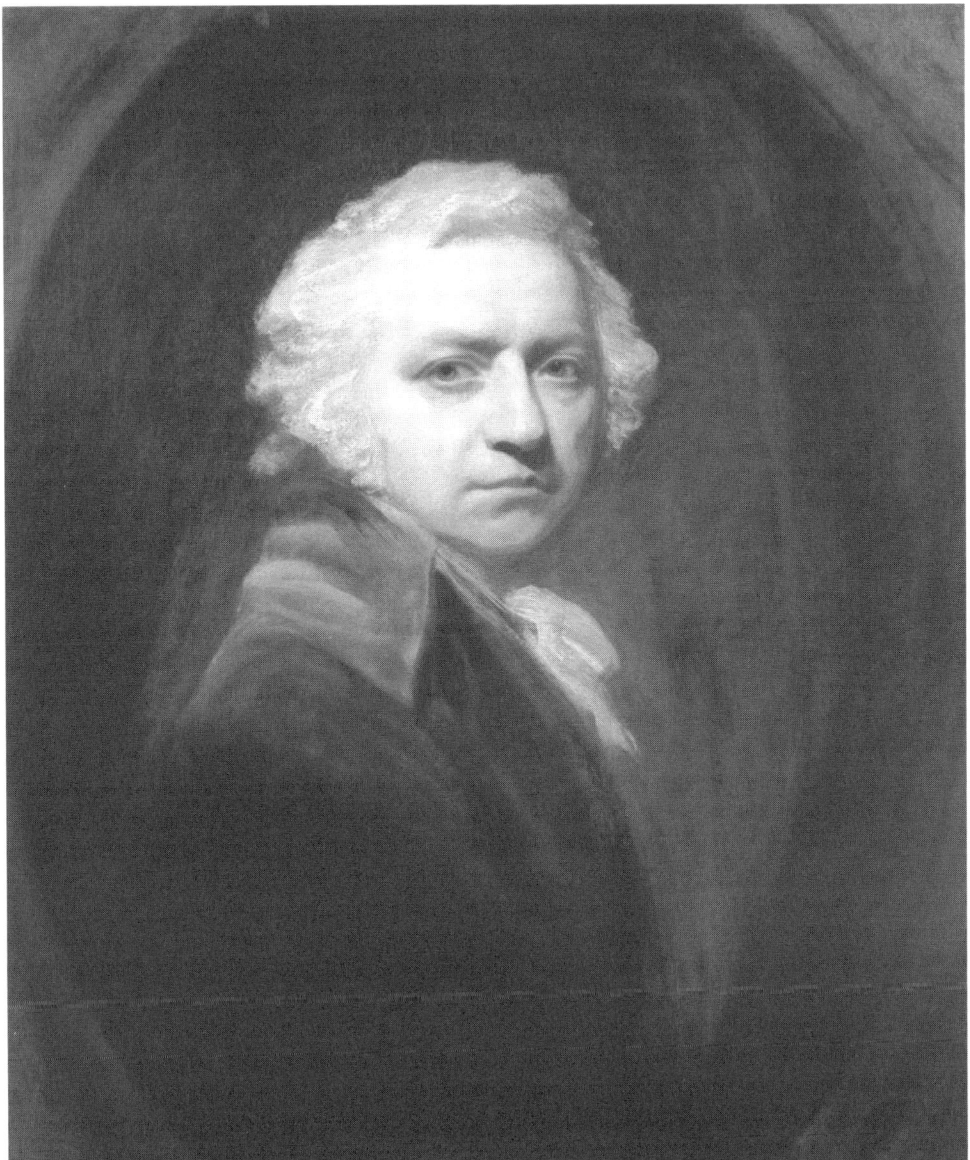

29
John Opie
Portrait of Henry Fuseli,
exh. 1794
Oil on canvas 76.3 × 63.5 cm
The National Portrait
Gallery, London

12 Organization is the mother of talent; practice its nurse; the senses its dominion; but hearts alone can penetrate hearts.

13 It is the lost of genius to be opposed, and to be invigorated by opposition: all extremes touch each other; frigid praise and censure wait upon attainable or common powers; but the successful adventurer in the realms of discovery leaps on an unknown or long-lost shore, ennobles it with his name, and grasps immortality.

20 Reality teams with disappointment for him whose sources of enjoyment spring in the elysium of fancy.

27 Some of the most genuine effusions of genius in art, some of the most estimable qualities in society, may be beholden for our homage to very disreputable principles.

51 Genius, inspired by invention, rends the veil that separates existence from possibility; peeps into the dark, and catches a shape, a feature, or a colour, in the reflected ray.

110 The epoch of rules, of theories, poetics, criticisms in a nation, will add to their stock of authors in the same proportion as it diminishes their stock of genius: their productions will bear the stamp of study, not of nature; they will adopt, not generate; sentiment will supplant images, and narrative invention; words will not longer be the dress but the limbs of composition, and feeble elegance will supply the want of nerves.

119 None but the first can represent the first. Genius, absorbed by the subject, hastens to the centre; and from that point disseminates, to that leads back the rays: talent, full of its own dexterities, begins to point the rays before they have a centre, and aggregates a mass of secondary beauties.

120 The ear absorbed in harmonies of its own creation, is deaf to all external ones.

137 Genius knows no partner. All partnership is deleterious to poetry and art: one must rule.

231 One of the most unexplored regions of are dreams, and what may be called the personification of sentiment: the Prophets, Sibyls and Patriarchs of Michael Angelo are so many branches of one great sentiment. The dream of Raffaelo is a characteristic representation of a dream; the dream of Michelangelo is moral inspiration, a sublime sentiment.

31 May 1790

The Public Advertiser

Fuseli

This Artist, whose works as a Painter are in such deserved esteem, is commended for nothing more than for that vivid imagination, whose creative exertions bring new beings into view, and which, pursuing the track of Shakespeare, calls forth objects beyond the boundaries of Nature,

> - - - 'and gives to airy Nothing
> A local Habitation and a Name.'

Of this creative faculty, if instances were wanted, his picture in the Shakespeare Gallery, from the *Midsummer Night's Dream*, could of itself furnish a sufficiency. The Fairies, Moth, Mustard, and Pease-Blossom, are beings as whimsical as ever were imagined.

But what makes this quality in the Artist the more singular, and induces us at present to mention it to our readers, is a circumstance not generally known, but which is equally interesting to the Poet, the Naturalist, and the Physician. It is a fact, that this creative fancy springs solely from an animal process, and is brought about after regular intervals, by Mr Fuseli's — eating raw PORK for supper!

The fact of indigestion producing a strong effect on the imagination, is fully ascertained. The monstrous forms which the latter brings forth, in consequence, are immediately sketched, and, when necessary, embodied on the canvas!

This account, however it may border on the ludicrous, our readers may rely on as strictly founded in truth.

1853

Benjamin Robert Haydon 1796–1846 *Autobiography*

Fuseli had a great reputation for the terrible. His sublime conception of Uriel and Satan had impressed me when a boy. I had a mysterious aw of him. Prince Hoare's apprehensions lest he might injure my taste or hurt my morals, excited in my mind a notion that he was a sort of gifted wild beast.

My father had the same feeling, and a letter I received from him, just before my calling, concluded with these words: 'God speed you with the terrible Fuseli.'

This sort of preparation made everything worse, and I was quite nervous when the day arrived. I walked away with my drawings up Wardour Street. I remembered that Berners Street had a golden lion on the right corner house and blundered on, till without knowing how or remembering why, I found myself at Fuseli's door! I deliberated a minute or two, and at last making up my mind to see the enchanter, I jerked up the knocker so nervously that it stuck in the air. I looked at it, as much as to say: 'Is this fair?' and then drove it down with such a devil of a blow that the door rang again. The maid came rushing up in astonishment. I followed her into a gallery or showroom, enough to frighten anybody at twilight. Galvanised devils — malicious witches brewing their incantations — Satan bridging Chaos, and springing upwards like a pyramid of fire — Lady Macbeth — Paolo and Francesca — Falstaff and Mrs Quickly — humour, pathos, terror, blood, and murder, met one at every look! I expected the floor to give way — I fancied Fuseli himself to be a giant. I heard his footsteps and saw a little bony hand slide round the edge of the door, followed by a little white-haired lion-faced

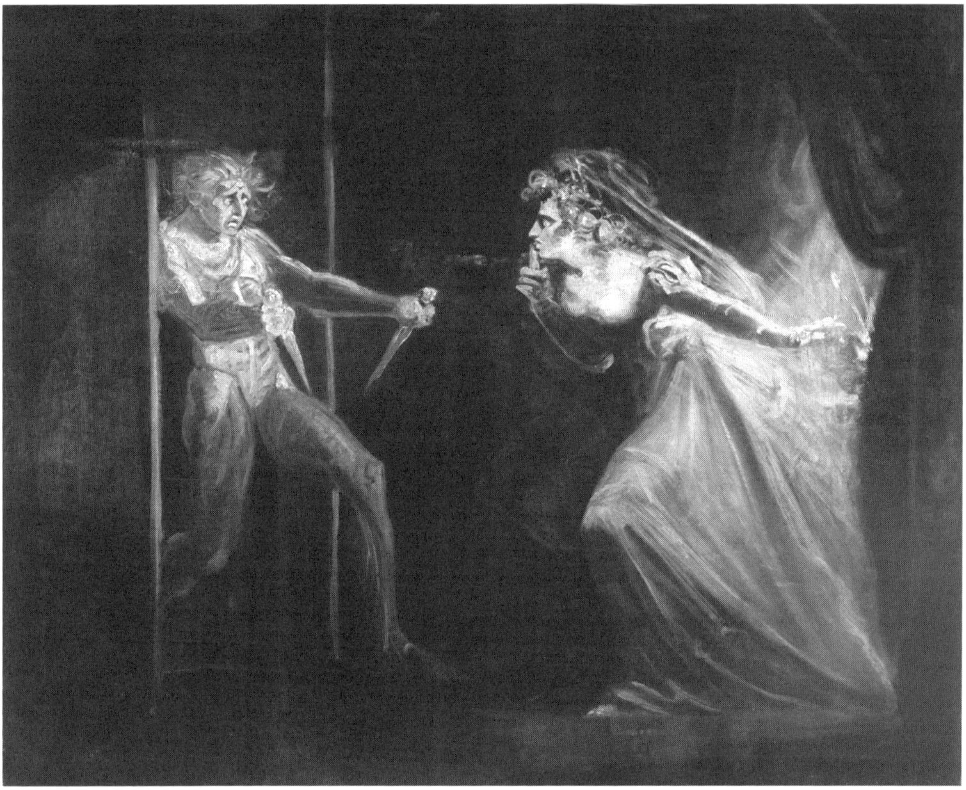

30
Henry Fuseli
Lady Macbeth Seizing the Daggers, ?exh. 1812
Oil on canvas 121.3 × 145.4 cm
Tate. Purchased 1965

man in an old flannel dressing-gown, tied round his waist with a piece of rope, and upon his head the bottom of Mrs Fuseli's work-basket.

'Well, well,' thought I, 'I am a match for you at any rate, if bewitching is tried': but all apprehension vanished on his saying in the mildest and kindest way: 'Well, Mr Haydon, I have heard a great deal of you from Mr Hoare. Where are your drawings?' In a fright I gave him the wrong book, with a sketch of some men pushing a cask into a grocer's shop; Fuseli smiled and said: 'By Gode, de fellow does his business at least with energy.' I was gratified at his being pleased in spite of my mistake.

'You are studying anatomy — you are right. Show me some drawings. I am Keeper of de Academy, and hope to see you dere de first nights.' I went away, feeling happy that my bones were whole and my breathing uninterrupted.

4.4

William Blake: The Visionary Artist

The nature — and veracity — of the visions apparently experienced by William Blake have always attracted comment. For the critics who made comment on his work, Blake's idiosyncratic iconography and stylised manner were the signs of a madman; as much as they derived from Fuseli, he perhaps outdid the older artist in the extent of his insanity and the depth of his delusion. Within Blake's circle, a variety of opinion was to be found. Fuseli thought there was 'something of madness about him', others considered him a true visionary. His patrons, William Hayley and latterly John Linnell and John Varley, may actively have encouraged his imaginative flights. There is a suspicion in modern scholarship that Blake played up his eccentricities in order to satisfy those of his supporters who wanted him to be genuinely inspired by encounters with spirits.

The two letters excerpted here show Blake explaining his visionary approach, first in relation to his development of distinctive technical and formal approaches, and secondly in poetic form, drawing in reference both to reality and to figures from his invented iconography. The biographical account of Allan Cunningham, also quoted here, was the most important early published source on the artist, and helped establish his memory as a great artistic eccentric.

16 August 1799

William Blake 1757–1827
to The Revd Dr Trusler

Revd Sir
I find more & more that my Style of Designing is a Species by itself. & in this which I send you have been compelld by my Genius or Angel to follow where he led if I were to act otherwise it would not fulfill the purpose for which alone I live. which is in conjunction with such men as my friend Cumberland to renew the lost Art of the Greeks

I attempted every morning for a fortnight together to follow your Dictate. but when I found my attempts were in vain. resolvd to shew an independence which I know will please an Author better than slavishly following the track of another however admirable that track may be At any rate my Excuse must be: I could not do otherwise, it was out of my power!

I know I begged of you to give me your Ideas & promised to build on them here I counted without my host I now find my mistake

The Design I have Sent. Is

A Father taking leave of his Wife & Child. Is watchd by Two Fiends incarnate. with intention that when his back is turned they will murder the mother & her infant — If this is not Malevolence with a vengeance I have never seen it on Earth. & if you approve of this I have no doubt of giving you Benevolence with Equal Vigor. as also Pride & Humility. but cannot previously describe in words what I mean to Design for fear I should Evaporate the Spirit of my Invention. But I hope that none of my Designs will be destitute of Infinite Particulars which will present themselves to the Contemplator. And tho I call them Mine I know that they are not Mine being of the same opinion with Milton when he says That the Muse visits his Slumbers & awakes & governs his Song when Morn purples The East. & being also in the predicament of that prophet who says I cannot go beyond the command of the Lord to speak good or bad

If you approve of my Manner & it is agreeable to you. I would rather Paint Pictures in oil of the same dimensions than make Drawings. & on the same terms. by this means you will have a number of Cabinet pictures. which I flatter myself will not be unworthy of a Scholar of Rembrant & Teniers. whom I have Studied no less than Rafael & Michael angelo — Please to send me your orders respecting this & In my next Effort I promise more Expedition

22 November 1802

William Blake 1757–1827
to Thomas Butts

After I had finishd my Letter I found that I had not said half what I intended to say & in particular I wish to ask you what subject you choose to be painted on the remaining Canvas which I brought down with me (for there were three) and to tell you that several of the Drawings were in great forwardness you will see by the Inclosed Account that the remaining Number of Drawings which you gave me orders for is Eighteen I will finish these with all possible Expedition if indeed I have not tired you or as it is politely calld Bored you too much already or if you would rather cry out Enough Off Off! tell me in a Letter of forgiveness if you were offended & of accustomd friendship if you were not. But I will bore you more with some Verses which My Wife desires me to Copy out & send you with her kind love & Respect they were Composed <above> a twelvemonth ago [in a] <while> Walk<ing> from Felpham to Lavant to meet my Sister

With happiness stretchd across the hills
In a cloud that dewy sweetness distills
With a blue sky spread over with wings
And a mild sun that mounts & sings
With trees & fields full of Fairy elves
And little devils who fight for themselves
Remembring the Verses that Hayley sung
When my heart knockd against the root of my tongue
With Angels planted in Hawthorn bowers
And God himself in the passing hours
With Silver Angels across my way
And Golden Demons that none can stay
With my Father hovering upon the wind
And my Brother Robert just behind
And my Brother John the evil one
In a black cloud making his mone
Tho dead they appear upon my path
Notwithstanding my terrible wrath
They beg they intreat they drop their tears
Filld full of hopes filld full of fears
With a thousand Angels upon the Wind
Pouring disconsolate from behind
To drive them off & before my way
A frowning Thistle implores my stay
What to others a trifle appears
Fills me full of smiles or tears
For double the vision my Eyes do see
And a double vision is always with me
With my inward Eye 'tis an old Man grey
With my outward a Thistle across my way
'If thou goest back the thistle said
Thou art to endless woe betrayd
For here does Theotormon lower
And here is Enitharmons bower
And Los the terrible thus hath sworn
Because thou backward dost return
Poverty Envy old age & fear
Shall bring thy Wife upon a bier
And Butts shall give what Fuseli gave
A dark black Rock & a gloomy Cave.'
I struck the Thistle with my foot
And broke him up from his delving root
'Must the duties of life each other cross'
'Must every joy be dung & dross'
'Must my dear Butts feel cold neglect'
'Because I give Hayley his due respect'
'Must Flaxman look upon me as wild'
'And all my friends be with doubts beguild'
'Must my Wife live in my Sisters bane'
'Or my sister survive on my Loves pain'
'The curses of Los the terrible shade'
'And his dismal terrors make me afraid'
So I spoke & struck in my wrath
The old man weltering upon my path
Then Los appeard in all his power
In the Sun he appeard descending before
My face in fierce flames in my double sight
Twas outward a Sun: inward Los in his might
'My hands are labourd day & night'
'And Ease comes never in my sight'
'My Wife has no indulgence given'
'Except what comes to her from heaven'
'We eat little we drink less'
'This Earth breeds not our happiness'
'Another Sun feeds our lifes streams'
'We are not warmed with thy beams'
'Thou measurest not the Time to me'
'Nor yet the Space that I do see'
'My Mind is not with thy light arrayd'
'Thy terrors shall not make me afraid'
When I had my Defiance given
The Sun stood trembling in heaven
The Moon that glowd remote below
Became leprous & white as snow
And every Soul of men on the Earth
Felt affliction & sorrow & sickness & dearth
Los flamd in my path & the Sun was hot
With the bows of my Mind & the Arrows of Thought
My bowstring fierce with Ardour breathes
My arrows glow in their golden sheaves
My brothers & father march before
The heavens drop with human gore
Now I a fourfold vision see
And a fourfold vision is given to me
Tis fourfold in my supreme delight
And three fold in soft Beulahs night
And twofold Always. May God us keep
From Single vision & Newtons sleep

I also inclose you some Ballads by Mr Hayley with prints to them by Your Hble. Servt. I should have sent them before now but could not get any thing done for You to please myself for I do assure you that I have truly studied the two little pictures I now send & do not repent of the time I have spent upon them
God bless you

1829-33

Allan Cunningham 1784-1842
Lives of the Most Eminent British Painters, Sculptors, and Architects

During the day he was a man of sagacity and sense, who handled his graver wisely, and conversed in a wholesome and pleasant manner: in the evening, when he had done his prescribed task, he gave loose to his imagination. While employed on those engravings which accompany the works of Cowper, he saw such company as the country where he resided afforded, and talked with Hayley about poetry with a feeling to which the author of *The Triumphs of Temper* was an utter stranger; but at the close of day away went Blake to the sea shore to indulge in his own thoughts and

'High converse with the dead to hold'

Here he forgot the present moment and lived in the past; he conceived, verily, that he had lived in other days, and had formed friendships with Homer and Moses; with Pindar and Virgil; with Dante and Milton. These great men, he asserted, appeared to him in visions, and even entered into conversation. Milton, in a moment of confidence, entrusted him with a whole poem of his, which the world had never seen; but unfortunately the communication was oral, and the poetry seemed to have lost much of its brightness in Blake's recitation. When asked about the look of those visions, he answered, 'They are all majestic shadows, gray but luminous, and superior to the common height of men.' It was evident that the solitude of the country gave him a larger swing in imaginary matters. His wife often accompanied him to these strange interviews; she saw nothing and heard as little, but she was certain that her husband both heard and saw.

Blake's mind at all times resembled the first page in the magicians book of gramoury, which made

'The cobweb on the dungeon wall,
Seem tapestry in lordly hall.'

His mind could convert the most ordinary occurrence into something mystical and supernatural. He often saw less majestic shapes than those of the poets old. 'Did you ever see a fairy's funeral, madam?' he once said to a lady, who happened to sit by him in company. 'Never, sir!' was the answer. 'I have,' said Blake, 'but not before last night. I was walking along in my garden, there was great stillness among the branches and flowers and more than common sweetness in the air; I heard a low and pleasant sound,

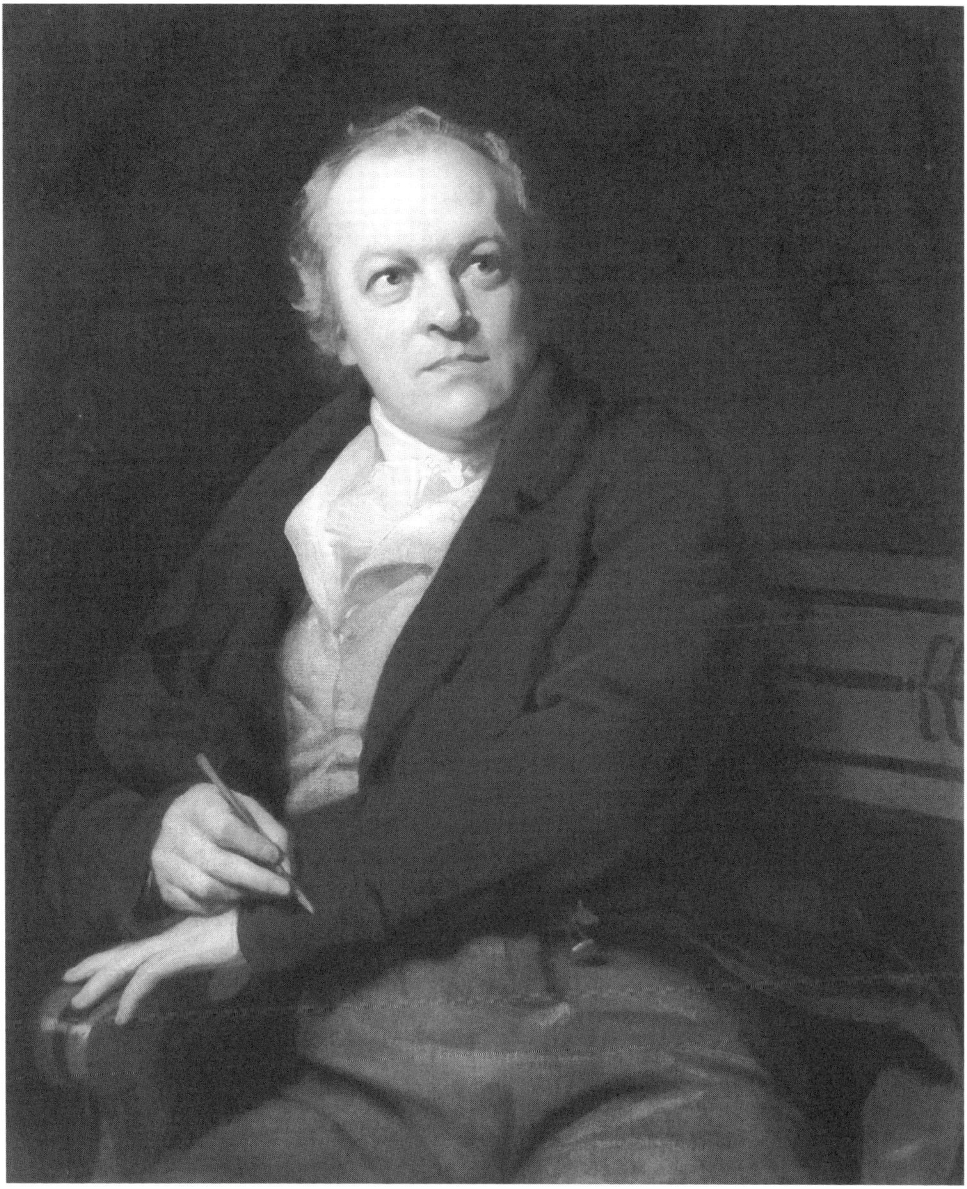

31
Thomas Phillips
Portrait of William Blake,
exh. 1807
Oil on canvas 92.1 × 72 cm
The National Portrait Gallery, London

and I knew not whence it came. At last I saw the broad leaf of a flower move, and underneath I saw a procession of creatures of the size and colour of green and gray grasshoppers, bearing a body laid out on a rose leaf, which they buried with songs, and then disappeared. It was a fairy funeral.' It would, perhaps, have been better for his fame had he connected it more with the superstitious beliefs of his country — amongst the elves and fairies his fancy might have wandered at will — their popular character would perhaps have kept him within the bounds of traditionary belief, and the sea of his imagination might have had a shore.

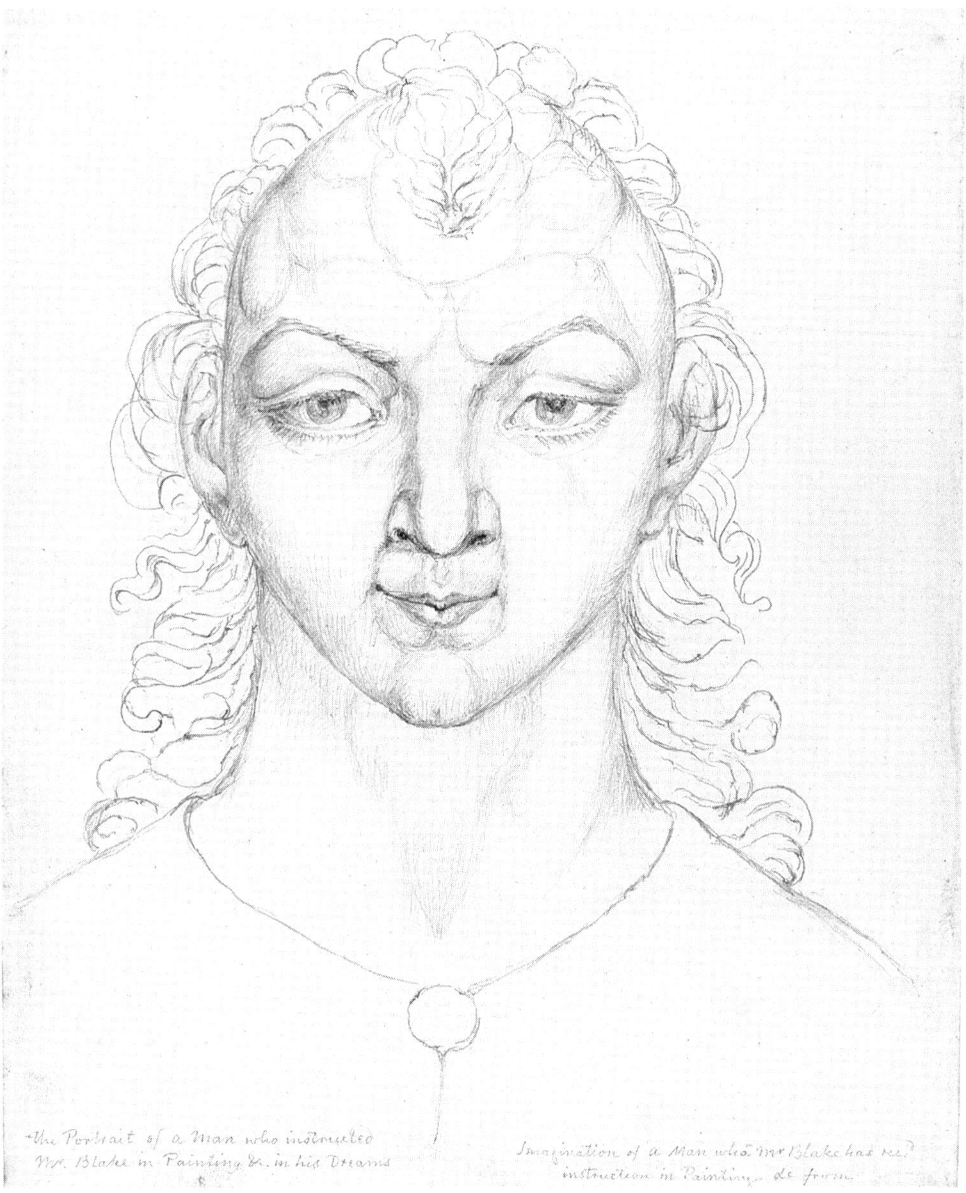

32
Probably John Linnell, after William Blake
The Man who Taught Blake Painting in his Dreams (Perhaps a Visionary Self-Portrait), after *c.*1819–20
Pencil on paper 26 × 20.6 cm
Tate. Bequeathed by Miss Alice G.E. Carthew 1940

33
William Blake
Vision: The Inspiration of the Poet (Elisha in the Chamber on the Wall), *c.*1819–20
Pencil and watercolour on paper 24.4 × 21.1 cm
Tate. Purchased with assistance from the American Fund for the Tate Gallery, courtesy of Edwin C. Cohen and Echoing Green 1989

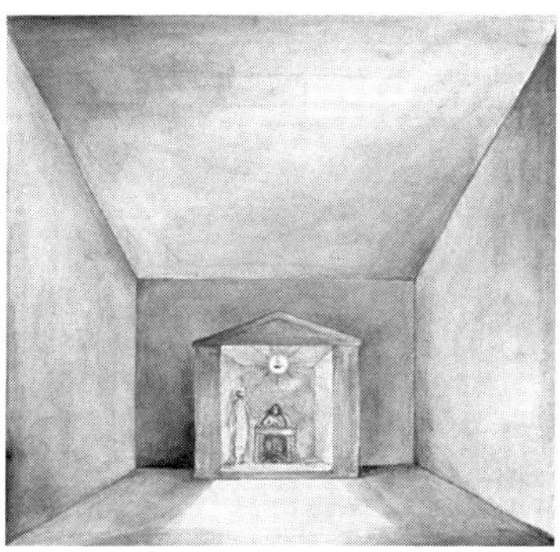

4.5

The Writing of Frankenstein: Mary Shelley's Account

Mary Shelley's Introduction to the 1831 edition of *Frankenstein* is considered a classic piece of Gothic writing in its own right. Dramatising the ghost-story session with Percy Bysshe Shelley, John Polidori and Lord Byron on 16 June 1816 in a villa overlooking Lake Geneva, Shelley has recourse to the creaking effects of the Gothic novel in its most conventional form. Yet her recollection, or creation, of the circumstances around the conception of the text are rich with personal associations, recalling the tragic loss of her own first child in March 1815 and the terrible dream of that infant's return to life which followed shortly thereafter. In this account she becomes mother to the monster, and in her own creative abilities a Frankenstein herself.

1831

Mary Shelley 1797–1851
Introduction to the 1831 edition of *Frankenstein*

The Publishers of the Standard Novels, in selecting 'Frankenstein' for one of their series, expressed a wish that I should furnish them with some account of the origin of the story. I am the more willing to comply, because I shall thus give a general answer to the question, so very frequently asked me — 'How I, then a young girl, came to think of, and to dilate upon, so very hideous an idea?' It is true that I am very averse to bringing myself forward in print; but as my account will only appear as an appendage to a former production, and as it will be confined to such topics as have connection with my authorship alone, I can scarcely accuse myself of a personal intrusion.

It is not singular that, as the daughter of two persons of distinguished literary celebrity, I should very early in life have thought of writing. As a child I scribbled; and my favourite pastime, during the hours given me for recreation, was to 'write stories.' Still I had a dearer pleasure than this, which was the formation of castles in the air — the indulging in waking dreams — the following up trains of thought, which had for their subject the formation of a succession of imaginary incidents. My dreams were at once more fantastic and agreeable than my writings. In the latter I was a close imitator — rather doing as others had done, then putting down the suggestions of my own mind. What I wrote was intended at least for one other eye — my childhood's companion and friend; but my dreams were all my own; I accounted for them to nobody; they were my refuge when annoyed — my dearest pleasure when free.

I lived principally in the country as a girl, and passed a considerable time in Scotland. I made occasional visits to the more picturesque parts; but my habitual residence was on the blank and dreary northern shores of the Tay, near Dundee. Blank and dreary on retrospection I call them; they were not so to me then. They were the eyry of freedom, and the pleasant region where unheeded I could commune with the creatures of my fancy. I wrote then — but in a most common-place style. It was beneath the trees of the grounds belonging to our house, on the bleak sides of the woodless mountains near, that my true compositions, the airy flights of my imagination, were born and fostered. I did not make myself the heroine of my tales. Life appeared to me too common-place an affair as regarded myself. I could not figure to myself that romantic woes or wonderful events would ever be my lot; but I was not confined to my own identity, and I could people the hours with creations far more interesting to me at that age, than my own sensations.

After this my life became busier, and reality stood in place of fiction. My husband, however, was from the first, very anxious

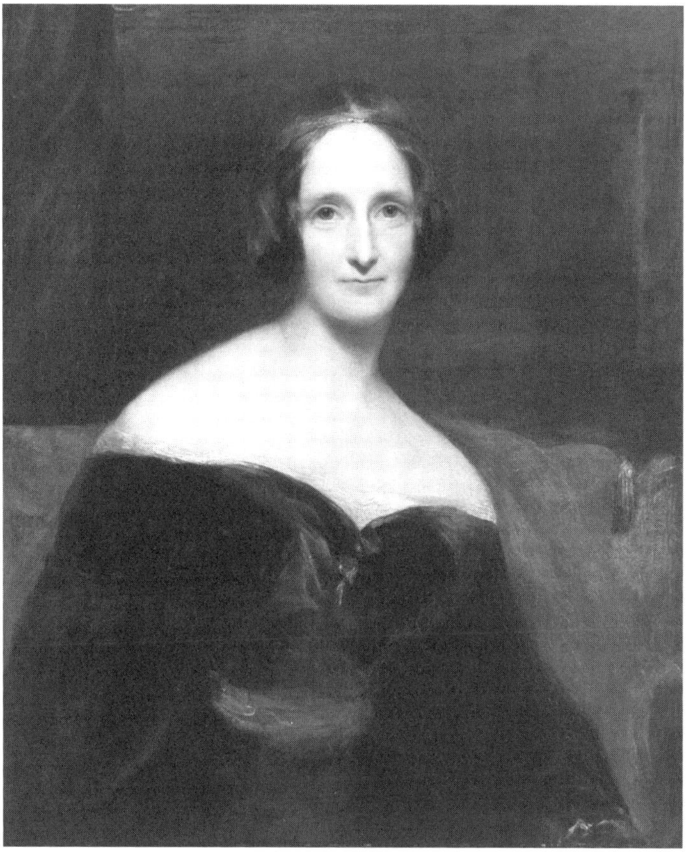

34
Richard Rothwell
Portrait of Mary Shelley,
exh. 1840
Oil on canvas 73.7 × 61cm
The National Portrait
Gallery, London

that I should prove myself worthy of my parentage, and enrol myself on the page of fame. He was for ever inciting me to obtain literary reputation, which even on my own part I cared for then, though since I have become infinitely indifferent to it. At this time he desired that I should write, not so much with the idea that I could produce any thing worthy of notice, but that he might himself judge how far I possessed the promise of better things hereafter. Still I did nothing. Travelling, and the cares of a family, occupied my time; and study, in the way of reading, or improving my ideas in communication with his far more cultivated mind, was all of literary employment that engaged my attention.

In the summer of 1816, we visited Switzerland, and became the neighbours of Lord Byron. At first we spent our pleasant hours on the lake, or wandering on its shores; and Lord Byron, who was writing the third canto of Childe Harold, was the only one among us who put his thoughts upon paper. These, as he brought them successively to us, clothed in all the light and harmony of poetry, seemed to stamp as divine the glories of heaven and earth, whose influences we partook with him.

But it proved a wet, ungenial summer, and incessant rain often confined us for days to the house. Some volumes of ghost stories, translated from the German into French, fell into our hands. There was the History of the Inconstant Lover, who, when he thought to clasp the bride to whom he had pledged his vows, found himself in the arms of the pale ghost of her whom he had deserted. There was the tale of the sinful founder of his race, whose miserable doom it was to bestow the kiss of death on all the younger sons of his fated house, just when they reached the age of promise. His gigantic, shadowy form, clothed like the ghost in Hamlet, in complete armour, but with the beaver up, was seen at midnight, by the moon's fitful beams, to advance slowly along the gloomy avenue. The shape was lost beneath the shadow of the castle walls; but soon a gate swung back, a step was heard, the door of the chamber opened, and he advanced to the couch of the blooming youths, cradled in healthy sleep. Eternal sorrow sat upon his face as he bent down and kissed the forehead of the boys, who from that hour withered like flowers snapt upon the stalk. I have not seen these stories since then; but their incidents are as fresh in my mind as if I had read them yesterday.

We will each write a ghost story, said Lord Byron; and his proposition was acceded to. There were four of us. The noble author began a tale, a fragment of which he printed at the end of his poem of Mazeppa. Shelley, more apt to embody ideas and sentiments in the radiance of brilliant imagery, and in the music of the most melodious verse that adorns our language, than to invent the machinery of a story, commenced one founded on the experiences of his early life. Poor Polidori had some terrible idea about a skull-headed lady, who was so punished for peeping through a key-hole — to see what I forget — something very shocking and wrong of course; but when she was reduced to a worse condition than the renowned Tom of Coventry, he did not know what to do with her, and was obliged to despatch her to the tomb of the Capulets, the only place for which she was fitted. The illustrious poets also, annoyed the platitude of prose, speedily relinquished their uncongenial task.

I busied myself *to think of a story*, — a story to rival those which had excited us to this task. One which would speak to the mysterious fears of our nature, and awaken thrilling horror — one to make the reader dread to look round, to curdle the blood, and quicken the beatings of the heart. If I did not accomplish these things, my ghost story would be unworthy of its name. I thought and pondered — vainly. I felt that blank incapability of invention which is the greatest misery of authorship, when dull Nothing replies to our anxious invocations. *Have you thought of a story?* I was asked each morning, and each morning I was forced to reply with a mortifying negative.

Every thing must have a beginning, to speak in Sanchean phrase; and that beginning must be linked to something that went before. The Hindoos give the world an elephant to support it, but they make the elephant stand upon a tortoise. Invention, it must be humbly admitted, does not consist in creating out of the void, but out of chaos; the materials must, in the first place, be afforded: it can give form to dark, shapeless substances, but cannot bring into being the substance itself. In all matters of discovery and invention, even of those that appertain to the imagination, we are continually reminded of the story of Columbus and his egg. Invention consists in the capacity of seizing on the capabilities of a subject, and in the power of moulding and fashioning ideas suggested to it.

Many and long were the conversations between Lord Byron and Shelley, to which I was a devout but nearly silent listener. During one of these, various philosophical doctrines were discussed, and among others the nature of the principle of life, and whether there was any probability of its ever being discovered and communicated. They talked of the experiments of Dr. Darwin, (I speak not of what the Doctor really did, or said that he did, but, as more to my purpose, of what was then spoken of as having been done by him,) who preserved a piece of vermicelli in a glass case, till by some extraordinary means it began to move with voluntary motion. Not thus, after all, would life be given. Perhaps a corpse would be re-animated; galvanism had given token of such things: perhaps the component parts of a creature might be manufactured, brought together, and endured with vital warmth.

Night waned upon this talk, and even the witching hour had gone by, before we retired to rest. When I placed my head on my pillow, I did not sleep, nor could I be said to think. My imagination, unbidden, possessed and guided me, gifting the successive images that arose in my mind with a vividness far beyond the usual bounds of reverie. I saw — with shut eyes, but acute mental vision, — I saw the pale student of unhallowed arts kneeling beside the thing he had put together. I saw the hideous phantasm of a man stretched out, and then, on the working of some powerful engine, show signs of life, and stir with an uneasy, half vital motion. Frightful must it be; for supremely frightful would be the effect of any human endeavour to mock the stupendous mechanism of the Creator of the world. His success would terrify the artist; he would rush away from his odious handywork, horror-stricken. He would hope that, left to itself, the slight spark of life which he had communicated would fade; that this thing, which had received such imperfect animation, would subside into dead matter; and he might sleep in the belief that the silence of the grave would quench for ever the transient existence of the hideous corpse which he had looked upon as the cradle of life. He sleeps; but he is awakened; he opens his eyes; behold the horrid thing stands at his bedside, opening his curtains, and looking on him with yellow, watery, but speculative eyes.

I opened mine in terror. The idea so possessed my mind, that a thrill of fear ran through me, and I wished to exchange the ghastly image of my fancy for the realities around. I see them still; the very room, the dark *parquet*, the closed shutters, with the moonlight struggling through, and the sense I had that the glassy lake and white high Alps were beyond. I could not so easily get rid of my hideous phantom; still it haunted me. I must try to think of something else. I recurred to my ghost story, — my tiresome unlucky ghost story! O! if I could only contrive one which would frighten my reader as I myself had been frightened that night!

Swift as light and as cheering was the idea that broke in upon me.

I have found it! What terrified me will terrify others; and I need only describe the spectre which had haunted my midnight pillow.

On the morrow I announced that I had *thought of a story*. I began that day with the words, *It was on a dreary night of November*, making only a transcript of the grim terrors of my waking dream.

At first I thought but of a few pages — of a short tale; but Shelley urged me to develope the idea at greater length. I certainly did not owe the suggestion of one incident, nor scarcely one train of feeling, to my husband, and yet but for his incitement, it would never have taken the form in which it was presented to the world. From this declaration I must except the preface. As far as I can recollect, it was entirely written by him.

And now, once again, I bid my hideous progeny go forth and prosper. I have an affection for it, for it was the offspring of happy days, when death and grief were but words, which found no true echo in my heart. Its several pages speak of many a walk, many a drive, and many a conversation, when I was not alone; and my companion was one who, in this world, I shall never see more. But this is for myself; my readers have nothing to do with these associations.

I will add but one word as to the alterations I have made. They are principally those of style. I have changed no portion of the story, nor introduced any new ideas or circumstances. I have mended the language where it was so bald as to interfere with the interest of the narrative; and these changes occur almost exclusively in the beginning of the first volume. Throughout they are entirely confined to such parts as are mere adjuncts to the story, leaving the core and substance of it untouched.

M.W.S.
London, October 15, 1831.

4.6

Suspiria de Profundis

Thomas De Quincey (1785–1859) has only recently been considered in relation to the Gothic. Essayist and critic, he achieved enormous fame with his *Confessions of an English Opium-Eater* (published in parts in 1821, and as a book in 1822). This autobiographical, dream and drug-fuelled narrative, represented a daring new kind of literary exploration into the realm of the subjective. *Suspiria de Profundis*, excerpted here, is a belated follow-up, including meditations on the power of dreams, and the potential of drugs to enhance the imagination. Although not, by any measure, simply Gothic texts, De Quincey's writings are profoundly informed by the Gothic — a literary form he encountered and consumed with a passion as a boy. The themes of mystery, ghosts, secret societies, Oriental luxuriance, vast caverns, dungeons and chambers, vengeance, violence and confession recur in his work, helping define complex psychological spaces. The resulting notion of the interior self both looks back to the Gothic and forward to the conventions of psychoanalysis.

1845

Thomas De Quincey 1785–1859
Suspiria de Profundis: Being a Sequel to the Confessions of an English Opium-Eater

In 1821, as a contribution to a periodical work — in 1822, as a separate volume — appeared the 'Confessions of an English Opium Eater.' The object of that work was to reveal something of the grandeur which belongs *potentially* to human dreams. Whatever may be the number of those in whom this faculty of dreaming splendidly can be supposed to lurk, there are not perhaps many in whom it is developed. He whose talk is of oxen, will probably dream of oxen: and the condition of human life, which yokes so vast a majority to a daily experience incompatible with much elevation of thought, oftentimes neutralizes the tone of grandeur in the reproductive faculty of dreaming, even for those whose minds are populous with solemn imagery. Habitually to dream magnificently, a man must have a constitutional determination to reverie. This in the first place; and even this, where it exists strongly, is too much liable to disturbance from the gathering agitation of our present English life. Already, in this year 1845, what by the procession through fifty years of mighty revolutions amongst the kingdoms of the earth, what by the continual development of vast physical agencies — steam in all its applications, light getting under harness as a slave for man, * powers from heaven descending upon education and accelerations of the press, powers from hell (as it might seem, but these also celestial) coming round upon artillery and the forces of destruction — the eye of the calmest observer is troubled; the brain is haunted as if by some jealousy of ghostly beings moving amongst us; and it becomes too evident that, unless this colossal pace of advance can be retarded, (a thing not to be expected,) or, which is happily more probable, can be met by counter-forces of corresponding magnitude, forces in the direction or religion or profound philosophy, that shall radiate centrifugally against this storm of life so perilously centripetal towards the vortex of the merely human, left to itself the natural tendency of so chaotic a tumult must be to evil; for some minds to lunacy, to others to a reagency of fleshly torpor. How much this fierce condition of eternal hurry, upon an arena too exclusively human in its interests, is likely to defeat the grandeur which is latent in all men, may be seen in the ordinary effect from living too constantly in varied company. The word *dissipation*, in one of its uses, expresses that effect; the action of thought and feeling is too much dissipated and squandered. To reconcentrate them into meditative habits, a necessity is felt by all observing persons for sometimes retiring from crowds. No man ever will unfold the capacities of his own intellect who does not at least chequer his

* Daguerrotype, &c

life with solitude. How much solitude, so much power. Or, if not true in that rigour of expression, to this formula undoubtedly it is that the wise rule of life must approximate.

Among the powers in man which suffer by this too intense life of the *social* instincts, none suffers more than the power of dreaming. Let no man think this a trifle. The machinery for dreaming planted in the human brain was not planted for nothing. That faculty, in alliance with the mystery of darkness, is the one great tube through which man communicates with the shadowy. And the dreaming organ, in connexion with the heart, the eye, and the ear, compose the magnificent apparatus which forces the infinite into the chambers of the human brain, and throws dark reflections fro eternities below all life upon the mirrors of the sleeping mind.

But if this faculty suffers from the decay of solitude, which is becoming a visionary idea in England, on the other hand, it is certain that some merely physical agencies can and do assist the faculty of dreaming almost preternaturally. Amongst these is intense exercise; to some extent at least, and for some persons: but beyond all others is opium, which indeed seems to possess a *specific* power in that direction; not merely for exalting the colours of dream-scenery, but for deepening its shadows; and, above all, for strengthening the sense of its fearful *realities*...

4.7

Poe's Fantastic Artist

The American poet and writer of tales Edgar Allan Poe (1809–49) has been subject to a tradition of mythmaking and psychological analysis which would cast him as a distinctly Gothic figure. Supposedly alcoholic and a drug-taker, prey to unhealthy sexual desires and damned to melancholia, the reality was probably rather less sensational. Which is not to say he lived a wholly conventional life; gambling, disease, marriage to a thirteen-year old cousin and depression certainly feature as undisputed facts of his biography. However, the extravagantly tragic and self-destructive artist he is sometimes imagined to be is more truly to be found in a literary creation of his — Roderick Usher. Poe's tale *The Fall of the House of Usher* (first published among his *Tales of the Grotesque and Arabesque*, 1840) recounts the demise of this melancholic and creative figure. Obsessed with the internment of his sister, he will eventually be carried to his death by her after she returns from a trance, and the house itself collapses in representation of the collapse of mental order and morality.

1840

Edgar Allan Poe 1809–49
The Fall of the House of Usher

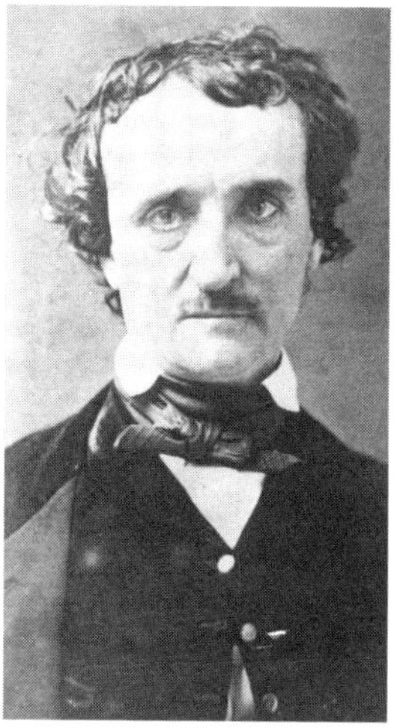

35
George Kendall Warren
Portrait of Edgar Allan Poe,
*c.*1874 (after *c.*1849
daguerreotype)
Albumen silver print
9.6 × 5.6 cm
National Portrait Gallery,
Smithsonian Institution,
Washington, DC

I shall ever bear about me a memory of the many solemn hours I thus spent alone with the master of the House of Usher. Yet I should fail in any attempt to convey an idea of the exact character of the studies, or of the occupations, in which he involved me, or led me the way. An excited and highly distempered ideality threw a sulphurous lustre over all. His long improvised dirges will ring forever in my ears. Among other things, I hold painfully in mind a certain singular perversion and amplification of the wild air of the last waltz of Von Weber. From the paintings over which his elaborate fancy brooded, and which grew, touch by touch, into vaguenesses at which I shuddered the more thrillingly, because I shuddered knowing not why; — from these paintings (vivid as their images now are before me) I would in vain endeavor to educe more than a small portion which should lie within the compass of merely written words. By the utter simplicity, by the nakedness of his designs, he arrested and overawed attention. If ever mortal painted an idea, that mortal was Roderick Usher. For me at least — in the circumstances then surrounding me — there arose out of the pure abstractions which the hypochondriac contrived to throw upon his canvas, an intensity of intolerable awe, no shadow of which felt I ever yet in the contemplation of the certainly glowing yet too concrete reveries of Fuseli.

One of the phantasmagoric conceptions of my friend, partaking not so rigidly of the spirit of abstraction, may be shadowed forth, although feebly, in words. A small picture presented the interior of an immensely long and rectangular vault or tunnel, with low walls, smooth, white, and without interruption or device. Certain accessory points of the design served well to convey the idea that this excavation lay at an exceeding depth below the surface of the earth. No outlet was observed in any portion of its vast extent, and no torch, or other artificial source of light was discernible; yet a flood of intense rays rolled throughout, and bathed the whole in a ghastly and inappropriate splendor.

I have just spoken of that morbid condition of the auditory nerve which rendered all music intolerable to the sufferer, with the exception of certain effects of stringed instruments. It was, perhaps, the narrow limits to which he thus confined himself upon the guitar, which gave birth, in great measure, to the fantastic character of his performances. But the fervid *facility* of his *impromptus* could not be so accounted for. They must have been, and were, in the notes, as well as in the words of his wild fantasias (for he not unfrequently accompanied himself with rhymed verbal improvisations), the result of that intense mental collectedness and concentration to which I have previously alluded as observable only in particular moments of the highest artificial excitement. The words of one of these rhapsodies I have easily remembered. I was, perhaps, the more forcibly impressed with it, as he gave it, because, in the under or mystic current of its meaning, I fancied that I perceived, and for the first time, a full consciousness on the part of Usher, of the tottering of his lofty reason upon her throne. The verses, which were entitled 'The Haunted Palace,' ran very nearly, if not accurately, thus:

I In the greenest of our valleys,
By good angels tenanted,
Once a fair and stately palace —
Snow-white palace — reared its head.
In the monarch Thought's dominion —
It stood there!
Never seraph spread a pinion
Over fabric half so fair.

II Banners yellow, glorious, golden,
On its roof did float and flow;
(This — all this — was in the olden
Time long ago)
And every gentle air that dallied,
In that sweet day,
Along the ramparts plumed
and pallid,
A winged odor went away.

III Wanderers in that happy valley
Through two luminous windows saw
Spirits moving musically
To a lute's well-tunéd law,
Round about a throne, where sitting
(Porphyrogene!)
In state his glory well befitting,
The sovereign of the realm was seen.

IV And all with pearl and ruby glowing
Was the fair palace door,
Through which came flowing,
flowing, flowing,
And sparkling evermore,
A troop of Echoes whose sweet duty
Was but to sing,
In voices of surpassing beauty,
The wit and wisdom of their king.

V But evil things, in robes of sorrow,
Assailed the monarch's high estate;
(Ah, let us mourn, for never morrow
Shall dawn upon him, desolate!)
And, round about his home, the glory
That blushed and bloomed
Is but a dim-remembered story
Of the old time entombed.

VI And travellers now within that valley,
Through the red-litten windows, see
Vast forms that move fantastically
To a discordant melody;
While, like a rapid ghastly river,
Through the pale door,
A hideous throng rush out forever,
And laugh — but smile no more.

I well remember that suggestions arising from this ballad led us into a train of thought wherein there became manifest an opinion of Usher's which I mention not so much on account of its novelty, (for other men have thought thus,) as on account of the pertinacity with which he maintained it. This opinion, in its general form, was that of the sentience of all vegetable things. But, in his disordered fancy, the idea had assumed a more daring character, and trespassed, under certain conditions, upon the kingdom of inorganization. I lack words to express the full extent, or the earnest *abandon* of his persuasion. The belief, however, was connected (as I have previously hinted) with the gray stones of the home of his forefathers. The conditions of the sentience had been here, he imagined, fulfilled in the method of collocation of these stones — in the order of their arrangement, as well as in that of the many *fungi* which overspread them, and of the decayed trees which stood around — above all, in the long undisturbed endurance of this arrangement, and in its reduplication in the still waters of the tarn. Its evidence — the evidence of the sentience — was to be seen, he said, (and I here started as he spoke,) in the gradual yet certain condensation of an atmosphere of their own about the waters and the walls. The result was discoverable, he added, in that silent, yet importunate and terrible influence which for centuries had moulded the destinies of his family, and which made him what I now saw him — what he was. Such opinions need no comment, and I will make none...

4.8

The Tragic Case of Richard Dadd

The association of madness and genius has roots in antiquity, and instances can be found wherever literary and artistic biography or anecdote is to be discovered. But the late eighteenth and nineteenth centuries saw a new emphasis on originality, novelty, magnitude, which compounded the idea of creativity and mental illness. Just as significantly, the unregulated and expansive nature of criticism in these years, and the changing character of the public for culture, raised concerns that the divisions between truth and illusion, deceit and authenticity, the solid and the airy, were permeable, or fragile.

In this context, critics and anecdotalists may have suggested that Fuseli and Blake were madmen, and in the latter case there may still be advocates for a certain mental disturbance as informing his work, but both had been able to conduct a professional life within regular society with greater or lesser reward. The case of Richard Dadd (1817–86) is rather different. Trained at the Royal Academy, Dadd was a promising young painter associated with William Powell Frith as part of an avant-garde group of artists, The Clique. He travelled in the Middle East in 1842 — an area of the world being newly explored by artists. But his mental state declined around this time, and in 1843 he stabbed and killed his own father while convalescing in Kent. He was committed to an asylum, and remained incarcerated for the rest of his life. The contemporary reports excerpted here imply a connection between madness and inspiration, while carefully drawing a line between inspired madness and the criminal violence he had perpetrated.

His works produced while confined draw from Fuseli and contemporary fairy-paintings (notably those of Daniel Maclise) but have an intensity that seems indelibly to mark them as the products of a disturbed mind. The content of his most famous work, *The Fairy-Feller's Master Stroke* was explained, or rather confused, by a poem of his, partly reproduced here.

1843

'The Late Richard Dadd'
The Art Union: Monthly Journal of the Arts

Alas! we must so preface the name of a youth of genius that promised to do honour to the world; for, although the grave has not actually closed over him, he must be classed among the dead. Those who regarded, respected, or loved him, must anticipate such an event as his restoration to a perfectly sane state only as an additional calamity; and pray, rather, that consciousness may be mercifully withheld from him; for a return to reason would infer a condition which we cannot contemplate without renewed horror.

Alas! it is, indeed, a heavy penalty — that which poor humanity pays for enjoying the gift of a fertile imagination.

'The brain too finely wrought
Preys on itself, and is consumed by thought!'

The history of the human mind, as exemplified by those who have exercised its nobler attributes, presents a melancholy record of high hopes or miserable disappointments — both too often ending alike in madness. Cases come before us very frequently, upon which we can offer no remarks without invading the circle of private life and augmenting private sorrow; the memory of them is consequently permitted to die away, for it is impossible to ask for the poor victim a public expression of grief. The awful fate of Richard Dadd, however, calls for no such delicacy. His madness, alas! has obtained notoriety by one of the most appalling events recorded in the history of modern times. It is needless to say how heavily the theme burthens our pen.

1848

The Art Union: Monthly Journal of the Arts

Richard Dadd — The calamitous termination of the moral existence of Richard Dadd, was too impressive to be forgotten. Since the awful calamity that has consigned him for the remainder of his earthly existence to the abode of lunatics, he has not, in the absence of reason, forgotten that he was a painter. By the kindness of the governer of Bethlehem Hospital, he has been furnished with canvasses, colours, &c, and paints! But how? — with all the poetry of imagination and the frenzy of insanity — in parts eminently beautiful, but other parts, in madness, without method. How singular these outpourings of disease and mind will be to future collectors.

36
Richard Dadd
Self-Portrait, 1841
Etching 14.9 × 11.4 cm
The National Portrait
Gallery, London

37
Richard Dadd
Sketch to Illustrate the Passions:
Agony — Raving Madness, 1854
Watercolour on brown paper
35.5 × 25.3 cm
Bethlem Royal Hospital
Museum, London

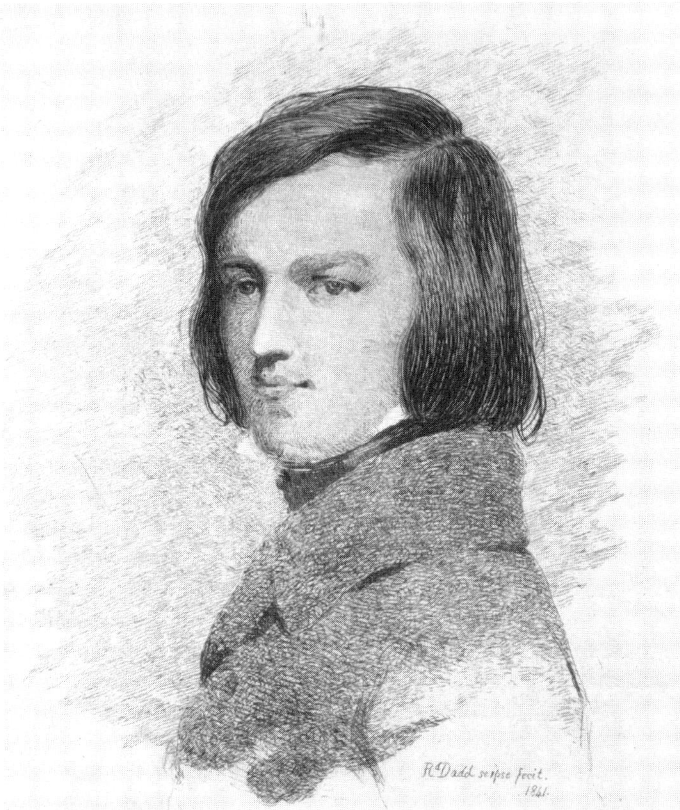

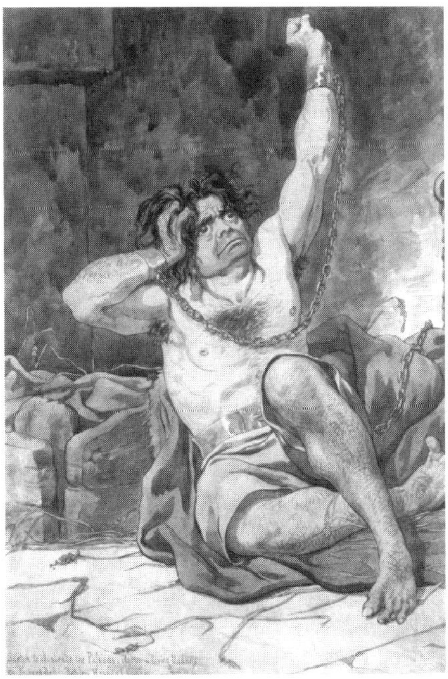

38
Richard Dadd
The Fairy Feller's Master-Stroke
1855–64
Oil on canvas 54 × 39.4 cm
Tate. Presented by Siegfried Sassoon in memory of his friend and fellow officer Julian Dadd, a great-nephew of the artist, and of his two brothers who gave their lives in the First World War 1963

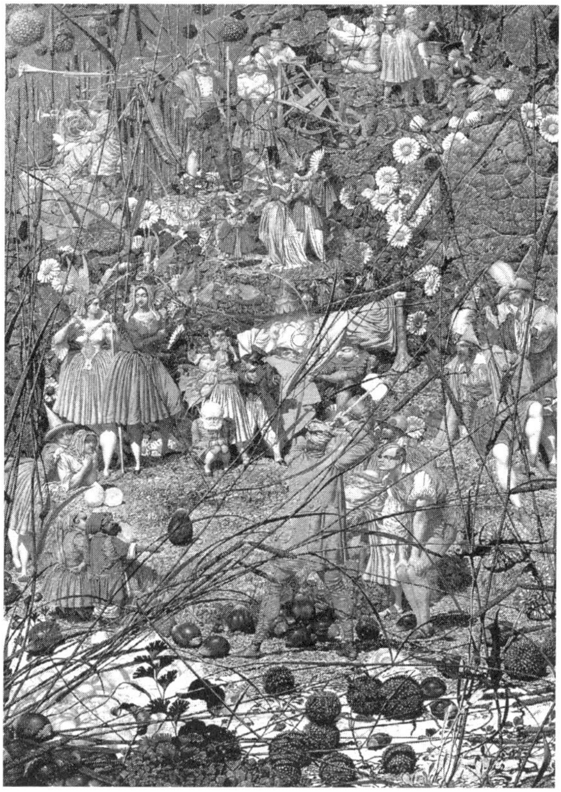

1865

Richard Dadd 1817–86

'Elimination of a Picture & Its Subject — Called the Feller's Master Stroke'

I thought on nought — a shift
As good perhaps as thinking hard.
Fancy was not to be evoked
From her ethereal realms
Or if so, then her purpose cloaked
And nuzzling the cloth, on which
The cloudy shades not rich,
Indefinite almost unseen
Lay vacant entities of chance,
Lent forms unto my careless glance
Without intent, pure fancy 't'is I mean
Design and composition thus —
Now minus and just here perhaps — plus —
Grew in this way — and so — or thus,
That fairly wrought they stand in view
A Fairy band, much as I say, just so 'tis true.

4.9

H.P. Lovecraft's Cosmic Artist

Lovecraft maintained a generally sceptical attitude to the art and literature of the earlier Gothic. As his comments on *The Castle of Otranto* reveal (p.279), these productions were too fussy or prosaic for his taste; he demanded a truly cosmic vision which only a few had achieved. The dismissive comments on Fuseli in his story 'Pickman's Model' chime with Poe's account of Roderick Usher in taking that Anglo-Swiss artist as the measure of the fantastic, even as they find him wanting.

1926

H.P. Lovecraft 1896–1937
Pickman's Model

You know, it takes profound art and profound insight into Nature to turn out stuff like Pickman's. Any magazine-cover hack can splash paint around wildly and call it a nightmare or a Witches' Sabbath or a portrait of the devil, but only a truly great painter can make such a thing really scare or ring true. That's because only a real artist knows the exact anatomy of the terrible or the physiology of fear — the exact sort of lines and proportions that connect up with latent instincts of hereditary memories of fright, and the proper colour contrasts and lighting effects to stir the dormant sense of strangeness. I don't have to tell you why a Fuseli really brings a shiver while a cheap ghost-story frontispiece merely makes us laugh. There's something those fellows catch — beyond life — that they're able to make us catch for a second. Doré had it. Sime has it. Angarola of Chicago has it. And Pickman had it as no man ever had it before or — I hope to Heaven — ever will again.

Don't ask me what it is they see. You know, in ordinary art, there's all the difference in the world between the vital, breathing things drawn from Nature or models and the artificial truck that commercial small fry reel off in a bare studio by rule. Well, I should say that the really weird artist has a kind of vision which makes models, or summons up what amounts to actual scenes from the spectral world he lives in. Anyhow, he manages to turn out results that differ from the pretender's mince-pie dreams in just about the same way that the life painter's results differ from the concoctions of a correspondence-school cartoonist. If I had ever seen what Pickman saw — but no! Here, let's have another drink before we get any deeper. Gad, I wouldn't be alive if I'd ever seen what that man — if he was a man — saw!

Moral Panics and Critical Debate: Opposition to Gothic Horror and Fantasy

Since Aristotle, critics and cultural authorities have always warned against the dangers of the over-indulged imagination and the creation of fantastic monsters. The classical tradition of literary criticism had little time for the outlandish, and was often prohibitive in its definition of the proper social scope and role of fiction. During the eighteenth century, even as literary and aesthetic criticism was developed in ways that now encompassed more readily elements of the fantastic, new anxieties arose about the social reach and influence of literature. The expanding market for novels and romances in the mid-century, and especially the rapidly growing female audience for culture, prompted fears that the standards of taste and judgement were being undermined.

Writers and artists using Gothic and fantasy imagery attracted particular moral opprobrium. Walpole, Radcliffe, and especially Matthew Lewis, attracted in turn sometimes virulent criticism. Criticism of the Gothic as a whole sharpened considerably in response to the events of the French Revolution; the imagination was thrown into suspicion, as an unruly influence on morals, and the supernatural and fantastic condemned as the unnatural progeny of the revolutionary political creed.

5.1

The Moral Dangers of Traditional Ghost Stories

In an era of self-conscious reason and social refinement, the sincere belief in the supernatural seemed to belong either to a lost period of ignorance, or to that ignorant sector of the populace who had no place alongside the educated upper- and (increasingly) middle-rank of society in running the affairs of the nation. Still, such tales were recovered in the context of polite literature as the subject of charmed fascination or nostalgia, as the excerpt from *The Spectator* (p.108) indicates. Here, an excerpt from the popular compilation *Round About our Coal Fire* makes the rather surprising suggestion that the telling of scary stories could lead directly to sexual immorality, although it does so in a decidedly entertaining manner. The second excerpt is from the moralising polite essay-journal *The Babler*, by the writer and attorney Hugh Kelly (1729–77). Damning ghost stories as an irrational influence on impressionable minds, he nonetheless implies a degree of ironic nostalgia for the time that such superstitions helped ensure a higher degree of moral order than that which prevailed in the modern era of materialism and social pretension.

c.1730

Round About our Coal Fire: Or, Christmas Entertainments

'Of Spectres, Ghosts, and Apparitions; the great Conveniences arising from them, and how to make them'

When the Men and the Maids have ended their Gambols, and Bed-time is drawing on, or all seated about the Fire, then *John* begins some dismal Story to the Company about Apparitions and Hobgoblins, and so about it goes till all the rest of the Society are drawn into the same kind of Discourse; and frightned out of their Wits with dreadful Apprehensions, a Mouse can't stir, but *Nan* creeps close to *John*, *Sue* hugs *Tom*, and none dare lie alone; then Love and the Devil Couples them together, and each one has a Mae for that Night, and when the Thing is once done, there is a little Ceremony used afterwards whenever a proper opportunity offers between the Parties; and ten to one but the Parish is fill'd with Bastards Nine Months after, unless the pregnant Maidens make their way to *London* in time, and top their Kids upon some smug Apprentice; by such means they get a spell of Money, deck themselves forth, renew their Maidenheads, and either set up an Alehouse with the Men that their Fear debauched, or else change the end of the Town, get acquainted with some eminent Bawd, and so are made the Fondlings of some Raking Coxcombs of Fortune for a while, and then turn'd off to walk the Streets. If it happens this way, when the Story of the Sprite was a dismal Story indeed; for the forsaking their first true Love, may bring the Ballad of *Bateman* before them; where they may plainly see in the Picture, that the Devil flies away with such false Wretches; but I have more Compassion for a tender-hearted Maiden than to think that where a Sixpence has once been crook'd between her and her Sweetheart she can ever forsake him, especially if she has any Notions of the Devil's Claws, and forked Tongue, or the direful Horrors she must be subject too from the Hauntings of Ghosts and Spectres, whenever she happens to be alone after Candlelight; then may she expect to see the Candle burn Blue, the Chairs gallop about the Room, be stun'd with Shrieks and Groans from every Quarter of the Place, when with a hideous Roar enters a ghastly Figure in a Winding-sheet, with a lighted Taper in one Hand, and a bloody Dagger in the other, crying out for Revenge, and stalking up to you with long Strides, and great Saucer Eyes, rattling of Chains and a Cloven-foot. This I am sure would be enough to frighten the stoutest Man that ever wore an Head, and much more a Woman, who is made of such tender Stuff as most Women are.

5 November 1763

Hugh Kelly 1729–97
The Babler, no. 39

The impressions which are made upon the human mind, during it's earliest states, being seldom if ever to be entirely eradicated, there is nothing in which we ought to be more careful than the education of our children, particularly in their infancy, when habits, in the strictest sense of the term, become an absolute part of our nature, and prejudices not only find a refuge in the heart, but twist themselves imperceptibly round its very strings.

I remember, when I was about four or five years of age, my grandmother took me entirely under her own care; and as the good woman, like the generality of her sex at that period, had a firm belief in witches, spirits and hobgoblins, she frequently entertained me with a variety of their pretty performances; and, if I happened to be any ways untoward, constantly threatened to send me to Robin Greenaway. This Mr Robin Greenaway was formerly a journeyman taylor in the neighbourhood, who had gone distracted for love, as the people said, and in one of his desperate fits cut his throat in the parson's garden. Various were the tricks related to this unhappy enamorato; sometimes he came in a storm, and threw a parcel of bricks down his sweetheart's chimney; at other times he assumed the figure of a grey mare; and at others, that of a spotted spaniel; but his most favourite mode of appearance was the form of an over-grown calf. Ridiculous as these accounts must have been considered on the smallest reflection, yet my poor grandmother believed them all with the most religious certainty, and thought it an indispensable part of her duty to make me believe them too. In this she succeeded to the utmost of her wishes: I was ten years old before I would venture to sleep alone; fourteen, before I had courage enough to go to bed in the dark; and to this very hour, if I happen to be by myself, the clock never strikes at night, but I think of Robin Greenaway, or some other worshipful member of the same community, to whom the blessing of an untimely death has granted a privilege of taking what form, and playing what tricks, he pleases till the cock crows next morning.

It would be unnecessary for me to observe, that nine out of every ten who may be turned of fifty, have like myself, in their infancy, been trained up in the greatest dread of spirits; and that the utmost exertion of reason, upon arriving at years of maturity, has not been sufficient to erase the impressions which have been unhappily made upon their imagination. Fortunately, however, the good sense of the present æra has provided the most effectual spells for our ghosts and spectres, and laid so many of them so effectually in the Red Sea, that harmless little boys may for the future sleep in the most perfect security, and the honest country people traverse the remotest church-yard after midnight without the smallest apprehension.

But, notwithstanding we have in a great measure got the better of our ghosts, there are yet some prejudices, and those of a very dangerous tendency, which we have in a manner substituted in their room, and which it would be much to our honour in this life, and to our happiness in the next, if we could get the better of too. These are the shameful indulgences to which we think ourselves entitled on Sundays. In the days of spectres and hobgoblins, we thought ourselves under an indispensable necessity of paying some regard to the Sabbath; and every man was obliged to pay a fine who omitted going to church that day, unless he could palliate his conduct by some very feasible excuse; but, now-a-days, Sunday is the time particularly set apart for riot and festivity; and the day, rendered holy by the express appointment of Omnipotence, is so often particularly appropriated for the violation of its laws. Has a great man a journey to make, or a company to invite, Sunday is an idle day, and he fixes either upon that. Has a woman of fashion an inclination to strip her best friends of the money which ought to pay a tradesman's bill, she sends cards for Sunday evening. And has a pretty little mechanic a mind to cut a figure, why he hires his horse, takes out his strumpet, and gets drunk on Sunday evening too.

5.2

The Castle of Otranto Criticised

Among the early Gothic novels, Walpole's *The Castle of Otranto* (1764) went relatively uncriticised. Its early reception was generally favourable; and even as criticism of the Gothic novel as a whole developed, Walpole's text was often excused from the more general condemnation of supernatural and shocking themes. Yet there were complaints, as apparent here, which anticipate later attacks on the silliness — indeed, girlishness — of the genre. H.P. Lovecraft's comments indicate the level of ignorance around this text at this later date, and the low esteem this curiously portentous fiction might be held in by an artist who expected a more fully cosmic vision to prevail in the work of art.

1765

Gilly Williams
to George Selwyn

A novel and such a novel, that no boarding-school Miss of thirteen could get through without yawning. It consists of ghosts and enchantments; pictures walk out of their frames, and are good company for half an hour together; helmets drop from the moon and cover half a family.

1765

John Langhorne 1735–79
Anonymous review of *The Castle of Otranto*

Those who can digest the absurdities of Gothic fiction, and bear with the machinery of ghosts and goblins, may hope, at least, for considerable entertainment from the performance before us: for it is written with no common pen; the language is accurate and elegant; the characters are highly finished; and the disquisitions into human manners, passions, and pursuits, indicate the keenest penetration, and the most perfect knowledge of mankind ... The principal defect of this performance does not remain unnoticed. That unchristian doctrine of visiting the sins of the fathers upon the children, is certainly, under our present system, not only a very useless, but a very unsupportable moral, and yet it is almost the only one deducible from this story. Nor is it at all rendered more tolerable through the insinuation that such evils might be diverted by devotion to St Nicholas; for there the good canon was evidently preaching in favour of his own household. However, as a work of genius, evincing great dramatic powers, and exhibiting fine views of nature, the *Castle of Otranto* may still be read with pleasure. To give the Reader an analysis of the story, would be to introduce him to a company of skeletons; to refer him to the book will be to recommend him to an assemblage of beautiful pictures.

14 February 1928

H.P. Lovecraft 1896–1937
to Bernard Austin Dwyer

... I thought you'd find the Railo book of interest, for it really goes into the matter of Gothic fiction far better than any other work extant, including the Birkhead treatise, hitherto the standard. Have you read *The Castle of Otranto* itself? If not, *don't!* Let the summary in Railo continue to give you a 'kick', for the original certainly won't! Walpole was too steeped in the classical tradition of the early 18th century to catch the Gothic spirit of the latter half. His choice of words and rhythms is the brisk, cheerful Addisonian one; and his nonchalant and atmosphereless way of describing the most prodigious horrors is enough to empty them of all their potency. Thanks to the second-hand way in which you received it, you have become the first reader to get a genuine shiver from *Otranto* since the days of Sir Walter Scott!

5.3

The Controversy of the 1790s

The years following the French Revolution were seminal in the development of a modern British political culture. Responding to the tumultuous events across the Channel, radicals, pursuing social and sometimes sexual equality, were further radicalised and subsequently ostracised. Fears about terror visited from abroad led to quite unprecedented levels of political repression; paranoia about secret societies was rife. In this new, relatively conservative consensus, ideas of moderation, common sense and plain speaking assumed importance in defining a supposedly communal national culture; abstract thought, democracy and the imagination were attacked as signs of wicked foreign influence.

Gothic literature and motifs had a dynamic role to play in these debates. Criticism of Gothic novels became a battleground, with the apparent excesses of Matthew Lewis and the new breed of Gothic novels translated from the German being a particular target. The repetitive, cannibalistic nature of this sensation literature, made more available than ever through the cheap editions issued by the Minerva Press and through the subscription-libraries, seemed to represent literary culture going down the plughole. For many critics, the time was nigh for the imposition of a new moral order in the realm of literature, as much as in public life.

17 September 1796

‘Aurelius’ in *The Flapper*, no.55

The moral which the Author in question professes to inculcate, is the necessity of resisting the first temptations to sin: but in order to press this with effect upon his reader, he should have represented those temptations, and those only, to which we are all exposed. The great enemy of mankind is at this day no otherwise discoverable among us than by his operations in our hearts. He ought therefore to be represented only by the effects which are there produced by him. We should then be duly affected by the moral, because there would be nothing in the case, that might not by possibility become our own. But when we see a wretch exposed to perpetual solicitation by the devil in person, suggesting evil things, and furnishing supernatural means of accomplishing them, the moral is lost in the improbability of the story: and we are more disposed to question the justice of a punishment which human nature had scarcely power to escape, than to deprecate a temptation to which we can never be subject.

I have, however, still weightier objections to this author on the ground of morality: that his professed moral does not flow naturally or necessarily from the story, might possibly be excused upon considering the nature of the work and of the materials which he had chosen. But the book abounds with passages plainly and unequivocally *immoral*: that author avails himself of every opportunity which his subject affords him, to introduce scenes of the most wanton and immodest nature, described in terms scarcely decent: too numerous to be overlooked by the most hasty, too circumstantial to be misunderstood by the most ignorant of his readers. In short, Sir, this book, affecting to have a moral tendency, and willed with gross impurity, reminds me of a celebrated trial of *crim. con.* which was published last winter, the preface of which bewailed in pompous terms, the rapid encrease of adultery in this kingdom, and humbly recommended to the youth of both sexes, as an antidote, a careful perusal of the scenes of licentiousness that were emblazoned in the subsequent pages.

One short observation more, Mr Flapper, upon a passage which, for the novelty of the position contained in it, deserves to be noticed. A female character is introduced, as accomplished as the author could make her: she has an only daughter whose education occupies her whole attention, and who repays her by her great proficiency: this young Lady is discovered reading — the holy scriptures are her study — but she studies them in a manuscript of her mother’s compilation; because, as we are gravely told, the sacred book itself it too full of gross indelicacy and indecency to be put into the hands of a virtuous young woman! what a pity that the author had not followed up this notable discovery, by presenting the world with a new edition of the Bible, purged of its immoralities by his own chaste hand, or that he has not at least referred us to those passages which in his opinion are so likely to pollute the mind of youth! And what ignorance have the most enlightened of the Infidel writers betrayed, who, amid their doubts of the authenticity of the sacred writings and their cavils on the evidence adduced to support it, scruple not to bear the fullest testimony to the inimitable delicacy of sentiment and purity of expression abounding in the Bible!

1798

From *Spirit of the Public Journals for 1797*

Sir,

I never complain of fashion, when it is confined to externals — to the form of a cap, or the cut of a lapelle; to the colour of a wig, or the tune of a ballad; but when I perceive that there is such a thing as fashion even in composing books, it is, perhaps, full time that some attempt should be made to recall writers to the old boundaries of common sense.

I allude, Sir, principally to the great quantity of novel with which our circulating libraries are filled, and our parlour tables covered, in which it has been the fashion to make *terror* the *order of the day*, by confining the heroes and heroines in old gloomy castles, full of spectres, apparitions, ghosts, and dead men's bones. This is now so common, that a Novelist blushes to bring about a marriage by ordinary means, but conducts the happy pair through long and dangerous galleries, where the light burns blue, the thunder rattles, and the great window at the end presents the hideous visage of a *murdered* man, *uttering* piercing groans, and developing shocking mysteries. If a curtain is withdrawn, there is a bleeding body behind it; if a chest is opened, it contains a skeleton; if a noise is heard, somebody is receiving a deadly blow; and if a candle goes out, its place is sure to be supplied by a flash of lightning. Cold hands grasp us in the dark, statues are seen to move, and suits of armour walk off their pegs, while the wind whistles louder than one of Handel's chorusses, and the still air is more melancholy than the dead march in *Saul*.

Such are the dresses and decorations of a modern novel, which, as Bayes says, is calculated to 'elevate and surprise'; but in doing so, carries the young reader's imagination into such a confusion of terrors, as must be hurtful. It is to great purpose, indeed, that we have forbidden our servants from telling the children stories of ghosts and hobgoblins, if we cannot put a novel into their hands which is not filled with monsters of the imagination, more frightful than are to be found in Glanvil, the famous *bug-a-boo* of our forefathers.

A novel, if at all useful, ought to be a representation of human life and manners, with a view to direct the conduct in the most important duties of life, and to correct its follies. But what instruction is to be reaped from the distorted ideas of lunatics, I am at a loss to conceive. Are we come to such a pass, that the only commandment necessary to be repeated is, 'Thou shalt do no murder?' Are the duties of life so changed, that all the instructions necessary for a young person is to learn to walk at night upon the battlements of an old castle, to creep hands and feet along a narrow passage, and to meet the devil at the end of it? Is the corporeal frame of the female sex so masculine and hardy, that it must be softened down by the touch of dead bodies, clay-cold hands, and damp sweats? Can a young lady be taught nothing more necessary in life, than to sleep in a dungeon with venemous reptiles, walk through a ward with assassins, and carry bloody daggers in their pockets, instead of pin-cushions and needle-books?

Every absurdity has an end, and as I observe that almost all novels are of the terrific cast, I hope the insipid repetition of the same bugbears will at length work a cure. In the meantime, should any of your female readers be desirous of catching the season of terrors, she may compose two or three very pretty volumes from the following recipe:

> *Take* — An old castle, half of it ruinous.
> A long gallery, with a great many doors, some secret ones.
> Three murdered bodies, quite fresh.
> As many skeletons, in chests and presses.
> An old woman hanging by the beck; with her throat cut.
> Assassins and desperadoes '*quant suff.*'
> Noise, whispers, and groans, threescore at least.

Mix them together, in the form of three volumes to be taken at any of the watering places, before going to bed.

1797

Samuel Taylor Coleridge 1772–1834
Review of *The Monk*

The horrible and the preternatural have usually seized on the popular taste, at the rise and decline of literature. Most powerful stimulants, they can never be required except by the torpor of an unawakened, or the langour of an exhausted, appetite. The same phenomenon, therefore, which we hail as a favourable omen in the belles lettres of Germany, impresses a degree of gloom in the compositions of our countrymen. We trust, however, that satiety will banish what good sense should have prevented: and that, wearied with fiends, incomprehensible characters, with shrieks, murders, and subterraneous dungeons, the public will learn, by the multitude of the manufacturers, with how little expense of though of imagination this species of composition is manufactured. But, cheaply as we estimate romances in general, we acknowledge, in the work before us, the offspring of no uncommon genius. The tale is similar to that of Santon Barsista in the *Guardian*. Ambrosio, a monk, surnamed the Man of Holiness, proud of his own undeviating rectitude, and severe to the faults of others, is successfully assailed by the tempter of mankind, and seduced to the perpetration of rape and murder, and finally precipitated into a contract in which he consigns his soul to everlasting perdition.

The larger part of the three volumes is occupied by the underplot, which, however, is skilfully and closely connected with the main story, and is subservient to its development. The tale of the bleeding nun is truly terrific; and we could not easily recollect a bolder or more happy conception than that of the burning cross on the forehead of the wandering jew (a mysterious character, which, though copied as to its more prominent features from Schiller's incomparable Armenian, does, nevertheless, display great vigour of fancy). But the character of Matilda, the chief agent in the seduction of Antonio [sic], appears to us to be the author's master-piece. It is, indeed, exquisitely imagined, and as exquisitely supported. The whole work is distinguished by the variety and impressiveness of its incidents; and the author everywhere discovers an imagination rich, powerful, and fervid. Such are the excellencies; — the errors and defects are more numerous, and (we are sorry to add) of greater importance.

All events are levelled into one common mass, and become almost equally probable, when the order of nature may be changed whenever the author's purposes demand it. No address is requisite to the accomplishment of the design; and no pleasure therefore can be received from the perception of *difficulty surmounted*. The writer may make us wonder, but he cannot surprise us. For the same reasons a romance is incapable of exemplifying a moral truth.

[...]

As far, therefore, as the story is concerned, the praise which a romance can claim, is simply that of having given pleasure during its perusal; and so many are the calamities of life, that he who has done this, has not written uselessly. The children of sickness and solitude thank him. — To this praise, however, our author has not entitled himself. The sufferings he describes are so frightful and intolerable, that we break with abruptness from the delusion, and indignantly suspect the man of a species of brutality, who could find a pleasure in wantonly imagining them: and the abominations which he portrays with no hurrying pencil, are such as the observation of character by no means demanded, such as 'no observation of character can justify, because no good man would willingly suffer them to pass, however transiently, through his own mind'. The merit of a novellist is in proportion (not simply to the effect, but) to the *pleasurable* effect which he produces. Situations of torment, and images of naked horror, are easily conceived; and a writer in whose works they abound, deserves our gratitude almost equally with him who should drag us by way of sport through a military hospital, or force us to sit at the dissecting-table of a natural philosopher. To trace the nice boundaries, beyond which terror and sympathy are deserted by the pleasurable emotions, — to reach those limits, yet never to pass them, — *hic labor, hic opus est*. Figures that shock the imagination, and narratives that mangle our feelings, rarely discover *genius*, and always betray a low and vulgar *taste*.

[...]

A more grievous fault remains, — a fault for which no literary excellence can atone, — a fault which all other excellence does but aggravate as adding subtlety to a poison by the elegance of its preparation. Mildness of censure would here be criminally misplaced, and silence would make us accomplices. Not without reluctance then, but in full conviction that we are performing a duty, we declare it to be our opinion, that the Monk is a romance, which if a parent saw in the hands of a son or daughter, he might reasonably turn pale. The temptations of Ambrosio are described with a libidinous minuteness, which, we sincerely hope, will receive its best and only adequate censure from the offended conscience of the author himself. The shameless harlotry of Matilda, and the trembling innocence of Antonia, are seized with equal avidity, as vehicles of the most voluptuous images; and though the tale is indeed a tale of horror, yet the most painful impression which the work left on our minds was that of great acquirements and splendid genius employed to furnish a *mormo* for children, a poison for youth, and a provocative for the debauchee. Tales of enchantments and witchcraft can never be *useful*: our author has contrived to make them *pernicious*, by blending, with an irreverent negligence, all that is most awfully true in religion, with all that is most ridiculously absurd in superstition. He takes frequent occasion, indeed, to manifest his sovereign contempt for the latter, both in his own person, and (more incongruously) in that of his principal characters; and that his respect for the *former* is not excessive, we are forced to conclude from the treatment which its inspired writings receive from him. Ambrosio discovers Antonia reading —

'He examined the book which he had been reading, and had now placed upon the table. It was the Bible.

'"How!" said the friar to himself, "Antonia reads the Bible, and is still so ignorant?"

'But, upon further inspection, he found that Elvira had made exactly the same remark. That prudent mother, while she admired the beauties of sacred writings, was convinced that, unrestricted, no reading more improper could be permitted to a young woman. Many of the narratives can only tend to excite ideas the worst calculated for a female breast: every thing is called plainly and roundly by its name: and the *annals of a brothel would scarcely furnish a greater choice of indecent expressions*. Yet this is the book which young women are recommended to study, which is put into the hands of children, able to comprehend little more than those passages of which they had better remain ignorant, and which but too *frequently inculcates the first rudiments of vice*, and gives the first alarm to the still sleeping passions. Of this was Elvira so fully convinced, that she would have preferred putting into her daughter's hands "Amadis de Gaul," or "The Valiant

Champion Tirante the White"; and *would sooner have authorised her studying the lewd exploits of Don Galaor, or the lascivious jokes of the Damsel Plazer di mi vida.*' Vol.II, p.247.

The impiety of this falsehood can be equalled only by its impudence. This is indeed as if a Corinthian harlot, clad from head to foot in the transparent thinness of the Cöan vest, should affect to view with prudish horror the naked knee of a Spartan matron! If it be possible that the author of these blasphemies is a Christina, should he not have reflected that the only passage in the scriptures, which could give a *shadow* of plausibility to the *weakest* of these expressions, is represented as being spoken by the Almighty himself? But if he be an infidel, he has acted consistently enough with that character, in his endeavours first to influence the fleshly appetites, and then to pour contempt on the only book which would be adequate to the task of recalming them. We believe it not absolutely impossible that a mind may be so deeply depraved by habit of reading lewd and voluptuous tales, as to use even the Bible in conjuring up the spirit of uncleanness. The most innocent expressions might become the first link in the chain of association, when a man's soul had been so poisoned; for we believe it not absolutely impossible that he might extract pollution from the word of purity, and, in a literal sense, *turn the grace of God into wantonness.*

We have been induced to pay particular attention to this work, from the unusual success which it has experienced. It certainly possesses much real merit in addition to its meretricious attractions. Nor must it be forgotten that the author is a man of rank and fortune. — Yes! the author of the *Monk* signs himself a LEGISLATOR! — We stare and tremble.

1798

Samuel Taylor Coleridge 1772–1834
Review of Ann Radcliffe's *The Italian*

It was not difficult to forsee that the *modern romance*, even supported by the skill of the most ingenious of its votaries, would soon experience the fate of every attempt to please by what is unnatural, and by a departure from that observance of real life, which has placed the works of Fielding, Smollett, and some other writers, among the permanent sources of amusement. It might for a time afford an acceptable variety to persons whose reading is confined to works of fiction, and who would, perhaps, be glad to exchange dullness for extravagance; but it was probably that, as its constitution (if we may so speak) was maintained only by the passion of terror, and that excited by a trick, and as it was not conversant in incidents and characters of a natural complexion, it would degenerate into repetition, and would disappoint curiosity. So many cries 'that the wolf is coming,' must at last lose their effect. In reviewing *The Mysteries of Udolpho*, we hazarded the opinion, that, if a better production could appear, it must come only from the pen of Mrs Radcliffe, but we were not totally blind to the difficulties which even she would have to encounter, in order to keep up the interest she had created in that work, and in the *Romance of the Forest*; and the present publication confirms our suspicions. *The Mysteries of Udolpho* fell short of the *Romance of the Forest*, by the tedious protraction of events, and by a redundancy of description: *The Italian* falls short of *The Mysteries of Udolpho*, by reminding us of the same characters and the same scenes; and, although the descriptive part is less prolix, the author has had recourse to it in various instances, in which it has no natural connexion with the story. There are, however, some scenes that powerfully seize the imagination, and interest the passions.

1801

From an anonymous review of Anne Ker *Adeline St Julien: or, The Midnight Hour. A Novel* (1800)

Why this performance is termed a *novel*, we are at a loss to determine: certainly not because it possesses any *novelty*; neither does the general acceptation of the word warrant its adoption in the present instance. According to the *modern school*, it falls under the denomination of ROMANCE; for, if *improbability* and *absurdity* constitute that species of writing, *Adeline St Julien* is sufficiently *romantic*. The story is *made up* from that *sublime* production, the *Castle Spectre*, and from Mr Whaley's tragedy of the *Castle of Montval*, with several incidents *freely* BORROWED from *Cervantes*; or, perhaps, at second-hand, from his *Shakespearean* dramatiser, the author of the *Mountaineers*. Had we any influence with Mr Astley, the Amphitheatrical Manager: we would recommend Mrs K. to his employment, as a kind of *journeyman manufacturer* of *ghosts, secret doors,* &c. &c.

1801

From a review of M.G. Lewis *Tales of Wonder* (1800)

Far from being inclined to join in the censure which has been directed against Mr Lewis for compiling the present volume, we think he is much better employed than in most of his former productions, at least, with reference to his well-known romance, entitled *The Monk*, a work that has tended more to vitiate juvenile minds, and poison the fountains of morality than any thing of the kind that has fallen within our notice for a long period. Indeed we hardly know of any work so licentious a complexion, and of so

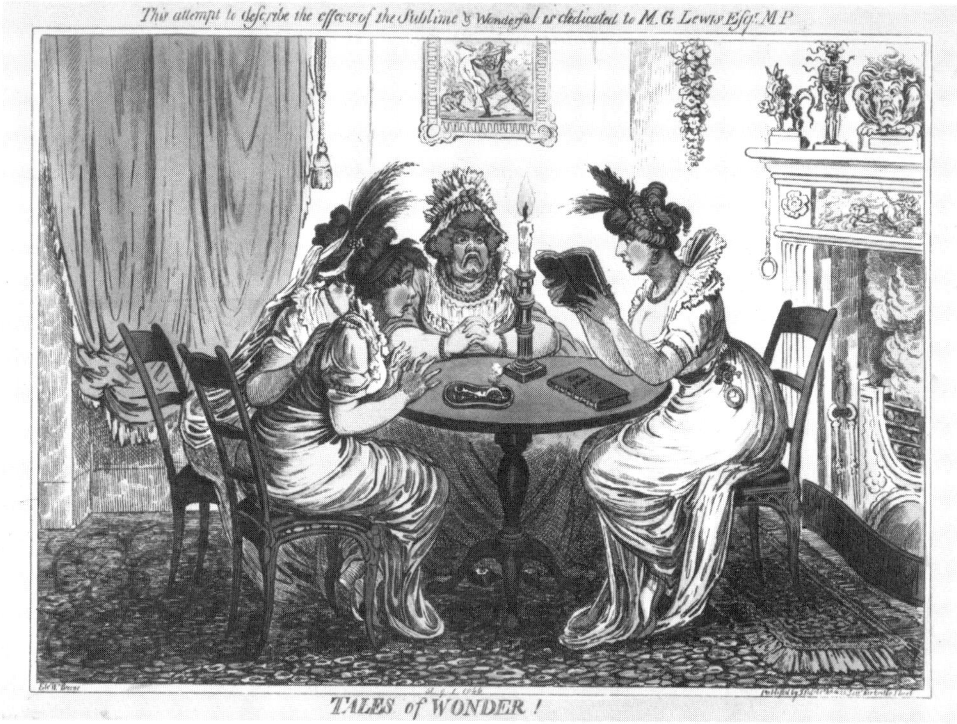

39
James Gillray
Tales of Wonder!
Published 1 February 1802
Handcoloured etching and aquatint 25.5 × 35.4 cm
The British Museum, London

mischievous a tendency, except the political crudities of the detestable Citizen PAINE. From all that we have read or heard of Mr Lewis and his works, he seems to us to possess a singular turn of mind. His fancy appears to be chiefly attracted by, and absorbed in, *the terrible, the horrible, the hideous,* and *the impossible*; nor can we conceive of what has been his bent of education that has led him into so uncommon a track of study. He certainly does not want abilities, or knowledge, but his talents are strangely perverted, and he sometimes seems even to be employed in throwing a ridicule upon himself. But to the present work. It consists of as many tales as the author could collect to scare the minds of children, and impress a terror upon the imagination through life. Some indeed of the compositions to be found in these volumes, are of a pathetic, interesting, and moral cast; but they bear a small proportion to the works of the other tendency. Several pieces were written by Mr Lewis himself, and others are well known. We shall extract an imitation from the German, by WALTER SCOTT, ['The Wild Huntsmen'] as a specimen of the works which these volumes contain, as he seems to be the best of the new species of *horror-breeding* Bards.

1801

Selected Reviews from *The Critical Review*, 1801

The Spirit of Turretville; or, the Mysterious Resemblance. A Romance of the Twelfth Century. 2 Vols. 12mo. 7s. sewed.
Dutton. 1800

In these times of scarcity and dearth, the author of the romance before us will be a servicable man indeed! The philosopher's stone is nothing to the secret he is in possession of. From the day lady Riverford commits her son to her servant James, with orders to convey him to a nurse, she sees no more this faithful confidant *who supplied her with food*; and yet, strange to tell! when the boy is out of age to head a company to the Holy Land, she comes out of her hiding place fat enough to pass upon the world for a monk! — As a novel writer we cannot, in justice to our readers, compliment *him* so highly: he is not likely to become a monk, or *the author of a Monk*. — Of ghosts, whether real or fictitious, we are heartily tired; and the flight of Jessy from her parents in Messina, to follow her beloved William as his page, is much better introduced in the History of Captain Robert Boyle, from which it is copied. We are doubly sorry that confinement from illness should have compelled our author to write his book to compensate for the loss of usual labour, and we sincerely hope that before this time he is well enough to resume his *proper* occupation, in which we trust he will meet with much better success.

***Jaqueline of Olzeburg; or, Final Retribution. A Romance. 12mo. 3s. 6d. sewed.* Chapple. 1800**

Another ghostly story, with a bombastic beginning, and a horrible termination, but with no incident between of the least consequence or interest. The author seems to have adopted the adage of the kitchen, 'Light the fire well at both sides, and the middle will take care of itself.'

***Tales of the Abbey, founded on Historical Facts. By A. Kendall, Author of Derwent Priory, &c. 3 Vols. 12mo. 10s 6d. Boards.* Symonds. 1800**

To attempt giving appropriate language and manners to the widow of Sidney and the successor of Essex is not a common task: it is the reverse of 'Edward's armour beaming on Cibber's breast;' and, in every step of the present production, we perceive modern manners, and the ideas of a very recent period. The sliding pannel, the passing sigh, with the various paraphernalia of modern novels, have been too often repeated to interest or attract. Our authoress, however, is not without merit; she is only unfortunate in her choice of the subject. The story is not unskilfully managed; the situations are often interesting; the romantic scenery in which the principal transactions occur is described with taste and propricty; and, probability is never greatly violated. A domestic tale would probably better suit the writer's talents.

***Rimualdo; or, the Castle of Badajos. A Romance. By W.S. Ireland, Author of the Abbess, &c. &c. 4 Vols. 12mo. 14s. sewed.* Longman *and* Rees. 1800**

We find too much of the fashionable machinery, of well-timed peals of thunder, of apparitions, &c. in these volumes; and our disgust at the frequent employment of these circumstances is increased by finding them in every instance useless. The story is artfully complicated, but too artificially developed; and the language unreasonably and injudiciously inflated. Yet the attention is kept alive in the midst of improbabilities; and we perceive that the author has talents, and knowledge of different countries and manners; which, with a little more experience and judgement, would enable him to produce a more perfect work. The poetry interspersed possesses a native wildness, truly interesting, and is introduced often with great effect.

***The Caverns of Strozzi. A Novel. 12mo. 3s. 6d. sewed.* Lane. 1800**

This is a supposed statement of the crimes, and consequent horrors and death of an abandoned woman of quality; but exhibited in a manner so impossible to have happened, that no one can mistake it for a true relation. There is a certain terseness in the style and energy in the description which shows that the author might have done better if he had chosen a better story. However as it is, in this age of rhodomóntade and fiction, it will most probably strut its hour among the other wonders and incongruities of the circulating library.

***Ancient Records; or, the Abbey of Saint Oswythe. A Romance. By T.J. Horsley Curties, Author of Ethelwina, or the House of Fitz-Auberne. 4 Vols. 12mo. 18s. Boards.* Lane. 1801**

More abbeys, with 'battlement ramparts,' and 'heavy *Gothic* pillars of the *Saxon* order!' — The novelist advertises his readers, in a preface, that he sent his last work into the world under the Christian name of Horsley; but the approbation which they have bestowed upon it makes him claim it now, with some degree of pride, by his sirname of Curties. But little more than fifty years ago, before turnpike-roads were so general through these kingdoms, a man who had a hundred miles to travel conceived himself about to undertake a tiresome journey; but, in the romance before us, sir Alfred St Oswythe and his family are conveyed in a covered car 'through the mountainous wilds of Scotland, and across more than half the kingdom of England,' in *six days*; a fact which we confess we should have doubted, as it happened five hundred years since, had the author not set his *sirname* to it. — As Mr Curties was so fortunate in the reception of his former work, we would advise him to try his hand at another, *A Treatise on the Mode of Posting in the Thirteenth and Fourteenth Centuries*; and if he should be so lucky as to prove that the fleet nags of that epoch owed the swiftness of their course to the spareness of their diet, we will ensure him the protection of all the hackney-men of the metropolis.

***The Mysterious Penitent; or, the Norman Château. A Romance. 2 Vols. 12mo. 6s. sewed.* Crosby *and* Letterman. 1801**

We cannot forbear to express our disapprobation of ghosts and mysteries, whenever and wherever it is our lot to meet with them: yet we must not throw by this little novel without bestowing upon it the portion of praise which it merits. Several of the characters are well conceived, amongst which the one of Valeria di Rozarno is peculiarly impressive. The lesson afforded by it to young minds is of the utmost consequence. When the passions are suffered to break down the bulwark of reason, and innocence is once lost, no one can determine how far the deluge shall spread. As the ghost turns out at last to be a monkey, we shall pass no further censure upon him than by generally remarking, that the more of supernatural agency is employed in a novel, the farther is the idea of its truth removed from the mind of its readers.

***Martyn of Fenrose; or, the Wizard and the Sword. A Romance. By Henry Summersett, Author of Leopold Warndorf, &c. 3 Vols. 12mo. 13s. Boards.* Dutton. 1801**

When we had perused only a few pages of this romance, we felt pleased with the performance; and, in spite of our objections to wizards and sorcery, could not avoid bestowing some commendation on the warm imagination of its author. But, before we had finished the second volume, disgust compelled us to throw the book on the floor, and we confess we have never since proceeded to the perusal.

Is it not enough that the English are already condemned by all Europe for the multiplicity of their oaths and blasphemies, that our circulating libraries must furnish their readers with a new set of anathemas? — 'May the spirit of my father strangle me in savageness!' and 'By the ruler of the world of angels, I will level all my rage and resentment at these smiling devils!' are the only two instances of our author's invention with which we would pollute our journal. But should any dragoon or boatswain's mate find himself disposed to improve in the delectable science of swearing, he will here meet with whole pages employed, between a mother and son, in curses and imprecations, for which, if he have taste, he may select many precious morsels for the use of the galley or the guard-room. The German dramatists are here absolutely *out-heroded*.

1798

Thomas James Mathias 1754–1835
The Pursuits of Literature, A Satirical Poem in Four Dialogues with Notes

From the First Dialogue

It is for me to creep, or soar, or doze,
In modish song, or fashionable prose?
To pen with garreteers obscure and shabby,
Inscriptive nonsense in a fancied Abbey;*
Or some Warkworthian hermit tale endite,
Such ditties as our gossip spinsters write?
Say, must I tempt some novel's lulling theme,

Bid the bright eye o'er Celestina stream;**
With fabled knights, and tales of slighted love,
Such as our Spanish Cato might approve?
In Travels for the heart, and not the head,
From post to pillar, and from board to bed,
Through climes of various woe the pilgrim lead,
Till Charlotte droops, and master misses bleed.

* Such trash as a vile pamphlet called Kilkhampton Abbey, *&c. &c. &c.*; in short, the whole mugitus Labyrinthi. Every age produces similar trash, and this name serves, as well as any other, to mark me meaning in this place.
** Put for almost any modern novel. Mrs Charlotte Smith, Mrs Inchbald, Mrs Mary Robinson, Mrs &c &c though all of them are very ingenious ladies, yet they are too frequently *whining* or *frisking* in novels, till our girls' heads turn wild with impossible adventures, and are now and then tainted with democracy, and sometimes with infidelity and loose principles.

Not so the mighty magician of THE MYSTERIES OF UDOLPHO, bred and nourished by the Florentine Muses in all their sacred solitary caverns, amid the paler shrines of Gothic superstition, and in all the dreariness of enchantment.

Preface to the Fourth Dialogue

> *Literature, well or ill conducted, is the great engine, by which all civilized states must ultimately be supported or be overthrown.*

I am now more impressed with this truth, if we consider the nature, the variety, and the extent of the word Literature.

We are no longer in an age of ignorance; and information is not partially distributed according to the ranks, the orders, the functions and the dignities of social life. All learning has an index, and every science its abridgement. I am scarcely able to name any man whom I consider as wholly ignorant. We no longer look exclusively for learned authors in the usual place, in the retreats of academick erudition, and in the seats of religion. Our peasantry now read the *Rights of Man* on mountains, and on moors, and by the way side; and shepherds make the analogy between their occupation and that of their governours: happy indeed, had they been taught to make no other comparison. Our *unsexed* female writers now instruct, or confuse, us and themselves in the labyrinth of politicks, or turn us wild with Gallick frenzy.

But there is one publication of the time too peculiar, and too important to be passed over in a general reprehension. There is nothing with which it may be compared. A Legislator in our own parliament, a member of the House of Commons of Great Britain, an elected guardian and defender of the laws, the religion, and the good manners of the country, has neither scrupled nor blushed to depict, and to publish to the world, the arts of lewd and systematic seduction, and to thrust upon the nation the most open and unqualified blasphemy against the very code and volume of our religion: and all this, with his name, style, and title, prefixed to the novel or romance called 'THE MONK' ... What is it to the kingdom at large, or what is it to all those whose office it is to maintain truth, and instruct the rising abilities and the hopes of England, that the author of THE MONK is *a very young man*? That forsooth he is a man of genius and of fancy? So much the worse. That there are very poetical descriptions of castles and abbies in this novel? So much the worse again, the novel is more alluring on that account. Is this a time to poison the waters of our land in their springs and fountains? Are we to add incitement to incitement, and corruption to corruption, till there neither is, nor can be, a return to virtuous action and to regulated life? Who knows *the age* of this author? I can presume very few. *Who does not know*, that he is a Member of Parliament? He has told us all so himself.

From the Fourth Dialogue

Novels of this seductive and libidinous tendency excite disgust, fear, and horrour in every man and woman who reflect upon those virtues which *alone* give support, comfort, and continuance to human society. The interests of society and its essential welfare, and even the very existence of this kingdom, authorise any man, though conscious of manifold frailties, to speak in the manner I have done. We cannot long deceive ourselves: poetical men, of loose and ungoverned morals, can offer to us, or to themselves, but feeble consolations from wit or from imagery, when left to solitary reflection and to the agony of remorse. I never found this subject so well represented, and so unanswerably enforced to every understanding, capable of *recalling itself* from vicious conduct and from irregular inclinations, as in this short sentence: '*Whoever* WHOLLY *gives themselves up to* Lust, *will soon find out it to be the least fault they are guilty of.*'

From the Fourth Dialogue

Speak then, the hour demands; Is learning fled?
Spent all her vigour, all her spirit dead?
Have Gallick arms and unrelenting war
Borne all her trophies from Britannia far?
Shall nought but ghosts and trinkets be display'd,
Since Walpole* ply'd the virtuoso's trade,
Bade sober truth reversed for fiction pass,
And mused o'er gothick toys through gothick glass?

* The late ingenious Earl of Orford, Horace Walpole. The spirit of inquiry which he introduced was rather frivolous, though pleasing, and his Otranto ghosts have propagated their species with unequal fecundity. The spawn is in every novel shop.

Henry Fuseli and William Blake

Henry Fuseli and William Blake were each repeatedly attacked in the most virulent terms by the critics of the day. From the outset of his career, Fuseli was equally admired and reviled as a wild eccentric. For his supporters, the oddities and shortcomings of his art and his confrontational personality, were signs of the depth of his genius; for his enemies, they were instead indications of his lack of talent, or his ability to seduce the gullible. Fuseli, meanwhile, in his published comments on the art, was reticent about the themes of terror and horror which drew so much attention in his own work. He suggests a degree of caution was necessary in the representation of such subjects, which his critics and perhaps many of his supporters would find surprising.

Fuseli was often enough condemned as a madman, and the visionary aspects of his art attributed to the influence of opium or of eating raw pork (see pp.244–5). In the case of William Blake, certainly an admirer of Fuseli and in some sense his follower, the same criticisms were applied even more vehemently. The infamous review of Blake's one-man show in 1809 links the two, and finds the younger artist culpable of a degree of eccentricity which has, by this date, dangerous political overtones.

October 1792

Henry Fuseli 1741–1825
Review of Hickey's *History of Painting and Sculpture, from the Earliest Accounts*

Mr H has added little to the criticisms of Pausanias, except in the instance of Neoptolemus, whom the painter, in his opinion with great judgment, has not represented slaying Priam, which would have shocked our feelings, but some obscure warrior, unknown even to Pausanias, one Elassits; and in a note he expatiates on the boundless licence granted to poetry, and the very narrow limits prescribed to painting with regard to the choice of objects: a notion, which owes its origins to the German critics.

The truth is, that horrour and loathsomness in all its branches are equally banished from the painter's and the poet's province. Terrour, as the chief ingredient of the sublime, composes in all instances, and in the utmost extent of the word, fit material for both.

December 1796

Henry Fuseli 1741–1825
Review of William Roscoe's *Life of Lorenzo de' Medici*

Let horror and loathsomeness be banished from the instruments of art, and the martyrdom of Stephen or Sebastian, Agnes or John becomes as admissible as that of Marsyas or Palamedes, Virginia or Regulus. It is the artist's fault, if the right moment be missed. If you see only blood-tipped arrows, brain-dashed stones, excoriating knives, the artist, not the subject, is detestable; this furnished heroism, celestial resignation, the features of calm fortitude and beauty endless but undismayed; the clown or brute alone, who handled it, pushed you down among the assassins from the hero's side. Humanity may avert our eyes with propriety from the murdered subjects of Pietro Testa, Joseph Ribera, sometimes even of Domenichino himself; but apathy, phlegm, effeminacy, alone would prefer an Adromeda, an Agave, or a Venus hanging over an expiring Adonis, to the 'Madonna del Spafmo' of Raffaelo, or M. Angelo's crucifixion of St Peter.

1805

Henry Fuseli 1741–1825
Fifth Lecture on Painting: 'Composition, Expression'

Sympathy and disgust are the irreconcilable parallels that must for ever separate legitimate terror and pity from horror and aversion. We cannot sympathise with what we detest or despise, nor fully pity what we shudder at or loathe. So little were these limits understood by the moderns, M. Angelo excepted, that even the humanity and delicacy of Raffaelo did not guard him from excursions into the realms of horror and loathsomeness: it is difficult to conceive what could provoke him to make a finished design of the inhumanities that accompany the martyrdom of St Felicitas at which even description shudders; a design made on purpose to be dispersed over Europe, perpetuated and made known to all by the graver of Marc Antonio: Was it to prove to Albert Durer and the Germans of his time that they had not exhausted the sources of abomination? He made an equal mistake in the Morbetto, where, though not with so lavish a hand as Poussin after him, instead of the moral effects of the plague, he has personified the effluvia or putrefaction. What *he* had not penetration to avoid, could not be expected to be shunned by his scholars. Julio Romano delighted in studied images of torture as well as of the most abandoned licentiousness. Among his contemporaries, Corregio even attempted to give zest to the most wanton cruelty by an affectation of grace in the picture of the Saints Placido and Flavia: but the enamoured trance of Placido with his neck half cut, and the anthem that quivers on the lips of Flavia whilst a sword is entering her side, in vain bespeak our sympathy, for whilst we detest the felons who slaughter them, we loathe to inspect the actual process of their crime; mangling is contagious, and spreads aversion from the slaughterman to the victim. If St Bartholomew and St Erasmus are subjects for painting, they can only be so before, and neither under nor after the operation of the knife or windlass. A decollated martyr represented with his head in his hand, as Rubens did, and a headless corpse with the head lying by it, as Corregio, can only prove the brutality, stupidity, or bigotry of the employer, and the callus or venality of the artist.

1788–1818

Henry Fuseli 1741–1825
Aphorisms on Art

48 All apparatus destroys terror, as all ornament grandeur: the minute catalogue of the cauldron's ingredients in *Macbeth* destroys the terror attendant on mysterious darkness; and the

seraglio-trappings of Rubens annihilate his heroes.

86 The loathsome is abominable, and no engine of expression. *Coroll.* — When Spenser dragged into light the entrails of the serpent, slain by the Red-cross Knight, he dreamt a butcher's dream and not a poet's: and Fletcher, or his partner, when rummaging the surgeon's box of cataplasms and trusses to assuage hunger, solicited the grunt of an applauding sty.

87 Sympathy and disgust are the lines that separate terror from horror: though we shudder at, we scarcely pity what we abominate.
Coroll. — Rowe, when he congratulates the ghost on bidding Hamlet spare his mother, accuses *her* of a crime which the poet never charged her: that Shakespeare might be hurried on to horror let the 'vile jelly' witness, which Cornwall treads from Gloster's bleeding sockets.

88 Expression animates, convulses, or absorbs form. The Apollo is animated; the warrior of Agasias is animated; the Laocoon is convulsed; the Niobe is absorbed.

89 The being seized by an enormous passion, be it joy or grief, hope or despair, loses the character of its own individual expression, and is absorbed by the power of the feature that attracts it: Niobe and her family are assimilated by extreme anguish; Ugolino is petrified by the fate that sweeps his sons; and every metamorphosis from that of Clytie to the transfusion of Gianni Fucci tells a new allegory of sympathetic power.

90 Reject with indignant incredulity all self-congratulations of conscious villainy, though they may be uttered by Richard or by Iago.

91 The axe, the wheel, saw-dust, and the blood-stained sheet are not legitimate substitutes of terror.

1793

Revd Robert Anthony Bromley
A Philosophical and Critical History of the Arts

...the dignity of moral instruction is degraded, whenever the pencil is employed on frivolous, whimsical, and unmeaning subjects. On this head, it is to be feared, there will ever be too much cause for complaint, because there will ever be persons incapable of solidity, although very capable of executing this art with power. Strength of understanding, and ability in art or science, are very different things; they are derived from different sources; and they are perfectly independent of each other. The one can no more be instrumental to the communication of the other, than either can communicate temper or disposition. The finest art in the world may therefore be combined with the lightest and most superficial mind. Books are written of a light and fantastic nature by those who cannot write otherwise, and yet will write something. And so it is with painting: the mind of the artist can but give such subjects as are consentaneous to its turn. The *night-mare, little red riding hood, the shepherd's dream,* or any dream that is not marked in authentic history as combined with the important dispensations of Providence, and many other pieces of a visionary and fanciful nature, are speculations of as exalted a stretch in the contemplation of such a mind as the finest lessons that ever were drawn from religion, or morals, or useful history. And yet the painter, who should employ his time on such subjects, would certainly amuse the intelligent no more than the man who should make those subjects the topics of a serious discourse. But what good has the world, or what honour has the art, at any time derived from such light and fantastic speculations? If it be right to follow Nature, there is nothing of her here, all that is presented to us is a *reverie* of the brain. If it be allowable to cultivate fancy; yet the fancy, which has little or nothing of Nature in its composition, becomes ridiculous. A man may carry the flights of imagination, even within the walks of the chastest art or science, till they become mere waking dreams, as wild as the conceits of a madman. The author of observations on Fresnoy *de arte graphica* very properly calls these persons 'Libertines of painting': as there are libertines of religion, who had no other law but the vehemence of their own inclinations; so these have no other model, he says, but a rodomontade-genius, which shews us a wild or savage nature that is not of our acquaintance, but of a new creation.

17 March 1809

The Examiner

If beside the stupid and mad-brained projects of their rulers, the sane part of the people of England required fresh proofs of the alarming increase of the efforts of insanity, they will be too well convinced from its having been spread into the hitherto sober regions of Art. I say hitherto, because I cannot think with many, that the vigorous genius of the present worthy Keeper of the Royal Academy is touched, though no one can deny that his Muse has been on the verge of insanity, since it has brought forth, with more legitimate offspring, the furious and distorted beings of an extravagant imagination. But, when the ebullitions of a distempered brain are mistaken for the sallies of genius by those whose works have exhibited the soundest thinking in art, the malady has indeed attained a pernicious height, and it becomes a duty to endeavour to arrest its development. Such is the case with the productions and admirers of WILLIAM BLAKE, an unfortunate lunatic, whose personal inoffensiveness secures him from confinement, and, consequently, of whom no public notice would have been taken, if it was not forced on the notice and animadversion of the EXAMINER, in having been held up to public admiration by many esteemed amateurs and professors as a genius in some respect original and legitimate. The praises which these gentlemen bestowed last year on this unfortunate man's illustrations of *Blair's Grave*, have, in feeding his vanity, stimulated him to publish his madness more largely, and thus again exposed him, if not to the derision, at least to the pity of the public. That work was a futile endeavour by bad drawings to represent immaterially by body personifications of the soul, while its partner the body was depicted in company with it, so that the soul was confounded with the body, as the personifying figure had none of the distinguishing characteristics of allegory, presenting only substantial flesh and bones. This conceit was dignified with the character of genius, and the tasteful hand of SCHIAVONETTI, who engraved the work, assisted to give it currency by bestowing an exterior charm on deformity and nonsense. Thus encouraged, the poor man fancies himself a great master, and has painted a few wretched pictures, some of which are unintelligible allegory, others an attempt at sober character by caricature representation, and the whole 'blotted and blurred' and very badly drawn. These he calls an Exhibition, of which he has published a Catalogue, or rather a farrago of nonsense, unintelligibleness, and egregious vanity, the wild effusions of a distempered brain.

New Reading Habits: Austen and Peacock

The ascent of the Gothic novel was inextricably linked to new ways of reading and disseminating literature. Advances in print technology, combining with the spread of circulating libraries, where books could be hired and returned, meant an enormous expansion in the potential market for any new book. These innovations attracted a range of concerns and critical doubts: would this help empower whole sectors of the populace previously excluded from the realm of reason and political influence? would the morals and minds of the impressionable be corrupted? would literature itself be cheapened, revitalised or inhibited?

The excerpts here present satirical comment on such issues. Jane Austen's *Northanger Abbey* (written *c*.1798–1803 but subsequently revised and published only in 1818) offers a sustained consideration of the significance of Gothic as a literary form for the middle- and upper-middle class of the early nineteenth century. In the first excerpt Catherine Morland and her new friend Eleanor Tinsley discuss the current crop of Gothic novels which absorb their interest. In the second excerpt, Catherine talks about a new Gothic novel, whose talk of novelty Eleanor mistakes as referring to actual political revolution. The passage is particularly striking, given the continuing debates about the nature or even possibility of political reference within the Gothic.

Thomas Love Peacock (1785–1866) created a series of acutely satirical novels, aimed at the pretensions and ambitions of the 'romantic' poets and readers of the day. With *Nightmare Abbey* he focused on what he referred to as 'the morbidities of modern literature'. The central protagonist is Scythrop Glowry. Troubled by disappointment in love, and living in isolation, Scythrop develops eccentric conspiracy theories and an obsession with German literature and philosophy. *The Sorrows of Werther* which is alluded to as Scythrop's youthful reading is, of course, Goethe's novel of that name. *Horrid Mysteries* is the same book as mentioned by Austen among her young characters' reading-list.

Peacock's immediate target was the poet Shelley; Scythrop shares the reading interests of the romantic writer, and draws from these a world-shaking revolutionary theory of a sort that was viewed with deep suspicion in post-French Revolution Britain. But more generally, Peacock outlines a suggestive association between masculine emotional neediness and a passion for the fantastic, which might find wider application.

1818

Jane Austen 1775–1817
Northanger Abbey

The following conversation, which took place between the two friends in the Pump-room one morning, after an acquaintance of eight or nine days, is given as a specimen of their very warm attachment, and of the delicacy, discretion, originality of thought, and literary taste which marked the reasonableness of that attachment.

They met by appointment; and as Isabella had arrived nearly five minutes before her friend, her first address naturally was — 'My dearest creature, what can have made you so late? I have been waiting for you at least this age!'

'Have you, indeed! — I am very sorry for it; but really I thought I was in very good time. It is but just one. I hope you have not been here long?'

'Oh! these ten ages at least. I am sure I have been here this half hour. But now, let us go and sit down at the other end of the room, and enjoy ourselves. I have an hundred things to say to you. In the first place, I was so afraid it would rain this morning, just as I wanted to set off; it looked very showery, and that would have thrown me into agonies! Do you know, I saw the prettiest hat you can imagine, in a shop window in Milsom-Street just now — very like yours, only with coquelicot ribbons instead of green; I quite longed for it. But, my dearest Catherine, what have you been doing with yourself all this morning? — Have you gone on with Udolpho?'

'Yes, I have been reading it ever since I woke; and I am got to the black veil.'

'Are you, indeed? How delightful! Oh! I would not tell you what is behind the black veil for the world! Are not you wild to know?'

'Oh! yes, quite; what can it be? — But do not tell me — I would not be told upon any account. I know it must be a skeleton, I am sure it is Laurentina's skeleton. Oh! I am delighted with the book! I should like to spend my whole life in reading it. I assure you, if it had not been to meet you, I would not have come away from it for all the world.'

'Dear creature! how much I am obliged to you; and when you have finished Udolpho, we will read the Italian together; and I have made out a list of ten or twelve more of the same kind for you.'

'Have you, indeed! How glad I am! — What are they all?'

'I will read you their names directly; here they are, in my pocketbook. Castle of Wolfenbach, Clermont, Mysterious Warnings, Necromancer of the Black Forest, Midnight Bell, Orphan of the Rhine, and Horrid Mysteries. Those will last us some time.'

'Yes, pretty well; but are they all horrid, are you sure they are all horrid?'

'Yes, quite sure; for a particular friend of mine, a Miss Andrews, a sweet girl, one of the sweetest creatures in the world, has read every one of them. I wish you knew Miss Andrews, you would be delighted with her. She is netting herself the sweetest cloak you can conceive. I think her as beautiful as an angel, and I am so vexed with the men for not admiring her! — I scold them all amazingly about it.'

'Scold them! Do you scold them for not admiring her?'

'Yes, that I do. There is nothing I would not do for those who are really my friends. I have no notion of loving people by halves; it is not my nature. My attachments are always excessively strong. I told Captain Hunt at one of our assemblies this winter that if he was to tease me all night, I would not dance with him, unless he would allow Miss Andrews to be as beautiful as an angel. The men think us incapable of real friendship, you know, and I am determined to show them the difference. Now, if I were to hear anybody speak slightingly of you, I should fire up in a moment: but that is not at all likely, for you are just the kind of girl to be a great favourite with the men ...'

The advantages of natural folly in a beautiful girl have been already set forth by the capital pen of a sister author; — and to her treatment of the subject I will only add, in justice to men, that though to the larger and more trifling part of the sex, imbecility in females is a great enhancement of their personal charms, there is a portion of them too reasonable and too well informed themselves to desire anything more in woman than ignorance. But Catherine did not know her own advantages — did not know that a good-looking girl, with an affectionate heart and a very ignorant mind, cannot fail of attracting a clever young man, unless circumstances are particularly untoward. In the present instance, she confessed and lamented her want of knowledge; declared that she would give anything in the world to be able to draw; and a lecture on the picturesque immediately followed, in which his instructions were so clear that she soon began to see beauty in everything admired by him, and her attention was so earnest that he became perfectly satisfied of her having a great deal of natural taste. He talked of fore-grounds, distances, and second distances — side-screens and perspectives — lights and shades; and Catherine was so hopeful a scholar, that when they gained the top of Beechen Cliff, she voluntarily rejected the whole city of Bath as unworthy to make part of a landscape. Delighted with her progress, and fearful of wearying her with too much wisdom at once, Henry suffered the subject to decline, and by an easy transition from a piece of rocky fragment and the withered oak which he had placed near its summit, to oaks in general, to forests, the enclosure of them, waste lands, crown lands and government, he shortly found himself arrived at politics; and from politics, it was an easy step to silence. The general pause which succeeded his short disquisition on the state of the nation was put an end to by

Catherine, who, in rather a solemn tone of voice, uttered these words, 'I have heard that something very shocking indeed will soon come out in London.'

Miss Tilney, to whom this was chiefly addressed, was startled, and hastily replied, 'Indeed! — and of what nature?'

'That I do not know, nor who is the author. I have only heard that it is to be more horrible than anything we have met with yet.'

'Good heaven! — Where could you hear of such a thing?'

'A particular friend of mine had an account of it in a letter from London yesterday. It is to be uncommonly dreadful. I shall expect murder and every thing of the kind.'

'You speak with astonishing composure! But I hope your friend's accounts have been exaggerated; — and if such a design is known beforehand, proper measures will undoubtedly be taken by government to prevent its coming to effect.'

'Government,' said Henry, endeavouring not to smile, 'neither desires nor dares to interfere in such matters. There must be murder; and government cares not how much.'

The ladies stared. He laughed, and added, 'Come, shall I make you understand each other, or leave you to puzzle out an explanation as you can? No — I will be noble. I will prove myself a man, no less by the generosity of my soul than the clearness of my head. I have no patience with such of my sex as disdain to let themselves sometimes down to the comprehension of yours. Perhaps the abilities of women are neither sound nor acute — neither vigorous nor keen. Perhaps they may want observation, discernment, judgment, fire, genius, and wit.'

'Miss Morland, do not mind what he says; — but have the goodness to satisfy me as to this dreadful riot.'

'Riot! —what riot?'

'My dear Eleanor, the riot is only in your own brain. The confusion there is scandalous. Miss Morland has been talking of nothing more dreadful than a new publication which is shortly to come out, in three duodecimo volumes, two hundred and seventy-six pages in each, with a frontispiece to the first, of two tombstones and a lantern — do you understand? — And you, Miss Morland — my stupid sister has mistaken all your clearest expressions. You talked of expected horrors in London — and instead of instantly conceiving, as any rational creature would have done, that such words could relate only to a circulating library, she immediately pictured to herself a mob of three thousand men assembling in St. George's Fields; the Bank attacked, the Tower threatened, the streets of London flowing with blood, a detachment of the Twelfth Light Dragoons, (the hopes of the nation,) called up from Northampton to quell the insurgents, and the gallant Capt. Frederick Tilney, in the moment of charging at the head of his troop, knocked off his horse by a brickbat from an upper window. Forgive her stupidity. The fears of the sister have added to the weakness of the woman; but she is by no means a simpleton in general.' [...]

1817

Thomas Love Peacock 1785–1866
Nightmare Abbey

Shortly after the disastrous termination of Scythrop's passion for Miss Emily Girouette, Mr Glowry found himself, much against his will, involved in a lawsuit, which compelled him to dance attendance on the High Court of Chancery. Scythrop was left alone at Nightmare Abbey. He was a burnt child, and dreaded the fire of female eyes. He wandered about the ample pile, or along the garden-terrace, with 'his cognitive faculties immersed in cogibundity of cognition'. The terrace terminated at the south-western tower, which, as we have said, was ruinous and full of owls. Here would Scythrop take his evening seat, on a fallen fragment of mossy stone, with his back resting against the ruined wall, — a thick canopy of ivy, with an owl in it, over his head, and *The Sorrows of Werther* in his hand. He had some taste for romance reading before he went to the university, where, we must confess, in justice to his college, he was cured of the love of reading in all its shapes; and the cure would have been radical, if disappointment in love, and total solitude, had not conspired to bring on a relapse. He began to devour romances and German tragedies, and, by the recommendation of Mr Flosky, to pore over ponderous tomes of transcendental philosophy, which reconciled him to the labour of studying them by their mystical jargon and necromantic imagery. In the congenial solitude of Nightmare Abbey, the distempered idea of metaphysical romance and romantic metaphysics had ample time and space to germinate into a fertile crop of chimeras, which rapidly shot up into vigorous and abundant vegetation.

He now became troubled with the *passion for reforming the world*. He built many castles in the air, and peopled them with secret tribunals, and bands of illuminati, who were always the imaginary instruments of his projected regeneration of the human species. As he intended to institute a perfect republic, he invested himself with absolute sovereignty over these mystical dispensers of liberty. He slept with *Horrid Mysteries* under his pillow, and dreamed of venerable eleutherachs and ghastly confederates holding midnight conventions in subterranean caves. He passed whole mornings in his study, immersed in gloomy reverie, stalking about the room in his nightcap, which he pulled over his eyes like a cowl, and folding his striped calico dressing-gown about him like the mantle of a conspirator.

'Action,' thus he soliloquised, 'is the result of opinion, and to new-model opinion would be to new-model society. Knowledge is power; it is in the hands of a few, who employ it to mislead the many, for their own selfish purposes of aggrandisement and appropriation. What if it were in the hands of a few who should employ it to lead the many? What if it were universal, and the multitude were enlightened? No. The many must be always in leading-strings; but let them have wise and honest conductors. A few to think, and many to act; that is the only basis of perfect society. So thought the ancient philosophers:

they had their esoterical and exoterical doctrines. So thinks the sublime Kant, who delivers his oracles in language which none but the initiated can comprehend. Such were the views of those secret associations of illuminati, which were the terror of superstition and tyranny, and which, carefully selecting wisdom and genius from the great wilderness of society, as the bee selects honey from the flowers of the thorn and the nettle, bound all human excellence in a chain, which, if it had not been prematurely broken, would have commanded opinion, and regenerated the world.'

Scythrop proceeded to meditate on the practicability of reviving a confederation of regenerators. To get a clear view of his own ideas, and to feel the pulse of the wisdom and genius of the age, he wrote and published a treatise, in which his meanings were carefully wrapt up in the monk's hood of transcendental technology, but filled with hints of matter deep and dangerous, which he thought would set the whole nation in a ferment; and he awaited the result in awful expectation, as a miner who has fired a train awaits the explosion of a rock. However, he listened and heard nothing; for the explosion, if any ensued, was not sufficiently loud to shake a single leaf of the ivy on the towers of Nightmare Abbey; and some months afterwards he received a letter from his bookseller, informing him that only seven copies had been sold, and concluding with a polite request for the balance.

Scythrop did not despair. 'Seven copies,' he thought, 'have been sold. Seven is a mystical number, and the omen is good. Let me find the seven purchasers of my seven copies, and they shall be the seven golden candle-sticks with which I will illuminate the world.'

Scythrop had a certain portion of mechanical genius, which his romantic projects tended to develope. He constructed models of cells and recesses, sliding panels and secret passages, that would have baffled the skill of the Parisian police. He took the opportunity of his father's absence to smuggle a dumb carpenter into the Abbey, and between them they gave reality to one of these models in Scythrop's tower. Scythrop foresaw that a great leader of human regeneration would be involved in fearful dilemmas, and determined, for the benefit of mankind in general, to adopt all the possible precautions for the preservation of himself.

The servants, even the women, had been tutored into silence. Profound stillness reigned throughout and around the Abbey, except where the occasional shutting of a door would peal in long reverberations through the galleries, or the heavy tread of the pensive butler would wake the hollow echoes of the hall. Scythrop stalked about like the grand inquisitor, and the servants flitted past him like familiars. In his evening meditations on the terrace, under the ivy of the ruined tower, the only sounds that came to his ear were the rustling of the wind in the ivy, the plaintive voices of the feathered choristers, the owls, the occasional striking of the Abbey clock, and the monotonous dash of the sea on its low and level course. In the mean time, he drank Madeira, and laid deep schemes for a thorough repair of the crazy fabric of human nature.

5.6

Modern Reticence: Bram Stoker and M.R. James

The themes of moderation and reticence have been a recurring motif in British literary criticism since the eighteenth century. While foreign (particularly French) writers and analysts have repeatedly been caricatured as misled by abstract theories and rigid conventions, Britain's national culture has been characterised by its supposed liberties, organic development and freedom from rules, each secured by a degree of compromise. From the 1790s in particular, in response to the French Revolution, a determinedly self-effacing idea of the literary enterprise has helped underpin a fundamentally bourgeois and conservative dominant culture. The excessive, explicit or cosmic have been held as peculiarly alien to the 'native' character.

How do the resilient threads of the fantastic apparent in British art and literature sit within this ideal? In a sense, very well indeed; for such productions help mark vividly the limits and extent of the legitimate, by exception, or by finely drawn distinctions. Moreover, the eccentricity or self-destructiveness of the fantastic artist have been important props for the bourgeois self-image; they provide proof of the peculiar liberties of British culture, even as they warn us of the dangers of exceeding the natural restraints emanating from our profound, collective common sense.

Here, Bram Stoker and M.R. James, each authors of strange and shocking fictions, succeed in appearing to support the libertarian nature of Britain's literary culture, while laying down proscriptive limits around the depiction of sexuality and horror. The resulting ambivalence reflects not so much personal idiosyncrasy, as the deep-rooted equivocation around issues of freedom, order and confinement in British (and in Stoker's case Anglo-Irish) culture and society, which has lent the Gothic such power for over two centuries.

July–December 1908

Bram Stoker 1847–1912
'The Censorship of Fiction', *The Nineteenth Century and After*, no.64

There is perhaps no branch of work amongst the arts so free at the present time as that of the writing of fiction. There are no official prohibitions, no embarrassing or hampering limitations, no oppressive restraints. Subject and method of treatment are both free. A writer is under no special obligation, no preliminary guarantee; he may choose his own subject and treat it in his own way. In fact, his duty to the public — to the State — appears to be *nil*. What one might call the cosmic police do not trouble him at all. Under these conditions, hitherto kept possible by the self-respect of authors, a branch of the art of authorship has arisen and gone on perfecting itself in mechanical excellence, until it has become an important factor of the life of the nation. To-day if the supply of fiction were to be suddenly withdrawn the effect would be felt almost as much as the failure of the supply of breadstuffs. Happily fiction is not dependent on the existence of peace, or the flourishing of trade, or indeed on any form of national well-being. War and business worries — distress in any form — are clamorous in their own ways for intellectual antidotes; so that though the nature of the output may be of every varying kind, the supply is undiminished. Herein it is that the wide scope of the art of fiction proves its excellence; as no subject and no form of treatment is barred it follows that changing needs may find settlement in suitable opposites. And so imaginative work becomes recognised in the higher stagecraft as a useful product.

But in the real world all things are finally relative. There is in reality, whose existence and progress must be based on cosmic laws, no such thing as absolute freedom. The needs and necessarily recognised rights of individuals and groups must at times become so conflicting that some sort of give-and-take rules or laws are necessary to the general good. Indeed we might put it in general form that freedom contains in its very structure the germs of constraint. The measure and method of that restraint have to be ascertained by experience, and in some measure by experiment, for if we wait till experience, following a simple course of *laissez faire*, has learned the worst that can happen, at least part of the protective force of common sense is thrown away.

This is a philosophy too simple to be put in books, and has its existence in the brain of every sane individual. Let us apply it to the subject in question — the union or at least the recognition of two values, the excellences of imagination and of restraint. Restraint may be one of two kinds — either that which is compelled by external forces, or that which comes from within. In art the latter in its usual phase is known as 'reticence'. This is the highest quality of art; that which can be and is its chief and crowning glory. It is an attribute practically undefinable. Its conditions are so varying and so multitudinous, its degrees so finely graded, its workings so mysterious, its end so elusive, that it is not possible to explain it adequately by words which are themselves defective and yet of every-varying meaning. Suffice it that it is recognisable, and recognised, by all true artists. In its consists largely, if not wholly, the ethics of art; and on it, or in it depends that quality of art which brings it within the classification of 'high' art. The measure of the ethics of the artist is expressed in the reticence shown in his work; and where such self-restraint exists there is no need for external compelling force. In fact, self-restraint is the bulwark of freedom, inasmuch as it makes other forms of restraint unnecessary. Some power must somewhere in the advance of things recognise the imperfection of humanity. When the integer of that great body recognises that imperfection and the evils consequent upon it, those evils are at their least...

That restraint in some form is necessary is shown by the history of the last few years with regard to works of fiction. The self-restraint and reticence which many writers have through centuries exercised in behalf of an art which they loved and honoured has not of late been exercised by the few who seek to make money and achieve notoriety through base means. There is no denying the fact nor the cause; both are only too painfully apparent. Within a couple of years past quite a number of novels have been published in England that would be a disgrace to any country even less civilised than our own. The class of works to which I allude are meant by both authors and publishers to bring

40
Francis Danby
Romantic Woodland, c.1824–5
Watercolour, gum arabic and pencil on paper 19.4 x 26 cm
Tate. Purchased as part of the Oppé Collection with assistance from the National Lottery through the Heritage Lottery Fund 1996

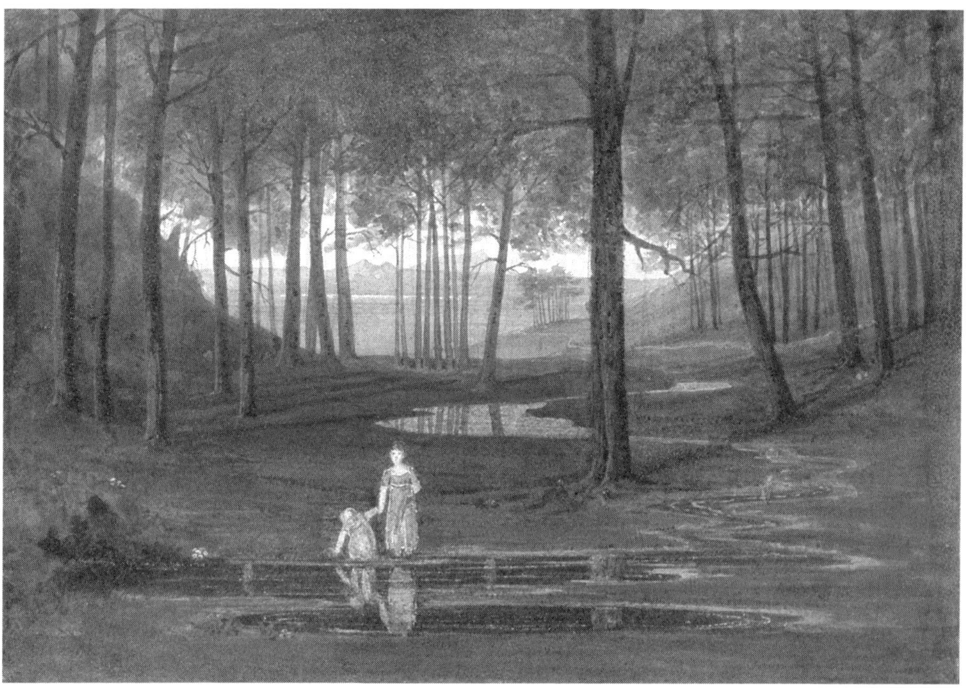

to the winning of commercial success the forces of inherent evil in man. The word man here stands for woman as well as man; indeed women are the worst offenders in this breach of moral law. As to the alleged men who follow this loathsome calling, what term of opprobrium is sufficient, what punishment could be too great? This judgment of work which claims to be artistic may seem too harsh, and punishment may seem vindictive — except in so far as all just judgment may seem harsh and all punishment vindictive. For look what those people have done. They have found an art wholesome, they made it morbid; they found it pure, they left it sullied. Up to this time it was free — the freest thing in the land; they so treated it, they so abused the powers allowed them and their own opportunities, that continued freedom becomes dangerous, even impossible. They in their selfish greed tried to deprave where others had striven to elevate. In the language of the pulpit, they have 'crucified Christ afresh.' The merest glance at some of their work will justify any harshness of judgment; the roughest synopsis will horrify. It is not well to name either these books or their authors, for such would but make known what is better suppressed, and give the writers the advertisement which they crave. It may be taken that such works as are here spoken of deal not merely with natural misdoing based on human weakness, frailty, or passions of the senses, but with vices so flagitious, so opposed to even the decencies of nature in its crudest and lowest forms, that the poignancy of moral disgust is lost in horror. This article is no mere protest against academic faults or breaches of good taste. It is a deliberate indictment of a class of literature so vile that it is actually corrupting the nation.

41
William Holman Hunt
The Haunted Manor, 1849
Oil on board 23.3 x 33.7 cm
Tate. Purchased 1967

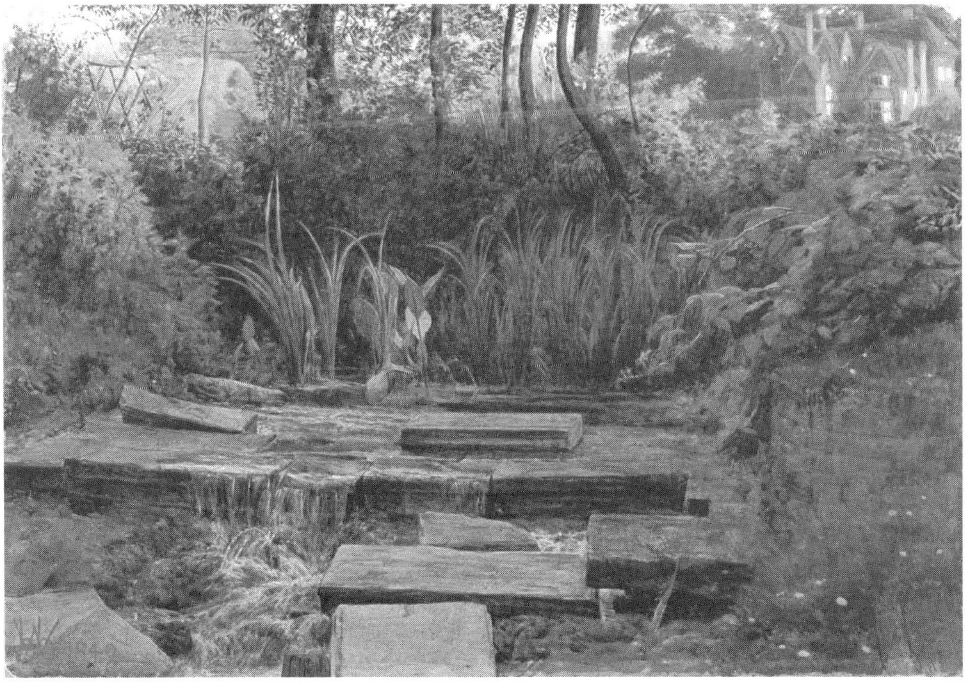

December 1929

M.R. James 1862–1936
'Some Remarks on Ghost Stories', *The Bookman*

Reticence may be an elderly doctrine to preach, yet from the artistic point of view I am sure it is a sound one. Reticence conduces to effect, blatancy ruins it, and there is much blatancy in a lot of recent stories. They drag in sex too, which is a fatal mistake; sex is tiresome enough in the novels; in a ghost story, or as the backbone of a ghost story, I have no patience with it.

At the same time don't let us be mild and drab. Malevolence and terror, the glare of evil faces, 'the stony grin of unearthly malice', pursuing forms in darkness, the 'long-drawn, distant screams', are all in place, and so is a modicum of blood, shed with deliberation and carefully husbanded; the weltering and wallowing that I too often encounter merely recalls the methods of M.G. Lewis.

Bibliographic references

Numbers in bold refer to page numbers

Part 1
The Gothic: A Sampling of Key Texts and Images

24 Richard Steele, *The Guardian*, no.148 (31 August 1713)

28 *The Adventures of Ferdinand Count Fathom. By the Author of Roderick Random*, 2 vols, London: W.Johnson 1753, vol.1, pp.129–35

31 *A Sentimental Journey through France and Italy by Mr Yorick*, 2 vols, London: T. Becket and P.A. De Hondt, 1768, vol.2, pp.29–32

34 *The Castle of Otranto, A Story. Translated by William Marshal, Gent. From the Original Italian of Onuphurio Murato, Canon of the Church of St Nicholas at Otranto*, London: T. Lownds 1765, pp.ii–viii and pp.12–26

43 *An Arabian Tale, From an Unpublished Manuscript: With Notes Critical and Explanatory*, London: J. Johnson, 1786, pp.90–8

48 Erasmus Darwin, *The Botanic Garden*, third edition, London: J. Johnson 1791, pp.97–9

50 Edmund Burke, *Reflections on the Revolution in France, and on the Proceedings in Certain Societies in London Relative to that Event. In a Letter Intended to Have Been Sent to a Gentleman in Paris*, London, J. Dodsley, 1790, pp.104–7

52 from David V. Erdman ed., *The Complete Poetry and Prose of William Blake*, rev. edn. New York: Doubleday, 1988

53 Helen Maria Williams, *Julia, A Novel; Interspersed with Some Poetical Pieces*, 2 vols, London: T. Cadell, 1790, vol.2, pp.218–23

55 Ann Radcliffe, *The Mysteries of Udolpho, A Romance; Interspersed with Some Pieces of Poetry*, 4 vols, London: G.G. and J. Robinson, 1794, vol.4, pp.241–53

61 Ann Radcliffe, *The Italian, Or the Confessional of the Black Penitents. A Romance*, 3 vols, London: T. Cadell and W. Davies, 1797, vol.2, pp.189–202

68 *The Monk: A Romance*, 3 vols, London: J. Bell, 1796, vol.2, pp.246–54 and vol.3, pp.236–58

79 *Tales of Wonder, Written and Collected by M.G. Lewis, Esq. M.P. ... in Two Volumes*, 2 vols, London: W. Bulmer and Co., 1801, vol.2, pp.62–9

80 from Thomas Hutchinson ed., corrected by G.M. Matthews, *Shelley: Poetical Works*, Oxford and New York 1971, p.853–6

85 *Frankenstein; Or, The Modern Prometheus*, 3 vols, London: Lockington, Hughes, Harding, Mavor and Jones, 1818, vol.1, pp.97–109

91 *Melmoth the Wanderer. A Tale. By the Author of 'Bertram' &c*, 3 vols, Edinburgh: Archibald Constable and Co., 1820, vol.1, pp.128–41

96 from *The Works of the Late Edgar Allan Poe. With Notes on his Life and Genius by N.P. Willis, J.R. Lowell, and R.W. Griswold*, 2 vols, New York: J.S. Redfield, 1850, vol.2, pp.7–11

100 *Dracula*, London: Archibald Constable and Co., 1897, pp.28–9, 34–5, 37–40

Part 2
The Psychological and Aesthetic Functions of Horror and the Fantastic

108 Joseph Addison, *The Spectator*, no.12 (14 March 1711)

109 Henry Bourne, *Antiquitates Vulgares; Or, The Antiquities of the Common People*, Newcastle:printed for the author, 1725, pp. 76–90

112 *Round about our Coal Fire: Or, Christmas Entertainments*, London: J. Roberts, c.1730, pp.12–13

113 *The Pleasures of the Imagination. A Poem. In Three Books*, London: R. Dodsley, 1744, p.24

115 Joseph Addison, *The Spectator*, no.412 (21 June 1712)

117 Joseph Addison, *The Spectator*, no.419 (1 July 1712)

118 David Hume, *Four Dissertations*, London: A. Millar, 1757, pp.185–93

123 *A Philosophical Enquiry into the Origin of our Ideas of the Sublime and Beautiful*,

2nd edn, London: R. and J. Dodsley, 1759, pp.43–7, 58–60, 72–5, 99–103, 110–11

130 John and Anna Aikin (later Barbauld), *Miscellaneous Pieces, In Prose*, London: J. Johnson, 1773, pp.119–27

132 James Beattie, *Dissertations Moral and Critical. On Memory and Imagination. On Dreaming. The Theory of Language. On Fable and Romance. On the Attachments of Kindred. Illustrations on Sublimity*, London: W. Strahan, 1783, 612–13, 615–17

136 *The Castle of Otranto, A Gothic Story*, 2nd edn, London: William Bathoe and Thomas Lownds, 1765, pp.v–vii

137 Clara Reeve, *The Old English Baron. A Gothic Story*, second edn. (first edn. published as *The Champion of Virtue*), London: Edward and Charles Dilly, 1778, pp.iii–viii

141 *The Castle of Otranto: A Gothic Story. By the Honourable Horace Walpole. With a Critical Introduction*, Edinburgh: John Ballantyne and Co., 1811, pp.xvii–xxii

145 *The Bee; Or, A Companion to the Shakespeare Gallery*, London: T. Cadell, [1789], p.54; *The Analytical Review*, quoted in Eudo C. Mason, *The Mind of Henry Fuseli: Selections from his Writings with an Introductory Study*, London: Routledge, Kegan and Paul, 1951, p.290

149 'On Ghosts', *The London Magazine*, vol.9 (1824), pp.253–4

151 Sir Walter Scott, *Letters on Demonology and Witchcraft. Addressed to J.G. Lockart, Esq.*, London: John Murray, 1830, pp.396–402

156 from *The Works of the Late Edgar Allan Poe. With Notes on his Life and Genius by N.P. Willis, J.R. Lowell, and R.W. Griswold*, 2 vols, New York: J.S. Redfield, 1850, vol.1, pp.353–9

162 Andrew Lang, 'Mrs Radcliffe's Novels', *The Cornhill Magazine* (July 1900), Montague Summers, *The Gothic Quest: A History of the Gothic Novel*, London: Fortune Press, 1938, pp.7, 12–13

163 Montague Summers ed., *The Supernatural Omnibus: A Collection of Stories of Apparitions, Witchcraft, Werewolves, Diabolism, Necromancy, Satanism, Divination, Sorcery, Goetry, Voodoo, Possession, Occult Doom and Destiny*, London: Victor Gollancz, 1931, p.10

165 Lafcadio Hearn, *Shadowings*, London: Sampson, Low and Co., 1900

167 Sigmund Freud, trans. Alix Strachey, in *The Collected* Papers, vol.3, London: The Hogarth Press, 1925

170 Ernest Jones, *On the Nightmare*, London: L & V. Woolf, 1931

175 V.H. Collins ed., *Ghosts and Marvels: A Selection of Uncanny Tales from Daniel Defoe to Algernon Blackwood*, Oxford: Oxford University Press, 1924

p.179 Howard Phillips Lovecraft, *Supernatural Horror in Literature*, with an introduction by August Derleth, New York: Ben Abramson, 1945, pp.12–15

Part 3
Rediscovering the Gothic

184 Joseph Addison, *The Spectator*, no.415 (26 June 1712); *Essays Moral and Political*, 2nd edn, 2 vols, Edinburgh: A. Kincaid, 1742, vol.2, p.195; *The Connoisseur*, no.120 (13 May 1756), in Bonnell Thornton and George Colman, *The Connoisseur*, 3rd edn., 4 vols, London: R. Baldwin, 1757–60, vol.4, pp.121, 125

185 *The Expedition of Humphry Clinker. By the Author of Roderick Random*, 3 vols, London: W. Johnston and B. Collins, 1771, vol.2, pp.137–40

189 Joseph Addison, *The Spectator*, no.26 (20 March 1711)

190 Robert Blair, *The Grave. A Poem*, London: M. Cooper, 1743, pp.3–5; *An Elegy Wrote in a Country Church Yard*, London: R. Dodsley, 1751

194 John Hughes, preface (1715) to *The Works of Spencer*, 6 vols, London: J & R Tonson, 1750, vol.1, pp.xlviii–xlviv; William Hogarth, *The Analysis of Beauty*, ed. Ronald Paulson, New Haven and London: Yale University Press 1997, pp.47–8; Horace Walpole, *Anecdotes of Painting in England*, 4 vols, Strawberry Hill, vol.1 (1762), p.114–15

195 *Letters on Chivalry and Romance*, London and Cambridge: A Millar, W. Thurlbourn and T. Woodyer, 1762, p.61

196 *An Essay on Original Genius*, London: Edward and Charles Dilly, 1767, pp.256–8; Horace Walpole, *Anecdotes of Painting in England*, 4 vols, Strawberry Hill, 1762–80,vol.4 (1780), p.vi

197 Robert Wark ed., *Reynolds: Discourses on Art*, New Haven and London: Yale University Press, 1975, pp.241–2 Henry Fuseli, 'Aphorisms on Art' (1788–1818), in John Knowles, *Thr Life and Writings of Henry Fuseli*, 3 vols, London: Henry Colburn and Richard Bentley, 1831, vol.3

199 *A Philosophical Enquiry into the Origin of our Ideas of the Sublime and Beautiful*, 2nd edn, London: R. and J. Dodsley, 1759, pp.132–7

200 *Essays on Gothic Architecture, by the Rev. T. W., Rev. J. Bentham, Captain Grose and the Rev. J. Milner ... Illustrated with ten plates of ornaments, etc. selected from ancient buildings*, 3rd edn., London: J. Taylor, 1808

206 William Mason, *The English Garden. A Poem. Book the Fourth*, York: A. Ward, 1781, pp.4–7; Richard Payne Knight, *The Landscape: A Didactic Poem*, in Three Books, Addressed to Uvedale Price, Esq., 2nd edn., London: W. Bulmer and Co, 1795, pp.53–4

207 *Observations Relative Chiefly to Picturesque Beauty, Made in the Year 1772, On Several Parts of England, Particularly the Mountains, and Lakes of Cumberland, and Westmoreland*, London: R. Blamire, 1786, pp.12–13

211 William Blake, 'On Virgil' (c.1810) and annotation to Sir Joshua Reynolds's *Discourses on Art* (c.1808), from David V. Erdman ed., *The Complete Poetry and Prose of William Blake*, rev. edn. New York: Doubleday, 1988

215 'An Architect'. in *The Gentleman's Magazine*, vol.74 (1804), pp.431–2, 735–7 p.220 *The Castle of Otranto: A Gothic Story. By the Honourable Horace Walpole. With a Critical Introduction*, Edinburgh: John Ballantyne and Co., 1811, pp.ix–x; *Northanger Abbey: And Persuasion. By the Author of 'Pride and Prejudice', 'Mansfield Park', &c*, 4 vols, London: John Murray, 1818, vol.2, pp.84–8

221 William Lisle Bowles, 'Lines on a First View of Fonthill Abbey, Aug. 21st, 1822', *The Gentleman's Magazine*, vol.92, part 2 (1822), p.102

222 'W.G.' in *The Gentleman's Magazine*, vol.92, part 2 (1822), pp.491–4

227 Lafcadio Hearn, *Shadowings*, London: Sampson, Low and Co., 1900, pp.213–22

Part 4
Fantastic Artists and Writers

234 Horace Walpole to William Cole, 9 March 1765, in W.S. Lewis ed,., *The Yale Edition of Horace Walpole's Correspondence*, 48 vols, New Haven and London: Yale University Press, 1937–83, vol.1, p.88; Horace Walpole to Madame Deffand, 13 March 1767, in *The Castle of Otranto: A Gothic Story. By the Honourable Horace Walpole. With a Critical Introduction*, Edinburgh: John Ballantyne and Co., 1811, pp.xiv–xv (cf. W.S. Lewis ed,., *The Yale Edition of Horace Walpole's Correspondence*, 48 vols, New Haven and London: Yale University Press, 1937–83, vol.3, pp.260–1)

237 *Biographical Memoirs of Extraordinary Painters*, London: J. Robson, 1780, pp.103–18

242 Henry Fuseli, 'Lectures on Painting', 'Invention' (1801), and 'Aphorisms on Art' (1788–1818), in John Knowles, *The Life and Writings of Henry Fuseli*, 3 vols, London: Henry Colburn and Richard Bentley, 1831, vol.2, pp.141–3 and vol.3, pp.64–145

245 Tom Taylor ed., *the Autobiography and Memoirs of Benjamin Robert Haydon, (1786–1846)* (1853), 2 vols, London: Peter Davies, 1926, vol.1, pp.21–2

248 William Blake to the Revd Dr Trusler, 16 August 1799, in David V. Erdman ed., *The Complete Poetry and Prose of William Blake*, rev. edn. New York: Doubleday, 1988

249 William Blake to Thomas Butts, 22 November 1802, in David V. Erdman ed., *The Complete Poetry and Prose of William Blake*, rev. edn. New York: Doubleday, 1988

250 Allan Cunningham, *Lives of the Most Eminent British Painters, Sculptors, and Architects*, (1929–33), quoted in G.E. Bentley, *Blake Records*, New Haven and London: Yale University Press, 2004, pp.639–41

254 Mary W. Shelley, *Frankenstein*, 3 vols, London: Colbourn and Bentley, 1831, vol.1, pp.v–xii

260 'Suspiria de Profundis: Being a Sequel to the Confesions of an English Opium-Eater: Introductory Notice', *Blackwood's Edinburgh Magazine*, vol.57, no.353 (March 1845), pp.269–70

263 from *The Works of the Late Edgar Allan Poe. With Notes on his Life and Genius by N.P. Willis, J.R. Lowell, and R.W. Griswold*, 2 vols, New York: J.S. Redfield, 1850, vol.1, pp.298–302

266 *The Art Union: Monthly Journal of the Arts*, October 1843, pp.267–71 and February 1848, p.66

268 from Richard Dadd, 'Elimination of a Picture & Its Subject – Called the Feller's Master Stroke', quoted in Patricia Allderidge, *The Late Richard Dadd 1817–1866*, exh. cat., Tate Gallery, London 1974, p.128

270 H.P. Lovecraft, 'Pickman's Model' (1926) in *The Best of H.P. Lovecraft: Bloodcurdling Tales of Horror and the Macarbre*, New York: Del Ray, 1982, p.34

Part 5
Moral Panics and Critical Doubts: Opposition to Gothic Horror and Fantasy

274 *Round about our Coal Fire: Or, Christmas Entertainments*, London: J. Roberts, c.1730

275 Hugh Kelly, *The Babler*, no.39 (5 November 1763), in *The Babler. Containing a careful selection from those ... essays Which have given ... so much satisfaction under that title ... in Owen's*

Weekly Chronicle, 2 vols, London: J. Newbery, 1767
278 Gilly Williams to George Selwyn, 19 March 1765 in W.S, Lewis ed., *The Yale Edition of Horace Walpole's Correspondence*, 48 vols, New Haven and London: Yale University Press, 1937–83, vol.30, p.177
279 H.P. Lovecraft to Bernard Austin Dwyer, 14 February 1928, in August Derleth and Donald Wandrei eds., *Howard Phillips Lovecraft: Selected Letters 1923–1929*, Wisconsin: Arkham House, 1968
282 *Spirit of the Public Journals for 1797*, vol.1 (1798), pp.223–5
283 *The Critical Review*, vol.19 (1797), pp.194–8
286 *The Critical Review*, vol.23 (1798), pp.166–7
287 from *The Anti-Jacobin Review and Magazine*, vo.7 (1801) and vol.8 (1801)
288 from *The Critical Review; Or, Annals of Literature* for 1801
291 Thomas James Mathias, *The Pursuit of Literature, A Satirical Poem in Four Dialogues with Notes*, 16th edn, London 1812
295 *The Analytical Review*, 14 (October 1792), p.161, and 24 (December 1796), p.561
296 Henry Fuseli, 'Fifth Lecture on Painting: Composition, Expression' (1805) and 'Aphorisms on Art' (1788–1818), in John Knowles, *The Life and Writings of Henry Fuseli*, 3 vols, London: Henry Colburn and Richard Bentley, 1831, vol.2, pp.262–4 and vol.3, pp.78–91
297 Robert Anthony Bromley, *A Philosophical and Critical History of the Arts*, 2 vols, London: printed for the author 1793–5, vol.1, pp.36–7
298 Robert Hunt in *The Examiner*, (17 March 1809), in G.E. Bentley ed., *Blake Records*, 2nd edn, New Haven and London: Yale University Press 2004, pp.282–5
301 *Northanger Abbey: And Persuasion. By the Author of 'Pride and Prejudice', 'Mansfield Park', &c*, 4 vols, London: John Murray, 1818, vol.1, pp.66–71
p.34 from Thomas Love Peacock, *Nightmare Abbey* (1817) in Raymond Wright ed., *Nightmare Abbey: Crochet Castle*, ed., Harmondsworth: Penguin 1969
307 Bram Stoker, 'The Censorship of Fiction', *The Nineteenth Century and After*, vol.64 (July-December 1908)
309 M.R. James, 'Some Remarks on Ghost Stories', *The Bookman* (December 1929)

Further reading

The literature on the Gothic as a literary phenomenon is vast, and to provide even a comprehensive bibliography of bibliographies would be a task quite beyond the scope of the present volume. However, the editor would like to draw attention to the following critical studies and compilations which have informed the selection and commentary:

José B. Monleón, *A Specter is Haunting Europe: A Sociological Approach to the Fantastic*, Princeton: Princeton University Press, 1990; Harriet Guest, 'The Wanton Muse: Politics and Gender in Gothic Theory After 1760' in Stephen Copley and John Whale eds, *Beyond Romanticism: New Approaches to Texts and Contexts 1780–1832*, London and New York: Routledge, 1992, pp.118–39; Terry Castle, *The Female Thermometer: Eighteenth Century Culture and the Invention of the Uncanny*, New York and Oxford: Oxford University Press, 1995; E. J. Clery, *The Rise of Supernatural Fiction, 1762–1800*, Cambridge: Cambridge University Press, 1995; James Watt, *Contesting the Gothic: Fiction, Genre and Cultural Conflict, 1764–1832*, Cambridge: Cambridge University Pres 1999; David Punter ed., *A Companion to the Gothic*, Oxford: Blackwell, 2000; Avril Horner ed., *European Gothic: A Spirited Exchange 1760–1960*, Manchester: Manchester University Press, 2002; Luke Gibbons, *Gaelic Gothic: Race, Colonization, and Irish Culture*, Galway 2004; David Punter and Glennis Byron, *The Gothic*, Oxford: Blackwell, 2004; E.J. Clery and Robert Miles eds, *Gothic Documents: A Sourcebook 1700–1820*, Manchester: Manchester University Press, 2000; Rictor Norton ed., *Gothic Readings: The First Wave, 1764–1840*, London and New York: Leicester University Press, 2000; Michael Charlesworth ed., *The Gothic Revival 1720–1870: Literary Sources and Documents*, 3 vols, Mountfield: Helm Information Ltd 2002. Further studies which have been important include: Ronald Paulson, *Representations of*

Revolution (1789–1820), New Haven and London: Yale University Press, 1983; John Bender, *Imagining the Penitentiary: Fiction and the Architecture of Mind in Eighteenth Century England*, Chicago and London: Chicago University Press, 1987; John Brewer, *The Pleasures of the Imagination: English Culture in the Eighteenth Century*, London: HarperCollins, 1997; John Barrell, *Imagining the King's Death: Figurative Treason, Fantasies of Regicide 1793–1796*, Oxford: Oxford University Press, 2000; Chris Baldick, *In Frankenstein's Shadow: Myth, Monstrosity, and Nineteenth-Century Writing*, Oxford: Clarendon 1987; Stephen Bann ed., *Frankenstein: Creation and Monstrosity*, London: Reaktion Books, 1994; Patrick Bridgwater, *De Quincy's Gothic Masquerade*, Amsterdam and New York: Rodopi, 2000. Among the modern editions consulted in preparing this volume, the editor is particularly indebted to: Susan Fraiman ed. *Jane Austen: Northanger Abbey: Authoritative Text, Backgrounds, Criticism*, New York and London: W.W. Norton and Co., 2004; Mary Shelley, *Frankenstein; Or, The Modern Prometheus: The 1818 Text*, D.L. Macdonald and Kathleen Scherf, eds, 2nd edn., Peterborough, Ontario: Broadview, 2003; Matthew Gregory Lewis, *The Monk: A Romance*, D.L. Macdonald and Kathleen Scherf eds, Peterborough, Ontario: Broadview, 2004; ed., Charles Maturin, *Melmoth the Wanderer*, ed. Douglas Grant, introduction by Chris Baldick,Oxford: Oxford University Press 1998; Ann Radcliffe, *The Italian, or, The Confessional of the Black Penitents: A Romance*, Frederick Garber ed., with an introduction and notes by E. J. Clery, Oxford: Oxford University Press 1998; Ann Radcliffe, *The Italian, or, The Confessional of the Black Penitents: A Romance*, introduction by Robert Miles, London: Penguin, 2000; Ann Radcliffe, *The Mysteries of Udolpho*, Bonamy Dobrée ed., with an introduction and notes by Terry Castle, Oxford: Oxford University Press, 1998; John Calhoun Stephens ed., *The Guardian*, Lexington: University Press of Kentucky, 1982; Donald F. Bond ed., *The Spectator*, 5 vols, Oxford: Clarendon Press, 1965.

Credits

Photographic credits

All photographs are © the institution or individual who owns the work, with the following exceptions and additions:

Photograph reproduced by kind permission of the Bethlem Art and History Collections Trust fig.37
Vancouver Art Gallery/
Photo: Trevor Mills fig.1
© V&A Images figs.7, 24

Index

Page numbers in bold refer to excerpted texts